BIRDS *of* ONTARIO

D1248576

Andy Bezener
With Contributions from Ross James

LONE PINE

The Publisher: Lone Pine Publishing
10145–81 Ave.
Edmonton, AB T6E 1W9
Canada

Website: http://www.lonepinepublishing.com

Canadian Cataloguing in Publication Data

Bezener, Andy
  Birds of Ontario

Includes bibliographical references and index.
ISBN 1-55105-239-X

  1. Birds—Ontario—Identification. 2. Bird watching—Ontario. I. Title.
QL685.5.O5B49 2000   598'.09713   C00-910370-8

Editorial Director: Nancy Foulds
Project Editor: Eloise Pulos
Editorial: Eloise Pulos, Roland Lines, Eli MacLaren
Production Manager: Jody Reekie
Layout & Production: Monica Triska
Book Design: Rob Weidemann
Cover Design: Rob Weidemann
Cover Illustration: Tundra Swan, by Gary Ross
Illustrations: Gary Ross, Ted Nordhagen, Ewa Pluciennik
Cartography: Volker Bodegom, Lana Anderson-Hale, Monica Triska, Elliott Engley
Separations & Film: Elite Lithographers Co., Edmonton, Alberta

We acknowledge the financial support of the Government of Canada through the Book Publishing Industry Development Program (BPIDP) for our publishing activities.

PC: P3

CONTENTS

ACKNOWLEDGEMENTS

It is impossible to mention every individual who has contributed to this project; nevertheless, there is a smaller cast of characters that have played an essential part in bringing this field guide to fruition. Many thanks go to Gary Ross and Ted Nordhagen, whose skilled illustrations have brought each page to life. The distribution maps are the work of Volker Bodegom, and his time and effort on this project is much appreciated. Gratitude is owed to my friend and editor, Eloise Pulos for her diligent work and tremendous support during this project. Special thanks is extended to Ross James for sharing his profound knowledge of Ontario's bird life in his review of the manuscript and distribution maps. Wayne Campbell, Chris Fisher, John Acorn and Roland Lines have contributed greatly toward the production of previously published projects, which have helped shape this guide's form and content. I am forever grateful to Jim Butler for his wisdom and guidance, and to my father, Jerry Bezener, who introduced me to the wonders of the natural world. Finally, I wish to thank my family and friends, and most of all my wife Kindrie Grove, for her love and unwavering support.

Red-throated Loon
size 65 cm • p. 34

Pacific Loon
size 66 cm • p. 35

Common Loon
size 80 cm • p. 36

Pied-billed Grebe
size 34 cm • p. 37

Horned Grebe
size 34 cm • p. 38

Red-necked Grebe
size 50 cm • p. 39

Eared Grebe
size 33 cm • p. 40

American White Pelican
size 160 cm • p. 41

Double-crested Cormorant
size 74 cm • p. 42

American Bittern
size 64 cm • p. 43

Least Bittern
size 33 cm • p. 44

Great Blue Heron
size 135 cm • p. 45

Great Egret
size 99 cm • p. 46

Snowy Egret
size 61 cm • p. 47

Cattle Egret
size 51 cm • p. 48

Green Heron
size 47 cm • p. 49

Black-crowned
Night-Heron
size 62 cm • p. 50

Turkey Vulture
size 74 cm • p. 51

Greater White-fronted
Goose
size 77 cm • p. 52

Snow Goose
size 78 cm • p. 53

Ross's Goose
size 60 cm • p. 54

Canada Goose
size 89 cm • p. 55

Brant
size 65 cm • p. 56

Mute Swan
size 150 cm • p. 57

Trumpeter Swan
size 165 cm • p. 58

Tundra Swan
size 135 cm • p. 59

Wood Duck
size 46 cm • p. 60

Gadwall
size 51 cm • p. 61

Eurasian Wigeon
size 47 cm • p. 62

American Wigeon
size 52 cm • p. 63

American Black Duck
size 57 cm • p. 64

Mallard
size 61 cm • p. 65

Blue-winged Teal
size 39 cm • p. 66

Northern Shoveler
size 49 cm • p. 67

Northern Pintail
size 62 cm • p. 68

Green-winged Teal
size 36 cm • p. 69

Canvasback
size 52 cm • p. 70

Redhead
size 51 cm • p. 71

Ring-necked Duck
size 41 cm • p. 72

Greater Scaup
size 45 cm • p. 73

Lesser Scaup
size 42 cm • p. 74

King Elder
size 56 cm • p. 75

Common Elder
size 63 cm • p. 76

Harlequin Duck
size 42 cm • p. 77

Surf Scoter
size 48 cm • p. 78

White-winged Scoter
size 55 cm • p. 79

Black Scoter
size 48 cm • p. 80

Long-tailed Duck
size 47 cm • p. 81

Bufflehead
size 36 cm • p. 82

Common Goldeneye
size 46 cm • p. 83

Barrow's Goldeneye
size 46 cm • p. 84

Hooded Merganser
size 45 cm • p. 85

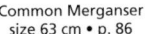

Common Merganser
size 63 cm • p. 86

Red-breasted Merganser
size 57 cm • p. 87

Ruddy Duck
size 40 cm • p. 88

Osprey
size 60 cm • p. 89

Bald Eagle
size 93 cm • p. 90

Northern Harrier
size 51 cm • p. 91

Sharp-shinned Hawk
size 31 cm • p. 92

Cooper's Hawk
size 43 cm • p. 93

Northern Goshawk
size 58 cm • p. 94

Red-shouldered Hawk
size 48 cm • p. 95

Broad-winged Hawk
size 42 cm • p. 96

Red-tailed Hawk
size 55 cm • p. 97

Rough-legged Hawk
size 55 cm • p. 98

Golden Eagle
size 89 cm • p. 99

American Kestrel
size 20 cm • p. 100

Merlin
size 28 cm • p. 101

Gyrfalcon
size 60 cm • p. 102

Peregrine Falcon
size 43 cm • p. 103

Gray Partridge
size 64 cm • p. 104

Ring-necked Pheasant
size 84 cm • p. 105

Ruffed Grouse
size 43 cm • p. 106

Spruce Grouse
size 37 cm • p. 107

Willow Ptarmigan
size 39 cm • p. 108

Sharp-tailed Grouse
size 45 cm • p. 109

Wild Turkey
size 97 cm • p. 110

Northern Bobwhite
size 25 cm • p. 111

Yellow Rail
size 18 cm • p. 112

King Rail
size 38 cm • p. 113

Virginia Rail
size 16 cm • p. 114

Sora
size 23 cm • p. 115

Common Moorhen
size 34 cm • p. 116

American Coot
size 37 cm • p. 117

Sandhill Crane
size 115 cm • p. 118

Black-bellied Plover
size 30 cm • p. 119

American Golden-Plover
size 32 cm • p. 120

Semipalmated Plover
size 18 cm • p. 121

Piping Plover
size 19 cm • p. 122

Killdeer
size 26 cm • p. 123

Greater Yellowlegs
size 36 cm • p. 124

Lesser Yellowlegs
size 27 cm • p. 125

Solitary Sandpiper
size 21 cm • p. 126

Willet
size 39 cm • p. 127

Spotted Sandpiper
size 19 cm • p. 128

Upland Sandpiper
size 30 cm • p. 129

Whimbrel
size 45 cm • p. 130

Hudsonian Godwit
size 38 cm • p. 131

Marbled Godwit
size 46 cm • p. 132

Ruddy Turnstone
size 24 cm • p. 133

Red Knot
size 27 cm p. 134

Sanderling
size 20 cm • p. 135

Semipalmated Sandpiper
size 16 cm • p. 136

Western Sandpiper
size 17 cm • p. 137

Least Sandpiper
size 15 cm • p. 138

White-rumped Sandpiper
size 19 cm • p. 139

Baird's Sandpiper
size 19 cm • p. 140

Pectoral Sandpiper
size 23 cm • p. 141

Purple Sandpiper
size 23 cm • p. 142

Dunlin
size 21 cm • p. 143

Stilt Sandpiper
size 22 cm • p. 144

Buff-breasted Sandpiper
size 20 cm • p. 145

Ruff/Reeve
size 26 cm • p. 146

Short-billed Dowitcher
size 29 cm • p. 147

Long-billed Dowitcher
size 30 cm • p. 148

Common Snipe
size 28 cm • p. 149

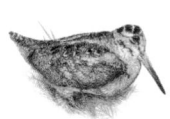

American Woodcock
size 28 cm • p. 150

Wilson's Phalarope
size 23 cm • p. 151

Red-necked Phalarope
size 18 cm • p.152

Red Phalarope
size 22 cm • p. 153

Pomarine Jaeger
size 55 cm • p. 154

Parasitic Jaeger
size 46 cm • p. 155

Long-tailed Jaeger
size 55 cm • p. 156

Laughing Gull
size 41 cm • p. 157

Franklin's Gull
size 36 cm • p. 158

Little Gull
size 27 cm • p. 159

Black-headed Gull
size 39 cm • p. 160

Bonaparte's Gull
size 33 cm • p. 161

Ring-billed Gull
size 49 cm • p. 162

Herring Gull
size 62 cm • p. 163

Thayer's Gull
size 60 cm • p. 164

Iceland Gull
size 56 cm • p. 165

Lesser Black-backed Gull
size 53 cm • p. 166

Glaucous Gull
size 69 cm • p. 167

Great Black-backed Gull
size 76 cm • p. 168

Sabine's Gull
size 35 cm • p. 169

JAEGERS, GULLS & TERNS

Black-legged Kittiwake
size 44 cm • p. 170

Caspian Tern
size 53 cm • p. 171

Common Tern
size 37 cm • p. 172

Arctic Tern
size 40 cm • p. 173

Forster's Tern
size 39 cm • p. 174

Black Tern
size 24 cm • p. 175

Rock Dove
size 32 cm • p. 176

Mourning Dove
size 31 cm • p. 177

DOVES & CUCKOOS

Black-billed Cuckoo
size 31 cm • p. 178

Yellow-billed Cuckoo
size 31 cm • p. 179

Eastern Screech-Owl
size 22 cm • p. 180

Great Horned Owl
size 55 cm • p. 181

OWLS

Snowy Owl
size 60 cm • p. 182

Northern Hawk Owl
size 41 cm • p. 183

Barred Owl
size 52 cm • p. 184

Great Gray Owl
size 73 cm • p. 185

Long-eared Owl
size 37 cm • p. 186

Short-eared Owl
size 38 cm • p. 187

Boreal Owl
size 27 cm • p. 188

Northern Saw-whet Owl
size 21 cm • p. 189

NIGHTHAWKS, SWIFTS & HUMMINGBIRDS

Common Nighthawk
size 24 cm • p. 190

Chuck-will's-widow
size 31 cm • p. 191

Whip-poor-will
size 24 cm • p. 192

Chimney Swift
size 13 cm • p. 193

Ruby-throated Hummingbird
size 9 cm • p. 194

Belted Kingfisher
size 32 cm • p. 195

WOODPECKERS

Red-headed Woodpecker
size 23 cm • p. 196

Red-bellied Woodpecker
size 25 cm • p. 197

Yellow-bellied Sapsucker
size 19 cm • p. 198

Downy Woodpecker
size 17 cm • p. 199

Hairy Woodpecker
size 22 cm • p. 200

Three-toed Woodpecker
size 23 cm • p. 201

Black-backed Woodpecker
size 24 cm • p. 202

Northern Flicker
size 33 cm • p. 203

FLYCATCHERS

Pileated Woodpecker
size 45 cm • p. 204

Olive-sided Flycatcher
size 19 cm • p. 205

Eastern Wood-Pewee
size 16 cm • p. 206

Yellow-bellied Flycatcher
size 14 cm • p. 207

Acadian Flycatcher
size 15 cm • p. 208

Alder Flycatcher
size 15 cm • p. 209

Willow Flycatcher
size 15 cm • p. 210

Least Flycatcher
size 13 cm • p. 211

Eastern Phoebe
size 18 cm • p. 212

Great-crested Flycatcher
size 22 cm • p. 213

Western Kingbird
size 22 cm • p. 214

Eastern Kingbird
size 22 cm • p. 215

SHRIKES & VIREOS

Loggerhead Shrike
size 23 cm • p. 216

Northern Shrike
size 25 cm • p. 217

White-eyed Vireo
size 13 cm • p. 218

Yellow-throated Vireo
size 14 cm • p. 219

Blue-headed Vireo
size 14 cm • p. 220

Warbling Vireo
size 14 cm • p. 221

Philadelphia Vireo
size 13 cm • p. 222

Red-eyed Vireo
size 15 cm • p. 223

JAYS & CROWS

Gray Jay
size 31 cm • p. 224

Blue Jay
size 30 cm • p. 225

Black-billed Magpie
size 50 cm • p. 226

American Crow
size 48 cm • p. 227

Common Raven
size 61 cm • p. 228

Horned Lark
size 18 cm • p. 229

Purple Martin
size 19 cm • p. 230

Tree Swallow
size 14 cm • p. 231

LARKS & SWALLOWS

Northern Rough-winged
Swallow
size 14 cm • p. 232

Bank Swallow
size 13 cm • p. 233

Cliff Swallow
size 14 cm • p. 234

Barn Swallow
size 18 cm • p. 235

CHICKADEES, NUTHATCHES & WRENS

Black-capped Chickadee
size 14 cm • p. 236

Boreal Chickadee
size 14 cm • p. 237

Tufted Titmouse
size 16 cm • p. 238

Red-breasted Nuthatch
size 11 cm • p. 239

White-breasted Nuthatch
size 15 cm • p. 240

Brown Creeper
size 13 cm • p. 241

Carolina Wren
size 14 cm • p. 242

House Wren
size 12 cm • p. 243

Winter Wren
size 10 cm • p. 244

Sedge Wren
size 11 cm • p. 245

Marsh Wren
size 13 cm • p. 246

KINGLETS, BLUE-BIRDS & THRUSHES

Golden-crowned Kinglet
size 10 cm • p. 247

Ruby-crowned Kinglet
size 10 cm • p. 248

Blue-gray Gnatcatcher
size 11 cm • p. 249

Eastern Bluebird
size 18 cm • p. 250

KINGLETS, BLUEBIRDS & THRUSHES

Veery
size 18 cm • p. 251

Gray-cheeked Thrush
size 19 cm • p. 252

Swainson's Thrush
size 18 cm • p. 253

Hermit Thrush
size 18 cm • p. 254

Wood Thrush
size 20 cm • p. 255

American Robin
size 25 cm • p. 256

Varied Thrush
size 24 cm • p. 257

STARLINGS, MIMICS & WAXWINGS

Gray Catbird
size 23 cm • p. 258

Northern Mockingbird
size 25 cm • p. 259

Brown Thrasher
size 29 cm • p. 260

European Starling
size 22 cm • p. 261

American Pipit
size 17 cm • p. 262

Bohemian Waxwing
size 20 cm • p. 263

Cedar Waxwing
size 18 cm • p. 264

WOOD-WARBLERS & TANAGERS

Blue-winged Warbler
size 12 cm • p. 265

Golden-winged Warbler
size 12 cm • p. 266

Tennessee Warbler
size 12 cm • p. 267

Orange-crowned Warbler
size 13 cm • p. 268

Nashville Warbler
size 12 cm • p. 269

Northern Parula
size 11 cm • p. 270

Yellow Warbler
size 13 cm • p. 271

Chestnut-sided Warbler
size 13 cm • p. 272

Magnolia Warbler
size 13 cm • p. 273

Cape May Warbler
size 13 cm • p. 274

Black-throated Blue Warbler
size 13 cm • p. 275

Yellow-rumped Warbler
size 14 cm • p. 276

Black-throated Green Warbler
size 12 cm • p. 277

Blackburnian Warbler
size 13 cm • p. 278

Yellow-throated Warbler
size 14 cm • p. 279

Pine Warbler
size 14 cm • p. 280

Prairie Warbler
size 13 cm • p. 281

Palm Warbler
size 13 cm • p. 282

Bay-breasted Warbler
size 14 cm • p. 283

Blackpoll Warbler
size 14 cm • p. 284

Cerulean Warbler
size 12 cm • p. 285

Black-and-white Warbler
size 13 cm • p. 286

American Restart
size 13 cm • p. 287

Prothonotary Warbler
size 14 cm • p. 288

Worm-eating Warbler
size 13 cm • p. 289

Ovenbird
size 15 cm • p. 290

Northern Waterthrush
size 14 cm • p. 291

Louisiana Waterthrush
size 15 cm • p. 292

Kentucky Warbler
size 13 cm • p. 293

Connecticut Warbler
size 14 cm • p. 294

Mourning Warbler
size 14 cm • p. 295

Common Yellowthroat
size 13 cm • p. 296

Hooded Warbler
size 14 cm • p. 297

Wilson's Warbler
size 12 cm • p. 298

Canada Warbler
size 14 cm • p. 299

Yellow-breasted Chat
size 19 cm • p. 300

Summer Tanager
size 19 cm • p. 301

Scarlet Tanager
size 18 cm • p. 302

Eastern Towhee
size 20 cm • p. 303

American Tree Sparrow
size 16 cm • p. 304

Chipping Sparrow
size 14 cm • p. 305

Clay-colored Sparrow
size 14 cm • p. 306

Field Sparrow
size 14 cm • p. 307

Vesper Sparrow
size 16 cm • p. 308

Savannah Sparrow
size 14 cm • p. 309

Grasshopper Sparrow
size 12 cm • p. 310

Henslow's Sparrow
size 13 cm • p. 311

Le Conte's Sparrow
size 12 cm • p. 312

Nelson's Sharp-tailed Sparrow
size 14 cm • p. 313

Fox Sparrow
size 18 cm • p. 314

Song Sparrow
size 16 cm • p. 315

Lincoln's Sparrow
size 14 cm • p. 316

Swamp Sparrow
size 14 cm • p. 317

White-throated Sparrow
size 18 cm • p. 318

Harris's Sparrow
size 19 cm • p. 319

White-crowned Sparrow
size 16 cm • p. 320

Dark-eyed Junco
size 16 cm • p. 321

Lapland Longspur
size 16 cm • p. 322

Smith's Longspur
size 15 cm • p. 323

Snow Bunting
size 17 cm • p. 324

Northern Cardinal
size 21 cm • p. 325

Rose-breasted Grosbeak
size 20 cm • p. 326

Blue Grosbeak
size 17 cm • p. 327

Indigo Bunting
size 14 cm • p. 328

Dickcissel
size 17 cm • p. 329

BLACKBIRDS & ORIOLES

Bobolink
size 17 cm • p. 330

Red-winged Blackbird
size 21 cm • p. 331

Eastern Meadowlark
size 24 cm • p. 332

Western Meadowlark
size 24 cm • p. 333

Yellow-headed Blackbird
size 24 cm • p. 334

Rusty Blackbird
size 23 cm • p. 335

Brewer's Blackbird
size 23 cm • p. 336

Common Grackle
size 31 cm • p. 337

Brown-headed Cowbird
size 17 cm • p. 338

Orchard Oriole
size 17 cm • p. 339

Baltimore Oriole
size 19 cm • p. 340

FINCH-LIKE BIRDS

Pine Grosbeak
size 23 cm • p. 341

Purple Finch
size 14 cm • p. 342

House Finch
size 14 cm • p. 343

Red Crossbill
size 15 cm • p. 344

White-winged Crossbill
size 16 cm • p. 345

Common Redpoll
size 13 cm • p. 346

Hoary Redpoll
size 14 cm • p. 347

Pine Siskin
size 12 cm • p. 348

American Goldfinch
size 13 cm • p. 349

Evening Grosbeak
size 20 cm • p. 350

House Sparrow
size 16 cm • p. 351

INTRODUCTION

BIRDWATCHING IN ONTARIO

In recent decades, birdwatching has evolved from an eccentric pursuit practised by a few dedicated individuals to a continent-wide activity that boasts millions of professional and amateur participants. There are many good reasons why birdwatching has become so popular. Many people find it simple and relaxing, while others enjoy the outdoor exercise that it affords. Some see it as a rewarding learning experience, an opportunity to socialize with like-minded people and a way to monitor the health of the local environment. Still others watch birds to re-connect with nature. These days, a visit to any of Ontario's premier birding locations, such as Point Pelee National Park, Algonquin Provincial Park, Presqu'ile Provincial Park or Lake of the Woods, would doubtless uncover still more reasons why people watch birds.

Blue Grosbeak

We are truly blessed by the geographical and biological diversity of our province. Because the Great Lakes moderate the climate, and the tip of the province juts so far south (extreme southwestern Ontario and Northern California share the same latitude), many birds remain in Ontario during the winter months. In addition to supporting a wide range of breeding birds and year-round residents, Ontario hosts a large number of spring and fall migrants that move between breeding and wintering grounds. In all, 472 bird species have been seen and recorded in Ontario, and more than 320 species make annual appearances.

Ontario also has a long tradition of friendly birdwatching. In general, Ontario birders are willing to help beginners and involve novices in their projects. Christmas bird counts, breeding bird surveys, nest box programs, migration monitoring and birdwatching lectures and workshops all provide a chance for novice, intermediate and expert birdwatchers to interact and share the splendour of birds. So, whatever your level, there is ample opportunity for you to get involved!

BEGINNING TO LEARN THE BIRDS
The Challenge of Birding

Black-throated Green Warbler

Birdwatching (also known as 'birding') can be extremely challenging and getting started is often the most difficult part. Learning to recognize all the birds in Ontario is a long process. But fear not! The species pictured in this guide will help you get started. Although any standard North American field guide will help you identify local birds, such guides can be daunting, because they cover the entire continent and present an overwhelming number of species. By focusing specifically on the bird life of Ontario, we hope to ease the beginner's difficulty.

Do not expect to become an expert overnight. To be able to identify any bird at a glance, you will have to spend more than a few hours in the field with binoculars and this guide. It could conceivably take a lifetime of careful study to master the art of birdwatching; after all, there are only a small number of birders and ornithologists in Ontario who can identify all of our species with confidence. Nevertheless, almost everyone finds the continual learning process of birding to be enjoyable, if not downright thrilling.

Classification: The Order of Things

To an ornithologist (a biologist who studies birds), the species is the fundamental unit of classification because the members of a single species look most alike and they naturally interbreed with one another. Each species has a scientific name (a Latin name, designating genus and species, which is always underlined or italicized) and a single accredited common name, so that the different vernacular names of a species do not cause confusion. A bird has been properly identified only when it has been identified 'to species'; most ornithologists use the accredited common name.

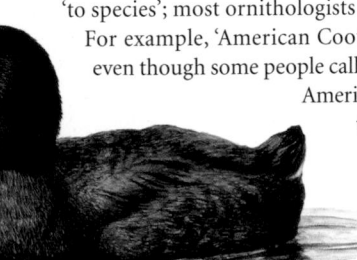

For example, 'American Coot' is an accredited common name, even though some people call it 'mudhen.' *Fulica americana* is the American Coot's scientific name. (*Fulica* is the genus, or generic name, and *americana* is the species, or specific name).

To help make sense of the hundreds of bird species in Ontario, scientifically oriented birdwatchers lump species into recognizable groups. The most commonly used groupings, in order of increasing scope, are genus, family and order. The American Coot and Common Moorhen are different species that do not share a genus (their generic names are different), but they are both members of the family Rallidae (the rail family). The rail, limpkin and crane families are in turn grouped within the order Gruiformes, which comprises the chicken-like birds.

American Coot

Ornithologists have arranged all of the orders to make a standard sequence. It begins with the loons (order Gaviiformes), which are thought by many to be most like the evolutionary ancestors of modern birds. It ends with those species thought to have been most strongly modified by evolutionary change and most departed from the ancestral norm. We have organized this book according to this standard sequence.

At first, the evolutionary sequence might not make much sense. Birders, however, know that all books of this sort begin with diving birds, followed by wading birds, waterfowl, shorebirds, birds of prey, chicken-like birds, and other birds that look more and more like songbirds (formally known as 'passerines'). Still, many readers will tell us that we should have arranged this book alphabetically. Although alphabetical organization may seem logical, it assumes that you already know all of the up-to-date, accredited names of the birds. In practice, the tried-and-true method of grouping birds according to similarities and differences provides the best format for learning.

Red-headed Woodpecker

TECHNIQUES OF BIRDWATCHING

Being in the right place at the right time to see birds in action involves both skill and luck. The more you know about a bird—its range, preferred habitat, food preferences and hours and seasons of activity—the better your chances will be of seeing it. It is much easier to find a Boreal Owl in the Boreal Forest than elsewhere, especially at night in spring, when adults are calling for mates. Snowy Owls, however, are most often seen on fenceposts or in fields during the day in winter.

Generally, spring and fall are the busiest birding times. Temperatures are moderate then, and a great number of birds are on the move, often cramming themselves into small patches of habitat before moving on. Male songbirds are easy to identify on spring mornings as they belt out their courtship songs. Throughout much of the year, diurnal birds are most visible in the early morning hours when they are foraging, but during winter they are often more active in the day when milder temperatures prevail. Timing is crucial, but because summer foliage often conceals birds and cold weather drives many species south of Ontario for winter, birdwatching also involves a great deal of luck.

Binoculars

The small size, fine details and wary behaviour of birds make binoculars an essential piece of equipment for birdwatching. Binoculars can cost anywhere from $50 to $1500, and at times it may seem that there are as many kinds of binoculars as species of birds. Most beginners pay less than $200 for their first pair. Many people are initially drawn to compact binoculars, which are small and lightweight. They are not always cheap, however; some of the most expensive binoculars can be considered compact.

*Golden-crowned
Kinglet*

Binoculars come in two basic types: porro-prism (in which there is a distinct, angular bend in the body of the binoculars) and roof-prism (in which the body is straight). Good porro-prism binoculars are less expensive than good roof-prism binoculars: a first-rate pair of 'porros' costs $300 to $400; good roof-prism binoculars, which are often waterproof and fog-resistant (nitrogen-filled), can cost $800 or more. Expensive binoculars usually have better optics and generally stand up better to abuse.

The optical power of binoculars is described with a two-number code. For example, a compact pair of binoculars might be '8 X 21,' while a larger pair might have '7 X 40' stamped on it. In each case, the first number states the magnification, while the second number records the diameter, in millimetres, of the front lenses. Seven-power binoculars are the easiest to hold and to find birds with; 10-power binoculars give a shakier but more magnified view. Larger lenses gather more light, so a 40-mm or 50-mm lens will perform much better at dusk than a 20-mm or 30-mm lens of the same magnification. For a beginner, eight-power, porro-prism binoculars with front lenses at least 35 mm in diameter (thus 8 X 35 or 8 X 40) are suitable. Some binoculars have a wider field of view than others, even if the two-number code is identical. We recommend the wider field of view, because many beginners have trouble finding birds in compact, narrow-view binoculars.

Look at many types of binoculars before making a purchase. Talk to birders about their binoculars and ask to try them. Go to a store that specializes in birdwatching—the sales people there will know from personal experience which models perform best in the field.

When birding, lift the binoculars up to your eyes without taking your eyes off the bird. This way you will not lose the bird in the magnified view. You can also note an obvious land-mark near the bird (a bright flower or a dead branch, for example) and then use it as a reference point to find the bird with the binoculars.

Wilson's Warbler

Spotting Scopes and Cameras

The spotting scope (a small telescope with a sturdy tripod) is designed to help you view birds that are beyond the range of binoculars. Most spotting scopes are capable of magnification by a factor of at least 20. Some scopes will even allow you to take photographs through them.

If you intend to photograph birds, you should buy a 35-mm single-lens reflex camera with a telephoto lens measuring at least 300 mm. A solid tripod for the camera is essential. The purpose of the good equipment is to help you take photos that are not marred by poor optics or shaky hands. Talk to knowledgeable camera sales staff, and be prepared to spend a lot of money.

Once you have a good camera, you must develop an equally good technique. Most successful bird photographs are taken by quiet, patient photographers—few birds stick around to have themselves photographed by noisy, stampeding admirers.

Birding by Ear

Recognizing birds by their songs and calls can greatly enhance your birding experience. When experienced birders conduct breeding bird surveys each June, they rely more on their ears than their eyes, because listening is far more efficient. There are numerous tapes and CDs that can help you learn bird songs, and a portable player with headphones can let you quickly compare a live bird with a recording.

The old-fashioned way to remember bird songs is to make up words for them. We have given you some of the classic renderings in the species accounts that follow, such as *who cooks for you? who cooks for you-all?* for the Barred Owl, as well as some nonsense syllables, such as *tsit tsit tsit* for the Blackpoll Warbler. Some of these approximations work better than others; birds often add or delete syllables from their calls, and very few pronounce consonants in a recognizable fashion. Be aware that songs usually vary from place to place. The words and recordings that have helped you identify birds successfully in one area might not work as well elsewhere.

Olive-sided Flycatcher

WATCHING BIRD BEHAVIOUR

Once you can confidently identify birds and remember their common names, you can begin to appreciate their behaviour. Studying birds involves keeping notes and records. The timing of bird migrations is an easy thing to record, as are details of feeding, courtship and nesting behaviour if you are willing to be patient. Flocking birds can also provide fascinating opportunities to observe and note social interactions, especially when individual birds can be recognized. Such observations have contributed greatly toward our knowledge of birds. However, casual note-taking should not be equated with more standardized, scientific methods of study.

Birding, for most people, is a peaceful, non-destructive recreational activity. One of the best ways to watch bird behaviour is to look for a spot rich with avian life and then sit back and relax. If you become part of the scenery, the birds, at first startled by your approach, will soon resume their activities and invite you into their world.

BIRDING BY HABITAT

Red-winged Blackbird

Ontario can be separated into five (or six) biophysical regions or 'bioregions': Carolinian Forest (deciduous forest), Great Lakes–St. Lawrence Forest (mixed forest), Boreal Forest, Hudson Bay Lowland Forest (boreal barrens) and Tundra. (The large surface area of the Great Lakes arguably forms a sixth bioregion.) Each bioregion is composed of a number of different habitats. Each habitat is a community of plants and animals supported by the infrastructure of water and soil and regulated by the constraints of topography, climate and elevation.

Simply put, a bird's habitat is the place in which it normally lives. Some birds prefer the open water, some birds are found in cattail marshes, others like mature coniferous forest, and still others prefer abandoned agricultural fields overgrown with tall grass and shrubs. Knowledge of a bird's habitat increases the chances of identifying the bird correctly. If you are birding in tundra wetlands, you will not be identifying tanagers or towhees; if you are wandering among the deciduous trees of the Carolinian Forest, do not expect to meet nesting Boreal Owls or Tundra Swans.

Habitats are just like neighbourhoods: if you associate friends with the suburb in which they live, you can easily learn to associate specific birds with their preferred habitats. Only in migration, especially during inclement weather, do some birds leave their usual habitat.

CALLING BIRDS CLOSER

Eastern Towhee

Some birders have learned that various birds will emerge from cover and come into view when a squeaking or 'pishing' sound is made. Although these sounds can be extremely annoying to other birders or passers-by, the practice of calling birds closer can distract birds from important activities and attract predators, which could lead to all manner of trouble for the birds. Suffice it to say that this practice is rapidly losing favour in many birding communities.

21

BIRD LISTING

Many birders list the species they have seen during excursions or at home. It is up to you to decide what kind of list—systematic or casual—you will keep, and you may choose not to make lists at all. However, lists may prove rewarding in unexpected ways, and after you visit a new area, your list becomes a souvenir of your experiences there. By reviewing it, you can recall memories and details that may otherwise be forgotten. Keeping regular, accurate lists of birds in your neighbourhood can also be useful for researchers. It can be interesting to compare the arrival dates and last sightings of hummingbirds and other seasonal visitors, or to note the first sighting of a new visitor to your area.

Although there are programs for listing birds available for computers, many naturalists simply keep records in field notebooks. Waterproof books and waterproof pens work well on rainy days, although many

White-winged Crossbill

birders prefer to use a pocket recorder in the field and to transcribe the observations into a dry notebook at home. Find a notebook that you like, and personalize it with it field sketches, observations, poetry or whatever you like.

BIRDWATCHING ACTIVITIES

Birdwatching Groups

It is recommended that you join in on such activities as Christmas bird counts, birding festivals and the meetings of your local birding or natural history club. Meeting other people with the same interests can make birding even more pleasurable, and there is always something to be learned when birders of all levels gather. If you are interested in bird conservation and environmental issues, natural history groups and conscientious birdwatching stores can keep you informed about the situation in your area and what you can do to help. Bird hotlines abound in Ontario and provide up-to-date information on the sightings of rarities, which are often easier to relocate than you might think. The following is a brief list of contacts that will help you get involved:

Federation of Ontario Naturalists (FON)
355 Lesmill Rd.
Don Mills, ON M3B 2W8
Tel: (416) 444-8419
Fax: (416) 444-9866
E-mail: fon@web.net
Web: http://www.ontarionature.org

Ontario Field Ornithologists (OFO)
Box 455, Station R,
Toronto, ON M4G 4E1
E-mail: ofo@interlog.com
Web:
http://www.interlog.com/~ofo/home.html

Bird Hotlines

Durham County (Oshawa) (905) 576-2738
Essex County (Windsor) (519) 252-2473
Hamilton (905) 648-9537
Kingston (613) 549-8023
London (519) 457-4593

Ottawa (613) 860-9000
Point Pelee National Park (519) 322-2371
Sault Ste. Marie (705) 256-2790
Simcoe County (Barrie) (705) 739-8585
Toronto & Area (416) 350-3000 (enter 2293)

Bird Conservation

Ontario is a good place to watch birds. After all, there are still large areas of wilderness here, including parks, wildlife reserves and public lands. Nevertheless, agriculture and forestry and development for housing are threatening viable bird habitat throughout the province. It is hoped that more people will learn to appreciate nature in the form of birding, and that those people will do their best to protect the nature that remains. Many bird enthusiasts support groups such as The Nature Conservancy of Canada and Ducks Unlimited, which help birds by buying and managing tracts of good habitat.

Yellow-billed Cuckoo

Landscaping your own property to provide native plant cover and natural foods for birds is an immediate way to ensure the conservation of bird habitat. The cumulative effects of such urban 'nature-scaping' can be significant. If your yard is to become a bird sanctuary, you may want to keep the neighbourhood cats out; every year, millions of birds are killed by cats. Check with the local Humane Society for methods of protecting both your feline friends and wild birds. Ultimately, cats are best kept indoors.

Bird Feeding

Many people set up a backyard birdfeeder to attract birds to their yard, especially in winter. It is possible to attract specific birds by choosing the right kind of food. If you have a feeder, keep it stocked through late spring. The weather may be balmy, but birds have a hard time finding food before flowers bloom, seeds develop and insects hatch. In summer, the Ruby-throated Hummingbird can be attracted to your yard with a special feeder filled with artificial nectar (a simple sugar solution of three to four parts water and one part white sugar). Be sure to follow the feeder's cleaning instructions.

Birdbaths will also bring birds to your yard, and heated birdbaths are particularly effective in winter. Avoid birdbaths that have exposed metal parts, because wet birds can accidentally freeze to them. In general, feeding birds is good, especially if you provide food in the form of native berry- or seed-producing plants grown in your backyard. Contrary to popular opinion, birds do not become dependent on feeders, nor do they subsequently forget to forage naturally. There are many good books written about feeding birds and landscaping your yard to provide natural foods and nest sites.

Eastern Bluebird

Nest Boxes

Another popular way to attract birds is to set out nest boxes, especially for wrens, bluebirds and swallows. Not all birds will use nest boxes: only species that normally use cavities in trees are comfortable in such confined spaces. Larger nest boxes can attract kestrels, owls and cavity-nesting ducks.

ONTARIO'S TOP BIRDING SITES

There are hundreds, if not thousands, of good birding areas throughout the province. The following areas have been selected to represent a broad range of bird communities and habitats, with an emphasis on accessibility. Common birds, as well as exciting rarities, are included in the accounts on the following pages.

Carolinian Forest

1. Ojibway Prairie, Windsor
2. Holiday Beach Conservation Area & Willow Beach
3. Point Pelee NP
4. Rondeau PP
5. Tremblay Beach Conservation Area
6. St. Clair NWA
7. The Pinery PP
8. Fanshawe Lake
9. Hawk Cliff
10. Long Point PP, Backus Woods & Wilson Tract
11. Wainfleet Bog
12. Niagara River
13. Short Hills PP
14. Beamer Point Conservation Area
15. Van Wagner's Beach & Dundas Marsh
16. Sudden Tract & Homer Watson Park
17. Beverly Swamp & Puslinch Swamp
18. Fisherman's Wharf & Spenser Smith Park
19. Rattray Marsh, Port Credit
20. Tommy Thompson Park & Toronto Islands
21. Rouge River PP

Great Lakes–St. Lawrence Forest

22. Mountsberg Conservation Area & Halton Regional Forest
23. Conestoga Lake (Reservoir) Conservation Area
24. Luther Lake/Marsh
25. Wawanosh Valley Conservation Area
26. Greenock Swamp
27. MacGregor Point PP
28. Walker's Woods, Rankin River & Spry Lake

29. Black Creek PP
30. Dyer's Bay
31. Minesing Swamp
32. Wye Marsh Wildlife Centre
33. Awenda PP & Georgian Bay Islands NP
34. Carden Plain
35. McRae Point PP
36. Sibbald Point PP
37. Lynde Shores Conservation Area & Cranberry Marsh
38. Darlington PP
39. Lake Scugog
40. Petroglyphs PP
41. Silent Lake PP
42. Bon Echo PP
43. Presqu'ile PP
44. Sandbanks PP
45. Big Island Marsh
46. Prince Edward Point NWA
47. Helen Quilliam Otter Lake Sanctuary
48. Charleston Lake PP
49. Frontenac PP
50. Foley Mountain Conservation Area
51. Upper Canada Migratory Bird Sanctuary & Long Sault Parkway
52. Guindon Park
53. Carillon PP
54. South Nation River
55. Mer Bleue Conservation Area
56. Richmond Fen
57. Deschênes Rapids & Lac Deschênes
58. Fitzroy PP
59. Ottawa River PP
60. Algonquin PP
61. Arrowhead PP
62. Killbear PP
63. Grundy Lake PP
64. Mattawa River PP
65. Marten River PP
66. Halfway Lake PP & Windy Lake PP

67. Killarney PP & Chutes PP
68. Manitoulin Island
69. St. Joseph Island
70. Whitefish Island & Hiawatha Highlands Conservation Area
71. Batchawana Bay PP
72. Lake Superior PP
73. Quetico PP
74. Rainy River area
75. Lake of the Woods PP
76. Rushing River PP

Boreal Forest

77. Hwy #11 from North Bay to Longlac
78. Kettle Lakes PP
79. Greenwater PP
80. Rene Brunelle PP
81. Fushimi Lake PP
82. Wakami Lake PP
83. The Shoals PP
84. Missinaibi River PP
85. Obatanga PP
86. Pukaskwa NP
87. Lake Nipigon PP
88. Hurkett Cove Conservation Area
89. Ouimet Canyon PP
90. Sleeping Giant PP
91. Mission Island Marsh
92. Hwy #599 to Pickle Lake
93. Albany River PP
94. Winisk River PP
95. Blue Lake PP
96. Woodland Caribou PP

Hudson Bay Lowlands

97. Severn River PP
98. Moosonee

Tundra

99. Polar Bear PP
100. Fort Severn

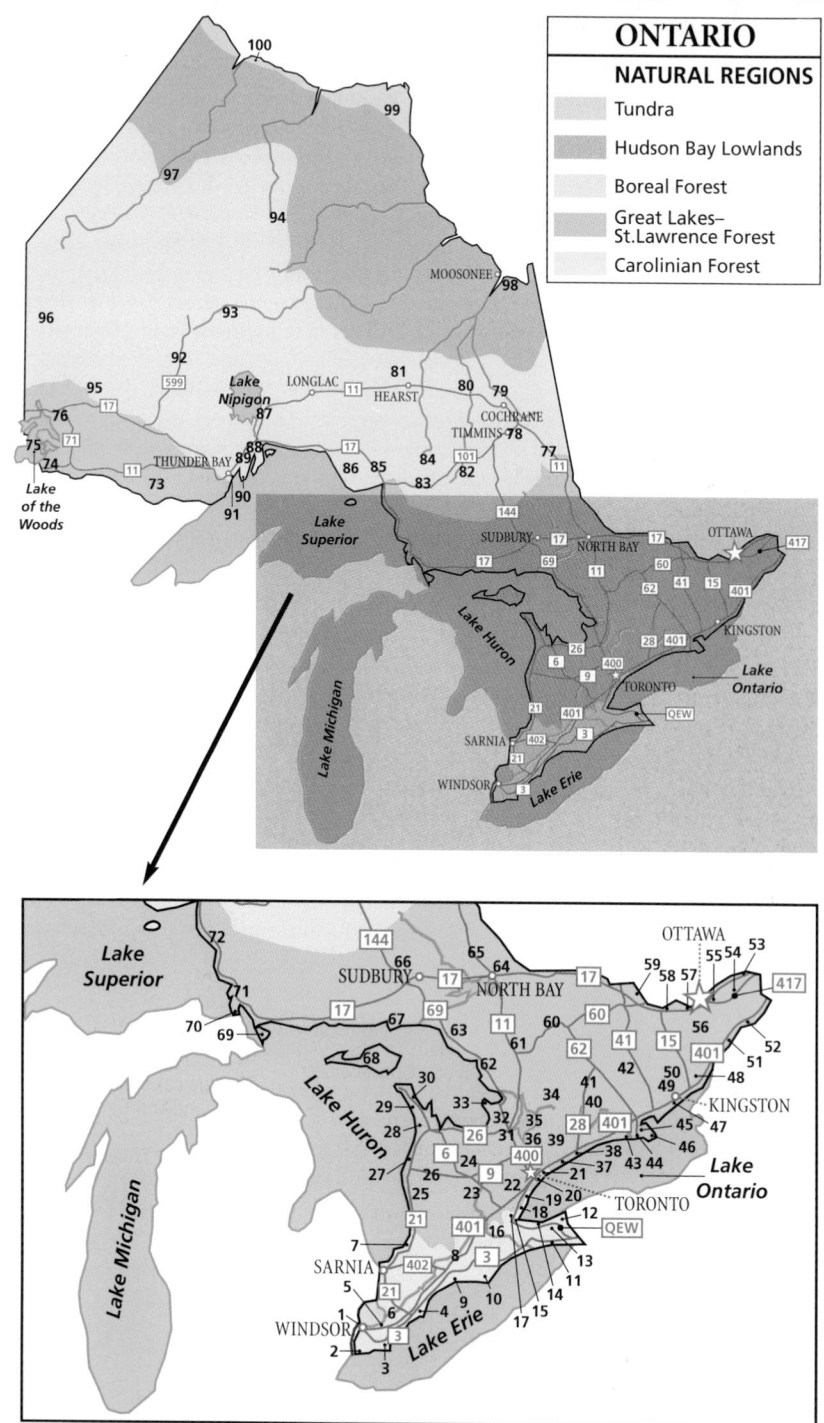

ONTARIO

NATURAL REGIONS

- Tundra
- Hudson Bay Lowlands
- Boreal Forest
- Great Lakes–St.Lawrence Forest
- Carolinian Forest

Point Pelee National Park

Jutting into Lake Erie, this tiny, triangular oasis of precious marshland and Carolinian Forest is the southernmost point of mainland Canada. The park's beaches, marshlands, forests and shrubby fields have attracted 368 recorded species, including 41 species of dazzling wood warblers. Experienced birders often meet more than 100 species in a day during the spring migration, which is world renowned in Point Pelee. But masses of birds attract masses of people—over 25,000 birders visit this park each spring!

Swamp Sparrow

During summer, you can rent a canoe or saunter along the boardwalk to look for Marsh Wrens, Swamp Sparrows, Common Yellowthroats, Great Egrets and Soras. In the swamp forest of the Woodland Nature Trail, Tree Swallows, Wood Ducks and rare Prothonotary Warblers may be seen attending to their nests. Many migrant shorebirds, waterfowl, raptors, hummingbirds and songbirds can be seen during the fall migration. Least Bitterns, Bald Eagles, King Rails, Purple Gallinules, Yellow-billed Cuckoos, White-eyed Vireos, Hooded Warblers and Orchard Orioles are some of the many rare species sighted here over the years.

Rondeau Provincial Park and Rondeau Bay

The forests, marshes, swamps and sandy beaches of the Rondeau Provincial Park promontory teem with both common and extremely rare bird life year-round. Sandhill Cranes, Chuck-will's-widows, Ruby-throated Hummingbirds, Red-bellied Woodpeckers, Brown Creepers, Carolina Wrens, Cerulean Warblers and Prothonotary Warblers all breed here. Fortunate observers may even find evidence of nesting Yellow-throated Vireos, Kentucky Warblers or Summer Tanagers.

In fall, Rondeau's shorelines occasionally support Purple Sandpipers and Red Phalaropes along with more regular yellowlegs, Sanderlings and other shorebirds. The bay itself may harbour the occasional King Eider or Harlequin Duck, but it more commonly supports Long-tailed Ducks, Buffleheads and Common Goldeneyes. Some birders may be shocked to hear pounding gunshots in the park's wetlands in fall, as hunters legally try to bag a waterfowl.

Long Point Provincial Park, Big Creek National Wildlife Area and Turkey Point Provincial Park

The diversity of habitats represented by these three neighbouring natural areas supports a tremendous abundance of bird life in all seasons. In late March and early April, the area boasts spectacular concentrations of staging waterfowl, including Green-winged Teals, Redheads, Canvasbacks, Lesser Scaups, Greater Scaups, American Wigeons and Ruddy Ducks. Trumpeter, Tundra and Mute swans have been recorded here, although the Tundra Swan is by far the most prominent.

Redhead

A special feature of the area is the Long Point Bird Observatory, the oldest bird observatory in North America. The Old Cut Field Station and visitor centre occasionally organize public viewing of bird banders in action, allowing superb, close-up views of both migrant and resident birds. (Contact the visitor centre in advance.) Rare and specialty birds that may be seen here include the Forster's Tern, Little Gull, Red-bellied Woodpecker, Sedge Wren, Blue-gray Gnatcatcher, Northern Mockingbird, Prothonotary Warbler and Louisiana Waterthrush.

The Niagara River

Bonaparte's Gull

Fall and winter seem to be the best time to bird along the Niagara River and its famous falls. From late October to December, enormous flocks of Bonaparte's Gulls, Herring Gulls and Ring-billed Gulls move through the area; they are accompanied by smaller flocks of less common gulls and exceptional rarities, such as Black-legged Kittiwakes. In November, waterfowl invade the area, and a lucky birder might catch sight of vagrants such as the Harlequin Duck and Barrow's Goldeneye. In winter, waxwings, mockingbirds and Evening Grosbeaks profit from the abundance of berry-producing plants found in these areas.

Dundas Marsh

Administered by the Royal Botanical Gardens, the wild lands and formal gardens surrounding Dundas Marsh provide a wide array of habitats for breeding, migrant and overwintering species. The marsh itself supports various waterfowl, herons and marsh-inhabiting songbirds, such as the Common Yellowthroat. Depending on water levels, mudflats bordering the wetland may host shorebirds during migration.

The Toronto Islands and Tommy Thompson Park (The Leslie Street Spit)

Accessible by ferry, the small Toronto Islands provide tremendous birding opportunities for much of the year, except in summertime, when crowds people scare away most birds. Many waterfowl and landbirds pass through in fall. Winter feeders and the unusually warm envelope of urban air sustain an exciting variety of overwintering birds. Beaches, marshes, wet meadows, sheltered coves, lawns, ornamental plantings and old cottonwood stands with dense, shrubby understories all attract a fine array of spring migrants.

The five-kilometre-long mainland spit encompassed by Tommy Thompson Park is not much more than a glorified landfill, but it remains one of Toronto's premier birding sites. Hordes of gulls, terns, cormorants and Black-crowned Night-Herons nest in the area, as do smaller numbers of Wilson's Phalaropes and waterfowl. Snowy Owls, Short-eared Owls, Snow Buntings and American Pipits are seen here in migration, as are a large number of unexpected rarities.

Black-crowned Night-Heron

Rouge River Provincial Park

Scarlet Tanager

The forests of sugar maple, beech and oak in Rouge River Provincial Park ring with the chimes of Red-eyed Vireos and Scarlet Tanagers. Hummingbirds, flycatchers, catbirds, sparrows and warblers may all be encountered in the park, too. Wood Thrushes stir the pungent, moist leaf litter of the forest floor, Field Sparrows buzz from atop their shrubby perches, the drumming of the wings of startled Ruffed Grouse reverberates through the air, and, when night falls, Great Horned Owls swoop through the forest in search of prey. It is here in the heart of the Rouge River Valley that you will find the wonders of the Carolinian Forest.

Cranberry Marsh and Lynde Shores Conservation Area

Located just outside of Toronto along the shores of Lake Ontario in the Ajax-Whitby area, these excellent birdwatching areas are a 'must see' for anyone interested in birds. Viewing platforms located around the periphery of Cranberry Marsh allow birders to observe a variety of herons, waterfowl, rails, gulls and other marshland birds. The adjacent Lynde Shores Conservation Area protects another marsh, some fields, a small woodland and thickets that at times seem to be pulsating with birds. Blue-winged Teals, Marsh Wrens, Virginia Rails, Spotted Sandpipers and Red-tailed Hawks are a few of the birds normally found here.

Presqu'ile Provincial Park

In the fall, shorebirds and pursuing raptors are best seen within Presqu'ile Provincial Park, a small, beach-lined peninsula. Smaller numbers of dowitchers, Black–bellied Plovers, Red Knots and Baird's, White-rumped and Purple sandpipers are seen among the larger numbers of Least Sandpipers, Semipalmated Sandpipers, Semipalmated Plovers, Sanderlings and Dunlins that regularly stop here to feed and rest before crossing Lake Ontario. At Owen Point, birders often see Merlins and Peregrine Falcons hunting. Waterfowl and wetland waders fill the park's eastern marshlands; migrant, breeding and overwintering songbirds enliven thickets and woodlands. October is a good time to see Brants and scoters.

The Bruce Peninsula

Although private cottages dominate the Bruce Peninsula, there are many small parks, picnic areas and nature preserves that are accessible to the public. The shores and islands of Lake Huron and Georgian Bay are good places to see shorebirds, gulls, terns, herons and waterfowl. Old fields, fencelines and ditches are usually bustling with bluebirds, swallows, sparrows and meadowlarks. Flycatchers, warblers, wrens, thrushes, tanagers and orioles are typical inhabitants of woodlands and cedar bogs in this area. MacGregor Point, Bruce Peninsula and Sauble Falls are the major parks. Black Creek, St. Jean Point, Crane River and Walker's Woods are smaller reserves that also offer good birding.

Baltimore Oriole

Carden Plain

Located east of Lake Simcoe and north of the small town of Kirkfield, the old fields, marginal farmland and sparse woodlands of Carden Plain are home to a unique community of species. Upland Sandpipers, Loggerhead Shrikes, Eastern Bluebirds, Purple Martins, Golden-winged Warblers, Western Meadowlarks and Grasshopper Sparrows are among the rarer Ontario birds that can be seen along the country roads during a late spring or early summer tour of the area.

Bon Echo Provincial Park

This celebrated park is a good place to introduce the whole family to the outdoors and the intriguing world of birds. In the campground alone, you will find Ruby-throated Hummingbirds and Yellow-bellied Sapsuckers, Hairy Woodpeckers, Pileated Woodpeckers, Black-capped Chickadees, Red-breasted Nuthatches, Blue Jays, Brown Thrashers and, if you are lucky, flamboyant flocks of Evening Grosbeaks. Huddled around the evening campfire, your family will no doubt be enchanted by the echoing tremolo of the Common Loon, the urgent call of the Whip-poor-will and the low hoots of owls preparing for the evening hunt. The ancient, red ochre paintings of Mazinaw Rock befit the seeming magic of Bon Echo Provincial Park.

Evening Grosbeak

Ottawa River Parklands

Residents of the nation's capital need not travel far to enjoy a fulfilling day of birding. The waters and shores of Lac Deschênes and the Deschênes Rapids are good places to see shorebirds and rare gulls and terns in migration. During winter, Common Goldeneyes, Common Mergansers and a variety of other waterbirds frequent this same area. Winter is a great time to visit Britannia and Rockcliffe parks to meet large flocks of Bohemian Waxwings, crossbills, Pine Siskins, Evening Grosbeaks and Purple Finches; these species all come to take advantage of well-stocked feeders and berry-producing plants. When winter snows arrive, keep your eyes peeled for the odd Gyrfalcon or Great Gray Owl.

Algonquin Provincial Park

Few parks are as enchanting as Algonquin, Ontario's oldest provincial park. Well-kept campgrounds, plenty of hiking and skiing trails and over 1600 km of canoe routes allow birders to thoroughly explore this park. The Boreal Forest and the Great Lakes–St. Lawrence forest meet in this park, which is laced with streams, lakes, beaver ponds and outcroppings of precambrian bedrock. In spring and summer, early mornings resound with the songs of Olive-sided Flycatchers, Red-eyed Vireos, Nashville Warblers, Northern Parula and Black-throated Blue Warblers.

Launching a canoe into the soft morning mist can be a magical experience when Common Loons issue their haunting wails and Great Blue Herons stand on the shoreline like statues. In winter, birding on cross-country skis or snowshoes can result in close encounters with Spruce Grouse, Northern Saw-whet Owls, Black-backed Woodpeckers, Gray Jays and Boreal Chickadees.

Grundy Lake and Killarney Provincial Parks

Precambrian outcroppings combined with mixed forest and interspersed in vibrant aquatic habitats typify the Grundy Lake area. On park trails, you can expect to meet Great Blue Herons (there is a large rookery in the park), Winter Wrens, Cedar Waxwings, Warbling Vireos and Pine Warblers. Further north lie stunning lakes, streams, beaver ponds, woodlands and towering rock ridges. Killarney Wilderness Park, home to well over 100 species of birds, has been celebrated in the paintings of the Group of Seven. Turkey Vultures, Common Ravens, Whip-poor-wills, Blackburnian Warblers and Rose-breasted Grosbeaks all breed in Killarney.

Turkey Vulture

Lake Superior Provincial Park

Resilient stands of majestic white pine, shaped by ferocious winter winds, support the activities of Pine Warblers and Olive-sided Flycatchers in Lake Superior Provincial Park. Beaver ponds reflect the images of breeding warblers, vireos and flycatchers, and kinglets, finches, grosbeaks and crossbills twitter in the stands of spruce and fir. This spectacular park could be the highlight of a northern birding adventure at any time of year.

Sleeping Giant Provincial Park

The Sleeping Giant, a high bluff with rugged cliffs, is a prominent feature of the Thunder Bay landscape and a sanctuary for many engaging birds. Here, Peregrine Falcons scan their world from cliffside eyries. Mature balsam fir forests provide excellent habitat for Bay-breasted Warblers and secretive Boreal Owls, and bogs of white cedar, black spruce and alder host a number of colourful warblers, including the Northern Parula. In spring and fall, the Thunder Cape Bird Observatory records amazing details of bird migration, including the astonishing arrival of southern rarities.

Quetico Provincial Park

Bald Eagle, Osprey, Merlin, Pine Siskins, Red Crossbills, Three-toed Woodpeckers, five species of owl and 21 species of warblers justify exploration of this beautiful wilderness park. All you need is some time, a canoe, a few supplies and some information from the park's interpretive staff.

Trans Canada North to Highway 11

Between the northern towns of North Bay, Kirkland Lake, Iroquois Falls, Kapuskasing, Hearst and Thunder Bay lie lonely expanses of spruce, fir, birch, aspen and tamarack that hold a quiet secret—the amazing bird life of the Boreal Forest. Sandhill Cranes, Spruce Grouse, Solitary Sandpipers, Bonaparte's Gulls, Boreal Owls, Black-backed Woodpeckers, Pine Grosbeaks, American Redstarts, Ovenbirds, White-throated Sparrows, Rusty Blackbirds, and Canada, Mourning and Black-and-white warblers all thrive in this northern landscape.

Sandhill Crane

Rainy River and Lake of the Woods

Nestled in a far corner of Ontario, bordering Manitoba and Minnesota, this unique area of islands, bays, woodlands and farmlands hosts a distinctive bird community that combines Boreal Forest species with species more typical of the Great Plains. American White Pelicans, Sharp-tailed Grouse, Black-billed Magpies, Yellow-headed Blackbirds and Western Kingbirds are rare Ontario breeders found in this region. Western waterbirds, including the Franklin's Gull, are also reported here.

Polar Bear Provincial Park

Polar Bear Provincial Park is a remote wilderness of tundra and water accessible only to those who have a great sense of adventure and expert camping skills. The only way in for humans is to charter a flight. Some birds here are found nowhere else in Ontario. This park supports nesting populations of Red-throated Loons, Pacific Loons, Tundra Swans, Snow Geese, King Eiders, Common Eiders, Rough-legged Hawks, Willow Ptarmigans, Whimbrels, Hudsonian Godwits, Dunlins, Stilt Sandpipers, Parasitic Jaegers, Arctic Terns, Gray-cheeked Thrushes, American Pipits, American Tree Sparrows and Smith's Longspurs. Birders should contact the Ministry of Natural Resources for access information.

ABOUT THE SPECIES ACCOUNTS

This book gives detailed accounts of the 318 species of birds that have nested or been confirmed nesting in Ontario at least 10 recorded times; these species can be expected on an annual basis. Thirty-seven occasional species and species of special note are briefly mentioned in an illustrated appendix. These species can be expected to be seen again because of anticipated range expansion, migration or well-documented wandering tendencies. The order of the birds and their common and scientific names follow the American Ornithologists' Union's *Check-list of North American Birds* (7th edition, July 1998).

As well as discussing the identifying features of the birds, each species account also attempts to bring the birds to life by describing their various character traits. Personifying a bird helps us relate to it, but the characterizations presented should not be mistaken for scientific propositions. Our limited understanding of non-human creatures, our interpretations and our assumptions most likely fall short of truly defining birds. Nevertheless, we hope that a lively, engaging text will communicate our scientific knowledge as smoothly and effectively as possible.

One of the challenges of birdwatching is that many species look different in spring and summer than they do in fall and winter. Many birds have what are generally called breeding and non-breeding plumages, and immature birds often look different from their parents. This book does not try to describe or illustrate all the different plumages of a species; instead, it focuses on the forms that are most likely to be seen in our area. Most the illustrations are of adult birds.

Mississippi Kite

ID: It is difficult to describe the features of a bird without being able to visualize it, so this section is best used in combination with the illustrations. Where appropriate, the description is subdivided to highlight the differences between male and female birds, breeding and non-breeding birds and immature and adult birds. The descriptions use as few technical terms as possible, and favour easily understood language. Birds may not have 'jaw lines,' 'moustaches' or 'chins,' but these and other terms are easily understood by all readers, in spite of their scientific inaccuracy. Some of the most common features of birds are pointed out in the glossary illustration.

Size: The size measurement, an average length of the bird's body from bill to tail, is an approximate measurement of the bird as it is seen in nature. The size of larger birds is often given as a range, because there is variation between individuals. In addition, wingspans are given for some of the larger birds that are often seen in flight. Please note that birds with long tails often have large measurements that do not necessarily reflect 'body' size.

Status: A general comment, such as 'common,' 'uncommon' or 'rare,' is usually sufficient to describe the relative abundance of a species. Situations are bound to differ somewhat since migratory pulses, seasonal changes and centres of activity tend to concentrate or disperse birds.

Habitat: The habitats we have listed describe where each species is most commonly found. In most cases, it is a generalized description, but if a bird is restricted to a specific habitat, the habitat is described precisely. Because of the freedom flight gives them, birds can turn up in almost any type of habitat, but usually they will be found in environments that provide the specific food, water, cover and, in some cases, nesting habitat that they need to survive.

Nesting: The reproductive strategies used by different bird species vary: in each species account, nest location and structure, clutch size, incubation period and parental duties are discussed. Remember that birdwatching ethics discourage the disturbance of active bird nests. If you disturb a nest, you may drive off the parents during a critical period or expose defenseless young to predators. The nesting behaviour of birds that do not nest in Ontario is not described.

Feeding: Birds spend a great deal of time foraging for food. If you know what a bird eats and where the food is found, you will have a good chance of meeting the bird you are looking for. Birds are frequently encountered while they are foraging; we hope that our description of their feeding styles and diets provides valuable identifying characteristics, as well as interesting dietary facts.

Voice: You will hear many birds, particularly songbirds, which may remain hidden from view. Memorable paraphrases of distinctive sounds will aid you in identifying a species by ear. These paraphrases only loosely resemble the call, song or sound produced by the bird. Should one of our paraphrases not work for you, feel free to make up your own—the creative exercise will reinforce your memory of the bird's sound.

Purple Martin

Similar Species: Easily confused species are discussed briefly. If you concentrate on the most relevant field marks, the subtle differences between species can be reduced to easily identifiable traits. You might find it useful to consult this section when finalizing your identification; knowing the most relevant field marks will shortcut the identification process. Even experienced birders can mistake one species for another.

White-breasted Nuthatch

Best Sites: If you are looking for a particular bird in Ontario, you will have more luck in some places than in others, even within the range shown on the range map. We have listed places that, besides providing a good chance of seeing a species, are easily accessible. As a result, many conservation areas and provincial and national parks are mentioned.

Range Maps: The range map for each species represents the overall range of the species in Ontario in an average year. Most birds will confine their annual movements to this range, although each year some birds wander beyond their traditional boundaries. These maps do not show differences in abundance within the range—areas of a range with good habitat will support a denser population than areas with poorer habitat. These maps also cannot show small pockets within the range where the species may actually be absent, or how the range may change from year to year. Unlike most other field guides, we have attempted to show migratory pathways—areas of the province where birds may appear while en route to nesting or winter habitat. Many of these migratory routes are 'best guesses,' which will no doubt be refined as new discoveries are made. The representations of the pathways do not distinguish high-use migration corridors from areas that are seldom used. Although most migratory birds will migrate over the Great Lakes, usually at high altitude, their migration patterns over these large expanses of water are not well known. Migration routes over the Great Lakes and Hudson Bay and James Bay have not been marked unless the species is known to feed or rest on open water during migration.

Range Map Symbols

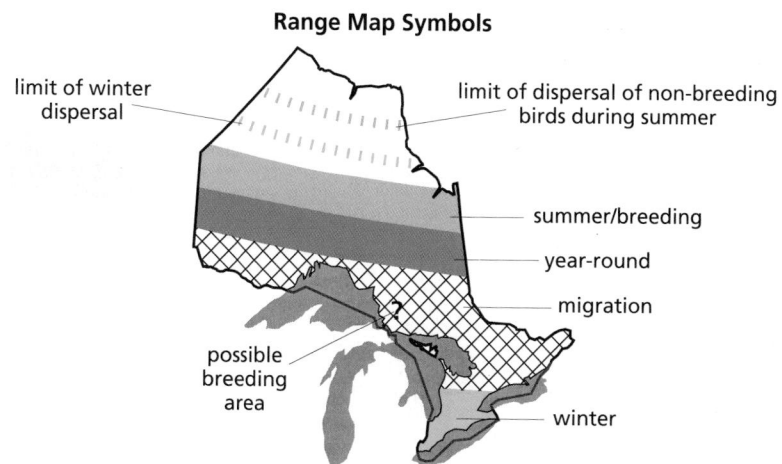

limit of winter dispersal

limit of dispersal of non-breeding birds during summer

summer/breeding

year-round

migration

possible breeding area

winter

RED-THROATED LOON

Gavia stellata

Red-throated Loons complete their annual nesting rites along the freshwater lakes and ponds of northern Ontario's coastal tundra and at the northern edge of the Hudson Bay Lowland. Only adventurous summer visitors to the often inhospitable Polar Bear Provincial Park can expect to see this dainty-bodied loon on its breeding territory. It typically swims low in the water with its bill held high, as if trying to accentuate its maroon throat in breeding plumage. • The Red-throat is our smallest loon, and it is able to stand upright and take flight with just a short take-off effort. As a result, it can nest on smaller bodies of water than its larger, less agile relatives. • Red-throats are reliable meteorologists: they often become very noisy before the onset of foul weather, possibly sensing changes in barometric pressure. • The scientific name *stellata* refers to the star-like, white speckles on this bird's back in its non-breeding plumage.

breeding

ID: slim bill is held upward. *Breeding:* red throat; grey face and neck; black and white stripes from the nape to the back of the head; plain brownish back. *Non-breeding:* back is speckled with white; white face; dark grey on the crown and the back of the head. *In flight:* hunched back; legs trail behind the tail; rapid wingbeats.
Size: *L* 60–70 cm; *W* 1–1.1 m.
Status: rare migrant; a few may be present in winter; rare to uncommon breeder.
Habitat: *Breeding:* small shallow lakes and ponds; often feeds at sea. *Non-breeding:* large freshwater lakes.
Nesting: on the shorelines of small ponds and wetlands; nest is a mass of aquatic vegetation piled very close to the water's edge; pair

incubates 2 eggs for up to 29 days.
Feeding: dives deeply and captures small fish; occasionally eats aquatic insects and amphibians; occasionally eats aquatic vegetation in early spring.
Voice: Mallard-like *kwuk-kwuk-kwuk-kwuk* in flight; mournful wail during courtship; distraction call is a loud *gayorwork*.
Similar Species: *Common Loon* (p. 36): larger; heavier bill; lacks the white speckling on the back in non-breeding plumage. *Pacific Loon* (p. 35): larger; purple throat and white speckling on the back in breeding plumage; all-dark back in non-breeding plumage.
Best Sites: Polar Bear PP; Ottawa River, Ottawa; Presqu'ile PP.

PACIFIC LOON

Gavia pacifica

In spring, Pacific Loons shimmer like aluminum vessels on our larger lakes during their stop-overs in Ontario. Unfortunately, they move quickly to their nesting grounds along the Hudson Bay, and there are few observations of these birds in breeding plumage. Birders in southern Ontario should watch for these loons from mid-April to late May and from late October to late December. • Pacific Loons nest in the same areas of the North as their red-throated relatives, but Pacifics incubate their eggs and raise their young along the shores of larger bodies of water. When approached by an intruder, nesting adults exhibit spectacular displays of energetic splashing and diving that are usually accompanied by loud yelps. • Pacific Loons winter exclusively along the Pacific coast from Alaska to southern California.

breeding

ID: *Breeding:* silver grey crown and nape; dark throat is framed by white stripes; white breast; dark back with large, bold, white spots. *Non-breeding:* well-defined light cheek and throat; dark upperparts; dark chin stripe. *In flight:* hunched back; legs trail behind the tail; rapid wingbeats.
Size: *L* 59–73 cm; *W* 1–1.3 m.
Status: rare migrant from mid-April to December; common local breeder.
Habitat: large coastal tundra sloughs and lakes; often feeds at sea; inhabits large freshwater lakes during migration.
Nesting: on grassy shorelines and islands; raised mass of vegetation is used as a nest site; pair incubates 1 or 2 dark olive,

black-spotted eggs for 28–30 days.
Feeding: dives deeply for fish and occasionally aquatic invertebrates; average dive is 45 seconds; occasionally eats aquatic vegetation.
Voice: calls include a dog-like yelp, a cat-like meow and a raven-like croak.
Similar Species: breeding plumage is distinctive. *Common Loon* (p. 36): larger; lacks the sharp definition between the black and the white on the face and neck; often has a light collar in non-breeding plumage. *Red-throated Loon* (p. 34): tilts its bill upward; extensive white spotting on the back in non-breeding plumage.
Best Sites: Polar Bear PP; Point Pelee NP; Lake Ontario, from Pickering to Hamilton.

COMMON LOON

Gavia immer

The Common Loon is a classic symbol of northern lakes, and it is honoured and celebrated as our provincial bird. Most summer cottagers and wilderness explorers revere the loon's haunting songs, which pierce the stillness of summer nights. • Loons are well adapted to their aquatic lifestyle: these divers have nearly solid bones that give them less buoyancy (most birds have hollow bones), and their feet are placed well back on their bodies for underwater propulsion. Small bass, perch, sunfish, pike and whitefish are all fair game for these excellent underwater hunters. On land, however, their awkward tendencies are very apparent. Their rear-placed legs make walking a nightmare, and their heavy bodies and small wing size means they require a lengthy sprint before taking off.

breeding

ID: *Breeding*: green-black head; stout, thick, black bill; white 'necklace'; white breast and underparts; black and white 'checkerboard' upperparts; red eyes. *Non-breeding*: much duller plumage; sandy brown back; light underparts. *In flight*: long wings beat constantly; hunchbacked appearance; legs trail behind the tail.

Size: *L* 71–89 cm; *W* 1.2–1.5 m.

Status: common migrant; rare winter resident; fairly common breeder.

Habitat: *Breeding*: large rivers and lakes, often with islands that provide undisturbed shorelines for nesting. *Non-breeding*: lakes with unfrozen, open water.

Nesting: on a muskrat lodge, small island or projecting shoreline; always very near water; nest mound is built from aquatic vegetation; pair shares all parental duties, including nest building, egg incubation and rearing of the young.

Feeding: pursues small fish underwater to depths of 55 m; occasionally eats large, aquatic invertebrates and larval and adult amphibians.

Voice: alarm call is a quavering tremolo, often called 'loon laughter'; contact call is a long but simple wailing note; breeding notes are soft, short hoots. *Male*: territorial call is an undulating, complex yodel.

Similar Species: *Red-throated Loon* (p. 34): smaller; slender bill; red throat in breeding plumage; sharply defined white face and white-spotted back in non-breeding plumage. *Pacific Loon* (p. 35): smaller; dusty grey head often looks silver; dark cap extends down over the eye and is lighter than the back in non-breeding plumage.

Best Sites: Algonquin PP; Lake of the Woods; Presqu'ile PP; large lakes of the Canadian Shield; MacGregor Point PP; Whitby-Pickering; Lake Ontario.

PIED-BILLED GREBE

Podilymbus podiceps

The odd, exuberant chortle of the Pied-billed Grebe fits right in with the boisterous cacophony of Ontario's wetland communities. Heard more frequently than seen, the Pied-billed Grebe is the smallest and least colourful of Ontario's grebes. • Pied-bills are extremely wary birds, and they are far more common than encounters would lead one to believe. They tend to swim inconspicuously in shallow waters of quiet bays and rivers, only occasionally giving their strange chuckle or whinny. Their floating nests are built among sparse vegetation, a strategy that allows them to see predators approaching from far away. When frightened by an intruder, they cover their eggs and slide underwater, leaving a nest that looks like nothing more than a mat of debris. A Pied-billed Grebe can slowly submerge up to its head, so that only its nostrils and eyes remain above the water. • The scientific name *podiceps*, which means 'rump foot,' refers to the way the bird's feet are located toward the back of its body. In flight, the feet extend beyond the tail and help the bird steer.

breeding

ID: *Breeding:* all-brown body; black ring on the light-coloured bill; laterally compressed 'chicken bill'; black throat; very short tail; white undertail coverts; pale belly; pale eye ring. *Non-breeding:* yellow eye ring; yellow bill lacks the black ring; white chin and throat; brownish crown.
Size: *L* 30–38 cm.
Status: fairly common migrant; a few may be present in winter; uncommon local breeder.
Habitat: ponds, marshes and backwaters with sparse emergent vegetation.
Nesting: among sparse vegetation in sheltered bays, ponds and marshes; floating platform nest, made of wet and decaying plants, is anchored to or placed among emergent vegetation; pair incubates 4 or 5

eggs and raises the striped young together.
Feeding: makes shallow dives and gleans the surface for aquatic invertebrates, small fish, adult and larval amphibians and occasionally aquatic plants.
Voice: loud, whooping call that begins quickly, then slows down: *kuk-kuk-kuk cow cow cow cowp cowp cowp.*
Similar Species: *Eared Grebe* (p. 40): red eyes; black and white head; golden ear tufts and chestnut flanks in breeding plumage; seldom seen in summer. *Horned Grebe* (p. 38): red eyes; black and white head; golden ear tufts and red neck in breeding plumage; seldom seen in summer. *American Coot* (p. 117): all-black body; pale bill extends onto the forehead.
Best Sites: Rondeau PP; Long Point PP; Presqu'ile PP; Ottawa River PP.

HORNED GREBE

Podiceps auritus

Cold, mucky wetlands might not seem very inviting, but nothing is more appealing to Horned Grebes than quiet, well-vegetated marshes. Their propensity for these habitats starts early in life, before the birds are born—Horned Grebe eggs often lie in a shallow pool of water on their floating nest. The wet vegetation and tea-coloured water may stain the eggs, improving their camouflage. When an incubating parent is frightened off its nest, it will frequently attempt to cover the eggs with soggy vegetation before leaving them. • Unlike the fully webbed front toes of most swimming birds, grebe toes are individually webbed, or 'lobed'—the three forward-facing toes have individual flanges that are not connected to the other toes. • This bird's common name and its scientific name, *auritus* (eared), refer to the golden feather tufts, or 'horns,' that these grebes acquire in breeding plumage.

breeding

ID: *Breeding*: rufous neck and flanks; black head; golden ear tufts ('horns'); black back; white underparts; red eyes; flat crown. *Non-breeding*: lacks the ear tufts; black upperparts; white cheek, foreneck and underparts. *In flight*: wings beat constantly; hunchbacked appearance; legs trail behind the tail.

Size: *L* 30–38 cm.

Status: locally common migrant; a few may be present in winter; rare breeder.

Habitat: *Breeding*: shallow, weedy wetlands. *In migration*: wetlands and larger lakes.

Nesting: usually singly or in groups of 2 or 3 pairs; in thick vegetation along lake edges, ponds, marshes and reservoirs; pair incubates 4–7 eggs and raises the young together.

Feeding: makes shallow dives and gleans the surface for aquatic insects, crustaceans, mollusks, small fish and adult and larval amphibians.

Voice: loud series of croaks and shrieking notes, and a sharp *kyark kyark* during courtship; usually quiet outside the breeding season.

Similar Species: *Eared Grebe* (p. 40): black neck in breeding plumage; black cheek and darker neck in non-breeding plumage. *Pied-billed Grebe* (p. 37): thicker, stubbier bill; mostly brown body. *Red-necked Grebe* (p. 39): larger; dark eyes; lacks the ear tufts; white cheek in breeding plumage; generally louder.

Best Sites: MacGregor Point PP; Point Pelee NP; Rondeau PP; Lake St. Clair marshes.

RED-NECKED GREBE

Podiceps grisegena

As spring evenings settle over Luther Marsh along the border of Dufferin and Wellington counties, the enthusiastic laughing calls of courting Red-necked Grebes punctuate the beginning of a new breeding season. Although Red-necked Grebes are not as vocally refined as loons, few loons can match the verbal vigour of a pair of Red-necks romancing the passions of spring. Typically, their wild laughter lasts through the nights in late May. • All grebes carry their newly hatched young on their backs. The heavily striped young can stay aboard even when the parents dive underwater. • The scientific name *grisegena* means 'grey cheek'—a distinctive field mark of this bird in winter plumage.

breeding

ID: *Breeding:* rusty neck; whitish cheek; black crown; straight, heavy bill is dark above and yellow underneath; black upperparts; light underparts; dark eyes. *Non-breeding:* greyish-white foreneck, chin and cheek.
Size: *L* 43–56 cm.
Status: fairly common migrant; a few may be present in winter; rare breeder.
Habitat: *Breeding:* emergent vegetation zone of lakes and ponds. *In migration:* open, deeper lakes.
Nesting: usually singly, but occasionally in loosely scattered colonies; floating platform nest of aquatic vegetation is anchored to submerged plants; 4 or 5 eggs in a clutch; eggs are initially white, but often become stained by the wet vegetation.
Feeding: dives and gleans the surface for small fish, aquatic invertebrates and amphibians.
Voice: often-repeated, laugh-like, excited *ah-ooo ah-ooo ah-ooo ah-ah-ah-ah-ah.*
Similar Species: *Horned Grebe* (p. 38): dark cheek and golden 'horns' in breeding plumage; red eyes, all-dark bill and bright white cheek in non-breeding plumage. *Eared Grebe* (p. 40): black neck in breeding plumage; black cheek in non-breeding plumage. *Pied-billed Grebe* (p. 37): thicker, stubbier bill; mostly brown body. *Western Grebe* (p. 352): red eyes; black and white neck in breeding plumage. *Ducks* (pp. 60–88): all lack the combination of a white cheek and a red neck.
Best Sites: Luther Lake/Marsh; Lillabelle Lake, Cochrane; Lake Ontario near Cranberry Marsh and Rattray Marsh.

EARED GREBE

Podiceps nigricollis

This little grebe is typically found in the West, but small numbers find their way into Ontario each year. Most Eared Grebes are only seen here in the lower Great Lakes region during spring or fall migration. Eared Grebes also inhabit parts of Europe, Asia, Central Africa and South America. • Like the rest of its clan, the Eared Grebe eats feathers. The feathers often pack the digestive tract, and it is thought that they might protect the stomach lining and intestines from sharp fish bones or parasites, or they might possibly slow the passage of food, giving more time for complete digestion. • The scientific name *nigricollis* means 'black neck'—a useful field mark for this species.

breeding

ID: *Breeding:* black neck, cheek, forehead and back; red flanks; fanned-out, golden ear tufts; white underparts; thin, straight bill; red eyes; slightly raised crown. *Non-breeding:* dark upperparts and cheek; light underparts; dusky upper foreneck and flanks. *In flight:* wings beat constantly; hunchbacked appearance; legs trail behind the tail.
Size: *L* 30–36 cm.
Status: very rare from April to November; 1 recent breeding record is known.
Habitat: *Breeding:* shallow, weedy wetlands. *In migration:* wetlands and larger lakes.
Nesting: usually colonial; in thick vegetation in lake edges, ponds and marshes; shallow, flimsy, floating platform nest of wet and decaying plants is anchored to or placed

among emergent vegetation; pair incubates the 3–5 eggs and raises the young together.
Feeding: makes shallow dives and gleans the surface for aquatic insects, crustaceans, mollusks, small fish and larval and adult amphibians.
Voice: mellow *poo-eee-chk* during courtship; usually quiet outside the breeding season.
Similar Species: *Horned Grebe* (p. 38): rufous neck in breeding plumage; white cheek in non-breeding plumage. *Pied-billed Grebe* (p. 37): thicker, stubbier bill; mostly brown body. *Red-necked Grebe* (p. 39): larger overall; longer bill; red neck and whitish cheek in breeding plumage; dusky white cheek in non-breeding plumage.
Best Sites: wetlands of the lower Great Lakes region; Rainy River sewage lagoons.

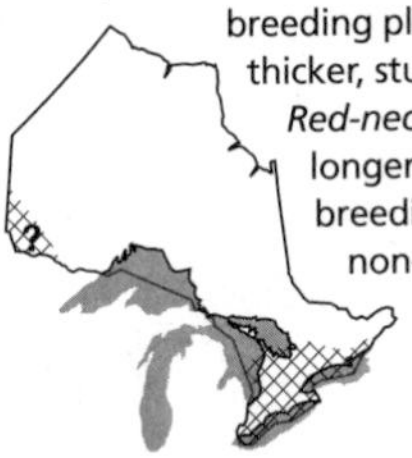

AMERICAN WHITE PELICAN

Pelecanus erythrorhynchos

Pelicans are massive waterbirds dramatically adapted for specialized feeding. Groups of foraging pelicans deliberately herd fish into schools, from which the birds dip and scoop the prey with their bills. In a single scoop, a pelican can hold up to 12 *l* of water and fish. As the pelican lifts its bill from the water, the fish are held within its flexible pouch as water is drained out. This impressive feat confirms Dixon Lanier Merritt's quotation: 'A wonderful bird is a pelican, his bill will hold more than his belican!' • Thousands of pelicans breed in colonies on Lake of the Woods and Lake Nipigon. Because these colonies are isolated from human activity and extremely sensitive to disturbance, this pelican is considered endangered in Ontario. Groups of post-breeding adult pelicans occasionally wander as far away from their nesting grounds as the lower Great Lakes and Hudson Bay.

non-breeding

ID: very large, stocky, white bird; long, orange bill and throat pouch; black primary and secondary wing feathers; short tail; naked orange skin patch around the eye. *Breeding:* small, keeled plate develops on the upper mandible; pale yellow crest on the back of the head. *Non-breeding* and *Immature:* white plumage is tinged with brown.
Size: *L* 1.4–1.8 m; *W* 2.8 m.
Status: locally abundant breeder; rare post-breeding wanderer from June to December.
Habitat: large lakes or rivers.
Nesting: colonial; on bare, low-lying islands; nest scrape is lined with pebbles and debris or is completely unlined; 2 eggs hatch asynchronously, after approximately 33 days; young are born naked and helpless.
Feeding: surface dips for small fish and amphibians; small groups of pelicans often feed cooperatively by herding fish into large concentrations.
Voice: generally quiet; adults rarely issue pig-like grunts; nestlings may give grunts and piercing screams.
Similar Species: No other large, white bird has a long beak with a pouch.
Best Sites: Lake of the Woods; Lake Nipigon; occasionally along Great Lakes shorelines.

41

DOUBLE-CRESTED CORMORANT

Phalacrocorax auritus

Ontario's large lakes and numerous isolated islands provide ideal habitat for the Double-crested Cormorant. This cormorant was once a rare sight through most of Ontario, but over the past century it has thrived and expanded its range to include many parts of the province. • The cormorant's beauty can take longer to appreciate than that of other birds. These slick-feathered birds often appear dishevelled, and extra-close encounters typically reveal the foul stench of fish oil. Their mastery of the aquatic environment, however, is virtually complete. Double-crested Cormorants have little ability to waterproof their feathers, which helps them during underwater dives by decreasing their buoyancy. After a bout of diving, this bird is often seen perched in a tree with its wings partially spread in an attempt to dry its feathers. The cormorant's long, rudder-like tail, excellent underwater vision and sealed nostrils also contribute to the success of its aquatic lifestyle.

breeding

ID: all-black body; long, crooked neck; thin bill, hooked at the tip; blue eyes. *Breeding:* throat pouch becomes intense orange-yellow; fine, black plumes trail from the eyebrows. *Immature:* brown upperparts; buff throat and breast; yellowish throat patch. *In flight:* rapid wingbeats; kinked neck.
Size: *L* 66–81 cm; *W* 1.3 m.
Status: uncommon to locally common from early April to early November; a few may be present in winter.
Habitat: large lakes and large, meandering rivers.
Nesting: colonial; on low-lying islands, often with pelicans, terns and gulls, or precariously high in trees; nest platform is made of sticks, aquatic vegetation and guano.

Feeding: long underwater dives of up to 9 m or more when after small schooling fish or, rarely, amphibians and invertebrates; feeds its young by regurgitation.
Voice: generally quiet; may issue pig-like grunts or croaks, especially near nest colonies.
Similar Species: *Great Cormorant:* larger bill and body; thicker neck; white 'chin-strap,' head plumes and flank patches in breeding plumage; immature has a white belly. *Common Loon* (p. 36): shorter neck; black bill lacks the hooked tip; spotted back in breeding plumage; white underparts in non-breeding plumage. *Canada Goose* (p. 55): white cheek; brown overall.
Best Sites: Pelee Island; Presqu'ile PP; Toronto Outer Harbour; north channel off Manitoulin Island; Lake of the Woods.

AMERICAN BITTERN

Botaurus lentiginosus

The American Bittern's deep and mysterious booming call is as characteristic of a spring marsh as the sound of croaking frogs, winnowing snipes and nighttime showers. This bittern is often common where productive marsh habitat can be found, but it's uncommon or even rare to actually see one. Even honed and patient eyes are no match for this elusive bird. • At the approach of an intruder, a bittern's first reaction is to freeze—its bill points skyward and its vertically streaked, brown plumage blends perfectly with the surroundings. An American Bittern will always face an intruder, moving ever so slowly to keep its camouflaged breast toward danger. It will adopt a reed-like position if it is encountered in an open area. In most cases, intruders simply pass by without ever noticing the cryptic bird.

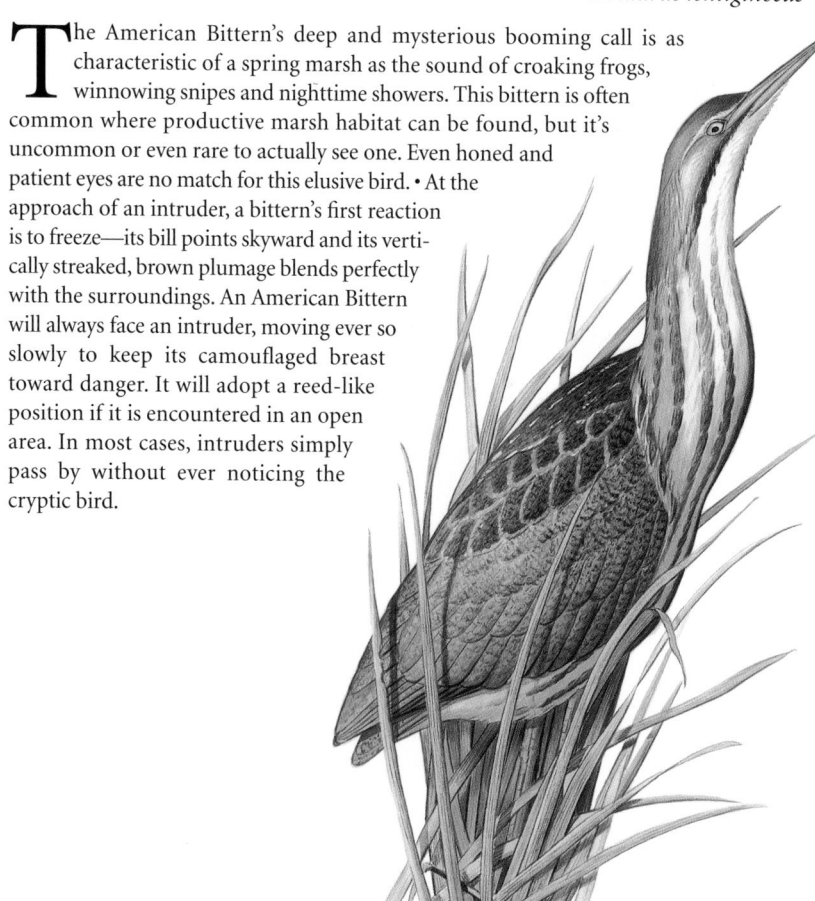

ID: brown upperparts; brown streaking from the chin through the breast; straight, stout bill; yellow legs and feet; black outer wings; black streaks from the bill down the neck to the shoulder; short tail.

Size: *L* 59–69 cm; *W* 1.1 m.

Status: rare to fairly common from late March to mid-November; a few may be present in winter.

Habitat: marshes, wetlands and lake edges with tall, dense grasses, sedges, bulrushes and cattails.

Nesting: singly; above the waterline in dense vegetation; nest platform is made of grass, sedges and dead reeds; nest often has separate entrance and exit paths.

Feeding: patient stand-and-wait predator; strikes at small fish, crayfish, amphibians, reptiles, mammals and insects.

Voice: deep, slow, resonant, repetitive *pomp-er-lunk* or *onk-a-BLONK*; most often heard in the evening or at night.

Similar Species: *Black-crowned Night-Heron* (p. 50), *Yellow-crowned Night-Heron* (p. 353), *Least Bittern* (p. 44) and *Green Heron* (p. 49): immatures lack the dark streak from the bill to the shoulder; immature night-herons have white flecking on their upperparts.

Best Sites: Long Point PP; Luther Marsh; Lake Scugog; Presqu'ile PP; Charleston Lake PP; Algonquin PP; Mission Island Marsh.

LEAST BITTERN

Ixobrychus exilis

The Least Bittern inhabits freshwater marshes where tall, impenetrable stands of cattails conceal most of its movements. This bird moves about with ease, its slender body passing freely and unnoticed through dense marshland habitat. An expert climber, it is often seen a metre or more above water, clinging to vertical stems and walking about without getting its feet wet. Least Bitterns are uncommon throughout most of Ontario, and sightings are rare, owing in part to their secretive behaviour and solitary lifestyle. • In southern Ontario, where this species reaches the northern limit of its North American range, the Least Bittern pushes the boundaries of its adaptability, particularly its tolerance to chilly summer nights.

ID: rich buff flanks and sides; streaking on the foreneck; white underparts; largely pale bill; yellowish legs; short tail; dark primary and secondary feathers. *Male:* black crown and back. *Female* and *Immature:* chestnut brown head and back; immature has darker streaking on the breast and back. *In flight:* large buffy shoulder patches.

Size: *L* 28–37 cm.

Status: uncommon from late April to October; a few may occur into December.

Habitat: freshwater marshes with cattails and other dense emergent vegetation.

Nesting: mostly the male constructs a platform of dry plant stalks on top of bent marsh vegetation; nest site is usually well concealed within dense vegetation; pair incubates 4 or 5 pale green or blue eggs for 17–20 days; pair feeds the young by regurgitation.

Feeding: stabs prey with its bill; eats mostly small fish; also takes large insects, tadpoles, frogs, small snakes, leeches and crayfish; may build a hunting platform.

Voice: guttural *uh-uh-uh-oo-oo-oo-ooah* is given by the male; ticking sound is made by the female; both issue a *tut-tut* call or a *koh* alarm call.

Similar Species: *American Bittern* (p. 43): bold brown streaking on the underparts; adult has a black streak from the bill to the shoulder. *Black-crowned Night-Heron* (p. 50) and *Yellow-crowned Night-Heron* (p. 353): immatures have dark brown upperparts and white flecking on the upperparts. *Green Heron* (p. 49): immature has dark brown upperparts.

Best Sites: Point Pelee NP; St. Clair NWA; Rondeau PP; Long Point PP; Presqu'ile PP; Luther Marsh; Lake Scugog; Chemong Lake; Rideau River and Canal.

GREAT BLUE HERON

Ardea herodias

The sight of a Great Blue Heron is always memorable for Ontarians with a passion for the outdoors. Whether you are observing its stealthy, often motionless hunting strategy, or tracking its graceful wingbeats as it returns to a rookery, it's difficult not to notice this bird's majesty. Its communal treetop nests, known as a rookeries, are sensitive to human disturbances, so if you are fortunate enough to discover a colony, it is best to observe the birds' behaviour from a distance. • It is rare, but not unheard of, for a few Great Blue Herons to successfully survive a winter in southern Ontario. Spotting one may even be a highlight of your local Christmas Bird Count. • This heron is often mistaken for a crane, but cranes hold their necks outstretched in flight, whereas the Great Blue folds its neck back over its shoulders.

breeding

ID: large, blue-grey bird; long, curving neck; long, dark legs; blue-grey wing covers and back; straight, yellow bill; chestnut thighs. *Breeding:* colours are more intense; plumes streak from the crown and throat. *In flight:* neck folds back over the shoulders; legs trail behind the body; slow and steady wingbeats.
Size: *L* 1.3–1.4 m; *W* 1.8 m.
Status: fairly common to locally abundant from late March to late November; a few typically overwinter.
Habitat: forages along the edges of rivers, lakes and marshes; also seen in fields and wet meadows.
Nesting: colonial; in a tree; flimsy to elaborate stick and twig platform is added onto, often over years, and can be up to 1.2 m in diameter; pair incubates the eggs for approximately 28 days.
Feeding: patient stand-and-wait predator; strikes at small fish,

amphibians, small mammals, aquatic invertebrates and reptiles; rarely scavenges.
Voice: usually quiet away from the nest; occasionally a deep, harsh *frahnk frahnk frahnk* (usually during take-off).
Similar Species: *Green Heron* (p. 49), *Black-crowned Night-Heron* (p. 50) and *Yellow-crowned Night-Heron* (p. 353): much smaller; shorter legs. *Egrets* (pp. 46–48): all are predominately white. *Sandhill Crane* (p. 118): red cap; flies with its neck outstretched. *Little Blue Heron* (p. 352): dark overall; purplish head; lacks the yellow on the bill. *Tricolored Heron* (p. 353): darker upperparts; white underparts.
Best Sites: Long Point PP; Lake Scugog; Beaver Meadow Conservation Area, Picton; Algonquin PP; Grundy Lake PP; Mission Island Marsh; Cranberry and Dundas marshes.

GREAT EGRET

Ardea alba

Great Egrets were first reported as potential breeders in the province in 1953, but breeding wasn't officially confirmed until 1975. Over the last few decades, nests have been found in a number of southwestern Ontario locales, with late summer and early fall wanderers sighted as far north as Thunder Bay and Kapuskasing. • The plumes of the Great Egret and Snowy Egret were widely used to decorate hats in the early 20th century. An ounce of egret feathers cost as much as $32—more than an ounce of gold at that time—and, as a result, egret populations began to disappear. Some of the first conservation legislation in North America was enacted to outlaw the hunting of Great Egrets. These egrets are now recovering and expanding their range, probably to where they formerly nested.

breeding

ID: all-white plumage; black legs; yellow bill. *Breeding:* white plumes trail from the throat and rump; green skin patch between the eyes and the base of the bill. *In flight:* neck folds back over the shoulders; legs extend backward.
Size: *L* 94–104 cm; *W* 1.3 m.
Status: rare to locally common from late March to mid-October; a few may remain into early winter.
Habitat: marshes, open riverbanks, irrigation canals and lakeshores.
Nesting: colonial, but may nest in isolated pairs; in a tree or tall shrub; pair builds a platform of sticks and incubates 3–5 pale blue-green eggs for 23–26 days.
Feeding: patient stand-and-wait predator; occasionally stalks slowly, stabbing at almost any small creature it can capture.
Voice: rapid, low-pitched, loud cuk-cuk-cuk.
Similar Species: *Snowy Egret* (p. 47): smaller; black bill; yellow feet. *Cattle Egret* (p. 48): smaller; stockier; orange bill and legs. *Whooping Crane* (p. 355): much larger; red crown; black and red facial mask; black primaries; extremely rare.
Best Sites: Point Pelee NP; Pelee Island; St. Clair NWA; Luther Lake; Bruce Peninsula.

SNOWY EGRET

Egretta thula

The elegant, snow white plumage, bright yellow feet and black legs of the Snowy Egret are rarely seen in Ontario—these birds are mainly wanderers here. Their propensity for far-ranging, post-breeding dispersal is much like that of the Great Egret, but only one pair of Snowies has ever been found nesting in Ontario. • Herons and egrets, particularly Snowy Egrets, make use of a variety of feeding techniques. By poking their bright yellow feet in the muck of shallow wetlands, these birds will try to spook potential prey out of hiding places. In an even more devious hunting strategy, Snowies are known to create shade by extending their wings over open water. When a fish is lured into the cooler, shaded spot, it is promptly seized and eaten. Some paleontologists have even suggested that this was one of the original functions of bird wings!

breeding

ID: white plumage; black bill and legs; bright yellow feet. *Breeding:* long plumes on the throat and rump; erect crown; orange-red lores. *Immature:* similar to an adult but with more yellow on the legs. *In flight:* yellow feet are obvious.

Size: *L* 56–66 cm; *W* 1 m.

Status: rare from mid-April to late October.

Habitat: open edges of rivers, lakes and marshes.

Nesting: colonial, often among other herons; in a tree or tall shrub; pair builds a platform of sticks and incubates 3–5 pale blue-green eggs for 20–24 days.

Feeding: stirs wetland muck with its feet; stands and waits; occasionally hovers and stabs; eats small fish, amphibians and invertebrates.

Voice: low croaks; bouncy *wulla-wulla-wulla* on breeding grounds.

Similar Species: *Great Egret* (p. 46): larger; yellow bill; black feet. *Cattle Egret* (p. 48): orange-yellow legs and bill.

Best Sites: check local bird hotlines for any recent sightings; St. Clair NWA; Rondeau PP; Point Pelee NP.

CATTLE EGRET

Bubulcus ibis

Over the last century—and without help from humans—the Cattle Egret has dispersed from Africa to inhabit every continent except Antarctica. Since the Cattle Egret was first recorded nesting in Ontario in 1962, over 50 nests have been discovered, usually among the nesting colonies of Black-crowned Night-Herons. This bird has not yet established itself as a regular breeder, however, and most nests remain active for only a year or two. Solitary Cattle Egrets are often seen flying through southwestern Ontario in spring, and larger flocks (but fewer sightings) are recorded in fall. • Cattle Egrets get their name from their habit of following grazing animals. They catch the insects and other small animals that the ungulates stir up. Unlike other egrets, the diet of this species consists primarily of terrestrial invertebrates. When foraging, this small egret is often seen in the company of similar-sized gulls. Like Franklin's Gulls, these egrets will sometimes follow ploughs, and like Ring-bills they occasionally scavenge at dumps.

breeding

ID: mostly white; yellow-orange bill and legs. *Breeding:* long plumes on the throat and rump; buff-orange throat, rump and crown; legs and bill turn orange-red; purple lores. *Immature:* similar to an adult, but with black feet.
Size: *L* 48–53 cm; *W* 90–95 cm.
Status: rare to locally uncommon from April to November.
Habitat: agricultural fields, ranchlands and marshes.
Nesting: colonial; often among other herons; in a tree or tall shrub; male supplies sticks for the female who builds a platform or shallow bowl; pair incubates 3 or 4 pale blue eggs for 21–26 days.
Feeding: picks grasshoppers, other insects, worms, small vertebrates and spiders from fields; often associated with livestock.
Voice: generally silent.
Similar Species: *Great Egret* (p. 46): larger; black legs and feet. *Snowy Egret* (p. 47): black legs; yellow feet. *Gulls* (pp. 157–69): do not stand as erect; generally have a grey mantle.
Best Sites: check local bird hotlines for any recent sightings; Point Pelee NP; Luther Marsh; Dundas Marsh; Presqu'ile PP.

GREEN HERON

Butorides virescens

This crow-sized heron is far less conspicuous than its Great Blue cousin. The Green Heron prefers to hunt for frogs and small fish in shallow, weedy wetlands, where it often perches just above the water's surface. While hunting, Green Herons have been observed dropping small debris, including twigs, vegetation and feathers, onto the water's surface as a form of 'bait' to attract fish within striking range. • If the light is just right, you may be fortunate to see a glimmer of green on the back and outer wings of this bird. Most of the time, however, this magical shine is not apparent, especially when this bird stands frozen under the shade of dense marshland vegetation. • The scientific name *virescens* is Latin for 'growing or becoming green,' and it refers to this bird's transition from a streaky brown juvenile to a greenish adult.

ID: stocky; green-black crown; chestnut face and neck; white foreneck and belly; blue-grey back and wings mixed with iridescent green; relatively short, green-yellow legs; bill is dark above and greenish below; short tail. *Breeding male:* bright orange legs. *Immature:* heavy streaks along the neck and underparts; dark brown upperparts.
Size: *L* 38–56 cm; *W* 66 cm.
Status: rare to locally common from mid-April to November.
Habitat: freshwater marshes, lakes and streams with dense shoreline or emergent vegetation.
Nesting: nests singly or in small, loose groups; male begins construction of the stick platform in a tree or shrub, usually very close to water; pair incubates 3–5 pale blue-green to green eggs for 19–21 days; pair feeds the young by regurgitation.

Feeding: eats mostly small fish; also takes frogs, tadpoles, crayfish, aquatic insects, small rodents, snakes, terrestrial insects, snails and worms; stabs prey with its bill after slowly stalking or standing and waiting.
Voice: generally silent; alarm and flight call are a loud *kowp, kyow* or *skow*; aggression call is a *harsh raah*.
Similar Species: *Black-crowned Night-Heron* (p. 50): larger; white cheek; pale grey and white neck; 2 long, white plumes trail down from the crown; immature has a streaked face and white flecking on the upperparts. *Least Bittern* (p. 44): buffy-yellow shoulder patches, sides and flanks. *American Bittern* (p. 43): more tan overall; black streak from the bill to the shoulder.
Best Sites: Point Pelee NP; Long Point PP; Dundas Marsh; Luther Marsh; Cranberry Marsh; Trent Canal.

BLACK-CROWNED NIGHT-HERON

Nycticorax nycticorax

When the setting sun has sent most wetland waders to their nightly roosts, Black-crowned Night-Herons arrive to hunt the marshy waters and to voice their hoarse squawks. *Nycticorax*, meaning 'night raven,' refers to these distinctive nighttime calls. These night-herons patrol the shallows for prey, which they can see in the dim light with their large, light-sensitive eyes. • Young night-herons are commonly seen around large cattail marshes in fall. Because of their heavily streaked underparts, they are easily confused with other immature herons and American Bitterns. • A popular hunting strategy for day-active Black-crowned Night-Herons is to sit motionless atop a few bent-over cattails. In this scenario, anything passing below the perch becomes fair game—even ducklings, small shorebirds or young muskrats are taken. On Leslie Street Spit in Toronto, these herons are predators of gull chicks.

breeding

ID: black cap and back; white cheek, foreneck and underparts; grey neck and wings; dull yellow legs; stout, black bill; large, red eyes. *Breeding:* 2 white plumes trail down from the crown. *Immature:* lightly streaked underparts; brown upperparts with white flecking.

Size: *L* 58–66 cm; *W* 1.1 m.

Status: uncommon to locally abundant from early April to November; a few may present in winter.

Habitat: shallow cattail and bulrush marshes, lakeshores and along slow rivers.

Nesting: colonial; in trees or shrubs; loose nest platform of twigs and sticks is lined with finer materials; male gathers the nest material; female builds the nest; pair incubates 3 or 4 pale green eggs for 21–26 days.

Feeding: often at dusk; stands motionlessly and waits for prey; stabs for small fish, amphibians, aquatic invertebrates, reptiles, young birds and small mammals.

Voice: deep, guttural *quark* or *wok*, often heard as the bird takes flight.

Similar Species: *Great Blue Heron* (p. 45): much larger; longer legs; blue-grey back. *Yellow-crowned Night-Heron* (p. 353): adult has a white crown and cheek patch, and white plumes on an otherwise black head; grey back; immature is very similar to and difficult to distinguish from a Black-crowned immature. *Green Heron* (p. 49): adult has a chestnut face and neck and a blue-grey back with green iridescence; immature has heavily streaked underparts. *American Bittern* (p. 43): similar to an immature Black-crowned Night-Heron, but the bittern has a black streak from the bill to the shoulder and is lighter tan overall.

Best Sites: Rondeau PP; Dundas Marsh; Niagara River; Presqu'ile PP; Cranberry Marsh; Toronto Harbour.

TURKEY VULTURE

Cathartes aura

Turkey Vultures are unmatched in Ontario at using updrafts and thermals—they tease lift out of the slightest pocket of rising air and patrol the skies when other soaring birds are grounded. • Vultures eat carrion almost exclusively, so their bills and feet are not nearly as powerful as those of hawks and falcons, which kill live prey. The Turkey Vulture may appear grotesque with its red, featherless head, but this adaptation allows it to remain relatively clean while digging through messy carcasses. • Vultures seem to have mastered the art of regurgitation. The ability to regurgitate meals allows parents to transport food over long distances and also enables engorged birds to repulse an attacker, or to 'lighten up' for an emergency take-off. • Recent studies have shown that American vultures are most closely related to storks, not hawks and falcons as previously thought. Molecular similarities with storks, and the shared tendency to defecate on their own legs to cool down, strongly support this taxonomic reclassification.

ID: all black; bare, red head. *Immature:* grey head. *In flight:* tilts side-to-side while soaring; silver grey flight feathers; black wing linings; wings are held in a shallow V; head appears small.

Size: *L* 66–81 cm; *W* 1.7–1.8 m.

Status: uncommon to fairly common from late March to early November; a few may be present in winter.

Habitat: usually seen flying over open country, shorelines or roads; rarely seen over forested areas.

Nesting: in a cave crevice or among boulders; rarely a hollow stump or log; no nest material is used; female lays 2 dull white eggs on bare ground; pair incubates the eggs for up to 41 days.

Feeding: entirely on carrion (mostly mammalian); young are fed by regurgitation; not commonly seen at roadkills.

Voice: generally silent; occasionally produces a hiss or grunt if threatened.

Similar Species: *Golden Eagle* (p. 99) and *Bald Eagle* (p. 90): wings are held flat in flight; do not rock when soaring; head is more visible in flight. *Black Vulture* (p. 353): rare visitor; grey head; silvery tips on otherwise black wings.

Best Sites: Beamer Point Conservation Area, Grimsby; Bruce Peninsula; Petroglyphs PP; Frontenac PP; Grundy Lake PP; Chutes PP; Blue Lake PP.

GREATER WHITE-FRONTED GOOSE

Anser albifrons

Greater White-fronted Geese are typically birds of the West, but they are occasionally spotted here in Ontario. They are best seen during spring and fall migration, when they stop to refuel on aquatic plants in shallow ponds and marshes or on freshly sprouted grains in fields and pastures. The small numbers that occasionally migrate through our province often travel among flocks of Canada Geese. The slightly smaller White-fronts can best be distinguished by their bright orange feet, which shine like beacons as the birds stand on frozen spring wetlands and fields. • The Greater White-fronted Goose is probably most familiar to hunters in the West, who know it as the 'speckle belly.'

ID: brown overall; black speckling on the belly; pinkish bill; white around the bill and on the forehead; white hindquarters; black band on the upper tail; orange feet. *Immature:* pale belly without speckles; little or no white on the face.
Size: *L* 69–84 cm; *W* 1.3–1.6 m.
Status: rare visitor from March to early May and from late September to late November; extremely rare in summer and winter.
Habitat: croplands, fields, open areas and shallow marshes in migration.

Nesting: does not nest in Ontario.
Feeding: dabbles in water and gleans the ground for grass shoots, spouting and waste grain and occasionally aquatic invertebrates.
Voice: high-pitched 'laugh.'
Similar Species: *Canada Goose* (p. 55): white 'chin strap'; black neck; lacks the speckling on its pale belly. *Snow Goose* (p. 53): blue morph has a white head and upperneck and an all-dark breast and belly.
Best Sites: check local bird hotlines for any recent sightings; Jack Miner's Bird Sanctuary; flooded fields near Carlsbad Springs (Ottawa).

VAGRANT

SNOW GOOSE

Chen caerulescens

In spring, flooded fields along the South Nation River between Plantagenet and St. Isidore team with Snow Geese flocks that typically number over 1000 birds. These cackling geese can be seen in farmers' fields as they fuel up on waste grain from the previous year's crops. • Snow Geese breed in large numbers in Ontario. In some years, the Cape Henrietta Maria colony (found in Polar Bear Provincial Park) supports 50,000 to 100,000 nests. Unfortunately, this area is so isolated that few people have the chance to witness the Snow Goose's annual nesting spectacle. Surveys of this colony have shown that up to 75 percent of the breeders are of the 'blue' colour morph. • Unlike Canada Geese, which fly in V formations, migrating Snow Geese usually form oscillating, wavy lines. • As with Sandhill Cranes, Snow Goose plumage is often stained rusty red from iron in the water.

ID: white overall; black wing tips; pink feet and bill; dark 'grinning patch' on the bill; plumage is occasionally stained rusty red. *Blue morph:* white head and upperneck; dark blue-grey body. *Immature:* grey or dusty white plumage; dark bill and feet.
Size: *L* 71–84 cm; *W* 1.4–1.5 m.
Status: rare to locally common migrant from March to May and from late September to mid-November; locally abundant breeder.
Habitat: *Breeding:* on tundra near a pond or lake shoreline or on an island. *In migration:* shallow wetlands, lakes and fields.
Nesting: loosely colonial; on a ridge or hummock; female fills a shallow depression with plant material and down; female incubates 3–5 whitish eggs for 22–23 days; both adults tend the young; pairs may mate for life.
Feeding: grazes on waste grain and new sprouts; also eats aquatic vegetation, grasses, sedges and roots.
Voice: loud, nasal, constant *houk-houk* in flight.
Similar Species: *Ross's Goose* (p. 54): smaller; shorter neck; lacks the black 'grin.' *Tundra* (p. 59), *Trumpeter* (p. 58) and *Mute* (p. 57) *swans:* larger; white wing tips. *American White Pelican* (p. 41): much larger bill and body.
Best Sites: South Nation River; Polar Bear PP; Jack Miner's Bird Sanctuary; Oliphant Beaches; Fanshawe Lake; Cranberry Marsh.

ROSS'S GOOSE

Chen rossii

This small goose looks so similar to the Snow Goose that inexperienced bird-watchers can easily get the two confused. The Ross's Goose is often overlooked, particularly when a few individuals are mixed within large flocks of migrating Snow Geese. • Most of the world's Ross's Geese nest along the coastline of Nunavut, but small numbers are thought to nest regularly among colonies of Snow Geese near Cape Henrietta Maria and Akimiski Island. The first Ross's nest known to ornithologists was discovered in 1938, and it was not until 1975 that this bird was a confirmed breeder in Ontario. • Bernard Rogan Ross, this bird's namesake, was a former chief factor of the Hudson's Bay Company and correspondent of the Smithsonian Institute.

white morph

ID: white overall; black wing tips; dark pink feet and bill; lacks a 'grinning patch'; small bluish or greenish 'warts' on the base of the bill; plumage is occasionally stained rusty by iron in the water. *Blue morph (very rare):* white head; blue-grey body plumage. *Immature:* grey plumage; dark bill and feet. **Size:** *L* 54–66 cm; *W* 1.2–1.3 m.
Status: rare to locally uncommon migrant from March to May and from late September to mid-November; rare and very local breeder.
Habitat: *Breeding:* on tundra along a pond or lake shoreline or on an island. *In migration:* shallow wetlands, lakes and fields.
Nesting: usually colonial; on a ridge or hummock of tundra;

female fills a shallow depression with plant material and down and incubates 2–6 dull white eggs for 21–23 days; both parents tend the young.
Feeding: grazes on waste grain and new sprouts; also eats aquatic vegetation, grasses, sedges and roots.
Voice: similar to the Snow Goose, but higher pitched.
Similar Species: *Snow Goose* (p. 53): larger; longer neck; dark 'grinning patch' on the bill. *Tundra* (p. 59), *Trumpeter* (p. 58) and *Mute* (p. 57) *swans:* much larger; white wing tips. *American White Pelican* (p. 41): much larger bill and body.
Best Sites: usually wherever Snow Geese are found.

CANADA GOOSE

Branta canadensis

Canada Geese are among the most recognizable birds in Ontario, but they are also among the most overlooked. In recent decades, these large, bold geese have inundated urban waterfronts, picnic sites, golf courses and city parks and today many people consider them pests. Few people realize, however, that at one time these birds were hunted almost to extinction in southern parts of the province. In fact, present-day flocks in southern Ontario are mainly derived from reintroductions. • Fuzzy goslings seem to compel people, especially children, to get closer. Unfortunately, Canada Goose parents can cause harm to unwelcomed strangers. Hissing sounds and low, outstretched necks are signs that you should give these birds some space.

ID: long, black neck; white 'chin strap'; white undertail coverts; light brown underparts; dark brown upperparts; short, black tail.
Size: *L* 55–122 cm; *W* up to 1.8 m.
Status: common to locally abundant migrant from March to May and from September to November; rare to locally common winter resident; uncommon to locally common breeder.
Habitat: lakeshores, riverbanks, ponds, farmlands and city parks.
Nesting: on islands and shorelines; usually on the ground; may use heron rookeries; female builds a nest of plant materials lined with down; female incubates 3–8 white eggs for 25–28 days while the male stands guard.
Feeding: grazes on new sprouts, aquatic vegetation, grass and roots; tips up for aquatic roots and tubers.
Voice: loud, familiar *ah-honk*.
Similar Species: *Greater White-fronted Goose* (p. 52): brown neck and head; lacks the white 'chin strap'; orange legs; white around the base of the bill; dark speckling on the belly. *Brant* (p. 56): lacks the white 'chin strap'; white 'necklace'; black upper breast. *Snow Goose* (p. 53): blue morph has a white head and upperneck. *Double-crested Cormorant* (p. 42): lacks the the white 'chin strap' and undertail coverts; crooked neck in flight.
Best Sites: Jack Miner's Bird Sanctuary; Niagara-on-the-Lake; Toronto Islands; Lac Deschênes; Sault Ste. Marie waterfront; Rene Brunelle PP; almost everywhere in migration.

55

BRANT
Branta bernicla

This cousin of the Canada Goose typically spends most of its time in saltwater environments, but during migration it passes over great expanses of land and fresh water, satisfying its hunger with freshwater plants and waste grain. • Most Brant are seen in eastern Ontario in spring and fall, either flying low in ragged formation or congregating on Hudson Bay and James Bay during migratory stop-overs. • Brant populations in eastern North America declined by almost 90 percent in the 1930s, when a virulent blight killed much of their winter source of saltwater eelgrass along the Atlantic coast. Fortunately, many of the birds switched to eating sea lettuce, a strategy that kept the population from disappearing altogether. • *Branta* is a Latinized form of an Anglo-Saxon word for 'burnt' or 'charred,' a reference to this bird's dark plumage.

ID: black neck, head and upper breast; dark upperparts; white 'necklace'; white hindquarters; black feet; pale brown sides and flanks; white belly. *Juvenile*: 'necklace' is less conspicuous.

Size: *L* 59–70 cm; *W* 1.1–1.2 m.

Status: rare to locally common migrant in May, June, October and November; a few may be present in summer and winter.

Habitat: lakeshores and agricultural fields.

Nesting: does not nest in Ontario.

Feeding: grazes on aquatic vegetation and waste grain in southern Ontario; elsewhere, eats eelgrass almost exclusively.

Voice: deep, prolonged *c-r-r-r-uk*, with hissing.

Similar Species: *Canada Goose* (p. 55): white 'chin strap'; brown upperparts and upper breast. *Greater White-fronted Goose* (p. 52): brown neck and head; orange legs; white around the base of the bill; dark speckling on the belly.

Best Sites: Kingston area north to Ottawa; Guindon Park, Cornwall; north end of Lake Temagami.

MUTE SWAN
Cygnus olor

Admired for its grace and beauty, this Eurasian native was introduced to eastern North America in the mid-1800s to adorn estates and city parks. Over the years, Mute Swans have adapted well to the North American environment. They have continued to expand their feral populations, and although they are not usually migratory, more northerly nesters have established short migratory routes to milder wintering areas. Mute Swans began nesting in Ontario in 1958, and 100 to 200 pairs now live in the province, largely concentrated along the shores and sheltered waters of Lake Erie and Lake Ontario. • Easy to recognize and beautiful to behold, swans are always a popular sight at local wetlands. Like many non-native species, however, Mute Swans are often fierce competitors for nesting areas and food sources. They can be very aggressive toward geese and ducks, often displacing many native species.

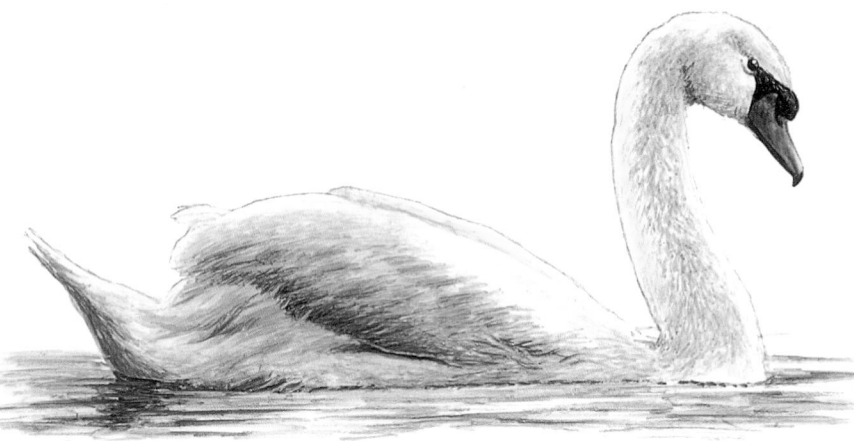

ID: all-white plumage; orange bill with a downturned tip and a bulbous, black knob extending from the forehead; neck is usually held in an S-shape; wings are often held in an arch over the back while swimming. *Immature:* plumage may be white to greyish brown.

Size: *L* 1.5 m; *W* 2.3–2.5 m.

Status: locally uncommon to fairly common year-round resident; a few may migrate short distances for winter.

Habitat: freshwater marshes, lakes and ponds.

Nesting: on the ground along a shoreline; female builds a mound of vegetation (male may help gather material) and incubates 5–10 pale green eggs for about 36 days; pair tends the young.

Feeding: tips up or dips its head below the water's surface for aquatic plants; grazes on land.

Voice: generally silent; may hiss or issue hoarse barking notes; loud wingbeats can be heard from up to 800 m.

Similar Species: *Tundra Swan* (p. 59) and *Trumpeter Swan* (p. 58): lack the orange bill with the black knob at the base; necks tend to be held straight.

Best Sites: Rondeau PP; Long Point PP; Dundas Marsh; Toronto Islands; Lynde Shores Conservation Area; Presqu'ile PP; Lake Ontario between the Humber River and Oakville.

TRUMPETER SWAN

Cygnus buccinator

The Trumpeter Swan was hunted nearly to extinction for its meat and feathers during the early 20th century. Breeding populations in Alaska and Alberta persisted, but eastern populations were less fortunate: by 1884, the Trumpeter Swan was extirpated in Ontario. Recent attempts have been made to reintroduce this species to its former range in Ontario, and the present population of nearly 250 pairs may be near to self-sustaining. Great success has been found by releasing young birds raised by captive Trumpeter parents, and a few birds have even spread to our province from restoration programs in the nearby U.S. By respecting the sensitivity of Trumpeter nesting sites and protecting Trumpeter habitat, Ontarians may once again hear the resonant bugling notes of this magnificent bird. • Both 'trumpeter' and *buccinator* refer to this bird's loud, bugling voice, which is produced when air is forced through the long windpipe that runs through the keel of the breast bone.

ID: all-white plumage; large, solid black bill; black skin extends from the bill to the eyes; black feet; neck is held with a kink at the base when standing or swimming. *Immature:* grey-brown plumage; grey bill.
Size: *L* 1.5–1.8 m; *W* 2.4 m.
Status: extremely rare migrant and reintroduced breeder.
Habitat: lakes and large wetlands; extremely local.
Nesting: often builds a large mound of vegetation on top of muskrat or beaver lodges, and occasionally along shorelines; female usually incubates 4–6 eggs; both adults tend the young.
Feeding: tips up, surface gleans and occasionally grazes for vegetation (primarily eats pondweed, duckweed, aquatic tubers and roots).
Voice: loud, resonant, bugle-like *koh-hoh*.
Similar Species: *Tundra Swan* (p. 59): smaller; more common; often shows yellow lores; softer, more nasal voice; neck and head are rounder. *Mute Swan* (p. 60): orange bill with a black knob on the upper base and a down-pointed bill; neck is usually held in an S-shape; wings are often held in an arch over the back while swimming. *Snow Goose* (p. 53): smaller; black wing tips; shorter neck; pinkish bill.
Best Sites: check local bird hotlines for any recent sightings; marshlands along the shores of Lake Ontario and Lake Erie.

TUNDRA SWAN

Cygnus columbianus

Before the last of the winter's snows have melted into the fields, Tundra Swans return to our province, bringing us the first whispers of spring. In early March, massive flocks of these swans soar over cities and fields in southwestern Ontario, occasionally stopping to refuel on waste grain and aquatic vegetation. The snow and ice that they encounter here will not be the last on their trip north—Tundra Swans usually reach their arctic breeding grounds well before the spring thaw. • During the early days of the fur trade, breeding Tundra Swans were extirpated from Ontario. Today, tens of thousands of Tundras migrate over our province, but only a handful of pairs actually nest here. • The Lewis and Clark exploration team found this bird near the Columbia River, after which its scientific name was later derived.

ID: white plumage; large, black bill; black feet; often shows yellow lores; neck is held straight up; neck and head show a rounded, slightly curving profile. *Immature:* grey-brown plumage; grey bill.
Size: *L* 1.2–1.5 m; *W* 2 m.
Status: locally uncommon to abundant migrant from late February to mid-April and from late October to early December; locally rare summer breeder; rare, local winter resident.
Habitat: *Breeding:* coastal arctic tundra. *In migration:* shallow areas of lakes and wetlands, agricultural fields and flooded pastures.
Nesting: on islands or along freshwater shorelines; pair builds a large mound of vegetation with a centre depression; female usually incubates 4 or 5 creamy white eggs for 31–32 days; both adults tend the young.

Feeding: tips up, dabbles and surface gleans for aquatic vegetation and invertebrates; grazes for tubers, roots and waste grain.
Voice: high-pitched, quivering *oo-oo-whoo* is constantly repeated by migrating flocks.
Similar Species: *Trumpeter Swan* (p. 58): larger; extremely rare in Ontario; loud, bugle-like voice; lacks the yellow lores; neck and head show a more angular profile. *Mute Swan* (p. 57): orange bill with a black knob on the upper base; neck is usually held in an S-shape; down-pointed bill; wings are often held in an arch over the back while swimming. *Snow Goose* (p. 53): smaller; black wing tips; shorter neck; pinkish bill.
Best Sites: Long Point PP; Lake St. Clair and rural fields near Carlsbad Springs; Dundas Marsh; Kettle Point; Point Pelee NP; Rondeau PP; Polar Bear PP.

WOOD DUCK

Aix sponsa

The male Wood Duck is one of the most colourful waterbirds in North America, and books, magazines, postcards and calendars routinely celebrate its beauty. No other duck can match its colourful, iridescent plumage. • Few birds are forced into the adventures of life as early as Wood Ducks. Newly hatched ducklings must jump to the ground from their nest cavity, which is often six metres high in a tree, to follow their mother to the nearest source of water. The little bundles of down are not exactly feather light, but they bounce fairly well and seldom sustain an injury. • Landowners with a tree-lined beaver pond or other suitable wetland may attract a family of Wood Ducks by building a nest box and erecting it close to the wetland shoreline. • The scientific name *sponsa* is Latin for 'promised bride,' suggesting that the male appears formally dressed for a wedding.

ID: *Male:* very colourful; glossy green head with a few white streaks; crest is slicked back from the crown; white chin and throat; purple-chestnut breast is spotted with white; black and white shoulder slash; golden sides; dark back and hindquarters. *Female:* white 'cleopatra' eye patch; mottled brown breast is streaked with white; brown-grey upperparts; white belly.

Size: *L* 38–53 cm.

Status: uncommon to locally fairly common from mid-March to late October; a few may be present in winter.

Habitat: beaver ponds, swamps, ponds, marshes and lakeshores with wooded edges.

Nesting: in a hollow or tree cavity (may be 9 m high or more); also in artificial nest boxes; usually near water; cavity is lined with down;

female incubates 9–14 white to buff eggs for 25–35 days.

Feeding: surface gleans and tips for aquatic vegetation, especially duckweed and aquatic sedges and grasses; eats more fruits and nuts than other ducks.

Voice: *Male:* ascending *ter-wee-wee*. *Female:* squeaky *woo-e-e-k*.

Similar Species: *Hooded Merganser* (p. 85): male has a black head with a white crest patch; slim, black bill; black and white breast. *Harlequin Duck* (p. 77): very rare in Ontario; male is blue-grey overall, with black and white patches; female has an unstreaked breast and a white ear patch.

Best Sites: Point Pelee NP; Long Point PP; Dundas Marsh; Lake Scugog; Charleston Lake PP; Algonquin PP; Britannia (Ottawa); Mission Island Marsh.

GADWALL

Anas strepera

Male Gadwalls lack the striking plumage of most other male ducks, but they nevertheless have a dignified appearance and a subtle beauty. Once you learn their field marks, Gadwalls are surprisingly easy to identify, whether they are on land, on water or in the air. • Ducks in the genus *Anas* (the dabbling ducks) are most often observed tipping up their hindquarters and submerging their heads to feed, but Gadwalls dive more often than others of this clan. • Gadwall numbers have greatly increased in Ontario since the 1970s, and this duck has expanded its range throughout North America. Large concentrations of Gadwalls can be seen in winter along the shores of Lake Ontario between Hamilton and the mouth of the Humber River.

ID: black and white wing patch (often seen in resting birds); white belly. *Male:* mostly grey; black hindquarters; dark bill. *Female:* mottled brown; brown bill with orange sides.

Size: *L* 46–56 cm.

Status: uncommon to locally common from late March to late November; rare to locally abundant winter resident.

Habitat: shallow wetlands, lake borders and beaver ponds.

Nesting: in tall vegetation, sometimes far from water; nest is well concealed in a scraped hollow, often with grass arching overhead; nest is made of grass and other dry vegetation and is lined with down; female incubates 8–11 white eggs for 24–27 days.

Feeding: dabbles and tips up for the leaves, stems, tubers and roots of water plants; grazes on grass and waste grain during migration; one of the few dabblers to dive routinely for food; also eats aquatic invertebrates, tadpoles and small fish.

Voice: *Male:* simple, singular quack; often whistles harshly. *Female:* high *kaak kaaak kak-kak-kak*, in series and oscillating in volume.

Similar Species: *American Wigeon* (p. 63): green speculum; male has a white forehead and a green swipe trailing from each eye; female lacks the black hindquarters. *Mallard* (p. 65), *Northern Pintail* (p. 68) and other dabbling ducks: generally lack the black and white wing patch, the black hindquarters of the male, and the orange-sided beak of the female.

Best Sites: almost any shallow wetland; St. Clair NWA; Long Point PP; Dundas Marsh; Lynde Shores Conservation Area; Presqu'ile PP; Britannia; Mission Island Marsh.

EURASIAN WIGEON

Anas penelope

Each year in Ontario a few birders will discover a conspicuous red-headed wigeon while scanning a flock of American Wigeons along the shores of the lower Great Lakes. Eurasian Wigeons might be among the most noticeable of the regularly occurring rarities to visit Ontario, and even beginning birders have little difficulty in confidently identifying this Asian duck. • The Eurasian Wigeons seen in Ontario are probably nothing more than misguided wanderers following their American cousins while on migration to the Atlantic coast. Although they are not recorded breeders in North America, the increased number of sightings each spring has convinced some people that there is a small breeding population somewhere in Canada, possibly in Ontario. American Wigeons are also wanderers—some of these birds have been seen among flocks of Eurasian Wigeons in Europe and eastern Russia.

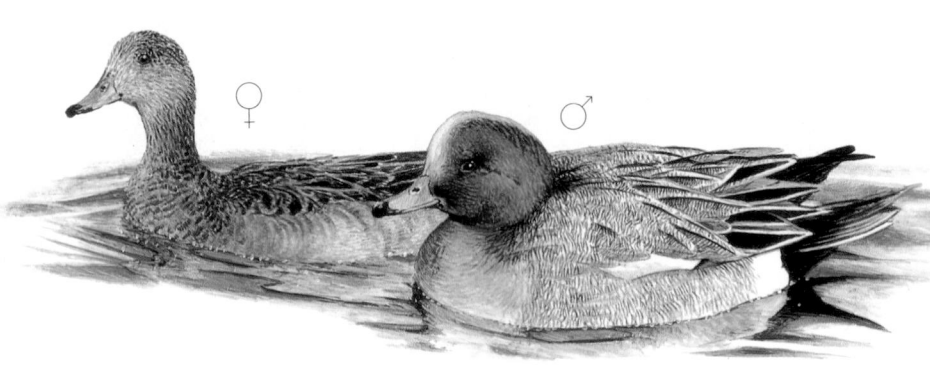

ID: black-tipped, grey-blue bill. *Male:* rufous head; cream forehead; rosy breast; grey sides; black hindquarters; dark feet; black-tipped, grey-blue bill. *Female:* rufous hints on a predominately brown head and breast. *In flight:* large, white wing patch; dusky grey wing pits.
Size: *L* 42–52 cm.
Status: rare migrant from March to June and from August to December.
Habitat: shallow wetlands, lake edges and ponds.

Nesting: not known to nest in Ontario.
Feeding: primarily a vegetarian; dabbles and grazes for grass, leaves and stems; occasionally pirates food from coots.
Voice: high-pitched, 2-toned whistle.
Similar Species: *American Wigeon* (p. 63): white wing pits; male lacks the reddish-brown head; female may have a browner head.
Best Sites: check local bird hotlines for any recent sightings; marshes and shorelines of Lake Erie and Lake Ontario; Ottawa River.

VAGRANT

AMERICAN WIGEON

Anas americana

The male American Wigeon's characteristic, wheezy laugh seems somewhat misplaced among the wetland orchestra of buzzes, quacks and ticks. Listen carefully, however, and you'll realize where toy makers got the sound for rubber duckies. • The American Wigeon is generally a vegetarian. Although it frequently dabbles for food, nothing seems to please a wigeon more than the succulent stems and leaves of pond-bottom plants. These plants grow far too deep for a dabbling duck, however, so pirating wigeons often steal from accomplished divers, such as American Coots, Canvasbacks, scaups and Redheads. • American Wigeons are commonly observed grazing on shore. They are good walkers, in contrast to other ducks. • The male's bright white crown and forehead has led some people, and especially hunters, to call it 'Baldpate.'

ID: large, white wing patch; cinnamon breast and sides; white belly; black-tipped, grey-blue bill; green speculum; white wing pits. *Male:* white forehead; green swipe running back from each eye. *Female:* greyish head; brown underparts.

Size: *L* 46–58 cm.

Status: uncommon to locally abundant spring and fall migrant; rare to locally common breeder; a few may be present in winter.

Habitat: shallow wetlands, lake edges and ponds.

Nesting: always on dry ground, often far from water; nest is well concealed in tall vegetation and is built with grass, leaves and down; female incubates 8–11 white eggs for 23–25 days.

Feeding: dabbles and tips up for aquatic leaves and the stems of pondweeds; also grazes and uproots young shoots in fields; may eat some invertebrates.

Voice: *Male:* nasal, frequently repeated whistle: *whee WHEE wheew. Female:* soft, seldom heard *quack.*

Similar Species: *Gadwall* (p. 61): white speculum; lacks the large, white wing patch; male lacks the green eye swipe; female has orange swipes on the bill. *Eurasian Wigeon* (p. 62): grey wing pits; male has a rufous head, cream forehead and rosy breast; lacks the green eye swipe; female may have a browner head.

Best Sites: Luther Marsh; Lynde Shores Conservation Area; Upper Canada Migratory Bird Sanctuary; Mission Island Marsh; Lillabelle Lake; Long Point PP; Presqu'ile PP.

AMERICAN BLACK DUCK

Anas rubripes

At one time, the American Black Duck was the most common and widely distributed duck in Ontario. In recent years, however, the eastern expansion of the Mallard has come at the expense of this dark dabbler. Unlike the American Black Duck, the Mallard is extremely adaptable and will thrive in almost any setting—it has even been known to swim about in backyard pools. A male Mallard will aggressively pursue a female Black Duck, and if unable to find a male its own kind, the female will often accept the offer. Hybrid offspring are less fertile and are usually unable to produce progeny of their own. To the abundant Mallard, it is not loss, but to the Black Duck it is a further set back. Fortunately, the rivers and lakes of northern Ontario still attract 'Blacks' but few Mallards.

ID: dark brown-black body; light brown head and neck; bright orange feet; violet speculum. *Male:* yellow olive bill. *Female:* dull green bill mottled with grey or black. *In flight:* whitish underwings; dark body.
Size: *L* 51–63 cm.
Status: uncommon to locally abundant migrant from late March to late May and from August to November; uncommon to fairly common breeder; rare to locally common winter resident.
Habitat: lakes, wetlands, rivers and agricultural areas.
Nesting: usually on the ground among clumps of dense vegetation near water; female fills a shallow depression with plant material and lines it with down;

female incubates 7–11 white to greenish-buff eggs for 23–33 days.
Feeding: tips up and dabbles in shallows for the seeds and roots of pondweeds; also eats aquatic invertebrates, larval amphibians and fish eggs.
Voice: *Male:* gives a *croak*. *Female:* loud quacks.
Similar Species: *Mallard* (p. 65): white belly; blue speculum bordered with black and white bars; female is lighter overall and has a white tail. *Gadwall* (p. 61): black hindquarters; black and white wing patch.
Best Sites: Conestoga Reservoir; Niagara River; Fisherman's Wharf, Bronte; Presqu'ile PP; Hwy 11 from Hearst to Cobalt; Mission Island Marsh.

MALLARD
Anas platyrhynchos

The male Mallard, with his iridescent green head and chestnut breast, is the classic duck of Ontario. Mallards can quite literally be seen every day of the year in our province, as long as there is a source of open water available to them. • Wild Mallards will freely hybridize with domestic ducks (which were originally derived from Mallards in Europe), and the resulting offspring, often seen in city parks, are a confusing blend of both parents. • Male ducks molt after breeding, losing much of their extravagant plumage. This 'eclipse' plumage stage lasts briefly before they molt again into their breeding colours, usually by early fall. • Most people think of the Mallard's quack as the classic duck call. • The scientific name *platyrhynchos* is Greek for 'broad, flat bill.'

ID: dark blue speculum bordered by white; orange feet. *Male:* glossy green head; yellow bill; chestnut breast; white 'necklace'; grey body plumage; black tail feathers curl upward. *Female:* mottled brown overall; orange bill is splattered with black.
Size: *L* 51–71 cm.
Status: rare to locally abundant migrant, breeder and winter resident.
Habitat: lakes, wetlands, rivers, city parks, agricultural areas and sewage lagoons.
Nesting: in tall vegetation or under a bush, often near water; nest of grass and other plant material is lined with down; female incubates 7–10 light green to white eggs for 26–30 days.
Feeding: tips up and dabbles in shallows for the seeds of sedges, willows and pondweeds; also eats aquatic invertebrates, larval amphibians and fish eggs.
Voice: *Male:* deep but quiet quacks. *Female:* loud quacks; very vocal.
Similar Species: *Northern Shoveler* (p. 67): much larger bill; male has a white breast. *American Black Duck* (p. 64): darker than a female Mallard; purple speculum lacks the white borders. *Common Merganser* (p. 86): male lacks the chestnut breast, blood red bill and white underparts.
Best Sites: almost any body of fairly still, open water.

BLUE-WINGED TEAL

Anas discors

The small, speedy Blue-winged Teal is renowned for its aviation skills. Small groups of teals can be identified in flight by their small size and by the sharp twists and turns that they execute with precision. • Despite the similarity of their names, the Green-winged Teal is not the Blue-winged Teal's closest relative. The Blue-wing is more closely related to the Cinnamon Teal and the Northern Shoveler. These birds all have broad, flat bills, pale blue forewings and green speculums. Female Cinnamon and Blue-winged teals are so similar in appearance that even expert birders and ornithologists have difficulty distinguishing them in the field. • The scientific name *discors* is Latin for 'without harmony,' which might refer to this bird's call as it takes flight.

ID: *Male:* blue-grey head; white crescent on the face; black-spotted breast and sides. *Female:* mottled brown overall. *In flight:* blue forewing patch; green speculum.

Size: *L* 36–41 cm.

Status: fairly common to common from April to early November; a few may be present in winter.

Habitat: shallow lake edges and wetlands; prefers areas of short but dense emergent vegetation.

Nesting: in grass along shorelines and in meadows; nest is built with grass and considerable amounts of down; female incubates 8–13 white eggs (may be tinged with olive) for 23–27 days.

Feeding: gleans the water's surface for sedge and grass seeds, pondweeds, duckweeds and aquatic invertebrates.

Voice: *Male:* soft *keck-keck-keck*. *Female:* soft quacks.

Similar Species: *Cinnamon Teal* (p. 354); female is virtually identical to the female Blue-winged Teal but is richer brown with a less-distinct eye line; very rare in Ontario. *Green-winged Teal* (p. 69): female has a black and green speculum and lacks the blue forewing patch. *Northern Shoveler* (p. 67): much larger bill; male has a green head and lacks the spotting on the body. *Harlequin Duck* (p. 77): male is blue-grey overall with many black and white patches; very rare in Ontario.

Best Sites: Rondeau PP; Dundas Marsh; Trent Canal; Upper Canada Migratory Bird Sanctuary; Ottawa River; Mission Island Marsh; Lake of the Woods.

NORTHERN SHOVELER

Anas clypeata

The initial reaction upon meeting this bird for the first time is often, 'Wow, look at the big honker on that Mallard!' A closer look, however, will reveal a completely different bird altogether—the Northern Shoveler. An extra large, spoon-like bill allows this strangely handsome duck to strain small invertebrates from the bottom of ponds. Shovelers eat much smaller organisms than do most other waterfowl, and their intestines are elongated to prolong the digestion these hard-bodied invertebrates. • The scientific name *clypeata* is Latin for 'furnished with a shield.' It refers to the shoveler's massive bill. This species was once placed in its own genus, *Spatula*, the meaning of which needs no explanation.

ID: large, spatulate bill; blue forewing patch; green speculum. *Male:* green head; white breast; chestnut sides. *Female:* mottled brown overall; orange-tinged bill.
Size: *L* 46–51 cm.
Status: uncommon to fairly common from mid-March to mid-May and from September to mid-November; rare, local breeder; a few may be present in winter.
Habitat: shallow marshes, bogs and lakes with muddy bottoms and emergent vegetation, usually in open and semi-open areas.
Nesting: in a shallow hollow on dry ground, usually within 50 m of water; female builds the nest with dry grass and down and incubates 10–12 pale greenish-buff eggs for 21–28 days.

Feeding: dabbles in shallow and often muddy water; strains out plant and animal matter, especially aquatic crustaceans, insect larvae and seeds; rarely tips up.
Voice: generally quiet; occasionally a raspy chuckle or quack; most often heard during spring courtship.
Similar Species: *Mallard* (p. 65): blue speculum bordered by white; lacks the pale blue forewing; male has a chestnut breast and white flanks. *Blue-winged Teal* (p. 66): much smaller bill; smaller overall; male has a spotted breast and sides.
Best Sites: Long Point PP; Grenadier Pond; Little Cataraqui Conservation Area; Long Sault Parkway; Kelley Lake, Sudbury; Mission Island Marsh; Lake of the Woods.

67

NORTHERN PINTAIL

Anas acuta

Elegant and graceful on the water and in the air, the male Pintail's beauty and style are unsurpassed by most of Ontario's birds. This bird's trademark is its long, tapering tail feathers, which are easily seen in flight and point skyward when the bird dabbles. In Ontario, only the male Long-tailed Duck shares this pintail feature. • Migrating pintails are often seen in flocks of 20 to 40 birds, but some flocks have been known to consist of nearly 10,000 individuals. Spring-flooded agricultural fields, such as those found along the South Nation and Nottawasaga rivers, tend to attract the largest pintail flocks. • Although the population of pintails in southern Ontario seems to be increasing slightly, this widespread duck appears to be in an overall decline across its range in central and western North America.

ID: long, slender neck; dark glossy bill. *Male:* chocolate brown head; long, tapering tail feathers; white of breast extends up the sides of the neck; dusty grey body plumage; black and white hindquarters. *Female:* mottled light brown overall. *In flight:* slender body; brownish speculum with a white trailing edge.

Size: *Male: L* 64–76 cm. *Female: L* 51–56 cm.

Status: fairly common to common from mid-March to May and from September to November; rare to locally common breeder; a few may be present in winter.

Habitat: shallow wetlands, fields and lake edges.

Nesting: in a small depression of vegetation; nest of grass, leaves and moss is lined with down; female incubates 6–12 greenish-buff eggs for 22–25 days.

Feeding: tips up and dabbles in shallows for the seeds of sedges, willows and pondweeds; also eats aquatic invertebrates and larval amphibians; eats waste grain in agricultural areas during migration.

Voice: *Male:* soft, whistling call. *Female:* rough quack.

Similar Species: *Mallard* (p. 65) and *Gadwall* (p. 61): females are chunkier and lack the tapering tail and the long, slender neck. *Blue-winged Teal* (p. 66): female is smaller; green speculum; blue forewing patch. *Long-tailed Duck* (p. 81): black or white head and neck; dark or light patch around the eye or on the cheek.

Best Sites: Rondeau PP; Minesing Swamp; western Bruce Peninsula; Severn Sound; Presqu'ile PP; Little Cataraqui Conservation Area; South Nation River floodplain and farmlands; Polar Bear PP.

GREEN-WINGED TEAL

Anas crecca

Small, tight-flying flocks of Green-winged Teals are among the most speedy and maneuverable of waterfowl. When intruders cause these small ducks to rocket up from wetlands, the ducks circle quickly overhead, returning only when the threat has departed. A predator's only hope of catching a healthy teal is to snatch it from the water or from a nest. Female Green-wings go to great lengths to conceal their nests among upland grasses and brush, but there are always those that are discovered by hungry weasels, skunks, foxes, coyotes and raccoons. • Green-winged Teals often undergo a partial migration before molting into their post-breeding, 'eclipse' plumage, in which they are flightless (because they do not possess a full set of flight feathers). • These lovely little teals often loiter on ponds and marshy wetlands until cold winter weather freezes the water's surface.

ID: small bill; green and black speculum. *Male:* chestnut head; green swipe running back from each eye; white shoulder slash; creamy breast is spotted with black; pale grey sides. *Female:* mottled brown overall; light belly.
Size: *L* 30–41 cm.
Status: uncommon to common from mid-March to mid-May and from late August to November; rare to uncommon breeder; rare winter resident.
Habitat: shallow lakes, wetlands, beaver ponds and meandering rivers.
Nesting: well concealed in tall vegetation; nest is built of grass and leaves and lined with down; female incubates 6–14 cream to pale buff eggs for 20–24 days.
Feeding: dabbles in the shallows for aquatic invertebrates, larval amphibians, sedge seeds and pondweeds.
Voice: *Male:* crisp whistle. *Female:* soft quack.
Similar Species: *American Wigeon* (p. 63): male lacks the white shoulder slash and the chestnut head. *Blue-winged Teal* (p. 66) and *Cinnamon Teal* (p. 354): females have a blue forewing patch.
Best Sites: St. Clair NWA; Lynde Shores Conservation Area; Bruce Peninsula; Ottawa-area farmlands; Kelley Lake, Sudbury; Clay Belt rivers and ponds; Mission Island Marsh; Lake Nipigon PP.

CANVASBACK

Aythya valisineria

Most male ducks sport richly decorated backs, but the male Canvasback has a bright clean back that, appropriately, appears to be wrapped in white canvas. This bird's back, sloping forehead and bill are unmistakable field marks. • Canvasbacks are devoted deep divers, and they seldom stray into areas of wetlands that are too shallow to allow foraging dives. Because Canvasbacks prefer the deepest areas of wetlands, birders often need binoculars to properly admire the male's wild red eyes, which nicely complement his rich mahogany head. Canvasbacks are most likely to be seen in Ontario during spring and fall migration, when flocks composed of 10,000 individuals occasionally converge on a suitable wetland. In search of winter sustenance, flotillas of Canvasbacks regularly ply the open shoreline waters of Lake Ontario, Lake Erie, the Niagara River and the St. Clair River. Canvasbacks are scarce in summer, and it is thought that fewer than 10 pairs breed in the province. • The scientific name *valisineria* refers to one of the Canvasback's favourite foods—wild celery (*Vallisneria americana*).

ID: head slopes upward from the bill to the forehead. *Male:* canvas white back; chestnut head; black breast and hindquarters; red eyes. *Female:* profile is similar to the male's; duller brown and grey plumage.

Size: *L* 48–56 cm.

Status: uncommon to fairly common from mid-March to mid-May and from October to December; rare breeder and winter resident.

Habitat: marshes, ponds, shallow lakes and other wetlands; large lakes on migration.

Nesting: basket nest of reeds and grass is lined with down and suspended above shallow water in dense stands of cattails and bulrushes;

may also nest on dry ground; female incubates 7–9 olive green eggs for up to 29 days.

Feeding: dives to depths of up to 9 m (average 3–4 m); feeds on roots, tubers, the basal stems of plants (including pondweeds and wild celery) and bulrush seeds; occasionally eats aquatic invertebrates.

Voice: generally quiet. *Male:* occasional coos and 'growls' during courtship. *Female:* low, soft, 'purring' *quack* or *kuck*; also 'growls.'

Similar Species: *Redhead* (p. 71): rounded rather than sloped forehead; male has a grey back and a bluish bill.

Best Sites: Lake St. Clair; Luther Marsh; Rondeau PP; Presqu'ile PP; St. Clair River; Niagara River; Long Point PP.

REDHEAD
Aythya americana

Like the Canvasback, the Redhead is most abundant in Ontario as a migrant and winter resident. Unlike the Canvasback, however, the Redhead maintains a more prominent presence in summer among the wetlands of southern Ontario: at Lake St. Clair and Luther Marsh, abundance has been estimated to be 11 to 100 nesting pairs for every 10 km². To distinguish a Canvasback from a Redhead, most birders will tell you to contrast their profiles, but the most obvious difference between them is the colour of their backs. • Female Redheads usually incubate their own eggs and brood their young as other ducks do, but they occasionally lay their eggs in the nests of other ducks. In Ontario, the Blue-winged Teal, Gadwall, Ring-necked Duck and Lesser Scaup have all been victims of Redhead egg dumping. • The Redhead is a diving duck, but it will occasionally feed on the surface of wetlands like a dabbler.

ID: blue-grey, black-tipped bill. *Male:* rounded, red head; black breast and hindquarters; grey back and sides. *Female:* dark overall; lighter foreneck and lower face.
Size: *L* 46–56 cm.
Status: common in March and April; fairly common from October to mid-December; rare breeder; uncommon winter resident.
Habitat: large wetlands, ponds, lakes, bays and rivers.
Nesting: deep basket nest of reeds and grass is lined with fine white down and suspended over water at the base of emergent vegetation; female incubates 9–14 eggs for 23–29 days; female may lay eggs in other ducks' nests.
Feeding: dives to depths of 3 m; primarily eats aquatic vegetation,

especially pondweeds and duckweeds and the leaves and stems of plants; occasionally eats aquatic invertebrates.
Voice: generally quiet. *Male:* cat-like meow in courtship. *Female:* rolling *kurr-kurr-kurr*; *squak* when alarmed.
Similar Species: *Canvasback* (p. 70): clean white back; bill slopes into the forehead. *Ring-necked Duck* (p. 72): female has a more prominent, white eye ring, a white ring on the bill and a peaked head. *Lesser Scaup* (p. 74): male has a dark purple head and whiter sides; female has more white at the base of the bill. *Greater Scaup* (p. 73): male has a dark green head and whiter sides; female has more white at the base of the bill.
Best Sites: Lake St. Clair; Long Point PP; Luther Marsh; Presqu'ile PP; Cache Bay; Lake Nipissing.

RING-NECKED DUCK

Aythya collaris

After observing the Ring-necked Duck in the wild, don't worry if you are left wondering why it wasn't named the 'Ring-billed Duck'—you are certainly not the first birder to ponder this perplexing puzzle. The official appellation is derived from the scientific name *collaris* (collar), which originated with an ornithologist looking at an indistinct cinnamon collar on a museum specimen, not a birdwatcher looking through binoculars. • The Ring-necked Duck is a fairly common nesting species throughout central and northern Ontario, where small, shy groups are often seen floating on boreal forest bogs, sedge-meadow wetlands and tree-edged beaver ponds. • Ring-necks are diving ducks, like scaups, Redheads and Canvasbacks, but they prefer to feed in shallower shoreline waters. They ride high on the water and they tend to carry their tails clear of the water's surface.

ID: *Male:* angular, dark purple head; black breast, back and hindquarters; white shoulder slash; grey sides; blue-grey bill with black and white bands at the tip; thin, white border around the base of the bill. *Female:* dark brown overall; white eye ring; dark bill with black and white bands at the tip; pale crescent on the front of the face.

Size: *L* 36–46 cm.

Status: uncommon to common from late February to late May; uncommon from mid-September to mid-November; rare to fairly common breeder; a few may be present in winter.

Habitat: wooded ponds, swamps, marshes and sloughs with emergent vegetation.

Nesting: frequently over water on a hummock or shoreline; bulky nest of grass and moss is lined with down; female incubates 8–10 olive tan eggs for 25–29 days.

Feeding: dives underwater for aquatic vegetation, including seeds, tubers and pondweed leaves; also eats aquatic invertebrates.

Voice: seldom heard. *Male:* low-pitched, hissing whistle. *Female:* growling *churr.*

Similar Species: *Lesser Scaup* (p. 74): lacks the white ring toward the tip of the bill; male lacks the white shoulder slash and the black back; female has a broad, clearly defined white border around the base of the bill. *Greater Scaup* (p. 73): lacks the white ring toward the tip of the bill; male has a dark green head and white sides; female has a broad, clearly defined white border around the base of the bill. *Redhead* (p. 71): female has a less prominent eye ring; rounded rather than peaked head; less white on the front of the face.

Best Sites: Big Creek NWA; Luther Marsh; Presqu'ile PP; Algonquin PP; Shirley's Bay, Ottawa; lakes along Hwy 11; Sleeping Giant PP.

GREATER SCAUP

Aythya marila

Since the introduction of zebra mussels into the Great Lakes, large flocks of Greater Scaup have begun wintering in southern Ontario, far away from their traditional wintering grounds on the Atlantic. It is believed that scaups eat large quantities of these freshwater mollusks, which have dramatically changed many of Ontario's underwater ecosystems. Large rafts of Greater Scaups can now be seen alongside Redheads, Long-tailed Ducks and Common Goldeneyes during winter on Lake Ontario.
• Greater Scaup are abundant throughout much of the province during spring and fall migration, and some locations boast concentrations of more than 27,000 individuals.
• Greater Scaup nesting in the province are primarily found on the open tundra of the Hudson Bay coast. • Look for the rounder (not peaked), more greenish head of the Greater Scaup to distinguish it from its Lesser relative.

ID: rounded, never peaked, head; golden eyes. *Male:* dark iridescent green head (often appears black); black breast, white belly, sides and flanks; light grey back; dark hindquarters; blue, black-tipped bill. *Female:* brown overall; well-defined white patch at the base of the bill. *In flight:* white flash through the wing extends well into the primary feathers.

Size: *L* 41–48 cm.

Status: uncommon to abundant migrant from early February to May and from September to November; rare to locally fairly common breeder; common to locally abundant winter resident.

Habitat: *Breeding:* ponds and small lakes on open tundra. *In migration:* lakes, large marshes and reservoirs, usually far from shore.

Nesting: on a grass- or sedge-covered shoreline; female lines a shallow depression with dry vegetation and down; may nest in small, loose colonies; female incubates 5–11 olive-buff eggs for 24–28 days.

Feeding: dives underwater for aquatic invertebrates and vegetation; amphipods, insect larvae and vegetation are taken in summer; freshwater mollusks are favoured in winter.

Voice: generally quiet in migration; alarm call is a deep *scaup*. *Male:* may issue a 3-note whistle and a soft *wah-hooo*. *Female:* may give a subtle growl.

Similar Species: *Lesser Scaup* (p. 74): shorter white wing flash in flight; slightly smaller bill; male has a peaked, purplish head; female has a peaked head. *Ring-necked Duck* (p. 72): black back; white shoulder slash; white ring around the base of the bill. *Redhead* (p. 71): female has less white at the base of the bill; male has a red head and darker sides.

Best Sites: Point Pelee NP; Long Point PP; Presqu'ile PP; Prince Edward Point NWA; St. Lawrence River at Ivy Lea; western Lake Ontario and Niagara River.

LESSER SCAUP

Aythya affinis

The male Lesser Scaup and its relative, the Greater Scaup, mirror the colours of an Oreo cookie: they are black at both ends and light in the middle. These readily identifiable birds are most at home among the lakes of the boreal regions of the province, but some can be found nesting in southern marshes. Although Greater and Lesser Scaup may occur together on larger lakes during migration, they tend not to mingle. • Lesser Scaups, also known as 'Bluebills,' leap up neatly before diving underwater, where they propel themselves with powerful strokes of their feet. • The scientific name *affinis* is Latin for 'adjacent' or 'allied'—a reference to this scaup's close association to other diving ducks. 'Scaup' might refer to a preferred winter food of this duck—shellfish beds are called 'scalps' in Scotland—or it might be a phonetic imitation of one of its calls.

ID: yellow eyes. *Male:* dark purplish head; black breast and hindquarters; dusty white sides; greyish back; blue-grey, black-tipped bill. *Female:* dark brown overall; well-defined white patch at the base of the bill.
Size: *L* 38–46 cm.
Status: uncommon to abundant migrant from late February to mid-May and from late August to November; rare breeder; rare to locally uncommon winter resident.
Habitat: *Breeding:* woodland and tundra ponds, wetlands and lake edges with grassy margins. *In migration:* lakes, large marshes and rivers.
Nesting: in tall, concealing vegetation, generally close to water and occasionally on an island; nest hollow is built of grass and lined with down; female incubates 8–14 olive-buff eggs for about 21–27 days.

Feeding: dives underwater for aquatic invertebrates, mostly mollusks, amphipods, insect larvae and vegetation.
Voice: alarm call is a deep *scaup*. *Male:* soft *whee-oooh* in courtship. *Female:* purring *kwah*.
Similar Species: *Greater Scaup* (p. 73): slightly larger bill; longer, white wing flash; male has a rounded, greenish head without a peak; female has a rounded head. *Ring-necked Duck* (p. 72): male has a white shoulder slash and a black back; female has a white-ringed beak. *Redhead* (p. 71): female has less white at the base of the bill; male has a red head and darker sides.
Best Sites: Lake St. Clair; Point Pelee NP; Long Point PP; Presqu'ile PP; Prince Edward Point NWA; St. Lawrence River; east end of Hamilton Harbour; Luther Marsh; Cranberry Marsh.

KING EIDER

Somateria spectabilis

I f you are saving up some luck for your next meeting with a spectacular bird, the dazzling King Eider is the bird to be saving for: the male boasts no less than six bold colours (blue, green, orange, red, black and white) on his magnificent head and bill.
• King Eiders are extremely rare breeders in Ontario. The southern limit of their breeding range extends only as far as Polar Bear Provincial Park in northern Ontario, so only during migration or over winter are birders able to get an intimate look at this impressive sea duck. Among waterfowl, only Long-tailed Ducks breed as far north as King Eiders.
• King Eiders are equipped with some of the finest insulation in the bird world (eider down), so these birds are well adapted for loafing on ice floes and taking deep, extended dives into frigid arctic water.

ID: *Male:* blue crown; green cheek; orange nasal disc; red bill; black wings; white neck, breast, back, upperwing patches and flank patches. *Female:* mottled rich rufous-brown overall; black bill extends into a nasal shield; sides have V-shaped markings. *Immature male:* dark overall; white breast; yellow-orange bill resembles the female's bill.
Size: *L* 48–64 cm; *W* 89–102 cm.
Status: rare to uncommon spring and fall migrant and breeder; rare winter visitor.
Habitat: *Breeding:* arctic tundra near fresh or salt water. *In migration:* large freshwater lakes.
Nesting: on dry tundra, usually close to water; female lines a scrape or natural depression with grass, sedges and large amounts

of down plucked from her own body; female incubates 3–7 pale olive eggs for 22–24 days; female tends the precocial young.
Feeding: primarily dives for aquatic mollusks; may dive more than 45 m deep; also takes small insects, crustaceans, echinoderms and some vegetation, especially in summer.
Voice: *Male:* soft cooing sounds in courtship. *Female:* low, twanging clucks.
Similar Species: *Common Eider* (p. 76): female has evenly barred sides; feathering on the sides of the long, droopy beak extend to the nostril; immature has white streaking on the back. *Female scoters* (pp. 78–80): more bulbous bills; lack the nasal shield; solid brown plumage.
Best Sites: Rondeau Bay and Lake Ontario west of Toronto; Niagara River gorge; Polar Bear PP.

COMMON EIDER

Somateria mollissima

Floating leisurely in rafts of thousands, Common Eiders regularly veil the frigid winter waters of Hudson Bay. Like scoters, these hefty birds are well adapted for living among the frothy ocean waves of cold, northern seas. Their high metabolic rate and dense down feathers facilitate their almost entirely marine lifestyle. • During the breeding season, female eiders pluck downy feathers from their own bodies to provide insulation and camouflage for their eggs. For centuries, people have prized eider down for its superior insulative qualities. • Both eiders and scoters are adept at feeding on mollusks. Pried from their benthic footholds, mollusks are swallowed whole, then crushed into small fragments in the birds' gizzards.

ID: *Male:* smoothly sloping forehead; black and white overall; green tinge on the nape and nasal shield. *Female:* grey to rusty brown overall; barred breast, flanks and back; grey bill and nasal shield. *Immature male:* dark head and body; white streaking on the back. *In flight:* flies close to the water's surface with its head lowered.
Size: *L* 58–68 cm; *W* 88–106 cm
Status: occasional winter visitor to locally abundant winter resident; rare and very local breeder.
Habitat: shallow coastal waters in all seasons; occasionally seen on large freshwater lakes. *Breeding:* rocky shorelines, islands or tundra in close proximity to water.
Nesting: colonial; in a shallow depression on a rocky shelf or in a rocky depression; nest is lined with plant material and large quantities of down; female incubates 3–6 olive grey eggs for 24–25 days; female tends young

of several broods grouped into a creche.
Feeding: mollusks pried from ocean depths are swallowed whole; may dive deeper than 45 m; crustaceans, echinoderms, insects and plant material are also taken when available.
Voice: *Male:* raucous, moaning *he-ho-ha-ho* or *a-o-waa-a-o-waa;* courtship calls are *ah-oo* and *k'doo. Female:* mallard-like *wak-wak-wak-wak-wak;* angry *wh-r-r-r-r;* courtship call is *aw-aw-aw.*
Similar Species: *White-winged* (p. 79), *Surf* (p. 78) and *Black* (p. 80) *scoters:* all lack the barring of the female and the white back and breast of the male. *King Eider* (p. 75): male has a colourful, blocky head; female has a long nasal shield; immature male has a yellow-orange bill and lacks the white streaking on the back. *Long-tailed Duck* (p. 81), *Bufflehead* (p. 82) and *Common Goldeneye* (p. 83): all lack the smoothly sloping facial profile.
Best Sites: inshore waters of Lake Ontario; Polar Bear PP.

HARLEQUIN DUCK

Histrionicus histrionicus

Harlequin Ducks are regular migrants and winter visitors to Ontario, but their numbers have declined over the years. The eastern Harlequin populations have dwindled to only about 1000 birds, but there seems to have been an increase in Ontario sightings, although by only a few each year. Most Harlequins are seen from October to December on the Great Lakes and on the Ottawa River, and a few linger through winter, riding the rough, open waters of Lake Ontario. Although their stay is usually brief, their dynamic appearance never fails to excite and impress fortunate onlookers.
• In eastern North America, Harlequins breed along the Atlantic coast from eastern Baffin Island to the Gaspé Peninsula, where tumbling coastal mountain streams are the favoured habitat of this bird. After a short breeding season, flocks of Harlequins move south to winter along the coast from Newfoundland to New York State.

ID: small, rounded duck; blocky head; short bill; raises and lowers its tail while swimming. *Male:* grey-blue body; chestnut sides; white spots and stripes outlined in black on the head, neck and flanks. *Female:* dusky brown overall; light underparts; 2 or 3 light patches on the head.
Size: *L* 36–48 cm.
Status: extremely rare from September to mid-April.
Habitat: large freshwater lakes.
Nesting: does not nest in Ontario.
Feeding: dabbles and dives for aquatic invertebrates, mostly caddisfly and stonefly larvae in rivers and crustaceans and mollusks in freshwater lakes; often searches river bottoms, probing rock crevices for invertebrates and fish eggs.
Voice: generally silent outside the breeding season.
Similar Species: *Bufflehead* (p. 82): smaller; never found on fast-flowing water; female lacks the white between the eye and the bill. *Surf Scoter* (p. 78): female has a bulbous bill. *White-winged Scoter* (p. 79): female has a white wing patch and a bulbous bill.
Best Sites: Rondeau Bay; Niagara River; Lake Ontario west of Toronto.

SURF SCOTER

Melanitta perspicillata

When spring storms put whitecaps on Ontario's big lakes, migrating Surf Scoters rest comfortably among the crashing waves. These scoters are most often seen during spring and fall migration, when tired flocks settle upon open water in large, dark rafts. Scoters spend their winters just beyond the breaking surf on both the Atlantic and Pacific coasts, and they are well adapted to life on rough water. • Small numbers of Surf Scoters have been recorded nesting in extreme northern Ontario, primarily along the boggy terrain of the Hudson Bay Lowland. Unfortunately, the inaccessibility of the region, combined with the bird's secretive nesting habits, means that few Surf Scoter nests have ever been studied. • The scientific name *Melanitta* means 'black duck'; *perspicillata* is Latin for 'spectacular,' which refers to this bird's colourful, bulbous bill.

ID: large, stocky, dark duck; large bill; sloping forehead; all-black wings. *Male:* black overall; white on the forehead and the back of the neck; orange bill and legs; black spot, outlined in white, at the base of the bill. *Female:* brown overall; dark grey bill; 2 whitish patches on the sides of the head.

Size: *L* 43–53 cm.

Status: common migrant from mid-April to December; rare breeder; a few may be present in winter.

Habitat: large, deep lakes and large rivers.

Nesting: in a shallow scrape under bushes or branches, often well away from open water; nest is lined with down; female incubates 5–9 buff-coloured eggs.

Feeding: dives underwater to depths of 9 m; eats mostly mollusks; also takes aquatic insect larvae, crustaceans and some aquatic vegetation.

Voice: generally quiet; infrequently utters low, harsh croaks. *Male:* occasionally gives a low, clear whistle. *Female:* guttural *krraak krraak*.

Similar Species: *White-winged Scoter* (p. 79): white wing patches; male lacks the white on the forehead and nape. *Black Scoter* (p. 80: male is all black; female has a well-defined, pale cheek.

Best Sites: St. Clair River; Point Edward; Rondeau PP; Stoke's Bay; Dyer's Bay; Niagara River; Hamilton Harbour (east end); southeastern Lake Simcoe; Presqu'ile PP; Prince Edward Point NWA; Guindon Park, Cornwall; North Bay; Polar Bear PP.

WHITE-WINGED SCOTER

Melanitta fusca

As White-winged Scoters race across Ontario's lakes, their flapping wings reveal a key identifying feature—the white inner-wing patches strike a sharp contrast with the bird's otherwise black plumage. The White-winged Scoter is the largest and most abundant of the three scoters seen in the province, and it is the only scoter seen consistently in large numbers throughout winter. In February 1993, approximately 13,000 White-winged Scoters were seen along the western end of Lake Ontario. • This bird probably breeds in very low densities throughout the Hudson Bay Lowlands, but few have ever been confirmed breeding there. • Scoters have small wings relative to the weight of their bodies, so they require long stretches of water for take-off. • The name 'scoter' may be derived from the way this bird scoots across the water's surface. Scooting can be a means of travelling quickly from one foraging site to another.

ID: stocky, all-dark duck; large, bulbous bill; sloping forehead; base of the bill is fully feathered. *Male:* black overall; white patch below the eye. *Female:* brown overall; grey-brown bill; 2 whitish patches on the sides of the head. *In flight:* white wing patches.

Size: *L* 48–61 cm.

Status: common year-round; rare breeder; rare to locally common winter visitor.

Habitat: *Breeding:* northern lakes, muskeg wetlands and slow-flowing rivers. *In migration:* large, deep lakes and large rivers.

Nesting: among bushes very near shorelines; in a shallow scrape lined with sticks, leaves, grass and down; often well concealed; female incubates 9–14 pinkish eggs for up to 28 days.

Feeding: deep, underwater dives lasting up to 1 minute; eats mostly mollusks; may also take crustaceans, aquatic insects and some small fish.

Voice: courting pair produces guttural and harsh noises, between a *crook* and a *quack*.

Similar Species: *Surf Scoter* (p. 78): lacks the white wing patches; male has a white forehead and nape. *Black Scoter* (p. 80): lacks the white patches in the wings and around the eyes. *American Coot* (p. 117): whitish bill and nasal shield; lacks the white patches in the wings and around the red eyes.

Best Sites: St. Clair River; Point Edward; Rondeau PP; Stoke's Bay; Niagara River; Lake Ontario west of Toronto; southeastern Lake Simcoe; Prince Edward Point NWA; Guindon Park, Cornwall; North Bay; South Baymouth, Manitoulin Island.

BLACK SCOTER

Melanitta nigra

Migration is a lengthy journey, especially after a rigorous breeding season, so many of these handsome scoters make rest stops on the Great Lakes and other large bodies of water as they travel south through Ontario. Some Black Scoters begin arriving in southern Ontario as early as Labour Day, but the majority arrive through late fall and early winter, just as the frigid cold beckons at the doors of Ontarians. • Of the three species of scoters in Ontario, the Black Scoter is the least common. On occasion, however, large flocks that number over 1000 birds can be seen along the shores of Presqu'ile Provincial Park and Kettle Point. • While floating on the water's surface, Black Scoters tend to hold their heads high, unlike the other scoters, which tend to look downward. • Large numbers of Black Scoters have been known to summer on Hudson Bay and James Bay, and smaller numbers have been reported to overwinter on the lower Great Lakes.

ID: *Male:* black overall; large orange knob on the bill. *Female:* light cheek; dark cap; brown overall; dark grey bill.

Size: *L* 43–53 cm.

Status: rare to uncommon from September to January; extremely rare from March to May.

Habitat: large, deep lakes, large rivers and sewage lagoons.

Nesting: does not nest in Ontario.

Feeding: dives underwater; eats mostly mollusks and aquatic insect larvae; occasionally eats aquatic vegetation and small fish.

Voice: generally quiet; infrequently an unusual *cour-loo*; wings whistle in flight.

Similar Species: *White-winged Scoter* (p. 79): white wing patches; male has a white slash below the eye. *Surf Scoter* (p. 78): male has white on the head; female has 2 whitish patches on the sides of the head.

Best Sites: check local bird hotlines for recent sightings; Kettle Point; Niagara River; Lake Ontario west of Toronto; Presqu'ile PP; Prince Edward Point NWA; Guindon Park, Cornwall; Ottawa River; North Bay.

NON-BREEDING

LONG-TAILED DUCK

Clangula hyemalis

These ancient mariners of the Great Lakes are able to survive violent winter gales like the great storm that scuttled the *Edmund Fitzgerald*. Long-tailed Ducks tend to remain in deeper waters well away from shore, but at times they may move to inshore waters, where observers can catch a glimpse of the birds' long, slender tails and winter finery. They are rare breeders along the coast of Hudson Bay, so most Ontarians meet them over winter or during spring and fall migration, when concentrations may exceed 10,000 individuals. Long-tailed Ducks are among the noisiest breeders on the tundra, but during migration and over winter they remain relatively silent. • The breeding and non-breeding plumages of these arctic-nesting sea ducks are like photo-negatives of each other: the spring breeding plumage is mostly dark with white highlights; the winter plumage is mostly white with dark patches. • King Eiders and Long-tailed Ducks are among the world's deepest diving waterfowl—both make regular dives to depths of more than 60 m. • Until recently, this duck was officially called the Oldsquaw, and many people still use that name.

summer

ID: *Breeding male:* dark head with a white eye patch; dark neck and upperparts; white belly; dark bill; long, dark central tail feathers. *Non-breeding male:* pale head with a dark patch; pale neck and belly; dark breast; long, white patches on the back; pink bill with a dark base; long, dark central tail feathers. *Breeding female:* short tail feathers; grey bill; dark crown, throat patch, wings and back; white underparts. *Non-breeding female:* similar, but generally lighter, especially on the head.
Size: *L* 43–51 cm.
Status: locally common to abundant from mid-November to early May; fairly common migrant in May and late October; rare breeder.
Habitat: large, deep lakes and wetlands.

Nesting: on dry ground near water; depression in the ground, usually partly concealed by vegetation or rocks, is lined with plant material and down; female incubates 5–11 olive-grey to olive-buff eggs for 24–29 days.
Feeding: dives for mollusks, crustaceans and aquatic insects; occasionally eats roots and young shoots; may also take some small fish.
Voice: courtship call—*owl-owl-owlet*—is rarely heard outside the breeding range.
Similar Species: *Northern Pintail* (p. 68): thin, white line extending up the sides of the neck; grey sides.
Best Sites: Rondeau PP; Niagara River; Toronto harbour; Dyer's Bay; Presqu'ile PP; Prince Edward Point NWA; St. Lawrence River at Ivy Lea; South Baymouth, Manitoulin Island; Polar Bear PP.

81

BUFFLEHEAD

Bucephala albeola

Each winter, the open waters of Lake Ontario become an avian battleground of sorts. Dozens of species of waterfowl patrol the waters in huge flotillas that are often composed of thousands of birds. Winter imposes many limiting factors on birds, so food and suitable habitat may be scarce at times. Fortunately for the Bufflehead, it is right at home on the lake amid its larger relatives. In summer, Buffleheads lead a more isolated life, choosing to breed, like goldeneyes, in secluded tree cavities or nest boxes alongside beaver ponds and quiet lakes. • The Bufflehead is actually a small goldeneye, as similarities in its profile, behaviour and scientific name will attest. • The common name refers to this duck's large head and sloped forehead, which are similar in shape to those of a buffalo. The scientific name *Bucephala* also refers to the shape of the head—it means 'ox-headed' in Greek; *albeola* is Latin for 'white,' a reference to the male's plumage.

ID: very small, rounded duck; white speculum in flight; short grey bill; short neck. *Male:* white wedge on the back of the head; head is otherwise dark iridescent green or purple, usually appearing black; dark back; white neck and underparts. *Female:* dark brown head; white, oval ear patch; light brown sides.
Size: *L* 33–38 cm.
Status: common to locally abundant from October to mid-May; rare to uncommon breeder.
Habitat: *Winter* and *In migration:* open water of lakes, large ponds and rivers. *Breeding:* small, wooded northern wetlands.
Nesting: in a tree cavity, usually an abandoned woodpecker nest or a natural cavity; often near water; nest chamber may be unlined or filled with down; female incubates 6–12 pale buff to cream eggs for 28–33 days; ducklings leave the nest within 3 days of hatching.

Feeding: dives for aquatic invertebrates; water boatmen and mayfly and damselfly larvae are taken in summer; mollusks (particularly snails) and crustaceans are favoured in winter; also eats some small fish and pondweeds.
Voice: *Male:* growling call. *Female:* harsh quack.
Similar Species: *Hooded Merganser* (p. 85): white crest is outlined in black. *Harlequin Duck* (p. 77): female has several light spots on the head. *Common Goldeneye* (p. 83) and *Barrow's Goldeneye* (p. 84): males are larger and have a white patch between the eye and the bill. *Other diving ducks:* females are much larger.
Best Sites: Big Creek NWA; Niagara River; Lake Ontario west of Toronto; Presqu'ile PP; Ottawa River; Hwy 11 from Hearst to Cobalt; Lake of the Woods.

COMMON GOLDENEYE

Bucephala clangula

The courtship display of the male Common Goldeneye looks much like an avian slapstick routine, although to the bird itself it is probably a serious matter. Beginning in winter, the male performs a number of odd postures and vocalizations, often to apparently disinterested females. In one common routine, he arches his puffy, iridescent head backward until his forehead seems to touch his back; then he catapults his neck forward like a coiled spring while producing a seemingly painful *peent* sound. • Common Goldeneyes are common, widespread breeders north of Georgian Bay. After hatching, ducklings remain in the nest cavity for one to three days before jumping out, often falling a long distance to the ground below. • Common Goldeneyes are frequently called 'whistlers,' because the wind whistles through their wings when they fly.

ID: steep forehead with a peaked crown; black wings with large, white patches; golden eyes. *Male:* dark, iridescent green head; round, white cheek patch; dark bill; dark back; white sides and belly. *Female:* chocolate brown head; lighter breast and belly; grey-brown body plumage; dark bill, tipped with yellow in spring and summer.
Size: *L* 41–51 cm.
Status: common to locally abundant from mid-October to mid-April; locally common breeder.
Habitat: *Breeding:* marshes, ponds, lakes and rivers. *Winter* and *In migration:* open water of lakes, large ponds and rivers.
Nesting: in a tree cavity; often close to water, but occasionally quite far from it; cavity is lined with wood chips and down; will use nest boxes; female incubates 6–10 blue-green eggs for 28–32 days.
Feeding: dives for crustaceans, mollusks and aquatic insect larvae; may also eat tubers, leeches, frogs and small fish.
Voice: wings whistle in flight. *Male:* courtship calls are a nasal *peent* and a hoarse *kraaagh*. *Female:* harsh croak.
Similar Species: *Barrow's Goldeneye* (p. 84): male has a large, white, crescent-shaped cheek patch and a purplish head; female has more orange on the bill and a more steeply sloped forehead.
Best Sites: widespread north of Georgian Bay; Niagara River; Lake Ontario west of Toronto; Presqu'ile PP; Ivy Lea; Deschênes Rapids.

BARROW'S GOLDENEYE

Bucephala islandica

The Barrow's Goldeneye is a rare but regular visitor to Ontario. The few welcomed strays that make an appearance in the province each year seem to fuel the determination of many dedicated winter birders hoping to see this rarity among the masses of Common Goldeneyes. Any birder will tell you that it is hard to forget the first meeting with a Barrow's Goldeneye. • Like the Common Goldeneye, the Barrow's has an amusing foraging style: after taking a deep dive for food, it pops back up to the surface like a colourful cork. • The majority of these birds breed in western North America, but smaller, highly isolated populations occur in Labrador, Greenland and Iceland. • This diving duck bears the name of Sir John Barrow, secretary to the British Admiralty, who was committed to finding the Northwest Passage.

ID: medium-sized, rounded duck; short bill; steep forehead. *Male:* dark purple head; white crescent on the cheek; white underparts; dark back and wings with white spotting. *Female:* chocolate brown head; orange bill is tipped with black in spring and summer; grey-brown body plumage.
Size: *L* 41–51 cm.
Status: rare from late October to mid-April.
Habitat: open lakes, rivers, ponds and sewage lagoons.

Nesting: does not nest in Ontario.
Feeding: dives for mollusks and crustaceans.
Voice: generally silent. *Male:* 'mewing' call in spring. *Female:* hoarse 'croaks' in spring.
Similar Species: *Common Goldeneye* (p. 83): male has a small, round, white cheek patch and a greenish head; female has a darker bill without the black tip.
Best Sites: St. Clair River at Sarnia; Niagara River; Lake Ontario west of Toronto; Presqu'ile PP; Cornwall Dam; Ivy Lea; Deschênes Rapids.

HOODED MERGANSER

Lophodytes cucullatus

Extremely attractive and exceptionally shy, the Hooded Merganser is one of Ontario's most sought after ducks from a birdwatcher's perspective. Most of the attention is directed toward the handsome male, whose flashy headgear may be the grooviest of all Ontario birds. Much of the time his crest is held flat, but in moments of arousal or agitation, he quickly unfolds his brilliant crest to attract a mate or signal approaching danger. • Hoodies attain their greatest density in summer in the Great Lakes region, wherever woodlands occur near waterways. • All mergansers have thin bills with small tooth-like serrations to help the birds keep a firm grasp on slippery prey. Before eating, Hoodies reposition their prey, using only their bill and slight tosses of the head, so that the prize can be swallowed headfirst—not an easy task to perform without the help of hands! The smallest of the mergansers, Hoodies have a more diverse diet than their larger relatives.

ID: slim body; crested head; dark, thin, pointed bill. *Male:* black head and back; bold white crest is outlined in black; white breast with 2 black slashes; rusty sides. *Female:* dusky brown body; shaggy, reddish-brown crest. *In flight:* small, white wing patches.

Size: *L* 41–48 cm.

Status: rare to locally fairly common from mid-March to mid-November; a few may be present in winter.

Habitat: forest-edged ponds, wetlands, lakes and rivers.

Nesting: usually in a tree cavity 4–12 m high; may also use nest boxes; cavity is lined with leaves, grass and down; female incubates 10–12 white eggs for 29–33 days.

Feeding: very diverse diet; dives for small fish, caddisfly and dragonfly larvae, snails, amphibians and crayfish.

Voice: low grunts and croaks. *Male:* frog-like *crrrrooo* in courtship display. *Female:* generally quiet; occasionally a harsh *gak* or a croaking *croo-croo-crook*.

Similar Species: *Bufflehead* (p. 82): male lacks the black outline to the crest and the 2 black breast and shoulder slashes. *Red-breasted Merganser* (p. 87) and *Common Merganser* (p. 86): females have a much longer, orange bill and a grey back. *Other small diving ducks:* females lack the crest.

Best Sites: Rondeau PP; Mountsberg Conservation Area; Luther Marsh; Silent Lake PP; Algonquin PP; Britannia, Ottawa; Honey Harbour; Killarney PP; lakes, ponds and rivers along Hwy 11; Sleeping Giant PP.

85

COMMON MERGANSER

Mergus merganser

Straining like a jumbo jet in take-off, the Common Merganser runs along the surface of the water, beating its wings until it gains sufficient speed to become airborne. Once up and away, this great duck flies arrow-straight, low over the water, making broad sweeping turns to follow the meanderings of rivers and lake shorelines. • The Common Merganser is the most widespread and abundant merganser in North America. It also occurs in Europe and Asia, where it is called the Goosander. • In Ontario, Common Mergansers breed among the forest-edged waterways of the Canadian Shield, wherever there are clear and unpolluted lakes and rivers. These ducks are highly social, and they often gather in large groups over winter and during migration. In winter, any source of open water with a fish-filled shoal may support good numbers of these skilled divers.

ID: large, elongated body. *Male:* glossy green head without a crest; blood red bill and feet; white body plumage; black stripe on the back; dark eyes. *Female:* rusty neck and crested head; clean white chin and breast; orange bill; grey body; orangish eyes. *In flight:* shallow wingbeats; body is compressed and arrow-like.

Size: *L* 56–69 cm.

Status: uncommon to common from late September to late April; rare to common breeder.

Habitat: large rivers and deep lakes.

Nesting: often in a tree cavity 4.5–6 m high; occasionally on the ground, under a bush or log, on a cliff ledge or in a large nest box; usually not far from water; female incubates 8–11 pale buff eggs for 30–35 days.

Feeding: dives underwater (up to 9 m) for small fish, usually whitefish, trout, suckers, perch and minnows; young eat aquatic invertebrates.

Voice: *Male:* harsh *uig-a*, like a guitar twang. *Female:* harsh *karr karr*.

Similar Species: *Red-breasted Merganser* (p. 87): male has a shaggy green crest and a spotted, red breast; female lacks the cleanly defined white throat. *Mallard* (p. 65): male has a chestnut breast and a yellow bill. *Common Goldeneye* (p. 83): male has a white cheek patch and a stubby, dark bill. *Common Loon* (p. 36): dark bill; white spotting on the back.

Best Sites: Niagara River; Lake Ontario; Cornwall Dam; Deschênes Rapids; Sault Ste. Marie's Whitefish Island; Bruce Peninsula; Georgian Bay Islands NP; Algonquin PP; Killarney PP; Lake Nipissing; lakes and rivers along Hwy 11; Sleeping Giant PP.

RED-BREASTED MERGANSER

Mergus serrator

Its glossy, slicked-back crest and wild red eyes give the Red-breasted Merganser the dishevelled, wave-bashed look of an adrenalized windsurfer. This bird was at one time called 'Sawbill' and 'Sea-Robin', so it's a good thing that bird names have since been standardized—who knows what we'd be calling this punk-haired bird now. • Each spring and fall, the shores of the lower Great Lakes host huge congregations of Red-breasted Mergansers. During the peak of migration, 60,000 or more of these birds may congregate along inshore waters to rest and refuel. • Shortly after their mates have begun incubating, males fly off to join large offshore rafts for the duration of summer. During this time, a brief moult makes the males largely indistinguishable from their female counterparts.

ID: large, elongated body; red eyes; thin, orange, serrated bill; shaggy, slicked-back head crest. *Male:* green head; light rusty breast is spotted with black; white collar; grey sides; black and white shoulders. *Female:* grey-brown overall; reddish head; white chin, foreneck and breast. *In flight:* male has a large, white wing patch crossed by 2 narrow, black bars; female has 1 dark bar separating the white speculum from the white upperwing patch.
Size: *L* 48–66 cm.
Status: uncommon to locally abundant migrant in April, May, October and November; uncommon winter resident; rare to uncommon breeder.
Habitat: lakes and large rivers, especially those with rocky shorelines and islands.
Nesting: usually on a rocky island or shoreline; on the ground, well

concealed under bushes, driftwood or in dense vegetation; female builds a nest lined with down and incubates 7–10 olive-buff eggs for 29–35 days.
Feeding: dives underwater for small fish; also eats aquatic invertebrates, fish eggs and crustaceans.
Voice: generally quiet. *Male:* cat-like *yeow* during courtship and feeding. *Female:* harsh *kho-kha.*
Similar Species: *Common Merganser* (p. 86): female's rusty foreneck contrasts gainst the white chin and breast; male has a clean white breast and a blood red bill and lacks the head crest.
Best Sites: Bruce Peninsula; Georgian Bay Islands NP; Lake Nipissing; Lake Superior PP; Sleeping Giant PP; Point Pelee NP; Big Creek NWA; Vineland Agricultural Research Station; Presqu'ile PP; western Lake Ontario.

RUDDY DUCK

Oxyura jamaicensis

Clowns of the wetlands, Ruddy Ducks display energetic courtship behaviour with comedic enthusiasm. The small males vigourously pump their bright blue bills, almost touching their breasts. The *plap, plap, plap-plap-plap* of the display increases in speed to its hilarious climax: a spasmodic jerk and sputter. • Female Ruddies commonly lay up to 10 eggs at a time—a remarkable feat, considering that their eggs are bigger than those of a Mallard, even though a Mallard is twice the size of a Ruddy Duck. • Some people might imagine birding paradise as a lush green forest or a dense, marshy wetland, but few birders visualize a local sewage lagoon. Birders searching for Ruddy Ducks, however, might find a sewage lagoon a desirable place to visit—Blenheim, Townsend, Strathroy, St. Isidore de Prescott, Casselman, Alfred, Winchester, Wawa and Rainy River all have sewage lagoons that are commonly visited by Ruddy Ducks.

breeding

ID: large bill and head; short neck; long, stiff tail feathers (often carried cocked upward). *Breeding male:* white cheek; chestnut red body; blue bill; black tail and crown. *Female:* brown overall; dark cheek stripe; darker crown and back. *Winter male:* like the female but with a white cheek.

Size: *L* 38–41 cm.

Status: uncommon migrant from April to May and from late September to mid-November; rare breeder; a few may be present in winter.

Habitat: *Breeding:* shallow marshes with dense emergent vegetation (such as cattails or bulrushes) and muddy bottoms. *Winter* and *In migration:* sewage lagoons and open, shallow water.

Nesting: in cattails, bulrushes or other emergent vegetation; female suspends a woven platform nest over water; may use an abandoned duck or coot nest, muskrat lodge or exposed log; female incubates 5–10 rough, whitish eggs for 23–26 days; an occasional brood parasite.

Feeding: dives to the bottom of wetlands for the seeds of pondweeds, sedges and bulrushes and for the leafy parts of aquatic plants; also eats a few aquatic invertebrates.

Voice: *Male:* courtship display is *chuck-chuck-chuck-chur-r-r-r. Female:* generally silent.

Similar Species: *Cinnamon Teal* (p. 354): lacks the white cheek and the blue bill. Other *diving ducks* (pp. 70–87): females lack the long, stiff tail and the dark facial stripe.

Best Sites: Sarnia's Canatara Park; Point Pelee NP; Long Point PP; St. Clair NWA; Luther Marsh; Port Colborne's Mud Lake; Cranberry Marsh; Lake Scugog; Cochrane's Lillabelle Lake.

OSPREY

Pandion haliaetus

Ospreys eat fish almost exclusively, and they are almost always found near water. While hunting, they survey local waterways from the air, often hovering far above the water's surface. Spotting a flash of silver or a slowly moving shadow near the surface, the bird locks itself in a perilous headfirst dive toward its target, thrusting its talons forward the instant before striking the water. Sometimes it will make a tremendous splash, and it will even disappear beneath the water's surface. Rising into the air and shaking its soggy feathers, the Osprey, if necessary, re-positions the fish to face forward for optimum aerodynamics. An Osprey's feet are specialized to prevent its catch from making a squirmy escape: two toes face forward, two face backward, and the soles are covered with sharp spines.

ID: dark brown upperparts; white underparts; dark eye line; light crown; yellow eyes. *Male:* all-white throat. *Female:* fine, dark 'necklace.' *In flight:* long wings are held in a shallow M; dark 'wrist' patches; brown and white banded tail.
Size: *L* 56–64 cm; *W* 1.7–1.8 m.
Status: uncommon to fairly common from late March to mid-October; a few birds occasionally linger into winter.
Habitat: lakes and slow-flowing rivers and streams.
Nesting: on treetops, usually near water; also on specially made platforms, utility poles or towers up to 30 m high; massive stick nest is reused over many years; pair incubates 2–4 eggs for about 38 days; both adults

feed the young, but the male hunts more.
Feeding: dramatic, feet-first dives into the water; fish, averaging 1 kg, make up almost all of the diet.
Voice: series of melodious ascending whistles: *chewk-chewk-chewk;* also an often-heard *kip-kip-kip.*
Similar Species: *Bald Eagle* (p. 90): larger; holds its wings straighter while soaring; adult has a clean white head and tail on an otherwise dark body; immatures lack the white underparts and the dark 'wrist' patches.
Best Sites: Luther Marsh; Lake Scugog; Trent and Rideau Canal waterways; Charleston Lake PP; Lake Nipissing; Georgian Bay Islands NP; Manitoulin Island; Lake of the Woods.

BALD EAGLE

Haliaeetus leucocephalus

The Bald Eagle is a source of inspiration and wonder for anyone longing for a wilderness experience. Bald Eagles also cast their spell on native peoples. The deep connection between these people, the land and this sacred bird is symbolically represented in aboriginal stories, apparel and spiritual rituals. • Bald Eagles are part of the sea eagle group, and they feed mostly on fish and scavenged carrion. Sometimes they will steal food from Ospreys, which often results in a spectacular aerial chase. • A pair of Bald Eagles may mate for life, each year renewing their pair bond by adding new sticks and branches to a massive nest. A Bald Eagle nest is the largest nest of any North American bird.

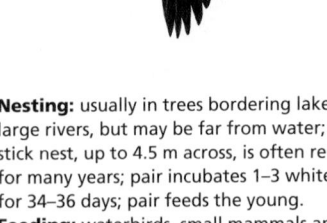

immature

Nesting: usually in trees bordering lakes or large rivers, but may be far from water; huge stick nest, up to 4.5 m across, is often reused for many years; pair incubates 1–3 white eggs for 34–36 days; pair feeds the young.

Feeding: waterbirds, small mammals and fish captured at the water's surface; frequently feeds on carrion; sometimes pirates fish from Ospreys.

Voice: thin, weak squeal or gull-like cackle: *kleek-kik-kik-kik* or *kah-kah-kah*.

Similar Species: Adult is distinctive. *Golden Eagle* (p. 99): adult is dark overall, except for the golden nape; tail may appear faintly banded with white; immature has a prominent white patch on each wing and at the base of the tail. *Osprey* (p. 89): like a 4th-year Bald Eagle, but has M-shaped wings in flight, dark 'wrist' patches and a dark bill.

ID: white head and tail on an otherwise dark brown body; yellow beak and feet; broad wings are held flat in flight. *Immature:* 1st-year is dark overall, with a dark bill and some white in the underwings; 2nd-year has a dark bib and white in the underwings; 3rd-year has largely white plumage, with yellow at the base of the bill and yellow eyes; 4th-year has a light head with a dark facial streak, variable pale and dark plumage, a yellow bill and paler eyes. *In flight:* broad wings are held flat.

Size: *L* 76–109 cm; *W* 1.7–2.4 m.

Status: rare to locally uncommon from mid-March to early November; rare but regular local winter resident.

Habitat: large lakes and rivers.

Best Sites: Willow Beach; Rondeau PP; Long Sault Parkway; Lake Superior PP; Lake of the Woods PP; Woodland Caribou PP; Holiday Beach; Hawk Cliff.

NORTHERN HARRIER

Circus cyaneus

The Northern Harrier may be the easiest raptor to identify on the wing, because no other hawk routinely flies so close to the ground. It cruises low over fields, meadows and marshes, grazing the tops of long grasses and cattails, relying on sudden surprise attacks to capture its prey. Although the harrier has excellent vision, its owl-like, parabolic facial disc allows it to hunt easily by sound. • The Northern Harrier was once known as the Marsh Hawk in North America, and it is still called the Hen Harrier in Europe. Britain's Royal Air Force was so impressed by this bird's maneuverability that it named its Harrier aircraft after this hawk. • The perilous courtship flight of the Northern Harrier is a spring event worth seeing. The male performs huge looping dives in a bid to secure the attention of onlooking females. • In recent years, Harrier numbers have declined greatly in Ontario, owing to a loss of wetland habitat.

ID: long wings and tail; white rump; black wing tips. *Male:* blue-grey to silvery-grey upperparts; white underparts; indistinct tail bands, except for the dark subterminal band. *Female:* dark brown upperparts; streaky brown and buff underparts. *Immature:* rich reddish-brown plumage; dark tail bands; streaked breast, sides and flanks.
Size: *L* 41–61 cm; *W* 1.1–1.2 m.
Status: uncommon to common from March to November; rare winter resident.
Habitat: open country, including fields, wet meadows, cattail marshes, bogs and croplands.
Nesting: on the ground, often on a slightly raised mound, usually in grass, cattails or tall vegetation; shallow depression or platform nest is lined with grass, sticks and cattails; female incubates 4–6 bluish-white eggs for 30–32 days.
Feeding: hunts in low, rising and falling flights, often skimming the tops of vegetation; eats small mammals, birds, amphibians, reptiles and some invertebrates.
Voice: most vocal near the nest and during courtship, but generally quiet; high-pitched *ke-ke-ke-ke-ke-ke* near the nest.
Similar Species: *Rough-legged Hawk* (p. 98): broader wings; dark 'wrist' patches; black tail with a wide, white base; dark belly. *Red-tailed Hawk* (p. 97): lacks the white rump and the long, narrow tail.
Best Sites: Luther Marsh; Lynde Shores Conservation Area; Lake Scugog; Presqu'ile PP; Carillon PP; Hwy 11 from North Bay to Hearst; Holiday Beach; Hawk Cliff.

SHARP-SHINNED HAWK

Accipiter striatus

After a successful hunt, the diminutive Sharp-shinned Hawk usually perches on a favourite 'plucking post,' grasping its prey in its razor-sharp talons. Sharpies prey almost exclusively on small birds, such as chickadees, finches and sparrows, chasing them in high-speed pursuits. • When delivering food to its nestlings, a male Sharp-shinned Hawk is cautious around his mate—she is typically one-third larger than he is. • Accipiters, named after their genus, are woodland hawks. Their short, rounded wings, long, rudder-like tails and flap-and-glide flight pattern give them the maneuverability necessary to negotiate a maze of forest foliage at high speed. • Rural birdfeeders can attract 'Sharpies,' especially during the winter months—not for the seeds, but for the finches and sparrows that the seeds attract.

Nesting: in a conifer; usually builds a new stick nest each year (about 60 cm across); might remodel an abandoned crow nest; female incubates 4 or 5 eggs for 34–35 days; male feeds the female during incubation.

Feeding: pursues small birds through forests; rarely takes small mammals, amphibians and insects.

Voice: silent, except during the breeding season, when an intense and often repeated *kik-kik-kik-kik* can be heard.

Similar Species: *Cooper's Hawk* (p. 93): larger; tail tip is more rounded and has a broader terminal band. *American Kestrel* (p. 100): long, pointed wings; 1 dark 'tear streak' and 1 dark 'sideburn'; typically seen in open country. *Merlin* (p. 101): pointed wings; rapid wingbeats; 1 dark 'tear streak'; brown streaking on buff underparts; dark eyes.

ID: short, rounded wings; long, straight, heavily barred, square-tipped tail; dark barring on the pale underwings; blue-grey back; red horizontal bars on the underparts; red eyes. *Immature:* brown overall; dark eyes; vertical brown streaking on the breast and belly. *In flight:* flap-and-glide flyer.

Size: *Male: L* 25–30 cm; *W* 51–61 cm. *Female: L* 30–36 cm; *W* 61–71 cm.

Status: common migrant from mid-March to early May and from late August to mid-November; rare to uncommon breeder; rare winter resident.

Habitat: dense to semi-open forests and large woodlots; occasionally along rivers; favours dense, moist coniferous forests and bogs.

Best Sites: Frontenac PP; Fitzroy PP; Algonquin PP; Pukaskwa NP; Hwy 11 from North Bay to Hearst; Quetico PP; Holiday Beach; Hawk Cliff; Beamer Point Conservation Area; Toronto's Grenadier Pond; backyard feeders.

COOPER'S HAWK

Accipiter cooperii

If songbirds dream, the Cooper's Hawk is sure to be the subject of their nightmares. This forest hawk hunts silently, using surprise and speed to ambush its wary prey. Bursting from an overhead perch, a Cooper's Hawk will pursue a songbird until it can use its long legs and sharp talons to snatch it in mid-air. • This forest hawk bears the name of William Cooper, one of the many hunters who supplied English and American ornithologists with bird specimens for museum collections during the early 19th century. • Now that they are protected by law, and the use of DDT has been banned throughout North America, Cooper's Hawks are slowly recolonizing former habitats in southern Ontario.

ID: short, rounded wings; long, straight, heavily barred, rounded tail; dark barring on the pale undertail and underwings; squarish head; blue-grey back; red horizontal barring on the underparts; red eyes; white terminal tail band. *Immature:* brown overall; dark eyes; vertical brown streaks on the breast and belly. *In flight:* flap-and-glide flyer.
Size: *Male: L* 38–43 cm; *W* 69–81 cm. *Female: L* 43–48 cm; *W* 81–94 cm.
Status: uncommon to fairly common migrant from mid-March to mid-April and from late September to late October; rare to uncommon breeder; rare winter resident.
Habitat: mixed woodlands, riparian woodlands and woodlots south of the Canadian Shield.
Nesting: nest of sticks and twigs is built 6–20 m high in the crotch of a deciduous or coniferous tree; often near a stream or pond; might reuse an abandoned crow nest; female incubates 3–5 bluish-white eggs for 34–36 days; male feeds the female during incubation.
Feeding: pursues prey in flights through forests; eats mostly songbirds, squirrels and chipmunks; uses plucking post or nest for eating.
Voice: fast, woodpecker-like *cac-cac-cac-cac.*
Similar Species: *Sharp-shinned Hawk* (p. 92): smaller; tail tip is not as rounded; thinner terminal tail band. *American Kestrel* (p. 100): smaller; long, pointed wings; 1 dark 'tear streak' and 1 dark 'sideburn'; typically seen in open country. *Merlin* (p. 101): smaller; pointed wings; rapid wingbeats; 1 dark 'tear streak'; brown streaking on the buff underparts; dark eyes.
Best Sites: Rondeau PP; The Pinery PP; Rouge River PP; Presqu'ile PP; Bon Echo PP; large SW Ontario woodlots; Point Pelee NP; Holiday Beach; Hawk Cliff; Toronto's Grenadier Pond; backyard feeders.

93

NORTHERN GOSHAWK

Accipiter gentilis

Northern Goshawks might be the most aggressive birds in Ontario. They will prey on any animal they can overtake, and once a capture has been made, these raptors stab repeatedly at their victim's internal organs with their long talons. They have even been known to chase their quarry on foot should elusive prey disappear under the cover of dense thickets. • Goshawks are devoted parents that are equally ferocious when defending their nest sites—unfortunate souls who wander too close to a goshawk nest are occasionally assaulted by an almost deafening, squawking dive-bomb attack. • Northern Goshawks require extensive areas of forests in which to hunt and raise their families. The clearing of forests for agricultural and residential development has caused goshawk populations to decline significantly throughout their range in Northern Europe, Asia and parts of North America.

Nesting: in deep woods; male builds a large, bulky stick plat-form in the crotch of a tree, usually 8–25 m above ground; nest is often reused for several years; female incubates 2–4 bluish-white eggs for 35–36 days; male feeds the female during incubation.

ID: rounded wings; long, banded tail with a white terminal band; white eyebrow; dark crown; blue-grey back; fine, grey vertical streaking on the pale breast and belly; grey barring on the pale undertail and underwings; red eyes. *Immature:* brown overall; brown vertical streaking on the whitish breast and belly; brown barring on the pale undertail and underwings; yellow eyes.

Size: *Male: L* 53–58 cm; *W* 1–1.1 m.
Female: L 58–64 cm; *W* 1.1–1.2 m.

Status: rare to uncommon throughout the year; very elusive in summer.

Habitat: *Breeding:* mature coniferous, deciduous and mixed woodlands. *Non-breeding:* forest edges, semi-open parklands and farmlands.

Feeding: low foraging flights through the forest; feeds primarily on grouse, rabbits and squirrels.

Voice: silent, except during the breeding season, when adults utter a loud, shrill and fast *kak-kak-kak-kak*.

Similar Species: *Cooper's Hawk* (p. 93) and *Sharp-shinned Hawk* (p. 92): smaller; adults have reddish breast bars and lack the white eyebrow stripe. *Buteo hawks* (pp. 95–98): shorter tails; broader wings. *Gyrfalcon* (p. 102): more pointed wings; dark eyes; often has a dark 'tear streak.'

Best Sites: Halton Regional Forest; Petroglyphs PP; Silent Lake PP; Algonquin PP; Arrowhead PP; Quetico PP; Holiday Beach; Hawk Cliff.

RED-SHOULDERED HAWK

Buteo lineatus

The Red-shouldered Hawk nests in mature trees, usually around river bottoms and along lowland tracts of woods along creeks. As spring approaches and pair bonds are formed, this normally quiet hawk utters loud and shrieking *kee-you, kee-you, kee-you* calls. During the summer months, the dense cover of this hawk's forested breeding habitat allows few viewing opportunities for hawkwatchers, but during spring and fall migration, Red-shouldered Hawks can be found hunting from exposed perches. Some individuals may even hunt as far as 800 m from the nearest stand of trees. Fortunately, this bird's seasonal use of telephone poles and fenceposts for hunting gives observers a better glimpse into its otherwise private life.

ID: chestnut red shoulders on otherwise dark brown upperparts; reddish underwing linings; narrow white bars on the dark tail; barred reddish breast and belly; reddish undertail coverts. *Immature:* large brown 'teardrop' streaks on the white underparts; whitish undertail coverts. *In flight:* light and dark barring on the underside of the flight feathers and tail; white crescents or 'windows' at the base of the primaries.
Size: *L* 48 cm; *W* 1 m.
Status: uncommon to fairly common from mid-March to late November; rare winter resident.
Habitat: mature deciduous and mixed forests, wooded riparian areas, swampy woodlands and large, mature woodlots.
Nesting: both sexes assemble a bulky nest of sticks and twigs, usually 5–25 m high in the crotch of a deciduous tree; nest is often reused; female incubates 2–4 darkly

blotched, bluish-white eggs for about 33 days; both adults raise the young.
Feeding: small mammals, birds, reptiles and amphibians are usually detected from a fencepost, tree or telephone pole and caught after a swooping attack; may catch prey flushed by low flight.
Voice: repeated series of high *key-ah* notes.
Similar Species: *Broad-winged Hawk* (p. 96): lacks the reddish shoulders; wings are broader, more whitish and dark-edged underneath; wide, white tail bands. *Red-tailed Hawk* (p. 97): lacks the barring in the tail and the light windows at the base of the primaries.
Best Sites: Cambridge's Sudden Tract; Petroglyphs PP; Frontenac PP; Charleston Lake PP; Six Mile Lake PP; Hawk Cliff; Beamer Point Conservation Area.

BROAD-WINGED HAWK

Buteo platypterus

Upon an encounter with a nesting Broad-winged Hawk, you may wonder why the bird has such broad, soaring wings—most hawks rarely soar among tree-trunks, branches and shrubbery. Its breeding-season foraging usually keeps the Broad-winged Hawk in the forest, but when the leaves change colour in fall, it unfolds its wings and takes to the sky. If the weather produces favourable flying conditions, it will spiral up into rising thermals and soar south. By the end of October, most of Ontario's Broad-winged Hawks will be experiencing the warm climes of Central and South America. Each fall, the mass exodus of Broad-wings offers Ontarians a chance to witness this migration in an unforgettable way. Typically between September 12th and 18th, Holiday Beach and Hawk Cliff, along the shores of Lake Erie, host the peak of the Broad-wing's southward migration. In good flight years, when cool temperatures, moderate northwest winds and sunny skies prevail, over 30,000 Broad-wings can be observed in a single day!

light morph

In migration: escarpments and shorelines; also uses riparian and deciduous forests and woodland edges.

Nesting: usually in a deciduous tree, often near water; bulky stick nest is built in a crotch 7–12 m high; usually builds a new nest each year; female usually incubates 2–4 brown-spotted, whitish eggs for 28–31 days; both adults raise the young.

Feeding: swoops from a perch for small mammals, amphibians, insects and young birds; often seen hunting from roadside telephone poles in northern areas.

Voice: high-pitched, whistled *peeeo-wee-ee*; generally silent during migration.

Similar Species: *Other buteos:* lack the broad banding on the tail and the dark-edged, broad wings with pointed tips. *Accipiters* (pp. 92–94): long, narrow tails with less distinct banding.

ID: broad, black and white tail bands; broad wings with pointed tips; heavily barred with rufous brown on the breast; dark brown upperparts. *Immature:* dark brown 'teardrop' streaks on the white breast, belly and sides; buff and dark brown tail bands. *In flight:* pale underwings (white primaries and buff linings in the adult and white linings with brown flecking on the immature) are outlined with dark trim.

Size: *L* 36–48 cm; *W* 81–99 cm.

Status: rare to common migrant from early April to mid-May; uncommon to fairly common breeder; common to abundant migrant in September.

Habitat: *Breeding:* dense, mixed and deciduous forests and woodlots.

Best Sites: Lake Scugog; Bon Echo PP; Parry Sound; Killarney PP; Sleeping Giant PP; Quetico PP; Holiday Beach; Hawk Cliff; Beamer Point Conservation Area; Ivy Lea.

RED-TAILED HAWK

Buteo jamaicensis

Red-tails are the most commonly seen hawks in Ontario, especially throughout the agricultural lands in the southwest parts of our province. An afternoon drive through the country at any time of year will likely reveal numerous Red-tails perching on exposed tree limbs, on fenceposts or on utility poles overlooking open fields and roadsides. • The Red-tailed Hawk's piercing call is as impressive as that of an eagle, and producers of television commercials and movies often cheat by putting the Red-tail's voice together with the image of an eagle. • During their spring courtship, excited Red-tailed Hawks will dive at each other, sometimes locking talons and tumbling through the air together before breaking off to avoid crashing to the ground. • This hawk's tail does not obtain its brick red colouration until it matures into a breeding adult.

immature

ID: red tail; dark upperparts with some white highlights; dark brown band of streaks across the belly. *Immature:* extremely variable; lacks the red tail; generally darker; band of streaks on the belly. *In flight:* fan-shaped tail; white or occasionally tawny brown underside and underwing linings; dark leading edge on the underside of the wing; light underwing flight feathers with faint barring.
Size: *Male: L* 46–58 cm; *W* 1.2–1.5 m. *Female: L* 51–64 cm; *W* 1.2–1.5 m.
Status: common to abundant throughout the year in suitable habitat.
Habitat: open country with some trees; roadsides, fields, woodlots, hedgerows, mixed forests and moist woodlands.
Nesting: in woodlands adjacent to open habitat; usually in a deciduous tree; rarely on cliffs or in conifers; bulky stick nest is usually added to each year; pair incubates 2–4 brown-blotched, whitish eggs for 28–35 days; male brings food to the female and young.

Feeding: scans for food while perched or soaring; drops to capture prey; rarely stalks prey on foot; eats voles, mice, rabbits, chipmunks, birds, amphibians and reptiles; rarely takes large insects.
Voice: powerful, descending scream: *Keeearrrr.*
Similar Species: *Rough-legged Hawk* (p. 98): white tail base; dark wrist patches on the underwings; broad, dark terminal tail band. *Broad-winged Hawk* (p. 96): broadly banded tail; broader wings with pointed tips; lacks the dark belt. *Red-shouldered Hawk* (p. 95): reddish wing linings and underparts; reddish shoulders. *Swainson's Hawk* (p. 355): all-dark back; dark flight feathers and pale wing linings while soaring; holds its wings in a shallow V; more pointed wing tips.
Best Sites: Hwy 11 from Hearst to Cobalt; Holiday Beach; Hawk Cliff; Beamer Point Conservation Area; Grenadier Pond; Ivy Lea.

ROUGH-LEGGED HAWK

Buteo lagopus

Populations levels of Rough-legged Hawks vary in cycles with densities of voles and northern lemmings. When lemming and vole numbers are high, Rough-legs can produce up to seven young, but in lean years a pair is fortunate to raise a single chick. • While hunting, the Rough-legged Hawk often 'wind-hovers' to scan the ground below, flapping to maintain a stationary position while facing upwind. • Only a small number of Rough-legged Hawks nest along the coast of Hudson Bay and James Bay. This hawk usually requires an elevated nest site on a high cliff ledge, crevice or boulder pile, but in the absence of such natural nest sites it will settle on a tower or an abandoned radar station. • The name *lagopus*, meaning 'hare's foot,' refers to this bird's distinctive feathered legs, which are an adaptation for survival in cold climates.

immature

Habitat: *Breeding:* coastal tundra; requires an elevated natural or artificial ledge for nesting. *Non-breeding:* tundra, fields, meadows, open bogs and agricultural croplands.

Nesting: in a large stick nest, possibly an abandoned raven nest, on an elevated structure; nests are reused over many years; mostly female incubates 3 or 4 brown- and violet-blotched, bluish-white eggs for 28–31 days; both adults raise the young.

ID: white tail base with a wide, dark subterminal band; dark brown upperparts; light flight feathers; legs are feathered to the toes. *Light-morph adult:* wide, dark abdominal 'belt'; darkly streaked breast and head; dark 'wrist' patches; light underwing linings. *Dark-morph:* dark wing linings, head and underparts. *Immature:* lighter streaking on the breast; bold belly band; buff leg feathers. *In flight:* most show the dark 'wrist' patches; frequently hovers.

Size: *L* 48–61 cm; *W* 1.2–1.4 m.

Status: irregularly rare to common visitor from late September to May; extremely rare breeder.

Feeding: soars and hovers while searching for prey; primarily eats small rodents; occasionally eats birds, amphibians and large insects.

Voice: alarm call is a cat-like *kee-eer*, usually dropping at the end.

Similar Species: *Other buteos:* rarely hover; adults lack the dark wrist patches and the white tail base. *Northern Harrier* (p. 91): facial disc; lacks the dark 'wrist' patches and the dark belly band; longer, thinner tail lacks the broad, dark subterminal band.

Best Sites: open fields throughout southwestern Ontario; Pearson International Airport; Amherst Island; the north shore of Lake Superior; Cochrane area; Polar Bear PP.

GOLDEN EAGLE

Aquila chrysaetos

For many centuries, the Golden Eagle has embodied the wonder and wildness of the North American landscape. Unfortunately, with the advent of widespread human development and intensive agricultural practices, this noble bird became the victim of a lengthy persecution. Perceived as a threat to livestock, bounties were offered supporting the shooting and poisoning of this regal bird. Today, the Golden Eagle is protected under Ontario's Endangered Species Act. • Most Golden Eagles are seen soaring over hawk-watching areas during fall migration or feeding on carrion in Algonquin and Petrogyphs provincial parks over winter. Few people ever forget the sight of a Golden Eagle soaring overhead— the average wingspan of an adult exceeds two metres!

immature

ID: very large; all brown, with a golden tint to the neck and head; brown eyes; dark bill; brown tail is slightly banded with greyish white; yellow feet; legs are fully feathered. *Immature:* white tail base; white patch at the base of the underwing primary feathers. *In flight:* relatively short neck; long tail; long, large, rectangular wings.
Size: *L* 76–102 cm; *W* 2–2.3 m.
Status: rare migrant from March to mid-April and from late September to November; very rare breeder and winter resident.
Habitat: *Breeding:* open and semi-open areas close to cliff faces, often along lakeshores or wide river canyons. *In migration:* along escarpments and lake shorelines. *Winter:* semi-open woodlands and fields.
Nesting: usually on a cliff near open foraging areas; infrequently in trees; rarely on the ground; huge nest of sticks, branches and roots measures up to 3 m across; often reuses a nest site for many years; nest might become stained from droppings; mostly the female incubates 1–3 brown-marked, whitish to buff eggs for 41–45 days; both adults raise the young.
Feeding: swoops on prey from a soaring flight; eats hares, grouse, ptarmigans, rodents, foxes and occasionally young ungulates; often eats carrion.
Voice: generally quiet; rarely a short bark.
Similar Species: *Bald Eagle* (p. 90): longer neck; shorter tail; immature lacks the distinct white underwing patches and tail base. *Turkey Vulture* (p. 51): naked pink head; pale flight feathers; dark wing linings. *Dark-morph Rough-legged Hawk* (p. 98): pale flight feathers; white tail base.
Best Sites: Holiday Beach; Hawk Cliff; Beamer Point Conservation Area; Grenadier Pond; Petroglyphs PP; Algonquin PP; Sutton Ridges.

AMERICAN KESTREL

Falco sparverius

The American Kestrel is the smallest and most common of Ontario's falcons. A kestrel perched on a telephone wire or fencepost along an open field is a familiar sight throughout the province in summer and in southern parts year-round. • Studies have shown that the Eurasian Kestrel can detect ultraviolet reflections from rodent urine on the ground. It is not known if the American Kestrel has this same ability, but it is frequently seen hovering above the ground while looking for small ground-dwelling prey.• In keeping with its robin-like size, this falcon preys on small rodents and songbirds, and old field guides and old-time birders refer to as the Sparrow Hawk. • The American Kestrel's diminutive size allows it to nest in the shelter of tree cavities, which helps protect defenceless young kestrels from hungry predators.

ID: 2 distinctive facial stripes. *Male:* rusty back; blue-grey wings; blue-grey crown with a rusty cap; lightly spotted underparts. *Female:* rusty back, wings and breast streaking. *In flight:* frequently hovers; long, rusty tail; buoyant, indirect flight style.
Size: *L* 19–20 cm; *W* 51–61 cm.
Status: common from late February to early November; irregular, very rare to fairly common winter resident.
Habitat: open fields, riparian woodlands, woodlots, forest edges, bogs, roadside ditches, grassy highway medians, grasslands and croplands.
Nesting: in a cavity in a standing dead tree (usually an abandoned woodpecker or flicker cavity); may use a nest box; incubates 4–6 brown

and grey-spotted, white to pale brown eggs for 29–30 days; both adults raise the young.
Feeding: swoops from a perch (a tree, fence-line, post, roadsign or powerline) or from a hovering position; eats mostly insects and some small rodents, birds, reptiles and amphibians.
Voice: loud, often repeated, shrill *killy-killy-killy* when excited; female's voice is lower pitched.
Similar Species: *Merlin* (p. 101): lacks the double facial stripes; less colourful; does not hover; flight is more powerful and direct. *Sharp-shinned Hawk* (p. 92): short, rounded wings; reddish barring on the underparts; lacks the facial stripes; flap-and-glide flight.
Best Sites: widespread along fields, woodlots and roadsides throughout southern Ontario.

MERLIN

Falco columbarius

The main weapons of this small falcon, like all its falcon relatives, are speed, surprise and sharp, dagger-like talons. The Merlin's sleek body, long, narrow tail and pointed wings increase its aerodynamic efficiency for high-speed songbird pursuits. • Owen Point, at the tip of Presqu'ile Provincial Park, is a good place to see Merlins in fall as they harass large flocks of shorebirds in the hopes of hunting down a few weakened individuals. • Most Merlins migrate to Central and South America each fall, but a few remain in our province over winter, capitalizing on the abundance of Cedar Waxwings, European Starlings and House Sparrows that are attracted to suburban ornamental shrubs and backyard feeders. • The Merlin was formerly known as the Pigeon Hawk, and the scientific name *columbarius* comes from the Latin for 'pigeon,' which it somewhat resembles in flight.

ID: banded tail; heavily streaked underparts; indistinct facial stripe; long, narrow wings and tail. *Male:* blue-grey back and crown; rusty leg feathers. *Female:* brown back and crown. *In flight:* very rapid shallow wingbeats.
Size: *L* 25–30 cm; *W* 58–66 cm.
Status: rare to uncommon from mid-March to mid-October; rare in winter.
Habitat: *Breeding:* open and second-growth, mixed and coniferous forests and plantations adjacent to open hunting grounds; sometimes found in suburban areas. *In migration:* open fields and lakeshores.
Nesting: in coniferous or deciduous trees, crevices or cliffs; usually reuses abandoned raptor, crow, jay or squirrel nests; mostly the female incubates 4 or 5 whitish eggs, marked with reddish-brown, for 28–32 days; male feeds the female away from the nest; both adults raise the young.
Feeding: overtakes smaller birds in flight; also eats rodents and large insects, such as dragonflies; may also take bats.

Voice: loud, noisy, cackling cry: *kek-kek-kek-kek-kek* or *ki-ki-ki-ki*; calls in flight or while perched, often around the nest.
Similar Species: *American Kestrel* (p. 100): 2 facial stripes; more colourful; less direct flight style; often hovers. *Peregrine Falcon* (p. 103): larger; well-marked, dark 'helmet'; pale, unmarked upper breast; black flecking on the light underparts. *Sharp-shinned Hawk* (p. 92) and *Cooper's Hawk* (p. 93): short, rounded wings; reddish barring on the breast and belly. *Rock Dove* (p. 176): broader wings in flight; shorter tail; often glides with its wings held in a V.
Best Sites: North Bay; Batchawana Bay PP; Lake Superior PP; Sleeping Giant PP; Holiday Beach; Hawk Cliff; Beamer Point Conservation Area; Presqu'ile PP.

GYRFALCON

Falco rusticolus

Every year, as the days get shorter and the snow begins to fall, Ontario birders anxiously await the return of the world's largest falcon. Rarely do Gyrfalcons leave the confines of the Hudson Bay Lowland and the northern arctic tundra, but even a brief glimpse of a handful of Gyrfalcons is enough to revive any birder who may have a bad case of the winter blues.

• Unlike the Peregrine Falcon, the Gyrfalcon rarely swoops from above with its wings closed—it prefers to outfly its prey, often launching a surprise attack from below. Soaring over open country, almost any sized bird it surprises is a potential meal. When a duck is the unlucky target, its only possible escape might be to plunge into the water headfirst. During their time in the Arctic, Gyrfalcons feed mostly on ptarmigans and hares.

grey morph

ID: long tail extends beyond the wing tips when it is perched; tail may be barred or unbarred. *Grey morph:* dark grey upperparts, facial stripe and streaking on the white underparts. *Brown morph:* dark brown upperparts, facial stripe and streaking on the white underparts. *White morph:* pure white head, breast and tail; white back and wings have dark flecking and barring. *Immature:* darker and more heavily streaked than the adult; grey (rather than yellow) feet and cere.
Size: *Male: L* 51–56 cm; *W* 1.2–1.3 m.
Female: L 56–64 cm; *W* 1.3–1.4 m.
Status: very rare from October to April.
Habitat: open and semi-open areas, including tundra marshes, fields and open wetlands, where prey concentrate.
Nesting: does not nest in Ontario.

Feeding: locates prey from an elevated perch or by flying low over the ground; takes prey in mid-air or chases it down; eats mostly birds, especially waterfowl, shorebirds and ptarmigans; takes Rock Doves in southern areas; also takes small mammals.
Voice: loud, harsh *kak-kak-kak.*
Similar Species: *Peregrine Falcon* (p. 103): prominent dark hood; shorter tail; adults have an unstreaked upper breast and throat. *Northern Goshawk* (p. 94): deceptively similar at times; prominent white eyebrow; dark cap; rounded wings in flight; greyer underparts with finer streaking; unstreaked white undertail coverts; red or yellow (immature) eyes.
Best Sites: Deschênes Rapids (Ottawa); Sudbury; Sault Ste. Marie waterfront; Thunder Bay waterfront and grain elevators; Moosonee.

PEREGRINE FALCON
Falco peregrinus

I n a perilous headfirst dive toward the beaches of Presqu'ile Provincial Park, a hunting Peregrine Falcon targets an unsuspecting group of shorebirds. As it reaches its top speed (it can dive at 360 km/h), the Peregrine clenches its feet and then strikes its prey with an irreparable blow. • The Peregrine's awesome speed and hunting skills were little defence against the pesticide DDT, which caused contaminated birds to lay eggs with thin shells. DDT was banned in North America in 1972, but it still persists in the food chain and is still used in parts of Latin America. With help from the Ministry of Natural Resources and the Canadian Wildlife Service, captive-bred Peregrines have been released into wild habitats in Ontario with much success.

immature

ID: blue-grey back; prominent, dark 'helmet'; light underparts with dark, fine spotting and flecking. *Immature:* similar patterning as the adult, but brown where the adult is blue-grey; heavier breast streaks; grey (rather than yellow) feet and cere. *In flight:* pointed wings; long, narrow, dark-banded tail.
Size: *Male: L* 38–43 cm; *W* 94–109 cm. *Female: L* 43–48 cm; *W* 1.1–1.2 m.
Status: rare to uncommon migrant from mid-March to mid-April and from mid-September to mid-October; very rare breeder.
Habitat: lakeshores, river valleys, river mouths, urban areas and open fields.
Nesting: usually on rocky cliffs or cutbanks; may use skyscraper ledges; no material is added, but the nest is littered with prey remains, leaves and grass; nest sites are often reused; mostly the female incubates 3 or 4 eggs for 32–34 days.

Feeding: high-speed, diving stoops; strikes birds with clenched feet in mid-air; prey is consumed on a nearby perch; pigeons, waterfowl, shorebirds, flickers, ptarmigans and larger songbirds are the primary prey; rarely takes small mammals or carrion.
Voice: loud, harsh, continuous *cack-cack-cack-cack-cack* near the nest site.
Similar Species: *Gyrfalcon* (p. 102): larger; lacks the dark hood; longer tail; seen only in winter in Ontario. *Merlin* (p. 101): smaller; lacks the prominent dark hood; heavily streaked breast and belly.
Best Sites: Red Rock; Sleeping Giant PP; Thunder Bay and Sarnia grain elevators; Holiday Beach; Hawk Cliff; Beamer Point Conservation Area; Presqu'ile PP.

GRAY PARTRIDGE

Perdix perdix

Throughout much of the year, Gray Partridges are probably best seen 'gravelling up' along quiet country roads, particularly during the early morning. Like other seed-eating birds, they regularly swallow small bits of gravel to help crush the hard seeds they feed on. The gravel accumulates in the bird's gizzard, a muscular pouch of the digestive system. • When flushed, Gray Partridges burst suddenly from cover, flapping furiously and then gliding to a nearby safe haven. During cold weather, they huddle together in a circle with each bird facing outward, always ready to burst into flight. When incubating their eggs, however, females will sit tightly on their nests and risk being stepped on, rather than alerting attention. • This Eurasian gamebird was first introduced to Ontario in 1909, with larger releases occurring from 1927 to 1938.

ID: small, rounded body; short tail with chestnut outer feathers; chestnut barring on the flanks; orange-brown face and throat; grey breast; mottled brown back; bare, yellowish legs. *Male:* chestnut brown patch on a white belly. *Female:* no belly patch; paler face and throat.

Size: *L* 28–36 cm.

Status: uncommon year-round resident.

Habitat: grassy and weedy fields and agricultural croplands; generally absent from alfalfa and tobacco fields.

Nesting: in hayfields, pastures and grassy-weedy fencelines and field margins; on the ground in a scratched-out depression lined with grass; female incubates 15–17 olive-coloured eggs for 23–25 days.

Feeding: at dawn and dusk during summer; throughout the day during winter; gleans the ground for waste, agricultural grains and seeds; might also eat leaves and large insects; often seen feeding on manure piles in winter.

Voice: at dawn and dusk; sounds like a rusty gate hinge: *kee-uck* or *scirl*; call is *kuta-kut-kut-kut* when excited.

Similar Species: *Ruffed Grouse* (p. 106): lacks the rusty face and outer tail feathers. *Northern Bobwhite* (p. 111): white crescents and spots edged in black on the chestnut sides and upper breast; male has a white throat and a long eye line; female has a buff throat and eye line.

Best Sites: agricultural fields, farmyards and roadside ditches in extreme southeastern Ontario from belleville to Arnprior; south-western Ontario from Long Point to Hamilton.

RING-NECKED PHEASANT

Phasianus colchicus

The spectacular Ring-necked Pheasant was introduced to Ontario from Eurasia in the late 1800s mainly as quarry for hunters. Few birds survived because they were unequipped for our cold winters, but today in Ontario, Ring-necked Pheasants persist in low-snowfall areas. Although they reproduce successfully, the provincial population is augmented by hatchery-raised birds. Unlike native grouse, Ring-necked Pheasants do not have feathered legs and feet to insulate them in cold weather, and they cannot survive on native plants alone. • Birders hear this bird more often than they see it, and the male's loud *ka-squawk* call is recognizable near farmyards, woodlots and brushy suburban parks. • Pheasants are not strong long-distance flyers, but they are able to fly in explosive bursts over small open areas to escape predators.

ID: large gamebird; long, barred tail; unfeathered legs. *Male:* green head; white collar; bronze underparts; naked, red face patch. *Female:* mottled brown overall; light underparts.

Size: *Male: L* 76–91 cm. *Female: L* 51–66 cm.

Status: uncommon year-round resident.

Habitat: *Breeding:* grasslands, grassy ditches, hayfields and grassy or weedy fields, fencelines, crop margins and woodlot margins. *Non-breeding:* grain and corn fields in fall; woodlots, cattail marshes and shrubby areas close to soybean or shell corn crops in winter.

Nesting: on the ground, among grass or sparse vegetation or next to a log or other natural debris; in a slight depression lined with grass and leaves; female incubates 10–12 olive-buff eggs for 23–28 days.

Feeding: *Summer:* gleans the ground and vegetation for weed seeds and insects. *Winter:* eats mostly seeds, corn kernels and buds.

Voice: *Male:* loud, raspy, rooster-like crowing: *ka-squawk*; whirring of the wings, mostly just before sunrise.

Similar Species: male is distinctive. *Other grouse:* generally smaller; shorter tails than a female pheasant.

Best Sites: fields, woodlots, croplands and grassy fencelines in Essex, Oxford, Niagara, Hamilton-Wentworth, Durham and Frontenac counties; Point Pelee NP.

RUFFED GROUSE

Bonasa umbellus

It always seems to happen without warning: a mysterious drumbeat echos through the forest and your body reverberates as if you've been caught in the shockwave of a mild earthquake. Actually, what you are feeling are the sounds of a 'drumming' Ruffed Grouse. Each spring, and occasionally in fall, the male Ruffed Grouse proclaims his territory, strutting along a fallen log with his tail fanned and his neck feathers ruffed, beating the air with accelerating wingstrokes. • The Ruffed Grouse is the most common and widespread grouse in Ontario, inhabiting a wide variety of woodland habitats ranging from small deciduous woodlots and suburban riparian woodlands to vast expanses of mixedwood and boreal forest. • Populations of Ruffed Grouse seem to fluctuate over about a 10-year cycle. Predators, such as the Northern Goshawk, that rely on this bird as a food source, show population fluctuations that closely follow Ruffed Grouse trends. • During winter, scales on the toes of these birds grow out along the sides, providing the bird with temporary snowshoes.

grey morph

ID: small head crest; mottled grey-brown overall; black feathers on the sides of the lower neck (visible when fluffed out in courtship); grey- or reddish-barred tail has a broad, dark, subterminal band and a white tip. *Female:* incomplete subterminal tail band.

Size: *L* 38–48 cm.

Status: common year-round resident.

Habitat: deciduous and mixed forests and riparian woodlands; in many areas it favours young second-growth stands with birch and poplar.

Nesting: in a shallow depression among leaf litter; often beside boulders, under logs or at the base of a tree; female incubates 9–12 buff-coloured eggs for 23–25 days.

Feeding: omnivorous diet includes seeds, buds, flowers, berries, catkins, leaves, insects, spiders and snails; may take small frogs; gleans from the ground and vegetation.

Voice: *Male:* uses his wings to produce a hollow, drumming courtship sound of accelerating, deep booms, like a lawnmower starting up and stalling. *Female:* clucks and 'hisses' around her chicks.

Similar Species: *Spruce Grouse* (p. 107): dark tail lacks the barring and the white tip; lacks the head crest; male has red combs above the eyes. *Sharp-tailed Grouse* (p. 109): lacks the fan-shaped tail and the black feathers on the lower neck. *Willow Ptarmigan* (p. 108): summer birds show white in the wings and legs.

Best Sites: MacGregor Point PP; Rouge River PP; Petroglyphs PP; Algonquin PP; Lake Superior PP; Hwy 11 from Cobalt to Hearst; Greenwater PP; Quetico PP; Lake of the Woods.

SPRUCE GROUSE

Falcipennis canadensis

This secretive grouse spends most of its time in upland black spruce stands and young jack pine forests searching for seasonally available food, such as trailing arbutus, blueberries, flowers, black spruce buds, moss spore capsules and insects. • Spruce Grouse trust their camouflaged plumage even in open areas—they often allow people to approach within a few metres—which is a reason they are often called 'fool hens.' Most of the time, however, their strategy seems to work. More Spruce Grouse probably escape our detection than we notice—setting out to find a Spruce Grouse is nowhere as easy as bumping into one by accident. • Spruce Grouse are most conspicuous in late April and early May, when females issue their vehement calls and strutting males magically appear in open areas along trails, roads and campgrounds. Their deep call is nearly undetectable to the human ear, but a displaying male attracts attention as he transforms from his usual dull camouflage to a red-eyebrowed, puff-necked, fan-tailed splendour.

grey morph

ID: black, unbarred tail with a chestnut tip; mottled grey, brown and black overall; feathered legs. *Male:* red comb over the eye; black throat, neck and breast; white-tipped undertail, lower neck and belly feathers. *Female:* barred, mottled underparts.
Size: *L* 33–41 cm.
Status: uncommon year-round resident.
Habitat: conifer-dominated forest; sometimes disperses into deciduous forests.
Nesting: on the forest floor; in a well-hidden, shallow scrape lined with a few grasses and needles; female incubates 4–7 eggs for up to 21 days.

Feeding: live buds and needles of spruce, pine and fir trees; also eats berries, seeds and a few insects in summer.
Voice: very low, guttural *krrrk krrrk krrrk*.
Similar Species: *Ruffed Grouse* (p. 106): head is crested; tail has a broad, dark, subterminal band and a white tip; lacks the black throat and breast. *Willow Ptarmigan* (p. 108): summer birds show white in the wings and legs. *Sharp-tailed Grouse* (p. 109): thinner, sharper tail; white throat; yellow eye combs.
Best Sites: Algonquin PP; Lake Superior PP; Hwy 11 from Cobalt to Hearst.

WILLOW PTARMIGAN

Lagopus lagopus

To visit the home of the Willow Ptarmigan in Ontario you must be willing to fly to the remote communities of Fort Severn or Peawanuck in Polar Bear Provincial Park. If you're up to the adventure, the best time to see this ptarmigan is from mid-June to early July when excited males strut about noisily voicing their bizarre clucking calls. Some individuals that are still adorned in their white winter plumage are highly conspicuous, but later in the season, both sexes acquire a more cryptic plumage to camouflage themselves from predators. • In some years, Willow Ptarmigans can be seen in high densities, but in other years, consider yourself lucky to find a few widely scattered individuals. Like many arctic animals, ptarmigans experience significant cyclical fluctuations in their numbers.

summer

ID: black outer tail feathers; short, rounded wings; black bill. *Spring male:* red comb above the eye; deep chestnut brown head and neck; dark upper breast and back; otherwise mostly white. *Summer male:* red comb; mottled brown and black overall; white wings, belly, legs and undertail coverts. *Summer female:* paler version of the male; lacks the red comb. *Winter:* all white, except for the black eyes, bill and outer tail; both sexes have a red comb.

Size: *L* 35–43 cm.

Status: very rare to abundant year-round resident; abundance varies from year to year.

Habitat: coastal tundra.

Nesting: on the ground in a shallow scrape lined with grass, leaves, moss and feathers; usually on a raised hummock or a raised ridge; female incubates 5–14 eggs for about 22 days; young leave the nest with their mother within a few hours of hatching.

Feeding: gleans vegetation and foliage for buds, flowers, leaves and small branches of willows and birch shrubs; eats insects in summer; eats berries in fall.

Voice: loud, crackling *go-back go-back go-back*.

Similar Species: *Rock Ptarmigan* (p. 355): winter male has a prominent black eye line and a thicker red eye comb; female is virtually indistinguishable from the winter female; lacks the black eye line and the red comb. *Spruce Grouse* (p. 107): lacks the white in the wings. *Ruffed Grouse* (p. 106): crested head; lacks the white in the wings.

Best Sites: Polar Bear PP; Fort Severn.

SHARP-TAILED GROUSE

Tympanuchus phasianellus

During the last weeks of April, male Sharp-tailed Grouse gather at traditional dancing grounds (leks) to perform courtship dances. With their wings drooping at their sides, their long, thin tails pointed skyward and their purple-pink air sacs fully inflated, males furiously pummel the ground with their feet, vigorously cooing and cackling for a crowd of prospective mates. Each male has a small stage within a larger circular lek, and the inner, central position features the greatest, most virile of dancers. • Like other grouse, Sharp-tail numbers rise and fall dramatically over time. In years of high abundance, large numbers of Sharp-tails move great distances, often colonizing new areas of suitable habitat. • 'Lek' is derived from the Swedish word for 'play.'

ID: mottled brown and black upperparts, neck and breast; dark crescents on a white belly; white undertail coverts and outer tail feathers; long central tail feathers; yellow eye combs; white throat; feathered legs. *Male:* purple-pink air sacs on the neck are inflated during the courtship display.
Size: *L* 38–51 cm.
Status: uncommon year-round.
Habitat: grasslands, abandoned pastures, fields and meadows, limestone plains, open bogs, fens and forest clearings with scattered shrubs and trees.
Nesting: on the ground; occasionally under cover; in a depression lined with grass and leaves; female incubates 10–14 eggs for 21 days.
Feeding: gleans the ground, trees and shrubs for buds, seeds, flowers, green shoots and berries;

also eats insects when available.
Voice: rarely heard outside of courtship events: male gives a mournful, *cooing* call and a *cackling* call on the lek just before sunrise.
Similar Species: *Ruffed Grouse* (p. 106): slight crest; broad, fan-shaped tail with a broad, dark, subterminal band; black patches on the neck. *Ring-necked Pheasant* (p. 105): female has a longer tail and unfeathered legs; paler markings on the underparts. *Spruce Grouse* (p. 107): black, fan-shaped tail; black or mottled throat; male has red eye combs. *Willow Ptarmigan* (p. 108): summer birds show white in the wings and legs.
Best Sites: Milford area; Barrie Island (Manitoulin Island); St. Joseph Island (Sault Ste. Marie); Rainy River area; Dryden area; Moosonee area; Polar Bear PP.

WILD TURKEY

Meleagris gallopavo

Wild Turkeys were once much more common in southern Ontario, but during the early part of the 20th century, habitat loss and overharvesting took a toll on these birds. Following failed attempts at reintroducing pen-reared stock into the province (an activity that is now illegal), agreements were made to relocate wild American turkeys from various U.S. states—a strategy that has met with considerable success. • Although turkeys prefer to feed on the ground and travel by foot— they can run faster than 30 km/h—they are able to fly short distances, and they roost in trees at night. • This charismatic bird is the only native North American animal that has been widely domesticated. The wild ancestors of chickens, pigs, cows, horses, sheep and most other domestic animals all came from Europe, Asia or Africa. In their natural habitat, Wild Turkeys are wary birds with acute senses and a highly developed social system.

ID: naked, red-blue head; dark, glossy, iridescent body plumage; barred, copper-coloured tail; largely unfeathered legs. *Male:* long central breast tassel; colourful head and body; red wattles. *Female:* smaller; blue-grey head; less iridescent body.
Size: *Male: L* 91–112 cm. *Female: L* 89–94 cm.
Status: rare to locally uncommon year-round resident.
Habitat: deciduous, mixed and riparian woodlands; occasionally uses grain and corn crops in late fall and winter.
Nesting: in woodlands or at field edges; in a depression on the ground under thick cover; nest is lined with grass and leaves; female incubates

10–12 eggs for up to 28 days.
Feeding: forages on the ground for seeds, fruits, bulbs and sedges; also eats insects, especially beetles and grasshoppers; may take small amphibians.
Voice: wide array of sounds; courting male gobbles loudly; alarm call is a loud *pert*; gathering call is a *cluck*; contact call is a loud *keouk-keouk-keouk*.
Similar Species: all other grouse and grouse-like birds are much smaller. *Ring-necked Pheasant* (p. 105): feathered head and neck; long, narrow tail.
Best Sites: Wilson Tract (western Haldimand-Norfolk County); Short Hills PP; Beverly Swamp; Campbellford area; Hill Island.

NORTHERN BOBWHITE

Colinus virginianus

Throughout fall and winter, Bobwhites typically travel in large family groups called 'coveys,' collectively seeking out sources of food and huddling together during cold nights. When they huddle, members of the covey all face outward, enabling the group to detect danger from every direction. With the arrival of summer, breeding pairs break away from their coveys to perform elaborate courtship rituals in preparation for another nesting season. • The Northern Bobwhite is the only native quail in eastern North America. Unable to survive the cold and heavy snow cover of winter and having lost most of its habitat to intensive farming practices, the few wild birds that remain in Ontario are found in the extreme southwest of the province. • The male's characteristic, whistled *bob-white* call, usually issued in spring, is often the only evidence of this bird's presence among the dense, tangled vegetation of its rural, woodland home.

ID: mottled brown, buff and black upper-parts; white crescents and spots edged in black are present on the upper breast and chestnut sides; short tail. *Male:* white throat; broad white eyebrow. *Female:* buff throat and eyebrow. *Immature:* smaller and duller overall; lacks the black on the underparts.
Size: *L* 25 cm.
Status: rare and local year-round resident
Habitat: farmlands, open woodlands, woodland edges, grassy fencelines, roadside ditches and brushy, open country.
Nesting: in a shallow depression on the ground, often concealed by surrounding vegetation or a woven, partial dome; pair lines the nest with grass and leaves and incubates 12–16 white to pale buff eggs.
Feeding: seasonally available seeds, berries, leaves, roots, nuts, insects and other invertebrates.
Voice: whistled *hoy* is given year-round. *Male:* a whistled, rising *bob-white* given in spring and summer.
Similar Species: *Ruffed Grouse* (p. 106): lacks the conspicuous throat patch and the broad eyebrow; long, fan-shaped tail has a broad, dark subterminal band; black patches on the sides of the neck. *Gray Partridge* (p. 104): orange-brown face and throat; grey breast; chestnut outer tail feathers.
Best Sites: from Sarnia south to Walpole Island.

YELLOW RAIL
Coturnicops noveboracensis

The Yellow Rail might be the most challenging breeding bird to meet in Ontario because it is most active at night, when most naturalists are dreaming of birds behind closed eyelids. Under a blanket of darkness, the Yellow Rail slips quietly through tall sedges and cattails, picking food from the ground and searching for snails and insects. By day, this shy bird hides behind a cover of dense, marshy vegetation. Only in spring does the Yellow Rail reveal its presence by issuing its distinctive, repetitive 'ticking' calls. • Rails are masters at slipping through tightly packed stands of marsh vegetation with their laterally compressed bodies, and they might get their name from the fact that they look 'as thin as a rail.' Their large feet, which help them rest atop thin mats of floating plant material, add to their strange appearance. • Agricultural expansion has claimed a large share of Yellow Rail habitat in southern Ontario. Holland Marsh, for example, has been drained and converted to cropland. Fortunately, such areas as the coastal wetlands of Polar Bear Provincial Park have not yet suffered a similar fate.

ID: short, pale bill; black and tawny stripes on the upperparts (the black stripes have fine, white barring); broad, dark line through the eyes; white throat and belly. *Juvenile:* darker overall; pattern on the upperparts extends onto the breast, sides and flanks. *In flight:* white trailing edge on the inner wing.
Size: *L* 17–19 cm.
Status: extremely rare in the south to locally common in the north from mid-May to mid-September.
Habitat: sedge marshes and wet sedge meadows.
Nesting: on the ground or low over water, hidden by overhanging plants; shallow cup nest is made of grass or sedges; female incubates 8–10 eggs for up to 18 days.

Feeding: picks food from the ground and aquatic vegetation; eats mostly snails, aquatic insects, spiders and possibly earthworms; occasionally eats seeds.
Voice: like 2 stones clicking together: *tik, tik, tik-tik-tik.*
Similar Species: *Sora* (p. 115): lacks the stripes on the back and the white patches in the wings; breeding birds have a black face and throat and a bright yellow bill; distinctly different call. *Virginia Rail* (p. 114): long, reddish bill; lacks the stripes on the back and the white patches in the wings; rusty breast; grey face.
Best Sites: Richmond Fen (south of Ottawa); western edge of the Rainy River area; Polar Bear PP.

KING RAIL

Rallus elegans

The King Rail is the largest rail in North America, even though it is only roughly the size of a farmyard chicken. Unlike some of the more secretive rails, it is often seen wading through shallow water along the edge of a freshwater marsh, stalking its prey within full view of eager onlookers. Crayfish, crabs, small fish, spiders, beetles, snails, frogs and a whole host of aquatic insects keep this formidable hunter occupied and well fed. • King Rail nests, which are commonly built above shallow water, often include a protective dome of woven vegetation and a well-engineered entrance ramp. Despite these deluxe features, young rails and their attending parents desert the nest mere hours after the eggs hatch. • King Rails reach the northern limit of their range in southern Ontario, and it is thought that only 25 to 50 pairs breed in our province.

ID: long, slightly downcurved bill; black back feathers have buffy or tawny edges; cinnamon shoulders and underparts; strongly barred, black and white flanks; greyish-brown cheeks. *Immature:* similar plumage patterning with lighter, washed-out colours.
Size: *L* 38 cm.
Status: very rare, local breeder from May to September.
Habitat: freshwater marshes, shrubby swamps, marshy riparian shorelines and flooded fields with shrubby margins.
Nesting: among clumps of grass or sedge just above the water or ground; male builds most of the platform nest with a canopy and entrance ramp using marsh vegetation; pair shares the incubation of 10–12 pale buff eggs, lightly spotted with brown, for about 21–23 days.
Feeding: aquatic insects, crustaceans and occasionally seeds; small fish and amphibians are caught by foraging in shallow water, often in or near dense plant cover.
Voice: chattering call is 10 or fewer evenly spaced *kek* notes.
Similar Species: *Virginia Rail* (p. 114): much smaller; brown back feathers; grey face; red bill. *Least Bittern* (p. 44): solid black back feathers lack the lighter edging; buff-orange face and wing patches; thicker bill.
Best Sites: Point Pelee NP; Rondeau PP; Long Point PP.

VIRGINIA RAIL

Rallus limicola

The best way to meet a Virginia Rail is to sit alongside a wetland marsh in spring, clap your hands three or four times and wait patiently. If you are lucky, this bird will reveal itself for a brief instant, but on most occasions you can only count on hearing its voice. • When pursued by an intruder or predator, a rail will almost always attempt to scurry away through dense, concealing vegetation, rather than risk exposure in a getaway flight. • Rails are very narrow birds that have modified feather tips and flexible vertebrae, all of which allow them to squeeze through the narrow confines of their marshy homes. • The Virginia Rail, and its relative the Sora, are often found living in the same marshes. The secret of their successful coexistence is found in their micro-habitat preferences and distinct diets. The Virginia Rail typically favours dry shoresides of marshes and feeds on invertebrates; the Sora prefers waterfront property and eats plants and seeds.

ID: long, downcurved, reddish bill; grey face; rusty breast; barred flanks; chestnut wing patch; very short tail. *Immature:* much darker overall; light bill.

Size: *L* 23–28 cm.

Status: uncommon to locally fairly common from mid-April to mid-September; a few may be present in winter.

Habitat: freshwater wetlands, especially cattail and bulrush marshes.

Nesting: concealed in emergent vegetation, usually suspended just over the water; loose basket nest is made of coarse grass, cattail stems or sedges; pair incubates 5–13, spotted, pale buff eggs for up to 20 days.

Feeding: probes into soft sub-strates and gleans vegetation for invertebrates, including beetles, snails, spiders, earthworms, insect larvae and nymphs; also eats some pondweeds and seeds.

Voice: call is an often-repeated, telegraph-like *kidick, kidick*; also 'oinks' and croaks.

Similar Species: *King Rail* (p. 113): much larger; dark legs; lacks the obviously reddish bill and the grey face; juvenile is mostly pale grey. *Sora* (p. 115): short, yellow bill; black face and throat. *Yellow Rail* (p. 112): short, pale yellowish bill; black and tawny striped back; white trailing edges of the wings are seen in flight.

Best Sites: Long Point PP; Luther Marsh; Spry Lake; Puslinch Wetland; Cranberry Marsh; Lake Scugog; Presqu'ile PP; Big Island Marsh; Rideau Canal; south end of Lake Simcoe.

SORA

Porzana carolina

Two ascending whistles followed by a strange, descending whinny abruptly announce the presence of the often undetectable Sora. Although it is the most common and widespread rail in North America, the Sora is seldom seen by birders. Its elusive habits and preference for dense marshlands force most would-be observers to typically settle for a quick look at this small bird. When attempting to meet a Sora, it also helps to embark upon a day in the field without your usual group of gabby birding partners! • Soras swim quite well over short distances, even though their feet are not webbed or lobed. • Northern Harriers, Great Horned Owls, weasels, raccoons, Northern Pikes and even Great Blue Herons are some of the many creatures that may prey on Soras.

breeding

ID: short, yellow bill; black face, throat and foreneck; grey neck and breast; long, greenish legs. *Immature:* no black on the face; paler underparts; bill is more greenish.
Size: *L* 20–25 cm.
Status: uncommon to common from early April to mid-September; a few may be present in winter.
Habitat: wetlands with abundant emergent cattails, bulrushes, sedges and grass.
Nesting: usually over water, but occasionally in a wet meadow under concealing vegetation; well-built basket nest is made of grass and aquatic vegetation; pair

incubates 10–12 eggs for 18–20 days.
Feeding: gleans and probes for seeds, plants, aquatic insects and mollusks.
Voice: alarm call is a sharp *keek*; courtship song begins *or-Ah or-Ah*, descending quickly in a series of maniacal *weee-weee-weee* notes.
Similar Species: *Virginia Rail* (p. 114) and *King Rail* (p. 113): long, downcurved bill; chestnut wing patch; rusty breast. *Yellow Rail* (p. 112): streaked back; tawny upperparts; white throat; white trailing edges of the wings are seen in flight.
Best Sites: Point Pelee NP; Rondeau PP; Luther Marsh; Cranberry Marsh; Lake Scugog; Big Island Marsh; Mission Island Marsh; Lake of the Woods.

COMMON MOORHEN

Gallinula chloropus

The Common Moorhen is a curious-looking creature that appears to have been assembled from bits and pieces left over from other birds: it has the bill of a chicken, the body of a duck and the long legs and large feet of a small heron. Although this bird looks gangly and awkward, its steps are well executed. As the Common Moorhen strolls around a wetland, its head bobs back and forth in synchrony with its legs, producing a comical, chugging stride. • Unlike most other members of the rail family, the Common Moorhen is quite comfortable feeding in open areas. • For moorhens, the responsibilities of parenthood do not end when their eggs have hatched—parents will feed and shelter their young until they are capable of feeding themselves and flying on their own.

breeding

ID: reddish forehead shield; yellow-tipped bill; grey-black body; white streak on the sides and flanks; long, yellow legs. *Breeding:* brighter bill and forehead shield. *Juvenile:* paler plumage; duller legs and bill; white throat.
Size: *L* 30–38 cm.
Status: fairly common to locally common from May to mid-October; migrants appear through April, October and much of November.
Habitat: freshwater marshes, ponds, lakes and sewage lagoons.
Nesting: pair builds a platform nest or a wide, shallow cup of bulrushes, cattails and reeds in shallow water or along a shoreline;

often built with a ramp leading to the water; pair incubates 8–11 eggs for 19–22 days.
Feeding: eats mostly aquatic vegetation, berries, fruits, tadpoles, insects, snails, worms and spiders; may take carrion and eggs.
Voice: various sounds include chicken-like clucks, screams, squeaks and a loud *cup*; courting males give a harsh *ticket-ticket-ticket*.
Similar Species: *American Coot* (p. 117): white bill and forehead shield; lacks the white streak on the flanks.
Best Sites: mouth of the Canard River; Long Point PP; Dundas Marsh; Lynde Shores Conservation Area; Lake Scugog; Presqu'ile PP; Rideau Canal; Carillon PP.

AMERICAN COOT

Fulica americana

The coot is truly an all-terrain bird: in its quest for food it dives and dabbles like a duck, grazes confidently on land and swims about skillfully with its lobed feet. • Coots are constantly squabbling. These odd birds can often be seen scooting across the surface of the water, charging rivals with flailing, splashing wings in an attempt to intimidate. • Outside the breeding season, coots gather together in large groups. During spring and fall, thousands congregate at a few select staging sites in southern Ontario. • Coots are colloquially known as 'Mud Hens,' and few birders realize that they are not a species of duck.

ID: grey-black, duck-like bird; white, chicken-like bill with a dark ring around the tip; reddish spot on the white forehead shield; long, green-yellow legs; lobed toes; red eyes. *Immature:* lighter body colour; darker bill and legs; lacks the prominent forehead shield.
Size: *L* 33–41 cm.
Status: uncommon to abundant migrant from March to mid-May and from September to mid-November; uncommon breeder; a few may be present in winter.
Habitat: shallow marshes, ponds and wetlands with open water and emergent vegetation; also sewage lagoons.
Nesting: in emergent vegetation; floating nest, built by the pair, is usually made of cattails and grass; pair incubates 6–11 greyish to buff, brown-spotted eggs for 21–25 days.

Feeding: eats aquatic vegetation, insects, snails, crayfish, worms, tadpoles and fish; gleans the water's surface; sometimes dives, tips up or even grazes on land; may steal food from ducks.
Voice: calls frequently in summer, day and night: *kuk-kuk-kuk-kuk-kuk*; also grunts.
Similar Species: *Ducks* (pp. 60–88): all lack the chicken-like, white bill and the uniform, black body colour. *Grebes* (pp. 37–40): lack the white forehead shield and the all-dark plumage. *Common Moorhen* (p. 116): reddish forehead shield; yellow-tipped bill; white streak on the flanks.
Best Sites: St. Clair NWA; Long Point PP; Luther Marsh; Lynde Shores Conservation Area; Lake Scugog; Presqu'ile PP; Mission Island Marsh.

SANDHILL CRANE

Grus canadensis

Deep, resonant, rattling calls announce the approach of a flock of migrating Sandhill Cranes long before they pass overhead. At first glance, the large, V-shaped flocks look very similar to flocks of Canada Geese, but cranes often soar and circle, and their calls are unlike the honking of geese. In Ontario, birders searching for Sandhill Cranes must to travel to Sault Ste. Marie to catch a glimpse of migrants or rare summer breeders. • Cranes mate for life, reinforcing their pair bond each spring with an elaborate courtship dance. It has often been equated with human dancing—a seemingly strange comparison until you see the ritual first hand. • Sandhill Cranes are sensitive nesters, so they prefer to raise their young in areas that are isolated from human disturbance.

ID: very large, grey bird with a long neck and legs; plumage is often stained a rusty colour from iron oxides in the water; naked, red crown; long, straight bill. *Immature:* lacks the red crown; reddish-brown plumage may appear patchy. *In flight:* extends its neck and legs; often glides, soars and circles.
Size: *L* 1–1.3 m; *W* 1.8–2.1 m.
Status: rare to locally uncommon from April to November; a few may be present in winter.
Habitat: *In migration:* agricultural fields and shorelines. *Breeding:* isolated, open marshes, fens and bogs surrounded by forests or shrubs; also coastal tundra.
Nesting: on a large mound of aquatic vegetation in the water or along the shoreline; pair incubates 2 eggs for 29–32 days; egg hatching is staggered; young fly at about 50 days.
Feeding: probes and gleans the ground for insects, soft-bodied invertebrates, waste grain, shoots and tubers; frequently eats small vertebrates.
Voice: loud, resonant rattling: *gu-rrroo gu-rrroo gurrroo.*
Similar Species: *Great Blue Heron* (p. 45): flies with its neck folded back over its shoulders; lacks the red forehead patch. *Whooping Crane* (p. 355): all-white plumage; black flight feathers; unlikely to be seen in Ontario.
Best Sites: Rondeau PP; Sault Ste. Marie area; Manitoulin Island; Lake of the Woods; Polar Bear PP.

BLACK-BELLIED PLOVER

Pluvialis squatarola

During the last days of May, the Black-bellied Plover's black and white plumage stands out against the drab soil of ploughed Ontario fields. Small groups of these arctic breeders pass through Ontario for a brief period in spring and for a longer period in fall. From time to time, flocks numbering over 13,000 birds have been seen in our province, but such occurrences are considered rare. The end of the fall passage, usually around October, is the best time to see the plain grey immature plovers following the adults in their worn-out breeding plumage. • These birds forage for small invertebrates with a robin-like run-and-stop technique, frequently pausing to lift their heads for a reassuring scan of their surroundings. • Most plovers have three toes, but the Black-belly has a fourth toe high on its leg, like most sandpipers.

breeding

ID: short, black bill; long, black legs. *Breeding:* black face, breast, belly and flanks; white undertail coverts; white stripe leading from the crown down the collar, neck and sides of the breast; mottled black and white back. *Non-breeding:* mottled grey-brown upperparts; lightly streaked, pale underparts. *In flight:* black 'wing pits'; whitish rump; white wing linings.
Size: *L* 27–33 cm.
Status: rare to locally abundant migrant from mid-April to early June and from August to mid-November; a few may be present in summer.

Habitat: ploughed fields, meadows, lakeshores and mudflats along the edges of reservoirs, marshes and sewage lagoons.
Nesting: does not nest in Ontario.
Feeding: run-and-stop foraging technique; eats insects, mollusks and crustaceans.
Voice: rich, plaintive whistle: *pee-oo-ee.*
Similar Species: *American Golden-Plover* (p. 120): upperparts are mottled with gold; black under-tail coverts in breeding plumage; lacks the black 'wing pits.'
Best Sites: Point Pelee NP and nearby onion fields; Long Point PP; Presqu'ile PP.

119

AMERICAN GOLDEN-PLOVER
Pluvialis dominica

The American Golden-Plover population was once among the largest of any bird in the world, but a century ago, market gunners mercilessly culled the great flocks in both spring and fall—a single day's shooting often yielded tens of thousands of birds. In recent times, populations have recovered somewhat, but they will never return to their former numbers. • Many thousands of American Golden-Plovers gather on the northern Ontario coast in fall in preparation for the long flight south. Because they migrate through central North America, however, few are seen here, although occasionally a flock of 1000 or so is observed in southern Ontario. • This bird's breeding plumage is a fine example of both disruptive and cryptic colouration. Although the bird is boldly marked, the pattern breaks up the image of the bird when it is seen in a wild setting. • The Eskimo Curlew, which is believed to be extinct, once migrated with the American Golden-Plover between the Canadian Arctic and South America. It is believed that if the Eskimo Curlew does still exist, it may be found travelling alongside the American Golden-Plover.

breeding

ID: straight, black bill; long, black legs. *Breeding:* black face and underparts, including the undertail coverts; S-shaped, white stripe from across the forehead down to the shoulders; dark upperparts are speckled with gold and white. *Non-breeding:* broad, pale eyebrow; dark streaking on the pale neck and underparts; much less gold on the upperparts. *In flight:* grey 'wing pits.'
Size: *L* 25–38 cm.
Status: rare to irregularly common migrant from mid-April to early June; common migrant from August to November; extremely rare breeder.
Habitat: cultivated fields, meadows, lakeshores and mudflats along the edges

of reservoirs, marshes and sewage lagoons.
Nesting: on the ground in dry tundra, in a shallow depression lined with grass, leaves, moss and lichen; pair incubates 4 cryptically coloured eggs for about 26–27 days; both adults tend the young.
Feeding: run-and-stop foraging technique; snatches insects, mollusks and crustaceans; seeds and berries are also taken.
Voice: soft, melodious whistle: *quee, quee-dle.*
Similar Species: *Black-bellied Plover* (p. 119): white undertail coverts; whitish crown; lacks the gold speckling on the upperparts.
Best Sites: Point Pelee NP; Long Point PP; Presqu'ile PP; Polar Bear PP.

120

SEMIPALMATED PLOVER

Charadrius semipalmatus

On their way to northern breeding grounds, small flocks of Semipalmated Plovers commonly touch down on Ontario shorelines. Watch for them in southern parts of the province in late May and early June, but keep your eyes peeled, because they are only around for a short time. If these birds seem to be in a hurry, they are! There is a tremendous amount of pressure for these long-distance migrants to begin breeding before the end of the short northern summer. If successful, the adults will leave their breeding grounds as early as July to enjoy a prolonged, leisurely migration to the coastlines of Central America and South America and the southern U.S. • The scientific name *semipalmatus* refers to the slight webbing between the toes of this plover. Webbed toes are also called 'palmate,' so partly webbed toes are 'semi-palmate.' The webbing is thought to give the bird's feet more surface area when it is walking on soft substrates.

breeding

ID: dark brown back; white breast with 1 black, horizontal band; long, orange legs; stubby, orange, black-tipped bill; white patch above the bill; white throat and collar; brown head; black band across the forehead; small, white eyebrow. *Immature:* dark legs and bill; brown banding. **Size:** *L* 18 cm.

Status: rare to common migrant in May and early June and from late July to mid-November; uncommon to common breeder.

Habitat: *Breeding:* tundra; sand and gravel bars along rivers and lake shorelines. *In migration:* sandy beaches, lakeshores, river edges and mudflats.

Nesting: on sand, gravel or tundra, usually near water; in a depression sparsely lined with vegetation; pair incubates 4 cryptic eggs for 23–25 days.

Feeding: run-and-stop feeding, usually on shorelines and beaches; eats crustaceans, worms and insects.

Voice: crisp, high-pitched, 2-part, rising whistle: *tu-wee.*

Similar Species: *Killdeer* (p. 123): larger; 2 black bands across the breast. *Piping Plover* (p. 122): lacks the dark band through the eyes; much lighter upperparts.

Best Sites: Point Pelee NP; Long Point PP; Presqu'ile PP; Polar Bear PP.

121

PIPING PLOVER

Charadrius melodus

A master of illusion, the Piping Plover is hardly noticeable when it settles on shorelines and beaches. Its plumage is the perfect camouflage against a sandy beach, and the dark bands across its forehead and neckline resemble scattered pebbles or strips of washed-up vegetation. This plover's cryptic plumage, however, has done little to protect it from wetland drainage, increased predation and disturbance by humans. The recreational use of beaches during summer, and an increase in human-tolerant predators, such as gulls, raccoons and skunks, has impeded its ability to reproduce successfully. The Piping Plover is an endangered species in Ontario. It is estimated that 150 to 160 pairs once bred along the shores of Lake Ontario, Lake Erie, Lake Huron and the St. Lawrence River, but successful breeding in these areas has not been recorded since 1977.

♂

breeding

ID: pale, sandy upperparts; white underparts; orange legs. *Breeding:* black-tipped, orange bill; black forehead band; black 'necklace' (sometimes incomplete, especially in the female). *Non-breeding:* no breast or forehead band; all-black bill.

Size: *L* 18–19 cm.

Status: extremely rare from mid-April to mid-September; a few may remain into October.

Habitat: sandy beaches and open lakeshores.

Nesting: on bare sand along an open shoreline; in a shallow scrape that is sometimes lined with pebbles and tiny shells; pair incubates 4 pale buff eggs, blotched with dark brown and black, for 26–28 days.

Feeding: run-and-stop feeding; eats worms and insects; almost all its food is taken from the ground.

Voice: clear, whistled melody: *peep peep peep-lo.*

Similar Species: *Semipalmated Plover* (p. 121): dark band over the eyes; much darker upperparts. *Killdeer* (p. 123): larger; 2 breast bands; much darker upperparts.

Best Sites: Point Pelee NP; Long Point PP; Lake of the Woods.

KILLDEER

Charadrius vociferus

The ubiquitous Killdeer is often the first shorebird a beginning birdwatcher will learn to identify, and its boisterous *kill-deer* call is easy to recognize. It has adapted well to urbanization, and it finds open fields, golf courses and abandoned industrial areas as much to its liking as shorelines. • If you happen to wander too close to a Killdeer nest, the parents will try to lure you away, issuing loud alarm calls and feigning a broken wing. Similar distraction displays are widespread phenomena in the bird world, but in Ontario, the Killdeer's broken wing act is by far the best known. • The scientific name *vociferus* aptly describes this vocal bird, but double-check all calls in spring—at that time of year the Killdeer is often imitated by frisky European Starlings.

ID: long, dark yellow legs; white breast with 2 black bands; brown back; white underparts; brown head; white eyebrow; tail projects beyond the wing tips; white face patch above the bill; black forehead band; rusty rump. *Immature:* downy; only 1 breast band.
Size: *L* 23–28 cm.
Status: common to abundant from April to late October; a few may be present in winter.
Habitat: open ground, fields, lakeshores, sandy beaches, mudflats, gravel streambeds, wet meadows and grasslands.
Nesting: on open ground; in a shallow, usually unlined depression; pair incubates 4 eggs for 24–28 days; occasionally raises 2 broods.
Feeding: run-and-stop feeder; eats mostly insects; also takes spiders, snails, earthworms and crayfish.
Voice: loud and distinctive *kill-dee kill-dee kill-deer* and variations, including *deer-deer*.
Similar Species: *Semipalmated Plover* (p. 121): smaller; only 1 breast band. *Piping Plover* (p. 122): smaller; lighter upperparts; 1 breast band.
Best Sites: extremely widespread; open areas and disturbed sites throughout the province.

GREATER YELLOWLEGS

Tringa melanoleuca

The Greater Yellowlegs is one of the birds that performs the role of lookout among mixed flocks of shorebirds. At the first sign of danger, these large sandpipers bob their heads and call incessantly. If forced to, the Greater Yellowlegs will usually retreat into deeper water, becoming airborne only as a last resort. • During migration, many shorebirds, including the Greater Yellowlegs, often stand or hop around beachflats on one leg. These stubborn 'one-leggers' may be mistaken for crippled individuals, but this stance is an adapation for the conservation of body heat. • Greater Yellowlegs nest primarily among wet bogs and fens on the Hudson Bay Lowland of Ontario's far north. Most attempts to find yellowleg nests are frustrating and fruitless—not only will your feet sink in waterlogged ground, but these birds will begin to issue high-pitched calls from atop a black spruce or tamarack long before you reach their nest.

breeding

ID: long, bright yellow legs; dark bill is slightly upturned and is noticeably longer than the head width. *Breeding:* brown-black back and wing covers; fine, dense, dark streaking on the head and neck; dark barring on the breast often extends onto the belly; subtle, dark eye line; light lores. *Non-breeding:* grey overall; fine streaks on the breast.
Size: *L* 33–38 cm.
Status: common to very common from May to October; rare in April and November.
Habitat: *In migration:* almost all wetlands, including lakeshores, marshes, flooded fields and river shorelines. *Nesting:* bogs, alluvial wetlands, sedge meadows, fens and beaver ponds.
Nesting: in a depression on a dry mound; usually on a ridge near open bogs or natural openings in muskeg;

never far from water; well-hidden nest is sparsely lined with leaves, moss and grass; female incubates 4 eggs for about 23 days.
Feeding: usually wades in water over its knees; commonly sweeps its bill from side to side; primarily eats aquatic invertebrates, but will also eat small fish; occasionally snatches prey from the water's surface.
Voice: quick, whistled series of *tew-tew-tew*, usually 3 notes.
Similar Species: *Lesser Yellowlegs* (p. 125): smaller; straight bill is not noticeably longer than the width of the head; call is generally a pair of notes: *tew-tew*. *Willet* (p. 127): black and white wings; heavier, straighter bill; dark, greenish legs.
Best Sites: Point Pelee NP; Rondeau PP; Long Point PP; Presqu'ile PP; Polar Bear PP.

LESSER YELLOWLEGS

Tringa flavipes

With a series of continuous, rapid-fire *tew-tew* calls, Lesser Yellowlegs streak across the surface of southern Ontario's wetlands and lakeshores. Visits by yellowlegs are relatively brief in spring, but the fall migration period is lengthy, and yellowlegs can been seen from mid-July to mid-October. • Greater Yellowlegs and Lesser Yellowlegs nest in the muskeg of Ontario's Hudson Bay Lowland, but Lessers tend to build their nests on higher, drier terrain, leaving the wetter, mushier ground for their long-legged relative. • Many birders find it a challenge to separate Lesser Yellowlegs and Greater Yellowlegs in the field. With practice, you will notice that the Lesser's bill is finer, straighter and not noticeably longer than the width of its head. If you are still puzzled at the bird's identity, it is acceptable to simply write 'yellowlegs' in your field notes.

breeding

ID: bright yellow legs; dark bill is not noticeably longer than the width of the head; brown-black back and wing covers; fine, dense, dark streaking on the head, neck and breast; lacks barring on the belly; subtle, dark eye line; light lores.
Size: *L* 25–28 cm.
Status: common to very common from May to mid-October; rare in late April and in late October and November.
Habitat: *Breeding:* grassy ponds and open forests. *In migration:* shorelines of lakes, rivers, marshes and ponds.
Nesting: usually in open muskeg or natural forest openings; in a depression on a dry mound; nest is sparsely lined with leaves and grass;

pair incubates 4 blotched eggs for 22–23 days.
Feeding: snatches prey from the water's surface; frequently wades in shallow water; primarily eats aquatic invertebrates, but will also take small fish and tadpoles.
Voice: typically a high-pitched pair of *tew* notes.
Similar Species: *Greater Yellowlegs* (p. 124): larger; bill is slightly upturned and noticeably longer than the width of the head; *tew* call is usually given in a series of 3 notes. *Solitary Sandpiper* (p. 126): white eye ring; greenish legs. *Willet* (p. 127): black and white wings; heavier bill; dark, greenish legs.
Best Sites: Point Pelee NP; Rondeau PP; Long Point PP; Presqu'ile PP; Polar Bear PP.

SOLITARY SANDPIPER

Tringa solitaria

True to its name, the Solitary Sandpiper is usually seen alone, bobbing its body like a spirited dancer as it forages for insects along Ontario wetlands. Once in a while, however, a lucky observer may happen upon a small group of Solitary Sandpipers during spring or fall. • The Solitary Sandpiper's nesting strategy remained a mystery until 1903, when a homesteader in Alberta peered into what he thought was a robin's nest, but found a sandpiper instead. For years, this wily shorebird had stumped amateur naturalists and professional ornithologists alike. Few would have dared dream that a shorebird would lay its eggs in an abandoned songbird nest! • Shorebirds lay very large eggs and incubate them for comparatively long periods of time. Once sandpiper chicks hatch, they are ready to run, hide and feed on their own. Highly developed hatchlings, known as precocial young, are immediately able to fend for themselves in a world of danger.

breeding

ID: white eye ring; short, green legs; dark yellowish bill with a black tip; brown-grey spotted back; white lores; brown-grey head, neck and breast have fine white streaks; dark upper tail feathers with black and white barring on the sides. *In flight:* dark underwings.
Size: *L* 19–23 cm.
Status: uncommon from May to early October; rare in late April and mid-October.
Habitat: *Breeding:* heavily forested wetlands, bogs, fens and streams. *In migration:* wet meadows, sewage lagoons, muddy ponds, beaver ponds and wooded streams.
Nesting: in a spruce tree in a bog or in muskeg; will use an abandoned songbird nest; pair incubates 4 eggs for 23–24 days.

Feeding: stalks shorelines, picking up aquatic invertebrates, such as waterboatmen and damselfly nymphs; also gleans for terrestrial invertebrates; occasionally stirs the water with its foot to spook out prey.
Voice: high, thin *peet-wheet* or *wheat wheat wheat* during summer.
Similar Species: *Lesser Yellowlegs* (p. 125): no eye ring; longer, bright yellow legs. *Spotted Sandpiper* (p. 128): incomplete eye ring; spotted breast in breeding plumage; orange, black-tipped bill. *Other sandpipers:* black bills and legs; lack the white eye ring.
Best Sites: Point Pelee NP; Presqu'ile PP; Sleeping Giant PP; Wakami Lake PP; Lake Superior PP; Obatanga PP; Kettle Lakes PP; Greenwater PP.

WILLET

Catoptrophorus semipalmatus

When it is grounded, the Willet cuts a rather dull figure. The moment it takes flight, however, its black and white wings flash in harmony while it calls out a loud, rhythmic *will-will willet, will-will-willet!* It is thought that the bright, bold flashes of the Willet's wings may serve as danger warnings to other shorebirds. The flashes may also intimidate predators during the bird's dive-bombing defence of its young. • Willets are rare but regular annual visitors to Ontario. Typically, they are best seen while foraging among larger mixed-species shorebird flocks along the shores of the lower Great Lakes from mid-April to late June. Most Willets that visit Ontario are probably lost individuals—traditional Willet breeding grounds are on the grasslands of southern Manitoba, western Minnesota and along the Maritime coast.

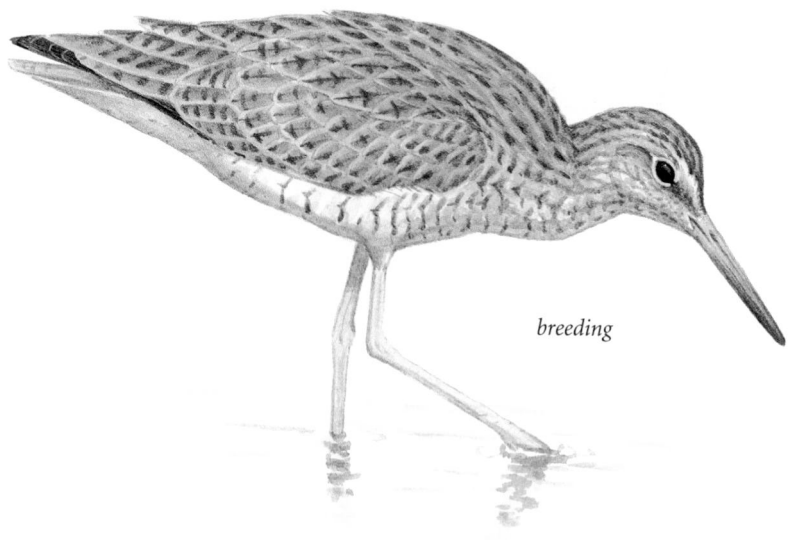

breeding

ID: plump; heavy, straight, black bill; light throat and belly. *Breeding:* dark streaking and barring overall. *In flight:* black and white wing pattern.
Size: *L* 36–41 cm.
Status: exceptionally rare to uncommon visitor from April to September.
Habitat: wet fields and shorelines of marshes, lakes and ponds.
Nesting: does not breed in Ontario.
Feeding: feeds by probing muddy areas; also gleans the ground for insects; occasionally eats shoots and seeds.

Voice: loud, rolling *will-will willet, will-will-willet.*
Similar Species: *Marbled Godwit* (p. 132) and *Hudsonian Godwit* (p. 131): much longer, yellow bill with a dark, slightly upturned tip; larger body; lacks the black and white wing pattern. *Greater Yellowlegs* (p. 124): long, yellow legs; slightly upturned bill; lacks the black and white wing pattern.
Best Sites: Point Pelee NP; Long Point PP; Mission Island Marsh.

VAGRANT

127

SPOTTED SANDPIPER

Actitis macularia

This diminutive shorebird is a widespread breeder in Ontario, and during summer it is the most frequently encountered sandpiper throughout much of the province. It wasn't until 1972 that the unexpected truths about the Spotted Sandpiper's breeding activities were realized. Like the phalaropes, female Spotted Sandpipers defend territories and mate with more than one male in a single breeding season, leaving the males to tend the nests and eggs. This unusual nesting behaviour, known as polyandry, is found in about one percent of all bird species on Earth. • Although its breast spots aren't noticeable from a distance, its stiff-winged, quivering flight pattern and tendency to burst from the shore are easily recognizable. Like the Solitary Sandpiper, it is also known for its continuous teetering behaviour as it forages.

breeding

ID: teeters almost continuously. *Breeding:* white underparts are heavily spotted with black; yellow-orange legs; yellow-orange, black-tipped bill; white eyebrow. *Non-breeding* and *Juvenile:* pure white breast, foreneck and throat; brown bill; dull yellow legs. *In flight:* flies close to the water's surface with very rapid, shallow wingbeats; white upperwing stripe.

Size: *L* 18–20 cm.

Status: common from late April to late September.

Habitat: shorelines, gravel beaches, ponds, marshes, alluvial wetlands, rivers, streams, swamps and sewage lagoons; occasionally seen in cultivated fields.

Nesting: usually near water; often under overhanging vegetation among logs or under bushes; in a shallow depression lined with grass; male almost exclusively incubates and raises the 4 young.

Feeding: picks and gleans along shorelines for terrestrial and aquatic invertebrates; also snatches flying insects from the air.

Voice: sharp, crisp *eat-wheat, eat-wheat, wheat-wheat-wheat-wheat.*

Similar Species: *Solitary Sandpiper* (p. 126): complete eye ring; lacks the spotting on the breast; yellowish bill with a dark tip. *Other sandpipers:* black bills and legs; lack the spotting on the breast.

Best Sites: along riverbanks and wetlands throughout Ontario; Canard River mouth; Dundas Marsh; Trent Canal; Carillon PP; Algonquin PP; Pukaskwa NP; Hwy 11; Rushing River PP.

UPLAND SANDPIPER

Bartramia longicauda

In spring, Upland Sandpipers are occasionally seen perched atop tall fenceposts belting out airy 'wolf-whistle' courtship tunes. Excited males will even launch into the air to perform a courtship flight, combining song with shallow, fluttering wingbeats. At the height of the breeding season, however, these large-eyed, inland shorebirds remain hidden in the tall grass of abandoned fields and ungrazed pastures. • For an Ontario naturalist who is accustomed to meeting the Upland Sandpiper among the province's grassy fields and meadows, meeting the same bird during a holiday in the grasslands of Argentina could be quite shocking. Twice each year, these wide-ranging shorebirds make the incredible journey between Canada and South America without jet propulsion or inflight movies. • During the late 1800s, high market demand for this bird's meat led to severe overharvesting and catastrophic declines in its population over much of North America. Its numbers have since rebounded in Ontario, but only in limited areas where grassland habitat persists.

ID: small head; long, streaked neck; large, dark eyes; yellow legs; mottled brownish upperparts; lightly streaked breast, sides and flanks; white belly and undertail coverts; bill is about as long the same length as the head.
Size: *L* 28–32 cm.
Status: rare to uncommon from mid-April to late September.
Habitat: hayfields, ungrazed pastures, grassy meadows, abandoned fields, natural grasslands and airports.
Nesting: in dense grass or along a wetland; in a depression, usually with grass arching overtop; pair incubates 4 pale to pinkish-buff eggs, lightly spotted with reddish-brown, for 22–27 days; both adults tend the young.

Feeding: gleans the ground for insects, especially grasshoppers and beetles.
Voice: courtship song is an airy, whistled *whip-whee-ee you;* alarm call is *quip-ip-ip.*
Similar Species: *Willet* (p. 127): longer, heavier bill; dark greenish legs; black and white wings in flight. *Buff-breasted Sandpiper* (p. 145): shorter neck; larger head; daintier bill; lacks the streaking on the cheek and foreneck. *Pectoral Sandpiper* (p. 141): abrupt end to the streaking on the breast; smaller eyes; shorter neck; usually seen in large numbers.
Best Sites: Bruce Peninsula; Pearson International Airport; Carden Plain; eastern Haldimand-Norfolk County; southern Prince Edward County; Prescott County; Russell County; Paipoonge Township.

WHIMBREL

Numenius phaeopus

Visitors to Polar Bear Provincial Park in late June or early July would probably remember the Whimbrel if they saw one. Whimbrels are protective parents, so anyone who wanders too close to a nest is certain to encounter the intimidating, high-speed, head-on flying attacks of angered adults. Most birders, however, are only likely to see these birds during migration as they pass along the shores of the lower Great Lakes. Whimbrels travel in flocks, so expect to see either a 'ton' of them or none at all. • It is impossible to talk about the Whimbrel without mentioning the Eskimo Curlew. Both of these birds suffered devastating losses to their populations during the commercial hunts of the late 1800s. Fortunately for the Whimbrel, it escaped the devastation suffered by the Eskimo Curlew because it migrates primarily over water. While the Whimbrel population slowly recovered, the Eskimo Curlew seemed to vanish into thin air—the last confirmed sighting of the curlew was in 1963. • *Numenius* is from the Greek for 'new moon,' and it refers to the curved shape of the bill.

ID: long, downcurved bill; striped crown; dark eye line; mottled brown body; long legs. *In flight:* dark underwings.

Size: *L* 45 cm.

Status: rare migrant from May to early June and from mid-July to mid-September; rare breeder.

Habitat: *Breeding:* coastal tundra. *In migration:* mudflats, sandy beaches, farmlands, grassy lakeshore fields and flooded agricultural fields.

Nesting: on a dry, raised area of wet tundra; in a shallow depression lined with grass, lichen and moss; pair incubates 4 brown-blotched, buff to olive eggs for 24–28 days.

Feeding: probes and pecks for invertebrates in mud or vegetation; also eats berries in fall.

Voice: usually quiet in migration; rolling *cur-lee-ou cur-lee-ou* heard mostly on breeding grounds.

Similar Species: *Long-billed Curlew:* much larger overall; much longer bill; lacks the bold striping on the head and through the eye. *Eskimo Curlew* (p. 356): unbarred primaries; pale cinnamon wing linings; shorter, slightly straighter bill; darker upperparts; thought to be extinct.

Best Sites: Point Pelee NP; Long Point PP; Presqu'ile PP; the south shore of Manitoulin Island; Polar Bear PP.

HUDSONIAN GODWIT

Limosa haemastica

Each fall, a great number of Hudsonian Godwits take flight from the shores of Hudson Bay and James Bay to embark on a non-stop journey to South America. This voyage is fueled solely by fat reserves that are built up on their north-coast staging grounds prior to departure. At least 30 percent of the entire North American population gathers in fall on the north coast of Ontario, but the breeding areas are so remote that we have only a vague idea of how many nest in the province and where. Fortunately, not all godwits fly south in early fall, so birders who are scouting the shores of southern Manitoulin Island, the Ottawa River and the lower Great Lakes in November are able to enjoy their presence.

breeding

♂

ID: long, yellow-orange bill with a dark, slightly upturned tip; white rump; black tail; long, black-blue legs. *Breeding:* heavily barred, chestnut red underparts; dark greyish upperparts; male is more brightly coloured. *Non-breeding adult:* greyish upperparts; whitish underparts may show a few short, black bars. *Juvenile:* dark grey-brown upperparts; pale underparts. *In flight:* white rump; black wing pits and wing linings.
Size: *L* 36–40 cm.
Status: rare migrant from late April to early June; rare to very uncommon migrant from late July to early November; rarely seen breeder.
Habitat: *Breeding:* coastal tundra. *In migration:* flooded fields, marshes, mudflats and lakeshores.
Nesting: in a sedge marsh; on a hummock, under a dwarf shrub or

in a grassy tussock; well-concealed, shallow depression is sparsely lined with leaves; pair incubates 4 dark, blotched, olive-brown eggs for 22–25 days.
Feeding: probes deeply into water or mud; eats insects and other invertebrates; also picks earthworms from ploughed fields.
Voice: sharp, rising *god-WIT!*
Similar Species: *Marbled Godwit* (p. 132): larger; mottled brown overall; lacks the white rump. *Greater Yellowlegs* (p. 124): shorter, all-dark bill; bright yellow legs; lacks the white rump. *Dowitchers* (pp. 147–48): smaller; straight, all-dark bills; yellow-green legs; mottled brown-black upperparts in breeding plumage.
Best Sites: Pickering Hydro Park; Presqu'ile PP; Ottawa River; southern shores of Manitoulin Island; Polar Bear PP.

131

MARBLED GODWIT

Limosa fedoa

The Marbled Godwit's bill looks long enough to reach buried prey, but this bird doesn't seem content with its reach. It is frequently seen with its head submerged beneath the water or with its face pressed into a mudflat. These deep probings seem to pay off for this large, resourceful shorebird, and a godwit looks genuinely pleased with a freshly extracted meal and a face covered in mud. • Sightings of Marbled Godwits are rare in Ontario. They migrate mostly over southern portions of the province in small numbers so sightings are limited to these areas. Furthermore, most godwits nest on the Canadian Prairies and American Great Plains, and the small, disjunct breeding population that remains in James Bay has never fully recovered from the uncontrolled slaughter of shorebirds in the 1800s. • The genus name *Limosa*, meaning 'muddy,' refers to this bird's preference for muddy foraging habitats.

breeding

ID: long, yellow-orange bill with a dark, slightly upturned tip; long neck and legs; mottled buff-brown plumage is darkest on the upperparts; long, black-blue legs. *In flight:* cinnamon wing linings.
Size: *L* 41–51 cm.
Status: extremely rare migrant from mid-April to mid-June and from early August to mid-November; rare breeder.
Habitat: *Breeding:* coastal marshes and prairies. *In migration:* flooded fields, wet meadows, marshes, mudflats and lakeshores.
Nesting: on dry ground in grass or sedges, usually near water; in a slight depression lined with grass; may have a partial canopy; pair probably shares the incubation of 4 brown-spotted, olive-buff

to greenish eggs for 21–23 days.
Feeding: probes deeply in soft substrates for worms, insect larvae, crustaceans and mollusks; picks insects from grass; may also eat the tubers and seeds of aquatic vegetation.
Voice: loud, duck-like, 2-syllable squawks: *co-rect co-rect* or *god-wit god-wit*.
Similar Species: *Hudsonian Godwit* (p. 131): smaller; chestnut red neck and underparts; white rump. *Greater Yellowlegs* (p. 124): shorter, all-dark bill; bright yellow legs. *Dowitchers* (pp. 147–48): smaller; straight, all-dark bill; white rump wedge; yellow-green legs. *Long-billed Curlew:* long, downcurved bill.
Best Sites: Mission Island Marsh; Rainy River–Lake of the Woods area; southern James Bay.

RUDDY TURNSTONE

Arenaria interpres

During late May and early June, small flocks of boldly patterned Ruddy Turnstones settle on blacktop fields and along the shores of Lake Erie and Lake Ontario to mingle and forage among the more populous shorebird migrants. Their costume-party faces and sharp black and red backs set them apart from the multitudes of little brown and white shorebirds. • Ruddy Turnstones are truly long-distance migrants. Individuals that nest along the shores of Canada's high arctic islands routinely fly to South America or western Europe to avoid frosty Canadian winters. • 'Turnstone' happens to be a perfect name for this bird, which uses its bill to flip over pebbles, shells and washed-up vegetation to expose hidden invertebrates. Its bill is short, stubby and slightly upturned, making it an ideal utensil for this unusual foraging style. Even with a specialized bill, however, the turnstone has a varied diet that may include the eggs of other birds.

♂

breeding

ID: white belly; black bib curves up to the shoulder; stout, black, slightly upturned bill; orange-red legs. *Breeding:* ruddy upperparts (female is slightly paler); white face; black collar; dark, streaky crown. *Non-breeding:* brownish upperparts and face.
Size: *L* 24 cm.
Status: rare to locally common migrant from late April to mid-June and from late July to early November; a few may remain in summer and early winter.
Habitat: shores of lakes, reservoirs, marshes and sewage lagoons; also in cultivated fields.

Nesting: does not nest in Ontario.
Feeding: probes under and flips rocks, weeds and shells for food items; picks, digs and probes for invertebrates from the soil or mud; also eats crabs, barnacles, berries, seeds, spiders and carrion.
Voice: low rattle; also a sharp *cut-a-cut* alarm call.
Similar Species: *Other shorebirds:* all lack the turnstone's bold patterning. *Plovers* (pp. 119–22): equally bold plumage but in significantly different patterns.
Best Sites: Point Pelee NP; Rondeau PP; Long Point PP; Presqu'ile PP.

133

RED KNOT

Calidris canutus

On the rich, dark fields that surround Lake Erie and Lake Ontario, small flocks of Red Knots appear for a brief period, usually around the last week of May. Never abundant in our province, these tubby, red-bellied knots are distinguished from the masses of migrating plovers and sandpipers by their reddish spring plumage. Along the shorelines and coastal wetlands of Hudson Bay and James Bay, huge flocks routinely gather to feed and rest before the long flight to overwintering areas on the Atlantic and Gulf coasts. • During the breeding season, their red plumage is a camouflage against a sea of arctic grasses and colourful wildflowers. In fall and winter, drab grey and white Red Knots are difficult to distinguish from other migrating and overwintering shorebirds, and they blend perfectly with the open sandy beaches that they inhabit at this time of year.

breeding

ID: chunky, round body; greenish legs. *Breeding:* rusty face, breast and underparts; brown, black and buff upperparts. *Non-breeding:* pale grey upperparts; white underparts with some faint streaking on the upper breast; faint barring on the rump; *Immature:* buffy wash on the breast; scaly-looking back. *In flight:* white wing stripe.
Size: *L* 27 cm.
Status: rare to fairly common migrant from late May to early June and from early August to early November; large numbers stage along the north coast.
Habitat: lakeshores, marshes and ploughed fields.
Nesting: does not nest in Ontario.

Feeding: gleans shorelines for insects, crustaceans and mollusks; probes soft substrates, creating lines of small holes.
Voice: melodious, soft *ker ek* in flight.
Similar Species: *Long-billed Dowitcher* (p. 148) and *Short-billed Dowitcher* (p. 147): much longer bills (at least 1$\frac{1}{2}$ times longer than the width of the head). *Buff-breasted Sandpiper* (p. 145): finer, shorter bill; dark flecking on the sides. *Other peeps:* smaller; most have black legs; only the Sanderling and Curlew Sandpiper show reddish colouration on the undersides in breeding plumage.
Best Sites: Oliphant waterfront; Presqu'ile PP; shorelines of the lower Great Lakes.

SANDERLING
Calidris alba

A stroll along the shores of Lake Erie or Lake Ontario is often punctuated by the sight of tiny Sanderlings running and playing in the waves. Their well-known habit of chasing waves has a simple purpose: to snatch washed-up aquatic invertebrates before the next wave rolls into shore. With a lack of crashing waves and coastal surf in Ontario, Sanderlings practise on smaller shores, often resorting to unenthusiastic probes into wet soil. When engaged in the rapid sprints of their beach-foraging strategy, Sanderlings move so fast on their dark legs that they appear to be gliding across the sand. When resting, Sanderlings often tuck one leg up to preserve body heat. • This sandpiper is one of the world's most widespread birds. It breeds across the Arctic in Alaska, Canada and Russia, and it spends winter running up and down sandy shorelines on every continent.

breeding

ID: straight, black bill; black legs. *Breeding:* dark spotting or mottling on the rusty head and breast. *Non-breeding:* white underparts; pale grey upperparts; black shoulder patch (often concealed).
Size: *L* 18–22 cm.
Status: fairly common migrant from early May to mid-June; fairly common to common from late July to mid-October; a few may remain through summer and into early winter.
Habitat: shores of lakes, marshes and reservoirs.
Nesting: does not nest in Ontario.
Feeding: gleans shorelines for insects, crustaceans and mollusks;

probes repeatedly, creating a line of small holes in the sand.
Voice: flight call is a sharp *kip*.
Similar Species: *Least Sandpiper* (p. 138): smaller and darker; yellowish legs; lacks the rufous breast in breeding plumage. *Dunlin* (p. 143): darker; slightly downcurved bill. *Red Knot* (p. 134): larger; grey-barred, whitish rump; breeding adult has a reddish belly. *Western Sandpiper* (p. 137) and *Semipalmated Sandpiper* (p. 136): lack the rufous breast in breeding plumage; sandy upperparts in non-breeding plumage.
Best Sites: Point Pelee NP; Rondeau PP; Long Point PP; Presqu'ile PP.

135

SEMIPALMATED SANDPIPER

Calidris pusilla

The small, plain Semipalmated Sandpiper can be difficult to identify among the swarms of similar-looking *Calidris* sandpipers that appear along the shores of the southern Great Lakes each spring. Known collectively as 'peeps,' because of the similiarity in their high-pitched calls, these strikingly similar miniatures, which include the Least, Western, White-rumped and Baird's sandpipers, can make shorebird identification either a complete nightmare or an uplifting challenge. • Each spring and fall, large numbers of 'Semis' touch down on Ontario shorelines, pecking and probing in mechanized fury to replenish their body fat for the remainder of their long journey. Semipalmated Sandpipers fly almost the entire length of the Americas during migration, so their staging sites must provide ample food sources.

breeding

ID: short, straight, black bill; black legs. *Breeding:* mottled upperparts; slight tinge of rufous on the ear patch, crown and scapulars; faint streaks on the upper breast and flanks. *Non-breeding:* white eyebrow; grey-brown upperparts; white underparts with a light brown wash on the sides of the upper breast. *In flight:* narrow, white wing stripe; white rump is split by a black line.
Size: *L* 14–18 cm.
Status: uncommon to common migrant from late April to mid-June; uncommon to abundant migrant from mid-July to early October; rare to locally fairly common breeder; a few may remain into November.
Habitat: *Breeding:* coastal tundra along Hudson Bay. *In migration:* mudflats and the shores of ponds and lakes.
Nesting: on a hummock or under a dwarf shrub; shallow depression in the ground is lined with grass, leaves and moss; pair incubates 4 darkly blotched, whitish to olive-buff eggs for about 20 days.
Feeding: probes soft substrates and gleans for aquatic insects and crustaceans.
Voice: flight call is a harsh *cherk*.
Similar Species: *Least Sandpiper* (p. 138): yellowish legs; darker upperparts. *Western Sandpiper* (p. 137): longer, slightly downcurved bill; bright rufous wash on the crown and ear patch. *Sanderling:* (p. 135): pale grey upperparts and a blackish trailing edge in the flight feathers in winter plumage. *White-rumped Sandpiper* (p. 139): larger; white rump; folded wings extend beyond the tail. *Baird's Sandpiper* (p. 140): larger; longer bill; folded wings extend beyond the tail.
Best Sites: Point Pelee NP; Long Point PP; Presqu'ile PP; Polar Bear PP.

WESTERN SANDPIPER

Calidris mauri

Most Western Sandpipers are seen only along the Pacific coast, but some adventurous individuals traverse the continent, often flying through Ontario to winter along the Atlantic. • Most identification guides will tell you to look for this bird's downcurved bill, and on paper this seems like a sensible plan. In the field, however, as angles and lighting change, the bills of peeps can look downcurved one moment, straight the next, and anything in between when double-checked. The only solution to this challenge is to spend some time getting to know the peeps before trying to identity them. A good strategy for meeting one of these rare shorebirds is to follow up on local sightings through Ontario's bird hotlines. Unless you are a particularly keen birder, there's no reason why you shouldn't let more experienced birders do most of the work for you!

breeding

ID: slightly downcurved, black bill; black legs. *Breeding:* rusty crown, ear patch and scapulars; V-shaped streaking on the upper breast and flanks; light underparts. *Non-breeding:* white eyebrow; grey-brown upperparts; white underparts; streaky, light brown wash on the upper breast. *In flight:* narrow, white wing stripe; a black line splits the white rump.
Size: *L* 15–18 cm.
Status: extremely rare to rare migrant in May and from mid-July to October.
Habitat: pond edges, lakeshores and mudflats.
Nesting: does not nest in Ontario.
Feeding: gleans and probes mud and shallow water; occasionally submerges its head; primarily eats aquatic insects, worms and crustaceans.
Voice: flight call is a high-pitched *cheep*.

Similar Species: *Semipalmated Sandpiper* (p. 136): shorter, straight bill; less rufous on the crown, ear patch and scapulars. *Least Sandpiper* (p. 138): smaller; yellowish legs; darker breast wash in all plumages; lacks the rufous patches. *White-rumped Sandpiper* (p. 139): larger; white rump; folded wings extend beyond the tail; lacks the rufous wing patches. *Baird's Sandpiper* (p. 140): larger; folded wings extend beyond the tail; lacks the rufous patches. *Dunlin* (p. 143): larger; black belly in breeding plumage; longer bill is thicker at the base and droops at the tip; greyer, unstreaked back in winter plumage. *Sanderling:* (p. 135): winter plumage shows pale grey upperparts, a blackish trailing edge of the flight feathers and a bold white upperwing stripe in flight.
Best Sites: check local bird hotlines for any recent sightings; shorelines of the lower Great Lakes.

LEAST SANDPIPER

Calidris minutilla

The Least Sandpiper is the smallest North American shorebird, but its size is not a deterrent to its migratory feats. Like most other 'peeps,' the Least Sandpiper migrates almost the entire length of the globe twice each year, from the Arctic to the southern tip of South America and back again. • Arctic summers are incredibly short, so shorebirds must maximize their breeding efforts. Least Sandpipers lay large eggs relative to other sandpipers, and when they nest, the entire clutch might weigh over half the weight of the female! The young hatch in an advanced state of development, getting an early start on preparations for the fall migration. These tiny shorebirds begin moving south as early as the first week of July, so they are some of the first migrants to arrive in southern Ontario. • Although light legs are a good field mark for this species, bad lighting or mud can confuse matters. Dark mud can make the legs look dark, while light mud can make them look light. • The genus name *Calidris* is a Greek word meaning 'a grey-speckled sandpiper.'

breeding

ID: black bill; yellowish legs; dark, mottled back; buff-brown breast, head and nape; light breast streaking. *Immature:* like the adult, but with a faintly streaked breast.
Size: *L* 13–17 cm.
Status: rare to common migrant from mid-April to early June and from early July to October; fairly common breeder; a few may remain into November.
Habitat: *Breeding:* coastal tundra, sedge or grass bogs and marshes. *In migration:* sandy beaches, lakeshores, ditches, sewage lagoons, mudflats and wetland edges.
Nesting: on a grassy or moss hummock surrounded by wet ground; in a shallow depression lined with grass, leaves and moss; pair incubates 4 brown-blotched, pale buff eggs.
Feeding: probes or pecks for insects, crustaceans, small mollusks and occasionally seeds.
Voice: high-pitched *kreee*.
Similar Species: *Semipalmated Sandpiper* (p. 136): black legs; lighter upperparts; tinge of rufous on the crown, ear patch and scapulars. *Western Sandpiper* (p. 137): slightly larger; black legs; lighter breast wash in all plumages; rufous patches on the crown, ear and scapulars in breeding plumage. *Other peeps:* all are larger; dark legs.
Best Sites: Point Pelee NP; Long Point PP; Presqu'ile PP; Polar Bear PP.

WHITE-RUMPED SANDPIPER

Calidris fuscicollis

When a die-hard shorebird watcher is about to go into a peep-induced stupor, one of the birds suddenly takes wing and flashes its pure white rump. Oh happy day! There is no doubt that the beautiful White-rumped Sandpiper has been identified. • The white rump on this bird might serve the same purpose as the tail of a White-tailed Deer—to alert other birds when danger threatens. • When flocks of White-rumps and other sandpipers take to the air, they often defecate in unison. This nervous evacuation might benefit the birds by reducing their weight for takeoff. Flocks of White-rumped Sandpipers have also been known to collectively rush at a predator and then suddenly scatter in its face. • The scientific name *fuscicollis* means 'brown neck,' a characteristic that this bird shares with many of its close relatives.

breeding

ID: black legs; black bill (about as long as the head width); brown-mottled upperparts; dark streaking on the breast, sides and flanks. *In flight:* white rump.
Size: *L* 18–20 cm.
Status: uncommon to common migrant from late May to mid-June and from mid-August to early November; a few may be present in summer.
Habitat: shores of lakes, marshes, sewage lagoons and reservoirs; flooded and cultivated fields.

Nesting: does not nest in Ontario.
Feeding: gleans the ground and shorelines for insects, crustaceans and mollusks.
Voice: flight call is a characteristic, squeal-like *tzeet.*
Similar Species: *Other peeps:* all have a dark line through the rump. *Baird's Sandpiper* (p. 140): lacks the clean white rump; breast streaking does not extend onto the flanks. *Stilt Sandpiper* (p. 144) and *Curlew Sandpiper* (p. 356): much longer legs trail beyond the tail in flight.
Best Sites: Presqu'ile PP.

BAIRD'S SANDPIPER

Calidris bairdii

Like its *Calidris* relatives, this modest-looking shorebird has extraordinary migratory habits—it flies twice annually between South America and the Arctic. In Ontario, there are typically less than four sightings of this bird in spring; in August and September, small numbers appear along the sandy beaches of the Great Lakes. • Like many shorebirds, the Baird's Sandpiper remains on its northern breeding grounds for only a short time. Soon after the chicks hatch and are able to fend for themselves, the adults flock together to begin their southward migration. After a few weeks of accumulating fat reserves, the young gather in a second wave of southbound migrants. Most move from their nesting areas through the centre of the continent, and the few strays that appear in Ontario are usually juvenile birds. • Spencer Fullerton Baird, an early director of the Smithsonian Institute, organized several natural history expeditions across North America. Elliott Coues named this bird in recognition of Baird's efforts.

breeding

ID: black legs and bill; faint, buff-brown breast speckling; large, black, diamond-like patterns on the back and wing covers; folded wings extend beyond the tail.
Size: *L* 18–19 cm.
Status: extremely rare migrant in mid-May; rare to locally uncommon migrant from mid-July to mid-October.
Habitat: sandy beaches, mudflats and wetland edges.
Nesting: does not nest in Ontario.
Feeding: gleans aquatic invertebrates; also eats beetles and grasshoppers; rarely probes.

Voice: soft, rolling *kriit kriit.*
Similar Species: *White-rumped Sandpiper* (p. 139): clean white rump; breast streaking extends onto the flanks. *Pectoral Sandpiper* (p. 141): dark breast ends abruptly at the edge of the white belly. *Least Sandpiper* (p. 138): smaller; yellowish legs. *Western Sandpiper* (p. 137) and *Sanderling* (p. 135): lack the streaked grey-buff breast. *Semipalmated Sandpiper* (p. 136): smaller; shorter bill; lacks the streaked breast in non-breeding plumage.
Best Sites: Great Lakes shorelines.

PECTORAL SANDPIPER

Calidris melanotos

This widespread traveller has been observed in every state and province in North America during its epic, annual migrations. In spring and fall, Pectoral Sandpipers are conspicuous along the shores of the lower Great Lakes and in wet, grassy fields, often in large flocks of over 1000 birds. In Ontario, peak numbers occur from late August to late October. • Although a Pectoral nest has not yet been discovered in Ontario, observations of fledgling young at Cape Henrietta Maria in Polar Bear Provincial Park imply that this shorebird has probably bred here. • Unlike most sandpipers, the Pectoral exhibits sexual dimorphism—the females are only two-thirds the size of the male. • When agitated, the male will inflate the air sacs in his neck, causing his feathers to rise. If threatened, flocks of Pectorals will suddenly launch into the air and converge into a single, swirling mass.

breeding

ID: brown breast streaks end abruptly at the edge of the white belly; white undertail coverts; black bill with a slightly downcurved tip; long, yellow legs; mottled upperparts; may have a faintly rusty dark crown and back; folded wings extend beyond the tail. *Juvenile:* less spotting on the breast; broader, white feather edges on the back form 2 white Vs.
Size: *L* 20–24 cm (female is slightly smaller).
Status: fairly common migrant from mid-April to early May; rare to common migrant from late July to mid-November; exceptionally rare breeder.
Habitat: *Breeding:* coastal tundra. *In migration:* along lakeshores,

marshes, mudflats and flooded fields.
Nesting: on flat, wet tundra with low shrub or grass-sedge cover; female makes a cup-shaped lining of grass and leaves in a shallow depression and incubates 4 brown-blotched, whitish to olive-buff eggs for 21–23 days.
Feeding: probes and pecks for small insects (mainly flies, but also beetles and some grasshoppers); may also take small mollusks, amphipods, berries, seeds, moss, algae and some plant material.
Voice: sharp, short, low *krrick krrick*.
Similar Species: *Other peeps:* all lack the well-defined, dark bib and yellow legs.
Best Sites: Point Pelee NP; Rondeau PP; Long Point PP; Presqu'ile PP; Polar Bear PP.

PURPLE SANDPIPER

Calidris maritima

While gazing at the frothing waters and icy spray of the Niagara River you might spot some ghostly, grey-hooded birds among the mist. Unlike most shorebirds, which prefer shallow marshy areas, sand beaches or mudflats, Purple Sandpipers are content to forage perilously close to crashing waves along rocky headlands, piers and breakwaters. They expertly navigate their way across rugged, slippery rocks while foraging for crustaceans, mollusks and insect larvae. • Purple Sandpipers winter along the Atlantic coast and breed on high arctic islands, so few are observed in Ontario each year. These birds have not been documented breeding in our province, but it is thought that some birds might be tempted to nest on the rocky ridges of Cape Henrietta Maria. • The name 'purple' was given to this sandpiper for a purplish iridescence that is occasionally observed on its shoulders.

breeding

ID: long, slightly drooping, black-tipped bill with an orange-yellow base; orange-yellow legs; dull streaking on the breast and flanks. *Breeding:* streaked neck; buff crown with dark streaks; dark back feathers with tawny to rusty-brown edges. *Non-breeding:* unstreaked, grey head, neck and upper breast form a hood; grey spots on the white belly.
Size: *L* 23 cm.
Status: extremely rare migrant from mid-May to early June; rare visitor from mid-October to February.
Habitat: sandy beaches, rocky shorelines, piers and breakwaters.
Nesting: not confirmed in Ontario.
Feeding: food is found visually and is snatched while moving over rocks and sand; eats mostly mollusks, insects, crustaceans and other invertebrates; also eats a variety of plant material.
Voice: call is a soft *prrt-prrt*.
Similar Species: *Other peeps:* all lack the unstreaked, grey hood in winter, the bicoloured bill and the yellow-orange legs.
Best Sites: Erieau pier; Presqu'ile PP; Niagara Falls.

DUNLIN

Calidris alpina

A visit to Point Pelee National Park or Presqu'ile Provincial Park in spring or fall is sure to reveal the extraordinary flocking behaviour of this droopy-billed shore-bird. Outside the breeding season, Dunlins form dynamic, synchronous flocks, and sometimes hundreds of these birds are seen flying wing tip to wing tip. In preparation for fall migration, tens of thousands gather on our northern coast to fatten before the long migratory flight out of the province. Once they take to the air, most pass through without even stopping. • Dunlins are fairly distinct in their breeding attire: their black bellies and legs make them look as though they have been wading belly-deep in puddles of ink. • This bird was originally called the 'Dunling' (meaning 'a small brown bird'), but with the passage of time, the 'g' was dropped.

breeding

ID: slightly downcurved, black bill; black legs. *Breeding:* black belly; streaked white neck and underparts; rusty wings, back and crown. *Non-breeding:* pale grey underparts; brownish-grey upperparts; light brown streaking on the breast and nape. *In flight:* white wing stripe.
Size: *L* 19–23 cm.
Status: rare to abundant migrant from mid-April to late June and from mid-July to November; rare to locally fairly common breeder.
Habitat: *Breeding:* coastal tundra. *In migration:* mudflats and the shores of ponds, marshes and lakes.
Nesting: on tundra; well hidden beneath grass or in a hummock; female chooses one of several shallow scrapes made by the male and lines it with leaves and grass; pair incubates 4 buff to blue-green eggs for 20–23 days.
Feeding: gleans and probes mudflats for aquatic crustaceans, worms, mollusks and insects.
Voice: flight call is a grating *cheezp* or *treezp*.
Similar Species: black belly in breeding plumage is distinctive. *Western Sandpiper* (p. 137) and *Semipalmated Sandpiper* (p. 136): smaller; non-breeding plumage is browner overall; bill tips are less downcurved. *Least Sandpiper* (p. 138): smaller; darker upperparts; yellowish legs. *Sanderling* (p. 135): paler; straight bill; usually seen running in the surf.
Best Sites: Point Pelee NP; Long Point PP; Presqu'ile PP; Polar Bear PP.

143

STILT SANDPIPER

Calidris himantopus

With the silhouette of a small Lesser Yellowlegs and the foraging behaviour of a dowitcher, the Stilt Sandpiper is easily overlooked by birders. Named for its relatively long legs, this shorebird prefers to feed in shallow water, where it digs like a dowitcher, often dunking its head completely underwater. Moving on tall 'stilts,' this sandpiper will also wade into deep water up to its breast in search of a meal. Stilt Sandpipers are omnivores, eating everything from insects to roots and seeds. To snag freshwater shrimp, insect larvae or tiny minnows from just below the water's surface, they may occasionally sweep their bills from side to side like an avocet. • Stilt Sandpipers never gather in large flocks as do many of their *Calidris* relatives. At the most, you may see a gathering of 50 or so at Point Pelee or Presqu'ile's marshes, usually between mid-August and the end of September.

breeding

ID: long, greenish legs; long bill droops slightly at the end. *Breeding:* chestnut red ear patch; white eyebrow; striped crown; streaked neck; barred underparts. *Non-breeding:* less conspicuous white eyebrow; dirty white neck and breast; white belly; dark brownish-grey upperparts. *In flight:* white rump; legs trail behind the tail; no wing stripe.
Size: *L* 20–23 cm.
Status: rare migrant in May; rare to uncommon migrant from late July to late October; uncommon breeder.
Habitat: *Breeding:* coastal tundra. *In migration:* shores of lakes, reservoirs and marshes.
Nesting: on a dry hummock or raised ground, usually surrounded by wet tundra; female chooses one of several shallow scrapes

made by the male; little or no nest lining is used; pair incubates 4 brown-dotted, pale cream to olive eggs for 19–21 days.
Feeding: probes deeply in shallow water; eats mostly invertebrates; occasionally picks insects from the water's surface or the ground; also eats seeds, roots and leaves.
Voice: simple, low-pitched *whu, querp* or a trilled *kirr* given in flight.
Similar Species: *Yellowlegs* (pp. 124–25): yellow legs; lack the red ear patch. *Curlew Sandpiper* (p. 356): bill has a more obvious curve; black legs; paler grey upperparts in non-breeding plumage.
Best Sites: Point Pelee NP; Presqu'ile PP; shallow marshes along the lower Great Lakes; Polar Bear PP.

BUFF-BREASTED SANDPIPER

Tryngites subruficollis

Shy in behaviour and humble in appearance, the Buff-breasted Sandpiper is a shorebird that many birders in Ontario hope to meet. This rare migrant is most regular and common along the north coast, but even there it is found in small numbers. Most sightings occur in early fall in the extreme southwestern parts of the province—Point Pelee, in particular, has proven to be the most reliable location for observing the Buff-breasted Sandpiper. Because most Buff-breasts migrate through the centre of the continent, the individuals that we see in Ontario are mainly dispersing juveniles heading south for winter. • Buff-breasted Sandpipers are often discovered in the course of scanning flocks of foraging Black-bellied Plovers and American Golden-Plovers. When feeding, these subtly coloured birds stand motionless, blending beautifully into a backdrop of furrowed cultivated fields, mudflats or grassy pastures, becoming visible only when they move.

breeding

ID: buffy, unpatterned face and foreneck; large, dark eyes; very thin, straight, black bill; buff underparts; small spots on the crown, hindneck, breast, sides and flanks; 'scaled' look to the back and upperwings; yellow legs. *In flight:* pure white underwings; no wing stripe.
Size: *L* 19–21 cm.
Status: extremely rare migrant from mid-May to mid-June; rare migrant from mid-August to late September.
Habitat: shores of lakes, reservoirs and marshes; also in cultivated and flooded fields.
Nesting: does not nest in Ontario.
Feeding: gleans the ground and shorelines for insects, spiders and small crustaceans; might eat some seeds.
Similar Species: *Upland Sandpiper* (p. 129): more boldly streaked on the breast; longer neck; smaller head; larger bill; streaking on the cheek and foreneck.
Best Sites: Sarnia's Hiawatha Race Track; the onion fields north of Point Pelee NP and Presqu'ile PP.

RUFF/REEVE

Philomachus pugnax

Sewage lagoons in the southern parts of the province seem to be the hotspots for Ruff sightings. In spring, males are particularly unmistakeable with their prominent neck and 'ear' ruffs. On average, there are about five official sightings of this Eurasian vagrant each year, usually during May. • The male of this species is called a 'Ruff,' while the female is known as a 'Reeve.' It is not known whether the male was named for his neck-feather ruffs, or if ruffs were named after the bird. 'Reeve' has even more obscure origins, but some suggest it is linked to the meaning 'observer' or 'bailiff'— the females oversee the tussling males, which, like Sharp-tailed Grouse, gather together in leks on their breeding grounds where they attempt to attract females through elaborate courtship posturing. • The scientific name *pugnax* means 'pugnacious,' which is an appropriate description of the courting males.

black morph breeding

ID: plump body; small head; yellow-green to red legs; yellow or black bill; brown-grey upperparts. *Breeding male:* black, white or orangey neck ruff, usually flattened, but erected during courtship; dark underparts. *Breeding female:* dark blotches on the underparts. *In flight:* thin, white wing stripe; oval, white rump divided by a dark central stripe.
Size: *Male: L* 26–31 cm. *Female: L* 22–25 cm.
Status: rare vagrant from April to September.
Habitat: shallow marshes and wetlands, flooded fields, mud-flats and sewage lagoons.

Nesting: not known to nest in Ontario.
Feeding: probes and picks at the surface of mudflats for aquatic invertebrates.
Voice: rarely vocal in Ontario; call is a short *tu-whit.*
Similar Species: *Yellowlegs* (pp. 124–25): slimmer bodies; longer legs; streaked underparts. *Red Knot* (p. 134): shorter legs; 'cleaner' breast in non-breeding plumage.
Best Sites: check local bird hotlines for any recent sightings; Point Pelee NP; Presqu'ile PP; sewage lagoons in Casselman, Alfred and Winchester.

VAGRANT

SHORT-BILLED DOWITCHER

Limnodromus griseus

Long before Ontario's deciduous trees burst into brilliant fall colours, Short-billed Dowitchers arrive from northern locales on the mudflats, marshes and beaches of the lower Great Lakes region. Short-bills are seen in good numbers during the spring migration, but these plump shorebirds are usually seen in the largest concentrations during the protracted fall migration. • Dowitchers tend to be stockier than most shorebirds, and they generally avoid venturing into deep water. While foraging along shorelines, these birds 'stitch' up and down into the mud with a sewing machine–like rhythm. Their performance is not only fascinating to watch, but this behaviour is helpful for long-range field identification. • Distinguishing between the Short-billed and Long-billed dowitcher is a difficult task for any birder, especially in Ontario, where two distinct subspecies of Short-billed Dowitcher, the *griseus* and *hendersoni*, occur together in the same habitats.

breeding

ID: straight, long, dark bill; white eyebrow; chunky body; yellow-green legs. *Breeding:* white belly; dark spotting on the reddish-buff neck and upper breast; prominent dark barring on the white sides and flanks. *Hendersoni ssp:* lighter back; more spots than bars on the underparts. *Non-breeding:* dirty grey upperparts; dirty white underparts. *In flight:* white wedge on the rump and lower back.
Size: L 28–30 cm.
Status: common migrant from mid-May to early June and from mid-July to early October; rare to uncommon breeder.
Habitat: *Breeding:* muskeg ponds and fens and coastal tundra. *In migration:* shores of lakes, reservoirs and marshes.
Nesting: near a muskeg pond or fen; in a shallow depression lined with twigs and vegetation; pair incubates 4 darkly marked, brown to olive-buff eggs for about 21 days; young leave the nest within days of hatching.
Feeding: aquatic invertebrates, including insects, mollusks, crustaceans and worms; may feed on seeds, aquatic plants and grasses; wades in shallow water or on mud, probing deeply into the substrate with a rapid drilling motion.
Voice: generally silent; flight call is a mellow, repeated *tututu, toodulu* or *toodu*.
Similar Species: *Long-billed Dowitcher* (p. 148): black and white barring on the red flanks in breeding plumage; very little white on the belly; dark spotting on the neck and upper breast; alarm call is a high-pitched *keek*. *Red Knot* (p. 134): much shorter bill; unmarked, red breast in breeding plumage; winter birds lack the barring on the tail and the white wedge on the back in flight. *Common Snipe* (p. 149): heavy streaking on the neck and breast; bicoloured bill; light median stripe on the crown; shorter legs. *American Woodcock* (p. 150): unmarked, buff underparts; yellow bill; light bars on the black crown and hindneck.
Best Sites: Point Pelee NP; Long Point PP; Presqu'ile PP; Polar Bear PP.

147

LONG-BILLED DOWITCHER
Limnodromus scolopaceus

Each spring and fall, Ontario mudflats and marshes host small numbers of enthusiastic Long-billed Dowitchers. These chunky, sword-billed shorebirds diligently forage up and down through shallow water and mud in a quest for invertebrate sustenance. A diet of insects, freshwater shrimp, mussels, clams and snails provides migrating birds with plenty of fuel for flight and essential calcium for bone and egg development. • In Ontario, migrating Long-bills are outnumbered by their close relative, the almost identical Short-billed Dowitcher. They are often seen together, and attention to their distinct calls and details in plumage will eventually enable you to distinguish between the two. • Dowitchers have shorter wings than most long-distance migrant shorebirds, making it more practical for them to take flight from shallow water. • Mixed flocks of shorebirds demonstrate a variety of foraging styles: some species probe deeply, while others pick at the water's surface or glean the shorelines. It is thought that large numbers of shorebird species are able to coexist because of their different foraging styles and specialized diets.

breeding

ID: very long, straight, dark bill; dark eye line; white eyebrow; chunky body; yellow-green legs. *Breeding:* black and white barring on the reddish underparts; some white on the belly; dark, mottled upperparts. *Non-breeding:* grey overall; dirty white underparts. *In flight:* white wedge on the rump and lower back.
Size: L 28–32 cm.
Status: very rare migrant in May and from mid-July to late November.
Habitat: lakeshores, shallow marshes and mudflats.
Nesting: does not nest in Ontario.
Feeding: probes in shallow water and mudflats with a repeated up-down motion of the bill; frequently plunges its head below the water; eats shrimps, snails, worms, larval flies and other soft-bodied invertebrates.
Voice: alarm call is a loud, high-pitched *keek*, occasionally given in series.
Similar Species: *Short-billed Dowitcher* (p. 147): white sides, flanks and belly; more spots than bars on the reddish sides and flanks; brighter feather edges on the upperparts; call is a lower-pitched *toodu* or *tututu*. *Red Knot* (p. 134): much shorter bill; unmarked, red breast in breeding plumage; winter birds lack the barring on the tail and the white wedge on the back in flight. *Common Snipe* (p. 149): shorter legs; heavy streaking on the neck and breast; bicoloured bill; light median stripe on the crown. *American Woodcock* (p. 150): unmarked, buff underparts; yellow bill; light bars on the black crown and hindneck.
Best Sites: Presqu'ile PP.

COMMON SNIPE

Gallinago gallinago

Visit almost any open Ontario wetland in spring or early summer and you will hear the eerie, hollow winnowing sound of courting Common Snipes. Their specialized outer tail feathers vibrate rapidly in the air as they perform daring, headfirst dives high above their marshland habitat. Snipes display most actively in the early morning, but evening performances are not uncommon. • Outside the courtship season, this well-camouflaged bird enters its shy and secretive mode, remaining concealed in vegetation. Only when an intruder approaches too closely will a snipe flush from cover, performing a series of aerial zig-zags—an evasive maneuver designed to confuse predators. Because of this habit, hunters that were skilled enough to shoot a snipe came to be known as 'snipers'—a term later adopted by the military.

ID: long, sturdy, bicoloured bill; relatively short legs; heavily striped head, back, neck and breast; dark eye stripe; dark barring on the sides and flanks; unmarked white belly. *In flight:* quick zig-zags as it takes off.
Size: *L* 27–29 cm.
Status: fairly common to common from April to mid-November; a few may overwinter near open water.
Habitat: cattail and bulrush marshes, sedge meadows, poorly drained floodplains, bogs, fens; willow and red osier dogwood tangles.
Nesting: usually in dry grass, often under vegetation; nest is made of grass, moss and leaves; female incubates 4 olive-buff to brown eggs, marked with dark brown, for about 20 days; both parents raise the young, often splitting the brood.
Feeding: probes soft substrates for larvae, earthworms and other soft-bodied invertebrates; also eats mollusks, crustaceans, spiders, small amphibians and some seeds.
Voice: eerie, accelerating courtship song is produced in flight: *woo-woo-woo-woo-woo-woo*; often sings *wheat wheat wheat* from an elevated perch; alarm call is a nasal *scaip*.
Similar Species: *Dowitchers* (pp. 147–48): lack the heavy striping on the head, back, neck and breast; longer legs; all-dark bills; usually seen in flocks. *Marbled Godwit* (p. 132): much larger; slightly upturned bill; much longer legs. *American Woodcock* (p. 150): unmarked buff underparts; yellowish bill; light bars on the black crown and hindneck.
Best Sites: Long Point PP; Luther Marsh; Oliphant waterfront marshes; Lynde Shores Conservation Area; Presqu'ile PP; Charleston Lake PP; Algonquin PP; Mission Island Marsh.

AMERICAN WOODCOCK

Scolopax minor

The American Woodcock's behaviour usually mirrors its cryptic and inconspic-uous attire. This denizen of moist woodlands and damp thickets usually goes about its business in a quiet and reclusive manner, but during courtship the male woodcock reveals his true character. Just before dawn or just after sunset, a male will strut provocatively in an open woodland clearing or a brushy, abandoned field, while calling out a series of loud *peeent* notes. He twitters through the air in a circular flight display, and then, with wings partly folded, he plummets to the ground in the zig-zag pattern of a falling leaf. • This secretive bird has endured many changes to its traditional Ontario nesting grounds. The clearing of forests and draining of woodland swamps has degraded and eliminated large tracts of productive woodcock habitat. The woodcock, therefore, is no longer as abundant in Ontario as it used to be.

ID: very long, sturdy bill; very short legs; large head; short neck; chunky body; large, dark eyes; unmarked, buff underparts; light-coloured bars on the black crown and hindneck. *In flight:* rounded wings; makes a twittering sound when flushed from cover.
Size: *L* 27–29 cm.
Status: fairly common to common breeder from March to early November; a few may overwinter near open water.
Habitat: moist woodlands and brushy thickets adjacent to grassy clearings or abandoned fields.
Nesting: on the ground in woods or overgrown fields; female builds a scrape lined with dead leaves and other debris; female incu-bates 4 brown and grey blotched,

pinkish-buff eggs for 20–22 days; female tends the young.
Feeding: probes in soft, moist or wet soil for earthworms and insect larvae; also takes spiders, snails, millipedes and some plant material, including seeds, sedges and grasses.
Voice: nasal *peent*; during courtship dance produces high-pitched, twittering, whistling sounds.
Similar Species: *Common Snipe* (p. 149): heavily striped head, back, neck and breast; dark barring on the sides and flanks. *Dowitchers* (pp. 147–48): all-dark bills; longer legs; lack the light-coloured barring on the dark crown and hindneck; usually seen in flocks.
Best Sites: swampy woodland edges with open, scrubby fields.

WILSON'S PHALAROPE

Phalaropus tricolor

Not only are phalaropes among the most colourful of shorebirds, they are also among the most unusual. Phalaropes practise an uncommon mating strategy known as polyandry in which each female mates with several males. After laying a clutch, the female often abandons her mate, leaving him to incubate the eggs and tend the precocial young. This reversal of gender roles also includes a reversal of plumage characteristics—females are more brightly coloured than their male counterparts. Even John James Audubon was fooled by the phalarope's strange breeding habits and unique colouration: he mislabeled the male and female birds in all his phalarope illustrations. • The Wilson's Phalarope is the only member of the phalarope clan that breeds in southern Ontario.

breeding

ID: dark, needle-like bill; white eyebrow, throat and nape; light underparts; black legs. *Breeding female:* very sharp colours; grey cap; chestnut sides of the neck; black eye line extends down the side of the neck and onto the back. *Breeding male:* duller overall; dark cap. *Non-breeding:* all-grey upperparts; white eyebrow and grey eye line; white underparts; dark yellowish or greenish legs.
Size: *L* 22–24 cm.
Status: rare to uncommon migrant from mid-May to mid-June and from mid-July to October; rare breeder from late May through July.
Habitat: *Breeding:* freshwater coastal marshes, cattail marshes and grass or sedge margins of sewage lagoons. *In migration:* lakeshores, marshes and sewage lagoons.
Nesting: often near water; in a depression lined with grass and other vegetation; nest is often well concealed; male incubates 4 brown-blotched, buff eggs for 18–27 days; male rears the young.

Feeding: whirls in tight circles in shallow or deep water to stir up prey from the substrate, then picks aquatic insects, worms and small crustaceans from the water's surface or just below it; makes short jabs on land to pick up invertebrates in open areas.
Voice: deep, grunting *work work* or *wu wu wu*, usually given on the breeding grounds.
Similar Species: *Red-necked Phalarope* (p. 152): rufous stripe down the side of the neck in breeding plumage; dark nape and line behind the eye in winter. *Red Phalarope* (p. 153): all-reddish neck, breast and underparts in breeding plumage; dark nape and a broad, dark line behind the eye in winter; rarely seen inland. *Lesser Yellowlegs* (p. 125): larger; yellow legs; streaked neck; mottled upperparts.
Best Sites: Luther Marsh; Amherst Island; Sudbury's Kelly Lake; sewage lagoons in Blenheim, Port Perry, St. Isidore de Prescott, Casselman, Alfred and Winchester; Rainy River sewage lagoon.

151

RED-NECKED PHALAROPE

Phalaropus lobatus

A birdwatching pilgrimage to a local sewage lagoon may not be your idea of an aesthically pleasing birding experience, but these areas are often the best places to meet many species of birds, including the Red-necked Phalarope. • Most Red-necked Phalaropes migrate to and from their arctic wintering grounds via the Atlantic coast, but every year small flocks of these tiny shorebirds take the inland route across Ontario. • When foraging on the water with other shorebirds, members of the phalarope clan can usually be singled out—phalaropes spin and whirl about in tight circles, stirring up tiny crustaceans, mollusks and other aquatic invertebrates. As prey funnels toward the water's surface, these birds daintily pluck them with their needle-like bills. • 'Phalarope' is the Greek word for 'coot's foot.' Like coots and grebes, phalaropes have individually webbed, or 'lobed,' toes, a feature that makes them proficient swimmers.

breeding

ID: thin, black bill; long, black legs. *Breeding female:* chestnut stripe on the neck and throat; white chin; blue-black head; incomplete, white eye ring; white belly; 2 rusty-buff stripes on each upperwing. *Breeding male:* white eyebrow; less intense colours than the female. *Non-breeding:* white underparts; black cap; broad, dark band from the eye to the ear; whitish stripes on the blue-grey upperparts.

Size: *L* 18 cm.

Status: very rare migrant from mid-April to early June and from late June to mid-November; rare to locally common breeder from June to September.

Habitat: *Breeding:* coastal tundra and freshwater coastal marshes. *In migration:* open waterbodies, including ponds, lakes, marshes and sewage lagoons.

Nesting: often near water; pair builds a scrape on a hummock lined with grass and lichens; male incubates 4 buff to olive, brown-blotched eggs for 17–21 days; male tends the precocial young.

Feeding: whirls in tight circles in shallow or deep water, picking insects, small crustaceans and small mollusks from the water; on land, makes short jabs to pick up insects.

Voice: often noisy in migration; soft *krit krit krit.*

Similar Species: *Wilson's Phalarope* (p. 151): female has a grey cap and a black eye line extending down the side of the neck and onto the back in breeding plumage. *Red Phalarope* (p. 153): all-red neck, breast and undersides in breeding plumage; lacks the white stripes on the upperwing in non-breeding plumage.

Best Sites: Dundas Marsh; Presqu'ile PP; municipal sewage lagoons; Polar Bear PP.

RED PHALAROPE

Phalaropus fulicaria

The Red Phalarope passes through Ontario in small numbers during its annual fall migration toward the Atlantic coast. Its dull wardrobe at this time of year does little to make it stand out among its more prevalent, similar-looking relative, the Red-necked Phalarope. Still, the Red Phalarope's heavier bill, larger size and plain blue-grey upperwings usually provide sufficient clues for sharp-eyed birders to distinguish between these two species in the field • While incubating the eggs, male phalaropes shed feathers on their abdomen and develop thick skin, which becomes swollen with blood. This 'brood patch' provides the required temperature for incubation and is a feature that usually develops in females of other species. • Phalaropes are the most aquatic of the shorebirds. They spend most of the non-breeding season floating on open ocean waters and feeding on plankton, small fish, jellyfish and crustaceans.

breeding

ID: *Breeding female:* chestnut red throat, neck and underparts; white face; black crown and forehead; black-tipped, yellow bill. *Breeding male:* mottled brown crown; duller face and underparts. *Non-breeding adult:* white head, neck and underparts; blue-grey upperparts; mostly dark bill; black nape; broad, dark patch extending from the eye to the ear. *Juvenile:* like the non-breeding adult, but is buff-coloured overall; dark streaking on the upperparts.
Size: *L* 21.5 cm.
Status: very rare migrant from late August to November.
Habitat: lakes, large wetlands and sewage lagoons.
Nesting: does not nest in Ontario.

Feeding: small crustaceans, mollusks, insects and other invertebrates; rarely takes vegetation or small fish; gleans from the water's surface, usually while swimming in tight, spinning circles.
Voice: calls include a shrill, high-pitched *wit* or *creep* and a low *clink clink.*
Similar Species: *Red-necked Phalarope* (p.152): smaller; thinner bill; breeding birds lack the all-red underparts; non-breeding birds have pale white stripes on the upperwing. *Wilson's Phalarope* (p. 151): breeding birds lack the all-red underparts; non-breeding birds lack the dark mask.
Best Sites: Erieau pier; Lake Ontario west of Toronto; Presqu'ile PP; municipal sewage lagoons.

153

POMARINE JAEGER

Stercorarius pomarinus

Jaegers are powerful, swift predators and notorious pirates of vast open oceans that seem to be forged from the moulds of gulls, terns and hawks. Most of their lives are spent in the air—they occasionally rest on the ocean surface—and they only seek the solid footing of land during the nesting season. • Fall and early winter appear to be the best seasons for observing the small number of Pomarine Jaegers that make regular appearances in Ontario. Keen fall birders patrolling piers or beaches along the Great Lakes shorelines probably have the best chance of meeting these migrant birds. • Novice birders often differentiate the three jaeger species based on the shape and length of their central tail feathers. This comparison seems to be an easy task, except that it only applies to adult jaegers. Knowing the subtleties of plumage, wingbeat rhythm and wing breadth is most important in making an accurate identification.

light morph breeding

dark morph breeding

ID: long, twisted tail streamers; black cap. *In flight:* wings are wide at the base of the body; powerful, steady wingbeats; white flash at the base of the underwing primaries. *Light morph:* dark, mottled breast band, sides and flanks; dark belly. *Dark morph:* dark body except for the white in the wing. *Juvenile:* central tail feathers extend just past the tail; white at the base of the upperwing primaries; variable dark barring on the underwings and underparts; lacks the black cap.
Size: *L* 51–58 cm; *W* 1.2 m.
Status: rare migrant from late August to early January; exceptionally rare in spring.
Habitat: open ocean; shorelines of large lakes and rivers.
Nesting: does not nest in Ontario.
Feeding: snatches fish from the ocean surface while in flight; chases down small birds; may also take small mammals and nestlings;

pirates food from gulls; may scavenge at landfills.
Voice: generally silent; may give a sharp *which-yew*, a squealing *weak-weak* or a squeaky whistled note during migration.
Similar Species: *Parasitic Jaeger* (p. 155): thin, pointed tail streamers; lacks the mottled sides and flanks; very little white on the upperwing primaries; immature and subadult have barred underparts. *Long-tailed Jaeger* (p. 156): very long, thin pointed tail streamers; very little white on the upperwing primaries; lacks the white on the base of the underwing primaries; lacks the very dark vent and the dark, mottled breast band, sides and flanks; juvenile has stubby, spoon-shaped tail streamers and solid dark markings on the throat and upper breast.
Best Sites: Sarnia waterfront; Van Wagner's Beach; Spenser Smith Park; Sibbald Point PP; Polar Bear PP.

PARASITIC JAEGER

Stercorarius parasiticus

Although 'jaeger' is a German word for 'hunter,' 'parasitic' more aptly describes this bird's foraging tactics. 'Kleptoparasitism' is the scientific term for the jaeger's pirating ways, and these birds are truly relentless. Parasitic Jaegers harass and intimidate terns and gulls until they regurgitate their partially digested meal. As soon as the food is ejected, these aerial pirates snatch it out of mid-air or pick it from the water's surface in a swooping dive. • When nesting, adult Parasitic Jaegers are extremely aggressive in defence of their eggs and young. Both adults often attack approaching danger in stooping, parabolic dives or aggressive, blazing pursuits. In such scenarios, the intruders are forced into a rapid retreat, often assessing how many feathers or how much hair has been lost! • The Parasitic Jaeger is the most numerous jaeger in the world and the most commonly seen in Ontario.

light morph breeding

ID: long, pointed, dark wings; slightly projecting, pointed tail streamers; brown upperparts; dark cap; light underwing tips. *Light morph:* white underparts; white to cream-coloured collar; light brown neck band. *Dark morph:* all-brown underparts and collar. *Juvenile:* barred underparts; central tail feather extends just past the tail.
Size: *L* 38–53 cm; *W* 91 cm.
Status: exceptionally rare migrant from early May to early June; rare migrant from August to mid-November (may appear as early late July and remain as late as January or February); rare to uncommon breeder.
Habitat: *Breeding:* coastal tundra. *In migration:* shorelines of large lakes and rivers, gravelbars, landfills and open water.
Nesting: in a shallow depression on tundra; lined sparsely with vegetation; pair incubates 2 brown-spotted,

olive to brown eggs for 25–28 days; first breeds at 4–5 years of age.
Feeding: pirates, scavenges and hunts for food; fish, eggs, large insects and small birds and mammals are taken; takes carrion and some berries while on land; often pirates food from other birds and scavenges at landfills.
Voice: generally silent; may make shrill calls while migrating or on nesting grounds.
Similar Species: *Pomarine Jaeger* (p. 154): adult has shorter, blunt and twisted tail streamers; dark mottled sides and flanks; white on the upperwing primaries. *Long-tailed Jaeger* (p. 156): much smaller; adult has much longer, pointed tail streamers; lacks the dark neck band.
Best Sites: Sarnia waterfront; Van Wagner's Beach; Spenser Smith Park; Sibbald Point PP; Hurkett Cove Conservation Area; municipal landfill sites; Polar Bear PP.

LONG-TAILED JAEGER

Stercorarius longicaudus

The graceful, buoyant flight of the Long-tailed Jaeger is a rare sight in Ontario. This jaeger may be a regular migrant along the coast of Hudson and James bays, but its presence there is not easily confirmed owing to the region's inaccessiblity to human observers. Most sightings are reported along the shores of Lake Erie and Lake Ontario in September and October. • While on their arctic nesting grounds, Long-tailed Jaegers prey heavily on lemmings, which they catch in powerful, swooping attacks. During migration, they hunt for fish over ocean waters and large lakes. They are less inclined than their jaeger relatives to pirate food from gulls, but they will certainly do so if a good opportunity arises. • *Stercorarius* is Latin for 'pertaining to dung'— a misleading reference to this bird's diet, which may include carrion and putrid food waste, but never excrement. • Jaegers are members of the Skua family.

light morph breeding

ID: long, twinned tail streamers; dark cap; clean white throat and belly; yellow collar; grey upperparts; dark flight feathers. *Sub-adult:* dark necklace; dark barring on the sides, flanks and rump. *Juvenile:* dark chin and throat; dark barring on the sides, flanks and rump; mottled underwing linings; brown upperparts; short, rounded tail streamers.
Size: *L* 51–58 cm; *W* 1 m.
Status: extremely rare to locally very uncommon migrant from April to May and from August to November.
Habitat: shorelines of ocean, large lakes and rivers, gravelbars, landfills and open water; may occasionally be seen over coastal tundra.
Nesting: does not nest in Ontario.
Feeding: eats mainly fish, which are sometimes pirated from other birds; small birds and mammals and large insects and eggs are taken while hovering or in a swooping attack; will also eat carrion and berries.
Voice: generally silent; may make shrill calls while migrating.
Similar Species: *Pomarine Jaeger* (p. 154): adult has shorter, spoon-shaped tail streamers and a dark, mottled breast band, sides and flanks; juvenile lacks the solid dark markings on the throat and upper breast and has more white on its upperwing primaries; both the adult and subadult can be very similar to an adult Long-tailed Jaeger but have a dark belly and white on the base of the underwing primaries. *Parasitic Jaeger* (p. 155): adult has much shorter central tail streamers and a dark neck band.
Best Sites: Polar Bear PP; Moosonee; the shorelines of Lake Erie and Lake Ontario.

LAUGHING GULL

Larus atricilla

The Laughing Gull moves easily among the urban landscape, gathering in harbours and parks to panhandle for food scraps. Its beautiful plumage and lilting laugh are readily accepted by humans today, but life has not always been so easy for the Laughing Gull. In the late 19th century, high commercial demand for egg collections and feathers for women's headresses resulted in the extirpation of this gull as a breeding species in many parts of its Atlantic coast range. Today, East Coast populations are gradually assuming their former abundance, and the Laughing Gull is now found in southern Ontario on a regular basis. Although this gull may appear in any month of the year, May, June, August and September support the most sightings.

breeding

ID: *Breeding:* black head; broken white eye ring; red bill. *Non-breeding:* white head with some pale grey bands; black bill. *3rd-year:* white neck and underparts; dark grey back; black-tipped wings; black legs. *Immature:* variable, brown to grey and white overall.

Size: *L* 38–43 cm; *W* 1 m.

Status: extremely rare visitor from March to October.

Habitat: shorelines of lakes and rivers, landfills and open water.

Nesting: does not nest in Ontario.

Feeding: omnivorous; gleans insects, small mollusks, crustaceans, spiders and small fish from the ground or water while flying, wading, walking or swimming; may steal food from other birds; may eat the eggs and nestlings of other birds; often scavenges at landfills.

Voice: loud, high pitched laughing call: *ha-ha-ha-ha-ha-ha.*

Similar Species: *Franklin's Gull* (p. 158): smaller overall; red legs; shorter, slimmer bill; winter adult has a black mask. *Black-headed Gull* (p. 160) and *Bonaparte's Gull* (p. 161): orange or reddish legs; slimmer bill (Bonaparte's has a black bill); lighter mantle; white wedge on the upper leading edge of wing; black hood on the breeding adult does not extend over the nape; white head and black head spot in winter. *Little Gull* (p. 159): paler mantle; reddish legs; dainty black bill; no eye ring; lacks the black wing tips.

Best Sites: Point Pelee NP; Long Point PP.

VAGRANT

FRANKLIN'S GULL

Larus pipixcan

Twice each year, small flocks of Franklin's Gulls drift into our province from the prairies. They are rare but regular visitors here, and most sightings are of individuals or small flocks intermingled among large groups of Bonaparte's and other gulls. Most Franklin's are seen in May and early June and from late August to early November, although keen birders occasionally detect a few strays in summer and winter.

• The Franklin's Gull is not simply a 'sea gull.' A large part of its life is spent inland, and on its traditional nesting territory on the prairies, it is affectionately known as the 'Prairie Dove.' It has a dove-like profile, and it often follows tractors across agricultural fields, snatching up insects from the tractor's path in much the same way its cousins follow fishing boats.

breeding

ID: grey mantle; broken white eye ring; white underparts. *Breeding:* black head; orange-red bill and legs; breast might have a pinkish tinge. *Non-breeding:* white head; dark patch on the sides of the head. *In flight:* black crescent on the white wing tips.
Size: *L* 33–38 cm; *W* 94 cm.
Status: rare to uncommon migrant from late April to early June and from mid-August to early December in the south; may be common in the Lake of the Woods area.
Habitat: agricultural fields, marshlands, river and lake shorelines, rivermouths and landfills.
Nesting: does not nest in Ontario.
Feeding: very opportunistic; gleans agricultural fields and meadows for grasshoppers and insects; often catches dragonflies, mayflies and other flying invertebrates in mid-air; also eats small fish and some crustaceans.

Voice: mewing, shrill *weeeh-ah weeeh-ah* while feeding and in migration.
Similar Species: *Bonaparte's Gull* (p. 161): adult has a black bill and a conspicuous white wedge on the forewing. *Little Gull* (p. 159): paler mantle; lacks the black crescent on the wing tips; breeding adult lacks the broken white eye ring and the white nape; winter adult lacks the black face mask. *Black-headed Gull* (p. 160): paler mantle; conspicuous white wedge on the forewing; breeding adult has much more white on the back of the head; winter adult lacks the black face mask. *Sabine's Gull* (p. 169): large black, white and grey triangles on the upperwings; yellow-tipped dark bill. *Laughing Gull* (p. 157): larger overall; black legs; longer, heavier bill; winter adult lacks the black mask.
Best Sites: Niagara River; lower Great Lakes; Sable Islands Channel in Lake of the Woods.

LITTLE GULL

Larus minutus

The Little Gull was first identified in North America around 1820 as a specimen collected on the first Franklin Expedition. It was considered an exceptionally rare vagrant until 1962, when the first documented nest in the New World was discovered near Oshawa's Second Marsh. In the 1980s, a breeding population was found in the Hudson Bay Lowland, and some speculate that the birds may have nested there long before the discovery in the South. Little Gulls never nest in a given site for more than a few years, and they are often found among established Black Tern colonies.

• Little Gulls are best seen around Blenheim, Long Point Provincial Park and the Niagara River in late fall and over winter. Look for their dark underwings, which are quite conspicuous among the masses of white-underwinged Bonaparte's Gulls, with which they usually mingle.

breeding

ID: white neck, rump, tail and underparts; grey back and wings; orange-red feet and legs. *Breeding:* black head; dark red bill. *Non-breeding:* black bill; dark ear spot and cap. *Immature:* pinkish legs; brown and black in the wings and tail. *In flight:* white wing tips and trailing edge of the wing; dark underwings.

Size: *L* 25–29 cm; *W* 61 cm.

Status: extremely rare to uncommon year-round; most common as a migrant from early May to mid-June and from late August to mid-November.

Habitat: *Breeding:* marshy areas of freshwater lakes, among fresh or brackish marshes and along saltwater coastlines. *In migration:* freshwater marshes, ponds and beaches.

Nesting: colonial, but occasionally in isolated pairs; on the ground near water; pair lines a shallow depression with vegetation or builds a raised mound on a wet site; pair incubates 1–5 brown-and-grey-marked, olive to buff eggs for 23–25 days.

Feeding: gleans insects from the ground or from the water's surface while flying, wading, walking or floating; may also take small mollusks and fish, crustaceans, marine worms and spiders.

Voice: repeated *kay-ee* and a low *kek-kek-kek*.

Similar Species: *Bonaparte's Gull* (p. 161) and *Black-headed Gull* (p. 160): black-tipped primary feathers; breeding adult has a broken white eye ring and a white nape; winter adult has a white cap; Bonaparte's has a larger, black bill and Black-headed has a larger, red bill. *Franklin's Gull* (p. 158): black wing tips; darker mantle; breeding adult has a broken white eye ring, a white nape and a brighter red bill; winter adult has a black face mask. *Laughing Gull* (p. 157): black wing tips; darker mantle; black legs; breeding adult has a broken white eye ring and a much larger bill. *Sabine's Gull* (p. 169): black forewing wedge; black legs; yellow-tipped bill.

Best Sites: Lambton sewage lagoons; Rondeau PP; Long Point PP; Niagara River; Sibbald Point PP; Sandbanks PP; Cornwall Dam; Deschênes Rapids.

159

BLACK-HEADED GULL

Larus ridibundus

Black-headed Gulls are typically found along the Atlantic coast, but a small number are seen annually in Ontario, usually cavorting with larger gatherings of Bonaparte's Gulls in fall. The shorelines and open inshore waters of the Niagara River and western Lake Ontario always seem to attract large, raucous concentrations of gulls, which occasionally include a few of these wanderers. • Like the Little Gull, the Black-headed is a relative newcomer to Canada, and the first sighting in North America was recorded in the 1920s. Small nesting colonies have been established on islands off the coasts of Newfoundland, Nova Scotia and Quebec, but there are no accounts of the Black-headed Gull nesting in Ontario. • In North America, there are many gulls with black heads; ironically, the Black-headed Gull has a brown head.

breeding

ID: white neck, rump, tail and underparts; grey mantle; red feet and legs. *Breeding:* red bill; dark brown facial hood appears blackish and does not extend onto the nape; broken, white eye ring. *Non-breeding:* dark ear patch; white cap; red bill. *Immature:* pale legs; white mottling on the hood in summer; dark tail band; black-tipped, yellow bill; dusky cap; brown in the wing in winter. *In flight:* white upper forewing wedge; black wing tips; dark underwing primaries.
Size: *L* 36–41 cm; *W* 1 m.
Status: rare fall visitor from late August through November; a few may remain through January; a few may appear from late March to early June.
Habitat: marshes, lakeshores and rivers.
Nesting: does not nest in Ontario.
Feeding: gleans insects, small mollusks, crustaceans, spiders and small fish from the ground or the water's surface while flying, wading, walking or swimming;

often catches insects in flight; may also take some seeds and berries; may steal food from other birds.
Voice: high-pitched *craah*.
Similar Species: *Bonaparte's Gull* (p. 161): smaller overall; daintier, black bill; largely white underwing primaries; more orange on the legs; black hood on the breeding adult extends onto the upper nape. *Little Gull* (p. 159): adult's primary feathers lack the black tips; breeding adult has an all-black head, a smaller bill and no eye ring; winter adult has a dark cap and a black bill. *Franklin's Gull* (p. 158) and *Laughing Gull* (p. 157): black crescent on the wing tips; lacks the white triangle on the upper leading edge of the wing; black hood on the breeding adult extends over the nape; winter Franklin's adult has a black face mask and a black bill. *Sabine's Gull* (p. 169): adult has a yellow-tipped, black bill and a black upper forewing wedge.
Best Sites: Niagara River; lower Great Lakes shorelines; southern Lake Simcoe; Sandbanks PP.

VAGRANT

BONAPARTE'S GULL

Larus philadelphia

Many Ontarians feel great disdain for gulls, but they might change their minds when they meet the Bonaparte's Gull. This graceful, reserved bird is nothing like its contentious, aggressive relatives. Delicate in plumage and behaviour, this small gull avoids landfills, preferring to dine on flying insects or from the surface of the water. Only when a flock of Bonaparte's spy a school of fish do they raise their soft, scratchy voices in excitement. • Unlike other gulls and terns, Bonaparte's Gulls nest in coniferous trees. Their nests are usually situated high in the canopy, and they choose sites that are often close to a lake or large beaver pond. • From October to early December, Lake Erie and the Niagara River host huge flocks of Bonaparte's Gulls, often numbering over 100,000 birds. In years when mild winter weather prevails, many of these gulls will remain in Ontario, flying about for hours on end, wheeling and flashing their pale wings. During cold winters, most Bonaparte's Gulls move south to the Atlantic coast.

breeding

ID: black bill; grey mantle; white underparts. *Breeding:* black head; white eye ring; orange legs. *Non-breeding:* white head; dark ear patch. *In flight:* white forewing wedge; black wing tips.
Size: *L* 30–36 cm; *W* 84 cm.
Status: common to very common migrant from March to early June and from late July through November; uncommon breeder from May to September; rare to locally abundant winter visitor.
Habitat: *Breeding:* boreal forest. *Winter* and *In migration:* large lakes, rivers and marshes.
Nesting: occasionally colonial; in coniferous trees; builds shallow nest-bowls on short, thick tree branches; pair incubates 3 brown-blotched, olive to buff eggs for about 24 days.
Feeding: dabbles and tips up for aquatic invertebrates, small fish and tadpoles while swimming;

gleans the ground for terrestrial invertebrates; also captures insects in the air.
Voice: scratchy, soft *ear ear* while feeding.
Similar Species: *Franklin's Gull* (p. 158): lacks the white upper forewing wedge; breeding adult has an orange bill; non-breeding adult has a black face mask. *Little Gull* (p. 159): daintier bill; adult has white wing tips; breeding adult's black hood lacks the white eye ring and extends over the nape; winter adult has a white cap. *Black-headed Gull* (p. 160): larger overall; larger, red bill; dark underwing primaries; more red than orange on the legs; breeding adult has a brownish hood. *Sabine's Gull* (p. 169): large black, white and grey triangles on the upperwings; yellow-tipped, dark bill; exceptionally rare in Ontario.
Best Sites: Lillabelle Lake; Hwy 11 from Kirkland Lake to Hearst; Polar Bear PP; Big Creek NWA; southern Lake Simcoe; Sandbanks PP; Hurkett Cove Conservation Area; Niagara River.

161

RING-BILLED GULL
Larus delawarensis

Few Ontarians can claim they have never come across a Ring-billed Gull in our province. Although this bird nests mainly along large bodies of water to the south and north of us, it wanders almost everywhere in Ontario. Its numbers have greatly increased over recent years, and its tolerance for humans has made it a part of our everyday lives—a connection that often involves Ring-bills scavenging our litter or fouling the windshields of our automobiles! Some people feel that Ring-billed Gulls have become pests; many parks, beaches, golf courses and even fast-food parking lots are often inundated with marauding gulls looking for food handouts. Few species, however, have fared as well as Ring-bills in the face of human development, which, in itself, is something to appreciate.

breeding

ID: white head; yellow bill and legs; black ring around the bill tip; pale grey mantle; yellow eyes; white underparts. *Immature:* grey back; brown wings and breast. *In flight:* black wing tips with a few white spots.
Size: *L* 46–51 cm; *W* 1.2 m (male is slightly larger).
Status: rare to locally very common migrant and winter visitor from August to May; uncommon to locally abundant breeder.
Habitat: *Breeding:* sparsely vegetated islands, open beaches, breakwaters and dredge-spoil areas. *Winter* and *In migration:* lakes, rivers, landfills, golf courses, fields, parks and garbage dumps.
Nesting: colonial; in a shallow scrape on the ground lined with plants, debris, grass and sticks; pair incubates 2–4 brown-blotched, grey to olive eggs for 23–28 days.
Feeding: gleans the ground for garbage, spiders, insects, rodents, earthworms, grubs and waste grain; scavenges for carrion; surface-tips for aquatic invertebrates and fish.
Voice: high-pitched *kakakaka-akakaka*; also a low, laughing *yook-yook-yook*.
Similar Species: *California Gull:* (p. 357) much larger; no bill ring; black and red spots near the tip of the lower mandible; dark eyes. *Herring* (p. 163), *Thayer's* (p. 164) *Glaucous* (p. 167), *Iceland* (p. 165) and *Slaty-backed gulls:* larger; adults have pinkish legs, lack the bill ring and have a red spot near the tip of the lower mandible. *Mew Gull* (p. 357): adults have less black on the wing tips, dark eyes, darker mantles and lack the bill ring. *Lesser Black-backed Gull* (p. 166): larger; much darker mantle; much less white on the wing tips; lacks the bill ring.
Best Sites: Point Pelee NP; Long Point PP; Hamilton Harbour; Niagara River; Tommy Thompson Park; waterfronts or landfills near Presqu'ile PP.

HERRING GULL

Larus argentatus

Although Herring Gulls are as adept as their smaller Ring-billed relatives at scrounging handouts on the beach, they are more likely to be found in wild areas than urban settings. Settling on lakes and large rivers where Ring-bills would never be found, Herring Gulls nest comfortably in large colonies, or they may choose a site kilometres from any other gulls. • Herring Gulls are skilled hunters, but they are also opportunistic birds that scavenge at landfills and in fast-food restaurant parking lots. Their foraging habits might seem unsanitary, but these birds have thrived by adopting the task of finishing off leftovers. • Like many gulls, Herrings have a small red spot on their lower mandible which serves as a target for nestling young. When a downy chick pecks at the lower mandible, the parent recognizes the cue and regurgitates its meal.

breeding

ID: large gull; yellow bill; red spot on the lower mandible; light eyes; light grey mantle; pink legs. *Breeding:* white head; white underparts. *Non-breeding:* white head and nape are washed with brown. *Immature:* mottled brown overall. *In flight:* white-spotted, black wing tips.
Size: *L* 58–66 cm; *W* 1.2 m.
Status: abundant migrant and locally abundant visitor from October to early April; common to locally abundant breeder from April to September.
Habitat: *Breeding:* undisturbed islands, peninsulas and cliffs. *Winter* and *In migration:* large lakes, wetlands, rivers, landfills and urban areas.
Nesting: singly or colonially; often nests with other gulls, pelicans and cormorants; on open beaches and islands; on the ground in a shallow scrape lined with plants and sticks;

pair incubates 3 darkly blotched, olive to buff eggs for 31–32 days.
Feeding: surface-tips for aquatic invertebrates and fish; gleans the ground for insects and worms; scavenges dead fish and garbage; eats other birds' eggs and young.
Voice: loud, bugle-like *kleew-kleew*; also an alarmed *kak-kak-kak*.
Similar Species: *California Gull* (p. 357): much smaller; dark eyes; yellowish legs; black and red spot on the lower mandible. *Ring-billed Gull* (p. 162): smaller; black bill ring; yellow legs. *Thayer's* (p. 164), *Glaucous* (p. 167) and *Iceland* (p. 165) *gulls:* paler mantle; all lack the black in the wings. *Lesser Black-backed Gull* (p. 166) and *Slaty-backed Gull:* much darker mantle.
Best Sites: Lake St. Clair; Rondeau PP; Presqu'ile PP; Lake Simcoe; Parry Sound; North Bay; Sault Ste. Marie; Thunder Bay; Lake Nipigon PP.

THAYER'S GULL

Larus thayeri

Thayer's Gulls are rare throughout Ontario, and since many of these visitors are immatures (the identification of which is beyond the scope of this book), only the most experienced birders tend to recognize them. If they are sighted, they are usually travelling inconspicuously among large flocks of Ring-billed and Herring gulls during winter. • Together with the Herring, Iceland, Glaucous, Glaucous-winged and Western gulls, the Thayer's Gull is part of a group of gulls that all have similar traits, indicating that they are relatively recently evolved species that could potentially still interbreed. In fact, the Thayer's Gull was once considered a subspecies of the very similar-looking Herring Gull, and some ornithologists continue to argue that this bird does not deserve full species status. Alternately, some believe that the Thayer's Gull is actually a subspecies of the Iceland Gull. • John Eliot Thayer was a Bostonian who provided the financial backing for natural history expeditions from Guadeloupe to the Canadian Arctic.

non-breeding

ID: white-spotted, dark grey wing tips; dark eyes; yellow bill with a red spot at the tip of the lower mandible; dark pink legs. *Breeding:* clean white head, neck and upper breast. *Non-breeding:* head, neck and upper breast are flecked with brown. *Immature:* variable mottled white and brown plumage; 1st-year has a black bill; 2nd-year has a black ring around a dusky bill.
Size: *L* 56–64 cm; *W* 1.3–1.4 m.
Status: rare visitor from October to May.
Habitat: landfills and open water on large lakes and rivers.
Nesting: does not nest in Ontario.
Feeding: diet includes carrion, small fish, crustaceans, mollusks and human food waste; gleans from the water's surface while in flight.
Voice: various raucous and laughing calls are given, much like the Herring Gull's *kak-kak-kak*.
Similar Species: *Herring Gull* (p. 163): black wing tips; light eyes; darker mantle. *Iceland Gull* (p. 165): light eyes; more white than dark grey on the wing tips. *Glaucous Gull* (p. 167): longer, heavier bill; light eyes; pure white wing tips; lighter pink legs. *Ring-billed Gull* (p. 162): smaller; dark ring on the yellow bill; yellow legs. *Lesser Black-backed Gull* (p. 166): darker mantle; black wing tips; yellow feet.
Best Sites: St. Clair, Niagara and Ottawa rivers.

ICELAND GULL

Larus glaucoides

This graceful glider spends much of its time searching for schools of fish over icy, open waters. When fishing proves unrewarding, this opportunistic gull has no qualms about digging through a landfill in search of food. Human onlookers might think that this bird's dirty brown head and breast streaking is a result of its filthy scavenging habits, but in truth, these are natural markings of its non-breeding plumage. • Iceland Gulls come in two well-recognized forms in Ontario: Kumlien's and European. Once considered a separate species, the Kumlien's form has grey on its wing tips and is the form most common in Ontario. On Baffin Island, the Kumlien's may interbreed with the highly similar Thayer's Gull, creating fertile hybrids that are occasionally spotted in Ontario. The European form of the Iceland Gull, which has white-tipped primary flight feathers, is less commonly seen in Ontario. Some scientists continue to debate the species status of the Iceland, the Thayer's and another close relative, the Glaucous Gull, asking themselves whether these gulls should be considered separate species or simply a series of races within the same species.

non-breeding

ID: *Breeding:* relatively short, yellow bill with a red spot on the lower mandible; rounded head; yellow eye with a dark ring; white wing tips with some dark grey; pink legs; white underparts; pale grey mantle. *Non-breeding:* head and breast streaked with brown. *Immature:* dark eyes, black bill and various plumages with varying amounts of grey on the upperparts and brown flecking over the entire body.
Size: *L* 56 cm; *W* 1.4 m.
Status: very rare to very uncommon visitor from October to May.
Habitat: landfills and open water on large lakes and rivers.
Nesting: does not nest in Ontario.

Feeding: eats mostly fish; may also take crustaceans, mollusks, carrion, seeds; scavenges at landfills.
Voice: high, screechy calls.
Similar Species: *Herring Gull* (p. 163): black wing tips; darker mantle. *Thayer's Gull* (p. 164): more dark grey than white on the wing tips; dark eyes. *Glaucous Gull* (p. 167): longer, heavier bill; pure white wing tips. *Ring-billed Gull* (p. 162): smaller; dark ring on a yellow bill; yellow legs. *Lesser Black-backed Gull* (p. 166): darker mantle; black wing tips; yellow feet.
Best Sites: Niagara River; Lake Ontario west of Toronto; Cornwall Dam; landfills throughout southern Ontario.

165

LESSER BLACK-BACKED GULL

Larus fuscus

Equipped with long wings for long-distance flights, small numbers of Lesser Black-backed Gulls leave their familiar European and Icelandic surroundings each fall to make their way to North America. Most of these gulls settle along the Atlantic coast during winter, but, inevitably, a few make their way into Ontario. In recent years, Lesser Black-backed sightings have increased in our province, so it is quite possible that this Eurasian species will soon colonize North America. Birders are advised to keep a close eye on local cliffs and shoreline rooftops—the most likely locations to support Lesser Black-backed Gull's nesting attempts.

non-breeding

ID: *Breeding:* dark grey mantle; mostly black wing tips; yellow bill with a red spot on the lower mandible; yellow eyes; yellow legs; white head and underparts. *Non-breeding:* head and neck streaked with brown. *Immature:* dark or light eyes; black or pale bill with a black tip; various plumages with varying amounts of grey on the upperparts and brown flecking over the entire body.

Size: *L* 53 cm; *W* 1.4 m.

Status: rare to uncommon visitor from September to May; rare summer resident.

Habitat: landfills and open water on large lakes and rivers.

Nesting: does not nest in Ontario.

Feeding: eats mostly fish, crustaceans, mollusks, insects, small rodents, carrion and seeds; scavenges for garbage.

Voice: screechy call is like a lower version of the Herring Gull's.

Similar Species: *Herring Gull* (p. 163): lighter mantle; pink legs. *Thayer's* (p. 164), *Glaucous* (p. 167) and *Iceland* (p. 165) *gulls*: pale grey mantle; white or grey wing tips; pink legs. *Ring-billed Gull* (p. 162): smaller; dark ring on the yellow bill; paler mantle. *Slaty-backed Gull:* larger; more white on the trailing edge of the wing; pink legs. *Greater Black-backed Gull* (p. 168): much larger; black mantle; pale pinkish legs.

Best Sites: Sarnia waterfront; Erieau pier; Niagara River; Lake Ontario west of Toronto; Guindon Park; Deschênes Rapids; landfills throughout southern Ontario.

VAGRANT

GLAUCOUS GULL

Larus hyperboreus

Its largely white underparts and pale grey mantle camouflage the Glaucous Gull against the cloud-filled skies of winter as it scans the open waters of the Great Lakes. Its pale plumage also helps birders to identify its large, ghostly figure from other, more numerous, overwintering gull species. This bird traditionally fished for its meals or stole food from smaller gulls. More recently, however, wintering Glaucous Gulls have traded the rigours of hunting for the job of defending plots of garbage at various landfills. • In summer, while other gulls are strolling along local beaches or hanging out in fast-food restaurant parking lots, the Glaucous Gull is far away in the arctic wilderness. • Although the adults are easier to identify, the immature Glaucous Gulls are more numerous in Ontario. Fortunately, these young birds are light enough to be easily recognized from other immature gulls. • The scientific name *hyperboreus* means 'of the far north.'

non-breeding

ID: *Breeding:* relatively long, heavy, yellow bill with a red spot on the lower mandible; pure white wing tips; flattened crown profile; yellow eyes; pink legs; white underparts; very pale grey mantle. *Non-breeding:* head, neck and breast are streaked with brown. *Immature:* dark eyes; pale, black-tipped bill; various plumages have varying amounts of brown flecking on the body.
Size: *L* 69 cm; *W* 1.5 m.
Status: rare to uncommon visitor from mid-November through May; exceptionally rare visitor from June to November.
Habitat: landfills and open water on large lakes and rivers.

Nesting: does not nest in Ontario.
Feeding: predator, pirate and scavenger; eats mostly fish, crustaceans, mollusks and some seeds; feeds on carrion and at landfills.
Voice: high, screechy calls similar to Herring Gull's *kak-kak-kak*.
Similar Species: *Thayer's Gull* (p. 164) and *Iceland Gull* (p. 165): smaller; slightly darker mantle; grey on the wing tips. *Herring Gull* (p. 163): slightly smaller; black wing tips; much darker mantle.
Best Sites: Sarnia waterfront; Bruce Nuclear Power Station; Erieau pier; Niagara River; Lake Ontario west of Toronto; Cornwall Dam; landfills throughout southern Ontario.

GREAT BLACK-BACKED GULL
Larus marinus

The Great Black-backed Gull's commanding size and bold disposition means that it almost always has first dibs at a fresh meal. This aggresssive feeder is highly domineering over other gulls, and it won't hesitate to steal a fish or prey on young hatchlings. • In recent years, the Great Black-backed Gull has chosen our province as a nesting location. Although it prefers to nest in colonies throughout most of its range, nesting efforts along Lake Huron and Lake Ontario have generally been limited to isolated pairs. In fall, good numbers of Great Black-backs can be found at landfills and areas of open water in southern Ontario. • Like many other North American gulls, the Great Black-backed Gull is a 'four-year gull,' meaning that it goes through various plumage stages until its fourth winter, when it develops its refined adult plumage. Most immature gulls have dark streaking, spotting or mottling, which allows them to blend into their surroundings and avoid detection by predators.

non-breeding

ID: very large gull; all white except for the grey underwings and the black mantle; pale pinkish legs; light-coloured eyes; large, yellow bill with a red spot on the lower mandible. *Immature:* variable, mottled gray-brown, white and black; black bill or black-tipped, pale bill.
Size: *L* 76 cm; *W* 1.6 m.
Status: uncommon to fairly common migrant and visitor from late August to mid-May; very rare breeder from May to September.
Habitat: *Breeding:* rocky islands; rarely on beaches. *Winter:* landfills and open water on large lakes and rivers.
Nesting: usually colonial, but mostly isolated pairs in Ontario; on islands, cliff tops or beaches; pair builds a mound of vegetation and debris on the ground, often near rocks; pair incubates 2 or 3 brown-blotched, olive to buff eggs for 27–28 days.
Feeding: opportunistic feeder; eats fish, eggs, birds, small mammals, berries, carrion, mollusks, crustaceans, insects and other invertebrates; scavenges at landfills; finds food by flying, swimming, or walking.
Voice: a harsh *kyow.*
Similar Species: *All other gulls:* smaller; lack the black mantle.
Best Sites: Basswood Island; Toronto Harbour; Peter Rock PP; Presqu'ile PP; Fish Point PP Reserve; Bruce Nuclear Power Station; Niagara River.

SABINE'S GULL

Xema sabini

It is unfortunate that few Ontarians will ever see a Sabine's Gull—it is truly a stunning bird, and a real rarity. The majority of these birds migrate over coastal waters, so they are not common in our province. Sabine's Gulls can best be observed in fall, when they trickle southward from the Arctic. • Sabine's Gulls share the same shape and head colour patterns of the common, black-headed *Larus* gulls, but their buoyant, dipping flight pattern and shallowly forked tail are characteristic of the *Sterna* terns. Thus, their taxonomic placement between the gulls and terns makes good sense. • This gull feeds while in flight, gently dipping down to the water's surface to snatch up prey without landing. • Sir Edward Sabine was a distinguished military man whose primary interests were astronomy and terrestrial magnetism. He joined an expedition to explore the Arctic Islands, and it was near Cape York that he collected the gull that was to be named in his honour.

non-breeding

ID: yellow-tipped, black bill; dark grey mantle; black feet. *Breeding:* dark slate grey hood trimmed with black. *Non-breeding:* white head; dark gray nape. *In flight:* 3-toned wing, grey at the base, then white, then black at the tip; shallowly forked tail.
Size: *L* 33–36 cm; *W* 91 cm.
Status: very rare migrant from late August to early December.
Habitat: lakes and large rivers.
Nesting: does not nest in Ontario.

Feeding: gleans the water's surface while swimming or flying; eats mostly insects, fish and crustaceans.
Voice: tern-like *kee-kee*; not frequently heard in migration.
Similar Species: *Bonaparte's* (p. 161), *Franklin's* (p. 158), *Little* (p. 159), *Laughing* (p. 157) and *Black-headed* (p. 160) *gulls:* lack the boldly patterned wing tips, forked tail and yellow-tipped bill.
Best Sites: Sarnia waterfront; Niagara River; Lake Ontario west of Toronto; Cornwall Dam.

VAGRANT

BLACK-LEGGED KITTIWAKE

Rissa tridactyla

The Black-legged Kittiwake is more closely associated with the marine environment than any other North American gull. For this reason, few birders will ever see this small, graceful gull from the comfort of Ontario's *terra firma*. Most of the small number of Black-legged Kittiwakes that move through the province usually migrate well offshore over the open waters of Lake Huron, Lake Ontario and Lake Erie. During late fall and early winter, watch for Black-legged Kittiwakes over the Niagara River, where mixed flocks of gulls often congregate. • Even during the most violent storms, Black-legged Kittiwakes will remain in open water, floating among massive freshwater swells that remind them of their saltwater homes. Because they spend most of their lives in saltwater environments, they have developed glands above their eyes that enable them to extract and secrete excess salt from the water. • Unlike the majority of gulls in Ontario, the Black-legged Kittiwake makes its living by fishing rather than by foraging in garbage dumps.

breeding

non-breeding

ID: *Breeding adult:* black legs; grey mantle; white underparts; white head; yellow bill. *Non-breeding adult:* grey nape; dark grey smudge behind the eye. *Immature:* black bill; wide, black half-collar; dark ear patch. *In flight:* adult has solid, black triangular wing tips; immature has a black M on the upper forewing from wing tip to wing tip and a black terminal tail band.
Size: *L* 41–46 cm; *W* 91 cm.
Status: rare migrant and visitor from mid-August to January; exceptionally rare visitor at other times of the year.
Habitat: open water on large lakes and rivers.
Nesting: does not nest in Ontario.

Feeding: small fish are preferred; also takes crustaceans, insects and mollusks; dips to the water's surface to snatch prey; may plunge under the water's surface or glean from the surface while swimming.
Voice: calls *kittewake* and *kekekek*.
Similar Species: *Franklin's* (p. 158), *Laughing* (p. 157), *Bonaparte's* (p. 161), *Black-headed* (p. 160) and *Little* (p. 159) *gulls:* lack the combination of black legs, yellow bill, grey nape and solid black, triangular wing tips. *Sabine's Gull* (p. 169): immature has grey-brown wash on the sides and head and lacks the dark M on the wings and the mantle.
Best Sites: Sarnia waterfront; Niagara River.

VAGRANT

CASPIAN TERN

Sterna caspia

In size and habits, the mighty Caspian Tern bridges the gulf between smaller terns and raucous gulls. It is the largest tern in North America, and its wingbeats are slower and more gull-like than those of most other terns—a trait that leads birders to confuse it with a gull. This tern's distinctive, heavy, red-orange bill and forked tail, however, usually give away its true identity. • Caspian Terns are often seen in association with gulls: during migration they often appear together on shoreline sandbars and mudflats, and during the breeding season they nest colonially on exposed islands and protected beaches. In Ontario, most Caspian Tern nesting colonies include Ring-billed Gulls. • A Caspian Tern foraging for alewife and other small, schooling fish might impress some observers: foraging high over open waters, this tern hovers, then folds its wings suddenly, plunging headfirst toward its target. • The Caspian Tern is strictly a migrant and summer breeder in Ontario; it retreats to the Gulf of Mexico for winter. • This species was first collected from the Caspian Sea, hence its name.

breeding

ID: black cap; heavy, red-orange bill with a faint black tip; light grey mantle; black legs; shallowly forked tail; white underparts; long, frosty, pointed wings; dark grey on the underside of the outer primaries. *Non-breeding:* black cap, streaked with white.
Size: *L* 48–58 cm; *W* 1.3–1.4 m.
Status: fairly common migrant and breeder from late April to mid-September; rare in mid-April and from mid-September to mid-October.
Habitat: *Breeding:* usually on islands in lakes and rivers. *In migration:* wetlands and shore-lines of large lakes and rivers.
Nesting: in a shallow scrape on bare sand, lightly vegetated soil or gravel; nest is sparsely lined with vegetation, rocks or twigs; pair incubates 1–3 brown- or black-spotted, pale buff eggs for 20–22 days.
Feeding: hovers over water and plunges headfirst after small fish, tadpoles and aquatic invertebrates; also feeds by swimming and gleaning at the water's surface.
Voice: low, harsh *ca-arr*; loud *kraa-uh*.
Similar Species: *Common* (p. 172), *Arctic* (p. 173) and *Forster's* (p. 174) *terns:* much smaller; daintier bills.
Best Sites: Point Pelee NP; Long Point PP; western Bruce Peninsula; Presqu'ile PP; Georgian Bay Islands NP; North Channel Islands.

COMMON TERN

Sterna hirundo

Common Terns patrol the shorelines of lakes and rivers during spring and fall and settle in large nesting colonies over the summer months. Both the males and the females perform aerial courtship dances, and for most pairs the nesting season commences when the female accepts her suitor's gracious fish offerings. • Tern colonies are noisy and chaotic, and they are often associated with even noisier gull colonies. Should an intruder approach a tern nest, the parent will dive repeatedly, often defecating on the offender. Needless to say, it is best to keep a respectful distance from nesting terns, and from all nesting birds, for that matter. • Terns are effortless flyers, and they are some of the most impressive long-distance migrants. Recently, a Common Tern banded in Great Britain was recovered in Australia.

breeding

ID: *Breeding:* black cap; thin, red, black-tipped bill; red legs; white rump; white tail with grey outer edges; white underparts. *Non-breeding:* black nape; lacks the black cap. *In flight:* shallowly forked tail; long, pointed wings; dark grey wedge near the lighter grey upperwing tips.
Size: *L* 33–41 cm; *W* 76 cm.
Status: common migrant and breeder from April to mid-December; may be extremely locally abundant in fall.
Habitat: *Breeding:* natural and dredge-spoil islands, breakwaters and beaches. *In migration:* large lakes, open wetlands and slow-moving rivers.
Nesting: primarily colonial; usually on islands with non-vegetated, open areas; in a small scrape lined sparsely with pebbles, vegetation or shells; pair incubates 1–3 variably marked eggs for up to 27 days.

Feeding: hovers over the water and plunges headfirst after small fish and aquatic invertebrates.
Voice: high-pitched, drawn-out *keee-are* is most commonly heard at colonies but also in foraging flights.
Similar Species: *Forster's Tern* (p. 174): grey tail with white outer edges; upper primaries have a silvery look; broad, black eye band in non-breeding plumage. *Arctic Tern* (p. 173): all-red bill; deeply forked tail; upper primaries lack the dark grey wedge; greyer underparts; rare in migration. *Caspian Tern* (p. 171): much larger overall; much heavier, red-orange bill.
Best Sites: Point Pelee NP; Rondeau PP; Long Point PP; Tommy Thompson Park; Presqu'ile PP; Awenda PP; McRae Point PP; Killarney PP; North Channel Islands; Lake of the Woods.

ARCTIC TERN

Sterna paradisaea

The Arctic Terns that nest in northern Ontario make annual, round-trip migrations to foreign lands that include South America, Antarctica, Europe and Africa. In some years, an Arctic Tern might fly a distance of 32,000 km! Because they experience 24 hours of daylight while on their northern nesting grounds, and long days of sunlight on their non-breeding grounds, Arctic Terns perpetually avoid winter and probably experience more daylight in an average year than most living creatures. • Arctic Terns are fairly vocal during their passage through our province, and they are even able to scream while holding a small fish in their bill. They are rare in our province, and most sightings occur along the Ottawa River valley in spring and fall and along the northern coast in summer.

breeding

ID: *Breeding:* blood red bill and legs; black cap and nape; short neck; white cheek; grey underparts; long, white, forked tail extends to the wing tips when perched. *Immature and Non-breeding:* white underparts; black band through the eyes and across the nape; black bill. *In flight:* appears neckless; deeply forked tail; even grey wings with a thin, dark trailing underwing edge.
Size: *L* 36–43 cm; *W* 74–84 cm.
Status: locally rare migrant from mid-May to mid-June; uncommon breeder from May to August; small numbers may be seen in southern Ontario from late April to mid-July and from September to mid-November.
Habitat: *Breeding:* marshy tundra, sand and gravel bars, sandspits,

barren islands, beaches and rocky shorelines. *In migration:* large lakes, rivers and wetlands.
Nesting: colonial; on sand, gravel, rock or marshy tundra; in a shallow, generally unlined scrape; pair incubates 2 or 3 black- and brown-blotched, pale olive to buff eggs for 20–24 days.
Feeding: dives into the water from a stationary hover; preys on small fish and aquatic invertebrates.
Voice: harsh, high-pitched *kee kahr!*
Similar Species: *Common Tern* (p. 172): black-tipped bill; dark grey wedge on the upper primaries; whiter underparts. *Forster's Tern* (p. 174): black-tipped bill; grey tail with white outer edges; upper primaries have a silvery look.
Best Sites: Ottawa River; Polar Bear PP.

173

FORSTER'S TERN

Sterna forsteri

It is often said that 'one good turn deserves another,' which is probably why we have both Common and Forster's terns here in Ontario. The Forster's Tern so closely resembles the Common Tern that the two often blend together in the eyes of many observers. It usually isn't until these terns acquire their distinct fall plumages that birders begin to note the Forster's presence. • Most terns are known for their extraordinary ability to catch fish in dramatic headfirst dives, but the Forster's excels at gracefully snatching flying insects in mid-air. • The Forster's Tern has an exclusively North American breeding distribution, but it bears the name of a man who never visited this continent: German naturalist Johann Reinhold Forster. Forster, who lived and worked in England, and who accompanied Captain Cook on his 1772 voyage around the world, examined tern specimens sent from Hudson Bay, and he was the first to recognize this bird as a distinct species. Taxonomist Thomas Nuttall agreed, and in 1832 he named the species 'Forster's Tern' in his *Manual of Ornithology*.

breeding

ID: *Breeding:* black cap and nape; thin, orange, black-tipped bill; orange legs; light grey mantle; pure white underparts; white rump; grey tail with white outer edges. *Non-breeding:* lacks the black cap; black band through the eyes. *In flight:* forked, grey tail; long, pointed wings.
Size: *L* 36–41 cm; *W* 79 cm.
Status: rare to locally common migrant from mid-April to early June and from July to mid-October; rare to locally uncommon breeder from May to August.
Habitat: *Breeding:* cattail marshes. *In migration:* lakes and marshes.
Nesting: colonial; in cattail marshes, atop floating vegetation (occasionally on a muskrat lodge or an old grebe nest); pair incubates

3 brown-marked, buff to olive eggs for 23–25 days.
Feeding: hovers above the water and plunges headfirst after small fish and aquatic invertebrates; catches flying insects and snatches items from the water surface.
Voice: flight call is a nasal, short *keer keer*; also a grating *tzaap*.
Similar Species: *Common Tern* (p.172): darker red bill and legs; mostly white tail; grey wash on the underparts; dark wedge near the tip of the primaries. *Arctic Tern* (p. 173): lacks the black-tipped bill; short, red legs; grey underparts; white tail with grey outer edges. *Caspian Tern* (p. 171): much larger overall; much heavier, red-orange bill.
Best Sites: Lake St. Clair marshes; Point Pelee NP; Rondeau PP; Long Point PP; Lake of the Woods.

BLACK TERN

Chlidonias niger

Wheeling about in foraging flights, Black Terns pick small minnows from the water's surface or catch flying insects in mid-air. Even on stormy days, these acrobats slice through the sky with grace. Black Terns are frail birds in many ways, but they have dominion over the winds. When they leave Ontario in August and September, they gather the wind in their wings and dance over warm foreign waters until their return in spring. • Foraging flocks of Black Terns in southern Ontario occasionally number over 100 birds, but populations have declined in recent years. • Black Terns are finicky nesters, refusing to return to areas that show slight changes in the water level or density of emergent vegetation. Commitment to restore and protect wetland habitat will eventually help this bird to reclaim its once-prominent place in our province. • In order to spell this tern's genus name correctly, one must misspell *chelidonias*, the Greek word for 'swallow.'

breeding

ID: *Breeding:* black head and underparts; grey back, tail and wings; white undertail coverts; black bill; reddish-black legs. *Non-breeding:* white underparts and forehead; molting fall birds may be mottled with brown. *In flight:* long, pointed wings; shallowly forked tail.
Size: *L* 23–25 cm; *W* 61 cm.
Status: locally uncommon to common migrant and breeder from mid-April to mid-September; a few may remain into mid-December.
Habitat: shallow, freshwater cattail marshes, wetlands, lake edges and sewage ponds with emergent vegetation.
Nesting: loosely colonial; nest of

dead plant material is built on floating vegetation, a muddy mound or a muskrat house; pair incubates 3 darkly blotched, olive to pale buff eggs for 21–22 days.
Feeding: snatches insects from the air, from tall grass and from the water's surface; also eats small fish.
Voice: greeting call is a shrill, metallic *kik-kik-kik-kik-kik*; typical alarm call is *kreea*.
Similar Species: *Other terns:* all are light in colour, not dark.
Best Sites: Lake St. Clair marshes; Point Pelee NP; Long Point PP; Luther Marsh; Rankin River crossing; Lake Scugog; Presqu'ile PP; Rideau Canal; St. Joseph Island.

ROCK DOVE
Columba livia

The Rock Dove was introduced to North America in the 17th century, and it has since settled wherever cities, towns, farms and grain elevators are found. Most seem content to nest on buildings or farmhouses, but 'wilder' members of this species can occasionally be seen nesting on tall cliffs, usually along lakeshores. • Rock Doves are believed to have been domesticated from Eurasian birds in about 4500 B.C. as a source of meat. Since then, they have been used as message couriers—both Caesar and Napoleon used them—as scientific subjects and even as pets. Much of our understanding of bird migration, endocrinology and sensory perception derives from experiments involving Rock Doves. • No other 'wild' bird varies as much in coloration—a result of semi-domestication and extensive inbreeding over time.

ID: colour is highly variable (iridescent blue-grey, red, white or tan); usually has a white rump and orange feet; dark-tipped tail. *In flight:* holds its wings in a deep V while gliding.
Size: *L* 31–33 cm (male is usually larger).
Status: locally abundant year-round resident.
Habitat: urban areas, railway yards, agricultural areas, grain elevators; high cliffs provide a more natural habitat for some.
Nesting: on ledges of barns, cliffs, bridges, buildings and towers; flimsy nest of sticks, grass and assorted vegetation; pair incubates 2 eggs for 16–19 days; pair feeds the young 'pigeon milk'; may raise broods year-round.
Feeding: gleans the ground for waste grain, seeds and fruits; occasionally eats insects.
Voice: soft, cooing *coorrr-coorrr-coorrr*.
Similar Species: *Merlin* (p. 101): not as heavy bodied; longer tail; does not hold its wings in a V; wings do not clap on take-off.
Best Sites: any town, city urban or suburban park, farm or grain elevator.

MOURNING DOVE

Zenaida macroura

The soft coos of the Mourning Dove that filter through Ontario's broken woodlands, farmlands and suburban parks and gardens are often confused with the sounds of a hooting owl. Tracking down the source of these calls, however, usually reveals one or two doves perched upon a fence, tree branch or utility wire. • Despite its fragile look, the Mourning Dove is a swift, direct flyer whose wings often whistle as it cuts through the air at high speed. When this bird bursts into flight, its wings clap above and below its body. • In Ontario, the largest concentrations of Mourning Doves are in the extreme southwest and southeast, among the abundance of open habitats, weed seeds and waste grain found there. In recent decades, birdfeeders and cropland grain in these regions have provided a food source for an increased number of overwintering doves. • All members of the pigeon family (including doves) feed 'milk' to their young. Because birds lack mammary glands, it isn't true milk, but a nutritious liquid produced by glands in the bird's crop. The chicks insert their bills down the adult's throat to eat the thick, protein-rich fluid. • This bird's common name reflects its sad song. The scientific name *Zenaida* honours Zenaide, Princess of Naples, the wife of Charles Lucien Bonaparte (the zoologist nephew of the French emperor).

ID: buffy, grey-brown plumage; small head; long, white-trimmed, tapering tail; sleek body; dark, shiny patch below the ear; dull red legs; dark bill; pale rosy underparts; black spots on the upperwing.
Size: *L* 28–33 cm.
Status: common to abundant year-round resident; less common in the north; absent in densely forested areas.
Habitat: open woodlands, riparian woodlands, woodlots, forest edges, agricultural and suburban areas and open parks; has benefited from human-induced habitat change.
Nesting: occasionally on the ground or in the fork of a shrub or tree; female builds a fragile, shallow platform nest from twigs supplied by the male; pair incubates 2 white eggs for 14 days; young are fed 'pigeon milk.'
Feeding: gleans the ground and vegetation for seeds; visits feeders; produces crop milk for its newly hatched young.
Voice: mournful, soft, slow *oh-woe-woe-woe*.
Similar Species: *Rock Dove* (p. 176): stockier; white rump; shorter tail; iridescent neck. *Yellow-billed Cuckoo* (p. 179) and *Black-billed Cuckoo* (p. 178): curved bill; long tail with a broad, rounded tip; brown upperparts; white underparts.
Best Sites: any suburban park or agricultural area.

BLACK-BILLED CUCKOO

Coccyzus erythropthalmus

hrubby field edges, hedgerows, tangled riparian thickets and abandoned, overgrown fields provide the elusive Black-billed Cuckoo with its preferred nesting haunts. Although this bird is uncommon or occasionally fairly common throughout much of southern Ontario, it remains an enigma to many would-be observers. Arriving in Ontario in late May, this cuckoo quietly hops, flits and skulks through low, dense deciduous vegetation in its ultra-secretive search for sustenance. Only when vegetation is in full bloom will males issue their loud, long irregular calls, advertising to females that it is time to nest. After a brief courtship, which may last for only a week, newly joined Black-billed Cuckoo pairs construct a makeshift nest, raise their young and then return promptly to their covert lives. • The Black-billed Cuckoo is one of few birds that thrives on hairy caterpillars, particularly Tent Caterpillars, and there is evidence to suggest that populations of this bird increase when a caterpillar infestation occurs in their area. • This cuckoo is reluctant to fly more than a short distance during nesting, but it will migrate as far as South America to avoid the North American winter.

ID: brown upperparts; white underparts; long, white-spotted undertail; downcurved, dark bill; reddish eye ring. *Juvenile:* buff eye ring; may have a buff tinge on the throat and undertail coverts.
Size: *L* 28–33 cm.
Status: rare to uncommon or irregularly fairly common breeder from mid-May to mid-September.
Habitat: dense second-growth woodlands, shrubby areas and thickets; often in tangled riparian areas and abandoned farmlands with low deciduous vegetation and adjacent open areas.
Nesting: in a shrub or small deciduous tree; flimsy nest of twigs is lined with grass and other vegetation; occasionally lays eggs in other birds' nests; pair incubates 2–5 blue-green, occasionally mottled eggs for 10–14 days.
Feeding: gleans hairy caterpillars from leaves, branches and trunks; also eats other insects and berries.
Voice: fast, repeated *cu-cu-cu* or *cu-cu-cu-cu-cu*; also a series of *ca, cow* and *coo* notes.
Similar Species: *Mourning Dove* (p. 177): short, straight bill; pointed, triangular tail; buffy, grey-brown plumage; black spots on the upperwing. *Yellow-billed Cuckoo* (p. 179): yellow bill; rufous tinge to the primaries; larger, more prominent, white undertail spots; lacks the red eye ring.
Best Sites: Rondeau PP; Long Point PP; Rouge River PP; Presqu'ile PP.

YELLOW-BILLED CUCKOO

Coccyzus americanus

Deep within the impenetrable deciduous undergrowth of Rondeau Provincial Park lurks the mysterious Yellow-billed Cuckoo. Most of the time it skilfully negotiates its tangled home in silence, relying on obscurity for survival. For a short period during nesting, however, the male cuckoo tempts fate, issuing a barage of loud, rhythmic courtship calls. Some folk have suggested that the cuckoo has a propensity for calling on dark, cloudy days in late spring and early summer—it is called 'Rain Crow' in some parts of its range. • In addition to consuming large quantities of hairy caterpillars, Yellow-billed Cuckoos feast on wild berries, young frogs and newts, small bird eggs and a variety of insects, including beetles, grasshoppers and cicadas. • Some Yellow-billed Cuckoos might lay eggs in the unattended nests of neighbouring Black-billed Cuckoos, but neither of these birds is considered to be an obligate 'nest parasite.' • Some Yellow-billed Cuckoos migrate as far south as Argentina for winter.

ID: olive-brown upperparts; white underparts; downcurved bill with a black upper mandible and yellow lower mandible; yellow eye ring; long tail with large white spots on the underside; rufous tinge to the primaries.
Size: *L* 28–33 cm.
Status: rare to locally fairly common breeder from early May to late September.
Habitat: semi-open deciduous habitats; dense tangles and thickets at the edges of orchards, urban parks, agricultural fields and roadways; some woodlots.
Nesting: on a horizontal branch in a deciduous shrub or small tree, within 2 m of the ground; builds a flimsy platform of twigs lined with roots and grass; pair incubates 3 or 4 pale bluish-green eggs for 9–11 days.
Feeding: gleans insect larvae, especially hairy caterpillars, from deciduous vegetation; also eats

berries, small fruits, small amphibians and occasionally the eggs of small birds.
Voice: long series of deep, hollow *kuks*, slowing near the end: *kuk-kuk-kuk-kuk kuk kop kow kowlp kowlp.*
Similar Species: *Mourning Dove* (p. 177): short, straight bill; pointed, triangular tail; buffy grey-brown plumage; black spots on the upperwing. *Black-billed Cuckoo* (p. 178): all-black bill; lacks the rufous tinge to the primaries; less prominent, white undertail spots; red rather than yellow eye ring; juveniles have a buff eye ring and may have a buff wash on the throat and undertail coverts.
Best Sites: Fish Point PP Reserve; Point Pelee NP; Rondeau PP; Long Point PP; orchards in Niagara County.

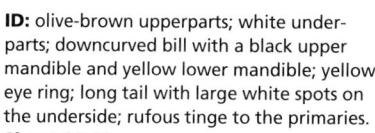

EASTERN SCREECH-OWL

Otus asio

The diminutive Eastern Screech-Owl is a year-round resident of Ontario's deciduous woodlands south of the Canadian Shield, but its presence is rarely detected. Most screech-owls sleep away the daylight hours snuggled safely inside a tree cavity or an artificial nest box. An encounter with a screech-owl is usually the result of a sound cue—the sounds of mobbing hordes of chickadees or squawking gangs of Blue Jays will occasionally alert you to an owl's presence during daylight hours (the smaller birds that mob screech-owls during the day may often do so after losing a family member during the night). More commonly, you will find this owl by listening for the male's eerie horse-whinny courtship calls and loud, spooky trills at night. • Despite its small size, the Eastern Screech-Owl is an adaptable hunter. It has a varied diet that ranges from insects, small rodents, earthworms and fish to birds larger than itself. • Unique among the owls found in Ontario, Eastern Screech-Owls are polychromatic: they show red or grey colour morphs. The red birds are less common because they are less able to withstand cold winters here; mixed-coloured pairs may produce intermediate-coloured young that are buffy brown.

grey morph

ID: short ear tufts; reddish or greyish overall; dark breast streaking; yellow eyes; pale greyish bill.
Size: *L* 20–23 cm; *W* 50–55 cm (female is slightly larger).
Status: uncommon year-round resident.
Habitat: mature deciduous forests, open deciduous woodlands, riparian woodlands, orchards and shade trees with natural cavities.
Nesting: in a natural cavity or artificial nest box; no lining is added; female incubates 4 or 5 white eggs for about 26 days; male brings food to the female during incubation.

Feeding: small mammals, earthworms, fish, birds and insects, including moths in flight; feeds at dusk and at night.
Voice: horse-like 'whinny' that rises and falls.
Similar Species: *Northern Saw-whet Owl* (p. 189): lacks the ear tufts; long, reddish streaks on the white underparts. *Long-eared Owl* (p. 186): much longer, slimmer body; longer, closer-set ear tufts; rusty facial disc; greyish, brown-white body. *Great Horned Owl* (p. 181): much larger; lacks the vertical breast streaks.
Best Sites: Ojibway Prairie; Point Pelee NP; Rondeau PP; Rouge River PP; Frontenac PP.

GREAT HORNED OWL

Bubo virginianus

The familiar *hoo-hoo-hoooo hoo-hoo* that resounds through campgrounds, suburban parks and farmyards is the call of the adaptable and superbly camouflaged Great Horned Owl. This formidable, primarily nocturnal hunter uses its acute hearing and powerful vision to hunt a wide variety of prey. Almost any small creature that moves is fair game for the Great Horned Owl. This bird, however, has a poorly developed sense of smell, which might explain why it is the only consistent predator of skunks. • Great Horned Owls often begin their courtship as early as January, at which time their hooting calls make them quite conspicuous. By February and March, they are already incubating their eggs, and by the time the last migratory birds have moved into Ontario, Great Horned owlets have already fledged. • The large eyes of owls are fixed in place, so to look up, down, or to the side, they must move their entire heads. Of course, owls have adapted to this situation, and they can swivel their necks 180 degrees!

ID: yellow eyes; tall ear tufts are set wide apart on the head; fine, horizontal barring on the breast; facial disc is outlined in black and is often rusty orange in colour; white chin; heavily mottled gray, brown and black upperparts; overall plumage varies from light gray to dark brown.

Size: *L* 46–64 cm; *W* 91–152 cm.

Status: fairly common to common year-round resident; absent from large areas of continuous forest.

Habitat: fragmented forests, agricultural areas, woodlots, meadows, riparian woodlands, wooded suburban parks and the wooded edges of landfills and town dumps.

Nesting: in the abandoned stick nest of another bird; may also nest on cliffs; adds little or no material to the nest; female mostly incubates the 2 or 3 dull whitish eggs for 28–35 days.

Feeding: mostly nocturnal, but also hunts at dusk or by day in winter; usually swoops from a perch; eats small mammals, birds, snakes, amphibians and even fish.

Voice: 4–6 deep hoots during the breeding season: *hoo-hoo-hoooo hoo-hoo* or *eat-my-food, I'll-eat you*; male gives higher-pitched hoots.

Similar Species: *Long-eared Owl* (p. 186): smaller; thinner; vertical breast streaks; ear tufts are close together. *Eastern Screech-Owl* (p. 180): much smaller; vertical breast streaks. *Great Gray* (p. 185), *Short-eared* (p. 187) and *Barred* (p. 184) *owls:* no ear tufts.

Best Sites: almost any fragmented or open woodland with an adjacent open area.

SNOWY OWL

Nyctea scandiaca

When the mercury drops and the landscape hardens in winter's icy grip, ghostly white Snowy Owls appear on fenceposts, utility poles, fields and lakeshores throughout the province. Motorists and landowners with an eye for Snowy Owls can often find them, even though they blend perfectly against almost any flat, open, snow-covered landscape. Snow cover is not a prerequisite for a Snowy Owl visit, however—many of these birds perch conspicuously on earth-tone fields in snowless portions of southern Ontario each winter. • Feathered to the toes, a Snowy Owl can remain active at cold temperatures that often send other owls to the woods for shelter. • As Snowy Owls age, their plumage becomes lighter in colour—old males are often pure white. • Snowy Owls are yearly visitors to Ontario, but their numbers can fluctuate quite dramatically. When lemming and vole populations crash in the Arctic, large numbers of Snowy Owls often venture south in search of food.

ID: predominantly white; yellow eyes; black bill and talons; no ear tufts. *Adult male:* almost entirely white, with very little dark flecking. *Adult female:* prominent dark barring or flecking on the breast and upperparts. *Immature:* heavier barring than an adult female.
Size: *L* 51–69 cm; *W* 1.4–1.7 m (female is noticeably larger).
Status: irregularly very rare to uncommon winter visitor from September to April; very rare summer visitor and potential breeder.
Habitat: open country, including croplands, meadows, airports and lakeshores; often perches on fenceposts, buildings and utility poles.
Nesting: nesting has not been confirmed in Ontario.
Feeding: swoops from a perch, often punching through the snow to take mice, voles, grouse, hares, weasels and rarely songbirds and water birds.
Voice: quiet during winter.
Similar Species: no other owl in Ontario is largely white and lacks ear tufts.
Best Sites: Sarnia Bay shoreline; Pearson International Airport; Tommy Thompson Park; Presqu'ile PP; Wolfe and Amherst islands; Marina Park in Thunder Bay; fields throughout Ontario.

NORTHERN HAWK OWL

Surnia ulula

The Northern Hawk Owl resides in Ontario's northern boreal forest, where muskeg and mosquitos dominate the summer landscape and cold arctic temperatures prevail in winter. Like the Snowy Owl, the Northern Hawk Owl is an 'irruptive' winter visitor to southern parts of the province, meaning that it may be common in some winters and rare in others. When a 'hawk owl year' comes around, be sure to make the best of the event—there might not be a repeat performance for a decade or more. • Northern Hawk Owls summer where the days are long, so they are comfortable hunting in daylight. Hawk Owls are by no means the only owls that hunt diurnally, but they are the ones most likely to rest on exposed perches. • With its long, slender, hawk-like features, and direct, accipiter-like flight pattern, it's easy to understand how this bird got its name. No matter how much it behaves like a hawk, however, there is no mistaking the face of an owl or its obvious use of sound to hunt prey.

ID: long tail; no ear tufts; fine horizontal barring on the underparts; white facial disc is bordered with black; pale bill; yellow eyes; white-spotted forehead.
Size: *L* 38–43 cm; *W* 80–90 cm.
Status: rare to very uncommon year-round resident.
Habitat: black-spruce bogs and muskegs, old burns and tree-bordered clearings.
Nesting: in an abandoned woodpecker cavity or on a broken treetop; adds no lining to the nest; female incubates

5–7 whitish eggs for 25–30 days.
Feeding: swoops from a perch; eats mostly voles, mice and birds; also eats some large insects in summer.
Voice: usually quiet; whistled breeding trill; call is an accipiter-like *kee-kee-kee*.
Similar Species: *Boreal* (p. 188), *Northern Saw-whet* (p. 189) and *Short-eared* (p. 187) *owls:* much shorter tail; vertical breast streaks.
Best Sites: check local bird hotlines for recent winter sightings in southern Ontario; Mer Bleue; Quetico PP; Wakami Lake PP; Moosonee area.

BARRED OWL

Strix varia

Each spring, the memorable sound of courting Barred Owls echoes through Ontario's forests: *Who cooks for you? Who cooks for you all?* The escalating laughs, hoots and gargling howls reinforce the bond between pairs. At the height of courtship and when raising young, a pair of Barred Owls may continue their calls well into daylight hours, and they may hunt actively day and night. They also tend to be more vocal during early evening or early morning when the moon is full and the air is calm. At other times of the year, Barred Owls are usually most active between midnight and 4:00 a.m., when the forest floor rustles with the movements of mice, voles and shrews. • Barred Owls have relatively weak talons, and they mainly prey on smaller animals, such as voles. • Barred Owls were once more common in southern Ontario, but their numbers have declined with the destruction of the moist, deciduous woodlands and swamps that covered much of the region before human settlement.

ID: dark eyes; horizontal barring around the neck and upper breast; vertical streaking on the belly; light-coloured bill; no ear tufts; dark grey-brown mottled plumage.

Size: *L* 43–61 cm; *W* 1–1.3 m (female is slightly larger).

Status: uncommon year-round resident.

Habitat: mature deciduous and mixed forests, especially in dense stands near swamps, streams and lakes.

Nesting: in a natural tree cavity, broken treetop or abandoned stick nest; adds very little to the nest; female incubates 2 or 3 white eggs for 28–33 days; male feeds the incubating female.

Feeding: nocturnal; swoops from a perch to pounce on prey; eats mostly mice, voles and squirrels; also eats amphibians and smaller birds.

Voice: most characteristic of all the owls; loud, hooting, rhythmic, laughing call is heard mostly in spring but also throughout the year: *Who cooks for you? Who cooks for you all?*

Similar Species: *Great Gray Owl* (p. 185): larger; yellow eyes; well-defined, ringed facial disc; black chin patch; lacks the horizontal barring on the upper breast. *Northern Hawk Owl* (p. 183): yellow eyes; finely barred underparts. *Great Horned Owl* (p. 181): ear tufts; light-coloured eyes. *Short-eared Owl* (p. 187): yellow eyes; lacks the horizontal barring on the upper breast.

Best Sites: Frontenac PP; Bon Echo PP; Algonquin PP; Killbear PP; Quetico PP.

GREAT GRAY OWL

Strix nebulosa

With a face designed like a satellite dish, the Great Gray Owl is able to detect and locate the quietest forest floor scurry or muskeg twitch. Even the faint sounds of a tiny rodent covered by 60 cm of snow can be detected by this owl. The Great Gray's facial discs funnel sound waves into its asymmetrically placed ears, enabling it, through triangulation, to pinpoint the precise location of its prey. • This regal owl is highly sought-after by Ontario birders, but its rare status and secretive lifestyle keep it well hidden. Finding a Great Gray Owl in its breeding habitat of northern spruce bogs and muskeg can be like finding a needle in a haystack. Fortunately for many southern Ontario residents, Great Grays occasionally appear in good numbers south of their breeding range, usually in years when northern small mammal populations have crashed. • Even though the Great Gray Owl is the largest North American owl, it is outweighed by as much as 15 percent by both the Snowy Owl and the Great Horned Owl.

ID: grey-brown overall; large, rounded head; no ear tufts; long tail; yellow eyes and bill; well-defined, ringed facial disc; black chin bordered by white.

Size: *L* 61–84 cm; *W* 1.4–1.5 m (female is slightly larger).

Status: rare to very uncommon year-round resident.

Habitat: forest clearings, open meadows, spruce or poplar stands adjacent to open muskeg, fens, bogs or meadows.

Nesting: usually near a spruce bog or muskeg; in an abandoned hawk, raven or eagle nest; occasionally nests atop a tall, broken stump; adds little nest material; female incubates 2–4 white eggs for 28–36 days; male feeds the female on the nest.

Feeding: listens and watches from a perch; swoops to catch voles, mice, shrews, lemmings, squirrels and hares.

Voice: slow, deep, almost inaudible resonating series of hoots; also a series of widely spaced, low, rising *wooo* notes.

Similar Species: *Barred Owl* (p. 184): dark eyes; horizontal barring on the upper breast. *Great Horned Owl* (p. 181): large ear tufts; dark bill. *Snowy Owl* (p. 182): mostly white. *Short-eared Owl* (p. 187): much smaller; black eye sockets; dark bill; black 'wrist' crescents.

Best Sites: Chapleau Crown Game Reserve; Lake Superior PP; Pukaskwa PP; Quetico PP.

185

LONG-EARED OWL

Asio otus

Long-eared Owls are widespread and probably fairly common throughout much of the province, but most Ontarians overlook these birds because of their cryptic plumage and reclusive habits. Only at dusk do these owls emerge from their secret hideouts to prey upon the small creatures of the night. Long-eared Owls are most noticeable during the winter months in southern parts of the province, where they roost together in groups of up to 75 birds in woodlots, hedgerows or isolated tree groves. • Long-eared Owls will either inflate or compress their feathers in response to certain situations: to scare off an intruder, the owl expands its air sacs, puffs its feathers and spreads its wings; to hide from an intruder, it compresses itself into a long, thin, vertical form. • All owls, as well as many other birds, such as herons, gulls, crows and hawks, regurgitate 'pellets'—the indigestible parts of their prey compressed into an elongated ball. The feathers, fur and bones that make up the pellets are interesting to analyze, because they reveal what the animal has eaten.

ID: long ear tufts are relatively close-set; slim body; vertical belly markings; rusty brown facial disc; mottled brown plumage; yellow eyes; white around the bill.

Size: *L* 33–41 cm; *W* 91–119 cm.

Status: rare to uncommon breeder; uncommon to locally common migrant and visitor in southern Ontario from September to April.

Habitat: *Breeding:* dense, coniferous, mixed and riparian forests and tall shrublands. *Winter:* woodlots, dense riparian woodlands, hedgerows and isolated tree groves in meadows, fields, cemeteries, farmyards or parks.

Nesting: often in an abandoned hawk or crow nest; female incubates 2–6 white eggs for 26–28 days; male feeds the incubating female.

Feeding: nocturnal; flies low, pouncing on prey from the air; eats mostly voles and mice, occasionally shrews, moles, small rabbits, small birds and amphibians.

Voice: breeding call is a low, soft, ghostly *quoo-quoo*; alarm call is *weck-weck-weck*; also issues various shrieks, hisses, whistles, barks, hoots and dove-like coos.

Similar Species: *Great Horned Owl* (p. 181): much larger; ear tufts are set further apart; stout body; rounder face. *Short-eared Owl* (p. 187): lacks the long ear tufts; nests on the ground. *Eastern Screech-Owl* (p. 180): much shorter, stout body; shorter, wider-set ear tufts.

Best Sites: Point Pelee NP; Shaefer's Woods; Amherst Island; Ojibway Prairie; Lynde Shores Conservation Area.

SHORT-EARED OWL

Asio flammeus

Like the Snowy Owl of the Arctic, the Short-eared Owl lacks conspicuous ear tufts and fills a niche that has been left unoccupied by forest-dwelling owls. This bird of open country occupies such habitats as wet meadows, marshes, fields, bogs and tundra, and it can be surprisingly difficult to locate, especially during the summer breeding season when females sit tightly on their ground nests. • In spring, Short-eared pairs perform visually dramatic courtship dances. Courting pairs fly together, and the male claps his wings on each downstroke as he performs short, periodic dives. Short-ears do not 'hoot' like forest-dwelling owls, because visual displays are more effective for communicating in open environments. • As with many other predators, Short-eared Owl populations grow and decline over many years in response to dramatic fluctuations in prey availability. Cold weather and declines in small mammal populations occasionally force large numbers of these owls to become temporary nomads, often sending them to areas well outside their breeding range.

ID: yellow eyes set in black sockets; heavy, vertical streaking on the buff belly; straw-coloured upperparts; short ear tufts are inconspicuous. *In flight:* dark 'wrist' crescents; deep wingbeats; long wings.
Size: *L* 33–43 cm; *W* 1–1.2 m (female is slightly larger).
Status: uncommon to locally fairly common migrant and visitor from October to April; rare breeder from April to October.
Habitat: open areas, including grasslands, wet meadows, marshes, fields, airports, forest clearings, muskeg and tundra.
Nesting: on wet ground in open areas; a slight depression is sparsely lined with grass; female incubates 4–7 white eggs for 24–37 days male feeds the incubating female.
Feeding: forages while flying low over marshes, wet meadows and tall vegetation; pounces on prey from the air; eats mostly voles and other small rodents; also takes insects, small birds and amphibians.
Voice: generally quiet; produces a soft *toot-toot-toot* during the breeding season; also squeals and barks like a small dog.
Similar Species: *Long-eared Owl* (p. 186) and *Great Horned Owl* (p. 181): long ear tufts. *Barred Owl* (p. 184): dark eyes; horizontal barring on the upper breast. *Great Gray Owl* (p. 185): much larger, lacks the black eye sockets and dark 'wrist' crescents; yellow bill. *Burrowing Owl:* exceptionally rare visitor to Ontario; much longer legs; shorter tail and wings.
Best Sites: Western Rainy River District; Wainfleet Bog; Beaverton; Polar Bear PP; Tommy Thompson Park; Nanticoke-area fields.

187

BOREAL OWL

Aegolius funereus

The Boreal Owl routinely ranks in the top five of the most-desired birds to see, according to birdwatcher surveys across North America. In Ontario, Boreal Owls are best seen from March to May, when they perch conspicuously on bare branches and call regularly during long northern nights. Look for them among the old-growth coniferous and mixed forests in Pukaskwa, Quetico and Sleeping Giant provincial parks. • Because of the Boreal Owl's remote habitat and nocturnal habits, ornithologists have yet to uncover many aspects of its ecology and behaviour. This small owl is known to be well adapted to snowy forest environments—it is quite capable of locating and catching prey that lives beneath the snow. • This approachable owl was named 'Blind One' by native peoples, because it was easily captured by hand.

ID: small; rounded head; whitish face with a dark border; white spots on the black forehead; yellowish bill; vertical, rusty streaks on the underparts; white-spotted, brown upperparts; black eyebrow; short tail. *Juvenile:* brown underparts; brown face with white between the eyes.
Size: *L* 23–31 cm; *W* 55–74 cm.
Status: rare to locally fairly common year-round resident; irregularly very rare to rare visitor outside its breeding range from October to March.
Habitat: mature coniferous and mixed forests.
Nesting: in an abandoned woodpecker cavity or natural hollow in a tree; lines the cavity with a few feathers; female incubates 4–6 white eggs for 26–32

days; male feeds the incubating female.
Feeding: swoops from a perch for voles, mice, shrews, flying squirrels and insects; often plunges through the snow to catch prey in winter; may cache food.
Voice: rapid, accelerating, continuous whistle: *whew-whew-whew-whew-whew-whew*; easily imitated.
Similar Species: *Northern Saw-whet Owl* (p. 189): adult has a dark bill, white forehead streaking and lacks the dark, vertical eyebrow; juvenile has reddish underparts. *Northern Hawk Owl* (p. 183): much longer tail; fine horizontal barring on the underparts.
Best Sites: Hwy 11 from Cochrane to Smooth Rock Falls; Pukaskwa PP; Sleeping Giant PP; Quetico PP; Woodland Caribou PP.

NORTHERN SAW-WHET OWL

Aegolius acadicus

This tiny owl is an opportunistic hunter, taking whatever it can, whenever it can. If temperatures are below freezing and prey is abundant, this small owl may choose to catch more than it can eat in a single sitting. The extra food is usually stored in a tree, where it quickly freezes. When hunting efforts fail, a hungry saw-whet will return to thaw out its frozen cache by 'incubating' it as if it were a clutch of eggs! • Saw-whets are usually heard more than they are seen, and from mid-winter to early spring, their slow, whistled notes are surprisingly common. They are most conspicuous in October, when they can be seen in considerable numbers on islands and peninsulas on the north shores of Lake Erie and Lake Michigan. • 'Owl prowls' during Christmas bird counts often concentrate much energy on saw-whets. These owls can be very numerous in parts of southeastern Ontario, but they are often frustratingly silent. • The scientific name *acadicus* is Latin for 'from Acadia,' the region where this bird was first collected.

ID: small body; large, rounded head; light, unbordered facial disc; dark bill; vertical, rusty streaks on the underparts; brown, white-spotted upperparts; white-streaked forehead; short tail. *Juvenile:* white patch between the eyes; rich brown head and breast; buff-brown belly.

Size: *L* 18–23 cm; *W* 43–55 cm.

Status: uncommon migrant from early February to mid-March and from late September to mid-November; rare visitor from October to March; rare to fairly common breeder.

Habitat: pure and mixed coniferous and deciduous forests; wooded city parks and ravines.

Nesting: in an abandoned wood-pecker cavity or natural hollow in a tree; female incubates 5 or 6 white eggs for 27–29 days; male feeds the incubating female.

Feeding: swoops from a perch; eats mostly mice and voles; also eats larger insects, songbirds, shrews, moles and occasionally amphibians; may cache food.

Voice: whistled, evenly spaced notes repeated about 100 times a minute: *whew-whew-whew-whew;* continuous and easily imitated.

Similar Species: *Boreal Owl* (p. 188): adult has a light-coloured bill, white spotting on the black forehead, a dark, vertical eyebrow and a dark border to the facial disc; juvenile has a dark chocolate brown breast. *Northern Hawk Owl* (p. 183): much longer tail; fine, horizontal barring on the underparts; white spotting on the black forehead.

Best Sites: Frontenac PP; Algonquin PP; Killbear PP; Killarney PP; Quetico PP; Point Pelee NP; Lynde Shores Conservation Area; Prince Edward Point NWA.

COMMON NIGHTHAWK

Chordeiles minor

Each May and June, male nighthawks fly high above forest clearings and lakeshores, gaining elevation in preparation for the climax of their noisy aerial dance. From a great height, they dive swiftly, thrusting their wings forward in a final braking action as they strain to pull out of the steep dive. This quick thrust of the wings produces a deep, hollow *vroom* that attracts female nighthawks. • Like other members of the nightjar family, the Common Nighthawk is adapted for catching insects in mid-air: its gaping mouth is surrounded by feather shafts that funnel insects into its mouth. • Nighthawks are generally less nocturnal than other nightjars, but they still spend most of the daylight hours resting on a tree limb or on the ground. These birds have very short legs and small feet, and they sit along the length of tree branches, rather than across the branch as do most perched birds.

ID: cryptic, mottled plumage; barred under-parts. *Male:* white throat. *Female:* buff throat. *In flight:* bold white patches on the long, pointed wings; shallowly forked, barred tail; flight is erratic.

Size: *L* 22–25 cm.

Status: uncommon migrant and breeder from May to August; fairly common to locally common migrant from mid-August to early September; a few may remain into October.

Habitat: *Breeding:* in forest openings or burns, bogs, rocky outcroppings, gravel rooftops and sometimes fields with sparse cover or bare patches. *In migration:* places where large numbers of flying insects can be found; usually roosts in trees, often near water.

Nesting: on bare ground; no nest is built; female incubates

2 well-camouflaged eggs for about 19 days; both adults feed the young.

Feeding: primarily crepuscular, but will also feed during the day and night; may fly around street lights at night to catch prey attracted to the light; catches insects in flight, often high in the air; eats mosquitoes, blackflies, midges, beetles, flying ants, moths and other flying insects.

Voice: frequently repeated, nasal *peent peent;* also makes a deep, hollow *vroom* with its wings during courtship flight.

Similar Species: *Whip-poor-will* (p. 192) and *Chuck-will's-widow* (p. 191): less common; lacks the white 'wrist' patches; shorter, rounder wings; rounded tail.

Best Sites: Detroit River waterfront; The Pinery PP; Trent Canal; Presqu'ile PP; Bon Echo PP; Ottawa River; Sault Ste. Marie waterfront; Niagara River.

CHUCK-WILL'S-WIDOW

Caprimulgus carolinensis

During daylight, you would be lucky to see this perfectly camouflaged bird roosting on the furrowed bark of a horizontal tree limb or sitting among scattered leaves on the forest floor. Even when it nests it is virtually undetectable: this bird incubates its eggs and raises its young on the forest floor. At dusk, however, the Chuck-will's-widow is easily detected as it calls its own name while it patrols the evening skies for flying insects. • This bird's core range is in the hot, humid southeastern U.S., so it is definitely pushing its luck at the northern limit of its range in southern Ontario. Fewer than 10 known pairs of Chuck-will's-widows currently nest in Ontario, confined mostly to protected stands of scarce Carolinian forest and pure pine plantations.

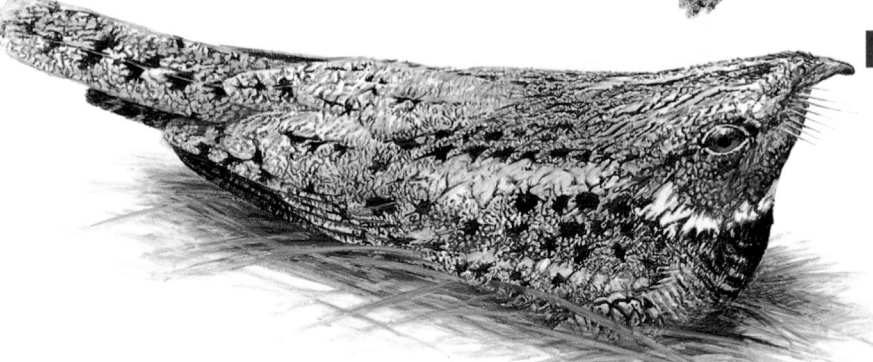

ID: mottled brown and buff body with an overall reddish tinge; pale brown to buff throat; whitish 'necklace'; dark breast; long, rounded tail. *Male:* inner edges of the outer tail feathers are white.

Size: *L* 28–33 cm; *W* 62–65 cm.

Status: rare and local breeder from late April through July.

Habitat: riparian woodlands, swamp edges and deciduous and pine woodlands.

Nesting: on bare ground; no nest is built; female incubates 2 heavily blotched, creamy white eggs for about 21 days and raises the young alone.

Feeding: catches insects on the wing or by hawking; eats beetles, moths and other large flying insects.

Voice: 3 loud whistling notes often paraphrased as *chuck-will's-widow.*

Similar Species: *Whip-poor-will* (p. 192): smaller; 'necklace' contrasts with the black throat; greyer colouration overall; male shows much more white in the tail feathers; female's dark tail feathers are bordered with buff on the outer tips. *Common Nighthawk* (p. 190): forked tail; white patches on the wings; male has a white throat; female has a buff throat.

Best Sites: Point Pelee NP; Rondeau PP; Long Point area.

191

RUBY-THROATED HUMMINGBIRD

Archilochus colubris

Ruby-throated Hummingbirds span the ecological gap between birds and bees—they feed on the sweet, energy-rich nectar that flowers provide in exchange for pollination. Many avid gardeners and birders have long understood the nature of this co-dependence and have planted native nectar-producing plants in their yards in hopes of attracting these delightful birds. Even non-gardeners can attract hummingbirds by maintaining a clean sugarwater feeder in a safe location. • Weighing about as much as a nickel, hummingbirds are briefly capable of speeds of up to 100 km/h; they are also among the few birds that are able to fly vertically and in reverse. In straight-ahead flight, they beat their wings up to 80 times a second (slightly less if hovering or reversing), and their hearts can beat up to 1200 times a minute! Each year, their long-distance migrations take them across the Gulf of Mexico—an incredible, non-stop journey of more than 800 km. • Ontarians can expect to see the delightful Ruby-throated Hummingbird wherever numerous nectar-filled tubular flowers brighten the landscape.

ID: tiny; long bill; iridescent green back; light underparts; dark tail. *Male:* ruby red throat; black chin. *Female* and *Immature:* fine, dark throat streaking.
Size: L 9–9.5 cm.
Status: fairly common migrant; uncommon breeder from May to August; common migrant from mid-August to mid-September; a few may remain into mid-November.
Habitat: open, mixed woodlands, wetlands, orchards, tree-lined meadows, flower gardens and backyards with trees and feeders.
Nesting: on a horizontal tree limb; tiny, deep cup nest of plant down and fibres is held together with spider silk; lichens and leaves are pasted on the exterior walls; female incubates 2 white eggs for 13–16 days; female feeds the young.

Feeding: uses its long bill and tongue to probe blooming flowers and sugar-sweetened water from feeders; also eats small insects and spiders.
Voice: most noticeable is the soft buzzing of the wings while in flight; also produces a loud *chick* and other high squeaks.
Similar Species: *Rufous Hummingbird* (p. 358): exceptionally rare in Ontario; male has red on the flanks and back; female has a red-spotted throat and reddish flanks.
Best Sites: backyard feeders and flower meadows throughout southern Ontario and parts of northern Ontario; Rondeau PP; Niagara Peninsula orchards.

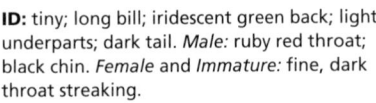

BELTED KINGFISHER

Ceryle alcyon

Many of Ontario's lakes, rivers, marshes and beaver ponds are monitored closely by the boisterous Belted Kingfisher. Never far from water, this bird is often found uttering its distinctive, rattling call while perched on a bare branch that extends out over a productive pool. With a precise headfirst dive, the Kingfisher can catch fish at depths of up to 60 cm, or snag a frog immersed in only a few centimetres of water.
• During the breeding season, a pair of kingfishers will typically take turns excavating the nest burrow. They use their bills to chip away at an exposed sandbank and then kick loose material out of the tunnel with their feet. Female kingfishers have the traditional female reproductive role for birds, but, like phalaropes, they are more colourful than their mates.
• Alcyon (Halcyone) was the daughter of the wind god in Greek mythology; she and her husband were transformed into kingfishers. • Kingfishers are found around the world, but the Belted Kingfisher is the only one found in Canada.

ID: bluish upperparts; shaggy crest; blue-grey breast band; white collar; long, straight bill; short legs; white underwings; small, white patch near the eye. *Male:* no 'belt.' *Female:* rust-coloured 'belt' (occasionally incomplete).
Size: L 28–36 cm.
Status: common breeder (rarer in the north) from April through October; rare visitor from November through March.
Habitat: rivers, large streams, lakes, marshes and beaver ponds, especially near exposed soil banks, gravel pits or bluffs.
Nesting: in a cavity at the end of an earth burrow, often up to 2 m deep,

dug by the pair with their bills and claws; pair incubates 6 or 7 eggs for 22–24 days; both adults feed the young.
Feeding: dives headfirst, either from a perch or from a hover above the water; eats mostly small fish, aquatic invertebrates and tadpoles.
Voice: fast, repetitive, cackling rattle, a little like a teacup shaking on a saucer.
Similar Species: *Blue Jay* (p. 225): more intensely blue; smaller bill and head; behaves in a completely different fashion.
Best Sites: almost any fish-bearing waterbody in Ontario.

RED-HEADED WOODPECKER

Melanerpes erythrocephalus

Although its numbers in Ontario might not be significant, the beauty of the Red-headed Woodpecker tips the esthetic scales in its favour. This woodpecker was once common throughout its range, but its numbers have declined dramatically over the past century. Red-headed Woodpeckers are commonly struck by traffic when they dart from their perches to catch flying insects, and since the introduction of the European Starling, they have been largely outcompeted for nesting cavities. • When Alexander Wilson, the 'father' of American ornithology, first arrived in North America, the Red-headed Woodpecker was one of the first birds to greet him. Inspired, Wilson wrote of this woodpecker: 'His tri-coloured plumage, so striking.... A gay and frolicsome disposition, diving and vociferating around the high dead limbs of some large tree, amusing the passenger with their gambols.'

ID: bright red head, chin, throat and bib with a black border; black back, wings and tail; white breast, belly, rump, lower back and inner wing patches. *Juvenile:* brown head, back, wings and tail; slight brown streaking on the white underparts.
Size: *L* 21–24 cm.
Status: fairly common migrant from late April to June and from late August to early November; uncommon breeder from May to September; rare visitor from November to April.
Habitat: open deciduous woodlands (especially oak woodlands), urban parks, river edges and roadsides with groves of scattered trees.
Nesting: male excavates a nest cavity in a dead tree or limb; pair

incubates 4 or 5 white eggs for 12–13 days; both adults feed the young.
Feeding: eats mostly insects, earthworms, spiders, nuts, berries, seeds and fruit; flycatches for insects; hammers dead and decaying wood for grubs; may also eat some young birds and eggs.
Voice: loud series of *kweer* or *kwrring* notes; occasionally a chattering *kerr-r-ruck*; also drums softly in short bursts.
Similar Species: adult is distinctive. *Red-bellied Woodpecker* (p. 197): whitish face and underparts; black and white barred back. *Yellow-bellied Sapsucker* (p. 198): large white wing patch.
Best Sites: Rondeau PP; The Pinery PP; Niagara Peninsula; Lake Scugog; Beaver Meadow Conservation Area.

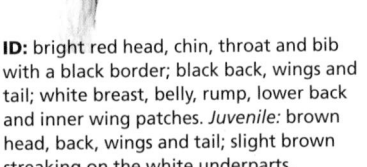

RED-BELLIED WOODPECKER

Melanerpes carolinus

Deep in southwestern Ontario, remnant stands of Carolinian forest serve as a stronghold for the rarest of Ontario woodpeckers, the Red-bellied Woodpecker. This bird reaches the extreme limit of its North American range in these forests, and although it is found year-round, its numbers fluctuate depending on the availability of habitat and the mildness of winter conditions. In recent years, mild winter weather has enabled the Red-bellied Woodpecker to increase its numbers in Ontario. • These birds often issue noisy, rolling *churr* calls as they poke about wooded landscapes in search of seeds and wood-boring insects. Unlike most woodpeckers, which eat mostly insects, Red-bellies consume large amounts of plant material. In the southwestern U.S., where they are more common, Red-bellied Woodpeckers are often considered pests because they feed on commercial fruit crops.

ID: black-and-white barred back; white patches on the rump and topside base of the primaries; reddish tinge on the belly. *Female:* red nape. *Male:* red nape extends to the forehead. *Juvenile:* dark grey crown; streaked breast.
Size: *L* 23–27 cm.
Status: rare year-round resident.
Habitat: mature deciduous woodlands, primarily Carolinian forest; occasionally in wooded residential areas.
Nesting: in a cavity; female selects one of several nest sites excavated by the male; pair may use natural cavities or abandoned cavities of other woodpeckers; pair incubates 4 or 5 white eggs over 12–14 days; both adults raise the young.
Feeding: eats mostly insects, seeds, nuts and fruit; may also eat tree sap, small amphibians, bird eggs or small fish; forages in trees, on the ground or occasionally on the wing.
Voice: call is a soft, rolling *churr*; drums in second-long bursts.
Similar Species: *Northern Flicker* (p. 203): yellow underwings; grey crown; brown back with dark barring; black bib; large, dark spots on the underparts. *Red-headed Woodpecker* (p. 196): all-red head; unbarred, black back and wings; white patch on the trailing edge of the wing.
Best Sites: Rondeau PP; Long Point PP; The Pinery PP; Dickson Wilderness Area; Sudden Tract.

197

YELLOW-BELLIED SAPSUCKER
Sphyrapicus varius

Yellow-bellied Sapsuckers are conspicuous in May, when they perform their characteristic courting rituals throughout woodlands in Ontario. The drumming of sapsuckers differs from that of other Ontario woodpeckers—it has an irregular, Morse–code-like rhythm. • Lines of parallel 'wells' freshly drilled in tree bark are sure sign a sapsucker is nearby. As the wells fill with sweet, sticky sap, they attract insects, and the sapsuckers make their rounds eating both the trapped bugs and the pooled sap. Sapsuckers don't actually suck sap; they lap it up with a tongue that resembles a paintbrush. Within their forest territory, a pair of sapsuckers might drill a number of sites. This variation of typical woodpecker foraging strategy has proven to be quite successful for the sapsucker. • Other species such as hummingbirds, kinglets, warblers and waxwings benefit from Yellow-bellied Sapsucker wells.

ID: black bib; red forecrown; black and white face, back, wings and tail; large, white wing patch; yellow wash on the lower breast and belly. *Male:* red chin. *Female:* white chin. *Juvenile:* brownish overall.
Size: *L* 18–20 cm.
Status: uncommon to common migrant and breeder from April to November; a few may be present in winter.
Habitat: deciduous and mixed forests, especially dry, second-growth woodlands.
Nesting: in a cavity; usually in a live poplar or birch tree with heart-rot; usually lines the cavity with wood chips; pair incubates 5 or 6 eggs for 12–13 days.
Feeding: hammers trees for insects; drills 'wells' in live trees where it collects sap and trapped insects; also flycatches for insects.
Voice: nasal, cat-like *meow*; territorial and courtship hammering has a Morse–code-like quality and rhythm.
Similar Species: *Red-headed Woodpecker* (p. 196): juvenile lacks the white patch on the wing. *Downy Woodpecker* (p. 199) and *Hairy Woodpecker* (p. 200): lack the large white wing patch and the red forecrown; red nape; white back. *Three-toed Woodpecker* (p. 201): lacks the white wing patch; yellow forecrown; black and white back.
Best Sites: Bruce Peninsula woodlands; Trent Canal woodlands; Bon Echo PP; Killbear PP; Grundy Lake PP; Hwy 11 from Cobalt to Hearst.

DOWNY WOODPECKER

Picoides pubescens

A regular patron of backyard suet feeders, the small and widely common Downy Woodpecker is often the first woodpecker a novice birdwatcher will identify with confidence. Downies are generally more approachable and tolerant of human activities, and once you become familiar with its dainty appearance, it won't be long before you recognize it by its soft taps and brisk staccato calls that filter through your neighbourhood. These encounters are not all confusion-free, however, because the closely related Hairy Woodpecker looks remarkably similar. • The Downy's small bill is extremely effective at poking into tiny crevices and extracting invertebrates and wood-boring grubs. Like many woodpeckers, it comes equipped with feathered nostrils, which serve to filter out the sawdust it produces when hammering. • To cushion the repeated shocks of a lifetime of hammering, woodpeckers have evolved a strong bill, strong neck muscles, a flexible, reinforced skull, and a brain that is tightly packed in its protective cranium.

ID: clear white belly and back; black wings are barred with white; black eye line and crown; short, stubby bill; mostly black tail; white outer tail feathers are spotted with black. *Male:* small, red patch on the back of the head. *Female:* no red patch.

Size: *L* 15–18 cm.

Status: generally common year-round resident; rare in the far north.

Habitat: all wooded environments, especially deciduous and mixed forests and areas with tall deciduous shrubs.

Nesting: pair excavates a cavity in a dying or decaying trunk or limb and lines it with wood chips; excavation lasts more than 2 weeks; pair incubates 4 or 5 white eggs for 11–13 days; both adults feed the young.

Feeding: forages on trunks and branches; chips and probes for insect eggs, cocoons, larvae and adults; also eats nuts and seeds; attracted to suet feeders.

Voice: long, unbroken trill; calls are a sharp *pik* or *ki-ki-ki* or whiny *queek queek*.

Similar Species: *Hairy Woodpecker* (p. 200): larger; bill is as long as the head is wide; no spots on the white outer tail feathers. *Yellow-bellied Sapsucker* (p. 198): large white wing patch; red forecrown; lacks the red nape and the clean white back. *Three-toed Woodpecker* (p. 201): yellow forecrown; black barring on the white back and sides.

Best Sites: almost any wooded area.

HAIRY WOODPECKER

Picoides villosus

A second or third look is often required to confirm the identity of the Hairy Woodpecker, because to uneducated eyes it is often confused with its smaller cousin, the Downy Woodpecker. A convenient way to distinguish one from the other might be at a backyard feeder, where it is not uncommon to see both of these birds vying for food. • The secret to woodpeckers' feeding success is hidden in their skulls. Most woodpeckers have very long tongues—in some cases more than four times the length of the bill—made possible by twin structures that wrap around the perimeter of the skull. These structures store the tongue in much the same way that a measuring tape is stored in its case. Besides being long and maneuverable, the tip of the tongue is sticky with saliva, and it is finely barbed to seize reluctant wood-boring insects. • Rather than singing during courtship, woodpeckers drum rhythmically on trees.

ID: pure white belly; black wings are spotted with white; black cheek and crown; bill is about as long as the head is wide; black tail, with unspotted, white outer feathers. *Male:* small red patch on the back of the head. *Female:* no red patch.

Size: *L* 19–24 cm.

Status: uncommon to fairly common year-round resident.

Habitat: deciduous and mixed forests.

Nesting: pair excavates a nest site in a live or decaying tree-trunk or limb; excavation lasts more than 2 weeks; lines the cavity with wood chips; pair incubates 4 or 5 white eggs for 12–14 days; both adults feed the young.

Feeding: forages on tree-trunks and branches; chips, hammers and probes bark for insect eggs, cocoons, larvae and adults; also eats nuts, fruit and seeds; attracted to feeders with suet, especially in winter.

Voice: loud, sharp call: *peek peek*; long, unbroken trill: *keek-ik-ik-ik-ik-ik*.

Similar Species: *Downy Woodpecker* (p. 199): smaller; shorter bill; dark spots on the white outer tail feathers. *Yellow-bellied Sapsucker* (p. 198): large white wing patch; red forecrown; lacks the red nape and the clean white back. *Three-toed Woodpecker* (p. 201): yellow forecrown; black barring on the white back and sides.

Best Sites: almost any large woodland.

THREE-TOED WOODPECKER

Picoides tridactylus

The Three-toed Woodpecker is a quiet, inconspicuous year-round resident of Ontario's northern boreal forest. In winter, this woodpecker finds solace under soft conifer boughs, and during the breeding season, it builds its nest in rotting trees and snags. Although it may appear to be rare throughout much of its range, it is often fairly common in areas where standing dead trees are infested with wood-boring beetle larvae. Burned-over areas and soggy muskeg bogs are also favourite haunts of this elusive bird. • While foraging, the Three-toed Woodpecker chisels off large flakes of bark from old or dying conifers, exposing the red inner surface of the trunk. Eventually the trees take on a distinct reddish look and are skirted with fragments of bark. • Both the Three-toed Woodpecker and the Black-backed Woodpecker have three toes rather than the usual four.

ID: black and white barring down the centre of the back; white underparts; black barring on the sides; predominantly black head with 2 white stripes; black tail with black-spotted, white outer tail feathers; 3 toes. *Male:* yellow crown. *Female:* black crown with occasional white spotting.
Size: *L* 21–24 cm.
Status: rare to uncommon year-round resident; irruptive, especially in winter.
Habitat: spruce and fir forests, bogs and disturbed areas.
Nesting: excavates a cavity, usually in a dead or dying conifer trunk; excavation can take up to 12 days; pair incubates 4 white eggs for 12–14 days; both adults feed the young.
Feeding: chips away bark to expose larval and adult wood-boring insects; occasionally eats berries and sap.

Voice: call is a low *pik* or *teek*; drumming is a prolonged series of short bursts.
Similar Species: *Black-backed Woodpecker* (p. 202): solid black back; unspotted white outer tail feathers. *Hairy Woodpecker* (p. 200): clean white back; lacks the dark barring on the sides. *Yellow-bellied Sapsucker* (p. 198): large white wing patch; red forecrown; black bib; yellow-tinged underparts.
Best Sites: The Shoals PP; Wakami Lake PP; Quetico PP; Albany River PP.

BLACK-BACKED WOODPECKER

Picoides arcticus

Even experienced naturalists can have difficulty finding the elusive, semi-nomadic Black-backed Woodpecker on its northern coniferous breeding grounds. This generally quiet woodpecker prefers a secretive life in remote, uninhabited tracts of boreal forest. Only during the brief courtship season does the male Black-backed Woodpecker advertise his presence by drumming on the top of a broken, standing dead tree or snag. • This reclusive bird is most active in recently burned forest patches where wood-boring beetles thrive under the charred bark of spruce, pine and fir trees. When it forages on blackened tree-trunks, its black-backed form can be difficult to spot, especially from a distance. • In years when food is scarce, this bird often moves south beyond its normal breeding range, occasionally showing up in wooded ravines near Toronto. Sighting records suggest that large, irruptive southern invasions of Black-backed and Three-toed woodpeckers occur at six- to eight-year intervals. • The scientific name *arcticus* reflects this bird's largely northern distribution.

ID: solid black back; white underparts; black barring on the sides; predominantly black head, with a single white line below the eye; black 'moustache' stripe; 3 toes; black tail with pure white outer tail feathers. *Male:* yellow crown. *Female:* black crown.
Size: *L* 23–25 cm.
Status: uncommon to locally fairly common year-round resident (but rarely seen); irruptive, especially in winter.
Habitat: coniferous forests, especially burned-over sites with many standing dead trees.
Nesting: excavates a cavity in a dead or dying conifer trunk or limb; excavation can take up to 12 days; pair incubates 4 eggs for 12–14 days; both adults feed the young.

Feeding: chisels away bark flakes to expose larval and adult wood-boring insects; may eat some nuts and fruits.
Voice: call is a low *kik*; drumming is a prolonged series of short bursts.
Similar Species: *Three-toed Woodpecker* (p. 201): white back with black, horizontal barring; black spots on the white outer tail feathers. *Hairy Woodpecker* (p. 200): clean white back; lacks the dark barring on the sides. *Yellow-bellied Sapsucker* (p. 198): black and whitish back; large white wing patch; red forecrown; black bib; yellow-tinged underparts.
Best Sites: Algonquin PP; Grundy Lake PP; Lake Superior PP; Quetico PP; Hwy 11 from Cobalt to Hearst.

NORTHERN FLICKER

Colaptes auratus

Unlike most woodpeckers, the Northern Flicker spends much of its time on the ground, feeding on ants and other insects. It appears almost robin-like as it hops about on grassy meadows, fields and along forest clearings. • Flickers are often seen bathing in dusty depressions. The dust particles absorb oils and bacteria that are harmful to the birds' feathers. To clean even more thoroughly, flickers will squish captured ants and then preen themselves with the remains (ants produce formic acid, which can kill small parasites on the flicker's skin and feathers). • All woodpeckers, including the Northern Flicker, are able to move vertically, up and down tree-trunks. Zygodactyl feet—two toes facing forward, another toe at a 90° angle, and a small hind toe pointing backward—and stiff tail feathers (to prop the body while scaling trees and excavating cavities), are two adaptations unique to woodpeckers.

ID: brown, barred back and wings; spotted buff to whitish underparts; black bib; yellow underwings and undertail; white rump; long bill; brownish to buff face; grey crown. *Male:* black 'moustache' stripe; red nape crescent. *Female:* no 'moustache.'
Size: *L* 32–33 cm.
Status: abundant migrant and breeder from April to late October; rare to locally uncommon visitor from November to March.
Habitat: open deciduous, mixed and coniferous woodlands and forest edges, fields, meadows, beaver ponds and other wetlands.

Nesting: pair excavates a cavity in a dead or dying deciduous tree; either sex chooses the nest site; excavation lasts for about 2 weeks; also uses nest boxes; lines the cavity with wood chips; pair incubates 5–8 white eggs for 11–16 days; both adults feed the young.
Feeding: forages on the ground for ants and other terrestrial insects; also eats berries and nuts; probes bark; occasionally flycatches.
Voice: loud, laughing, rapid *kick-kick-kick-kick-kick-kick*; *woika-woika-woika* issued during courtship.
Similar Species: none.
Best Sites: almost any open woodland, woodlot or forest edge.

PILEATED WOODPECKER

Dryocopus pileatus

With its flaming red crest, swooping flight and maniacal call, this impressive deep forest dweller can stop hikers in their tracks. Using its powerful, dagger-shaped bill and stubborn determination, the Pileated Woodpecker chisels out uniquely shaped rectangular cavities in its unending search for grubs and ants. Not surprisingly, a woodpecker's bill becomes shorter as the bird ages. In Audubon's historic painting of the Pileated Woodpecker, he correctly depicted the bills of the juveniles as slightly longer than those of the adults. • Because they have a large home territory, these magnificent birds are not encountered with much frequency. A pair of breeding Pileated Woodpeckers generally requires more than 40 ha of mature forest to settle. • As a primary cavity nester, the Pileated Woodpecker plays an important role in forest ecosystems. Other birds and even mammals depend on the activities of this woodpecker—ducks, small falcons, owls and even flying squirrels are frequent nesters in abandoned Pileated cavities. • There is no real consensus on whether this bird's name should be pronounced 'pie-lee-ated' or 'pill-e-ated'—it's generally a matter of preference and good-natured debate.

ID: predominantly black; white wing linings; flaming red crest; yellow eyes; stout, dark bill; white stripe running from the bill to the shoulder; white chin. *Male:* red 'moustache'; red crest extends from the forehead. *Female:* no red 'moustache'; red crest starts on the crown.
Size: *L* 41–48 cm.
Status: rare to uncommon year-round resident.
Habitat: in extensive tracts of mature deciduous, mixed or coniferous forest; some occur in riparian woodlands or woodlots in suburban and agricultural areas.
Nesting: pair excavates a cavity in a dead or dying tree-trunk; excavation can take 3–6 weeks; lines the cavity with wood chips; pair incubates 4 white eggs for 15–18 days; both adults feed the young.
Feeding: often hammers the base of rotting trees, creating fist-sized or larger, rectangular holes; eats carpenter ants, wood-boring beetle larvae, berries and nuts.
Voice: loud, fast, laughing, rolling *woika-woika-woika-woika*; long series of *kuk* notes; loud resonant drumming.
Similar Species: *Other woodpeckers*: much smaller. *American Crow* (p. 227) and *Common Raven* (p. 228): lack the white underwings and the flaming red crest.
Best Sites: Rondeau PP; Niagara Escarpment woodlands; Trent Canal woodlands; Macauley Mountain Conservation Area; Bon Echo PP; Sleeping Giant PP; Quetico PP.

OLIVE-SIDED FLYCATCHER

Contopus cooperi

An early morning hike through the lush conifers of Ontario's northern boreal forest often reveals a most curious and incessant wild call: *Quick-three-beers! Quick-three-beers!* This strange interpretation of the male Olive-sided Flycatcher's courtship song may seem silly, but it is surprisingly accurate. Once nesting has begun, this flycatcher quickly changes its tune to an equally enthusiastic, but less memorable, territorial *pip-pip-pip.* • Olive-sided Flycatchers nest high in the forest canopy far above the daily hubbub of the forest floor. Among the towering, lofty spires of spruce, pine and fir, they have easy access to an abundance of flying insects that inhabit the sunny forest heights. These feisty birds are difficult to spot, so look for big-headed silhouettes perched at the tip of a mature conifer. • Like all flycatchers, this olive-vested songbird perches with a distinctive, upright and attentive profile. Its ready stance allows it to quickly launch out and snatch flying insects in mid-air.

ID: dark olive grey 'vest'; light throat and belly; olive grey to olive brown upperparts; white tufts on the sides of the rump; dark upper mandible; base of the lower mandible is dull yellow-orange; inconspicuous eye ring.
Size: *L* 18–20 cm.
Status: rare to fairly common migrant from early May to early June and from mid-August to late September; uncommon to locally fairly common breeder from June to September.
Habitat: semi-open mixed and coniferous forests near water; burned areas and wetlands are preferred.
Nesting: high in a conifer, usually on a horizontal branch far from the trunk; nest of twigs and plant fibres is bound with spider silk; female incubates 3 white to pinkish-buff

eggs, with dark spots concentrated at the larger end, for 14–17 days.
Feeding: flycatches insects from a perch.
Voice: *Male:* chipper and lively *quick-three-beers*, with the 2nd note highest in pitch; descending *pip-pip-pip* when excited.
Similar Species: *Eastern Wood-Pewee* (p. 206): smaller; lacks the white rump tufts; grey breast; 2 faint wing bars. *Eastern Phoebe* (p. 212): lacks the white rump tufts; all-dark bill; often wags its tail. *Eastern Kingbird* (p. 215): lacks the white rump tufts; all-dark bill; white-tipped tail.
Best Sites: Algonquin PP; Grundy Lake PP; Lake Superior PP; Ouimet Canyon PP; sideroads off Hwy 11 from Cobalt to Hearst.

EASTERN WOOD-PEWEE

Contopus virens

Often perched on an exposed tree branch in a suburban park, woodlot edge or neighbourhood yard, the male Eastern Wood-Pewee whistles its plaintive *pee-ah-wee pee-oh* all day long. Some of the keenest pewee suitors will even sing their charms late into the evening, long after most birds have silenced their weary courtship songs. • Like other flycatchers, the Eastern Wood-Pewee loops out from exposed perches to snatch flying insects in mid-flight, a technique often referred to as 'flycatching' or 'hawking.' • Many insects have evolved defence mechanisms to avert potential predators such as the Eastern Wood-Pewee and its flycatching relatives. A number of flying insects are camouflaged; others are distasteful or poisonous, and flaunt their foul nature with vivid colours. Interestingly, some insects even mimic their poisonous allies, displaying warning colours even though they are perfectly tasty.

ID: olive grey to olive brown upperparts; 2 narrow, white wing bars; whitish throat; grey breast and sides; whitish or pale yellow belly, flanks and undertail coverts; dark upper mandible; base of lower mandible is dull yellow-orange; no eye ring.

Size: *L* 15–16 cm.

Status: common migrant and breeder from mid-May to late September; some may arrive as early as late April and remain until late November.

Habitat: open mixed and deciduous woodlands with a sparse understorey, especially woodland openings and edges; rarely in open coniferous woodlands.

Nesting: open cup of grass, plant fibres and lichen, bound with spider webs, is saddled on the fork of a horizontal deciduous branch well away from the trunk; female incubates 3 whitish eggs, with dark blotches concentrated at the larger end, for 12–13 days.

Feeding: flycatches insects from a perch; may also glean insects from foliage, especially while hovering.

Voice: *Male:* clear, slow, plaintive *pee-ah-wee*, with the 2nd note lower, followed by a downslurred *pee-oh*, given with or without intermittent pauses; also a *chip* call.

Similar Species: *Olive-sided Flycatcher* (p. 205): larger; white rump tufts; olive grey 'vest'; lacks the conspicuous white wing bars. *Eastern Phoebe* (p. 212): lacks the conspicuous white wing bars; all-dark bill; often pumps its tail. *Eastern Kingbird* (p. 215): larger; white-tipped tail; brighter white underparts; all-dark bill. *Empidonax flycatchers* (pp. 207–11): smaller; more conspicuous wing bars; eye rings.

Best Sites: almost any open deciduous or mixed woodland or woodland edge.

YELLOW-BELLIED FLYCATCHER

Empidonax flaviventris

Deep within soggy, mosquito-infested bogs and fens in Ontario's northcountry lives the reclusive Yellow-bellied Flycatcher. In late spring and early summer, the male Yellow-bellied Flycatcher spends much of his time singing plain, soft, liquidly *chelek* songs and occasionally zipping out from inconspicuous perches to help reduce the insect population. Once nesting has begun, the male changes his tune to a slow, rising *per-wee* and focuses his attention on defending his nesting territory and supplying food to his growing young. • Ontario offers fine opportunities for birders to develop their empidonax flycatcher identification skills—our province boasts a large assemblage of nearly indistinguishable flycatchers. The Yellow-bellied Flycatcher is the most elusive and secretive of this confusing clan—it does not habitually perch in the open—but it distinguishes itself from other 'empids' by nesting on the ground. A good pair of binoculars and close attention to fine details in plumage and voice should help you accurately identify this flycatcher and lead you to even greater birding challenges.

ID: olive green upperparts; 2 whitish wing bars; yellowish eye ring; white throat; yellow underparts; pale olive breast.
Size: *L* 13–15 cm.
Status: fairly common migrant from mid-May to mid-June and from mid-August to mid-September; uncommon to fairly common breeder from May to August.
Habitat: coniferous bogs and fens and shady spruce and pine forests with a dense shrub understorey.
Nesting: on the ground in dense sphagnum moss or in the upturned roots of a fallen tree; small cup nest of moss, rootlets and weeds is lined with grass, sedges and fine rootlets; female incubates 3 or 4 whitish eggs, lightly spotted with brown, for 12–14 days.

Feeding: flycatches for insects at low to middle levels of the forest; also gleans vegetation for larval and adult invertebrates while hovering.
Voice: *Male:* song is a soft *cheluck* or *chelek* (2nd syllable is lower pitched); calls include a chipper *pe-wheep*, *preee*, *pur-wee* or *killik*.
Similar Species: *Acadian* (p. 208), *Willow* (p. 210), *Alder* (p. 209) and *Least* (p. 211) *flycatchers:* all lack the extensive yellow wash from the throat to the belly; white eye rings; different songs; all but the Acadian have browner upperparts.
Best Sites: Algonquin PP; Wakami Lake PP; Lake Superior PP; Ouimet Canyon PP; Quetico PP.

ACADIAN FLYCATCHER

Empidonax virescens

As most experienced birders will tell you, one of the keys to identifying a flycatcher is to listen for its distinctive song. The Acadian Flycatcher is virtually indistinguishable from other empidonax flycatchers until it utters its quick, forceful *peet-sa*. Unfortunately, this summer resident is rare and unlocalized in Ontario, so male singers feel little pressure to issue their hallmark song in defence of a breeding territory. • Learning to identify this bird is only half the fun. Its speedy aerial courtship chases and the male's hovering flight displays are sights to behold, that is if you can survive the swarming hordes of blood-sucking mosquitoes deep within the swampy woodlands of extreme southwestern Ontario. • Maple and beech trees are preferred nesting sites for the Acadian Flycatcher. The nest is built on a horizontal branch up to four metres from the ground, and it can be quite conspicuous because loose material often dangles from the nest, giving it a sloppy appearance.

ID: narrow, yellowish eye ring; 2 buff to yellowish wingbars; large bill has a dark upper mandible and pinkish-yellow lower mandible; white throat; faint olive yellow breast; yellow belly and undertail coverts; olive green upperparts; primaries are very long. *Immature:* greenish head and back have buff edges, creating a scaly effect; yellow wash on the underparts may extend onto the throat.
Size: L 14–15 cm.
Status: rare breeder from May to late August; a few may remain into late September.
Habitat: fairly mature deciduous woodlands, riparian woodlands and wooded swamps.
Nesting: low in a beech or maple tree, usually 2–4 m above the ground; female builds a loose, sloppy-looking cup nest from vegetative material; female incubates 3 creamy white eggs, lightly spotted with brown, for 13–15 days; both parents raise the young.
Feeding: wasps, bees, spiders and ants are readily taken; berries and small fruits may be eaten; forages primarily by hawking or by gleaning from foliage while hovering.
Voice: best identified by its forceful *peet-sa* or *pizza* song; call is a softer *peet*; may issue a loud, flicker-like *ti-ti-ti-ti-ti* during the breeding season.
Similar Species: flycatchers are best distinguished by songs and calls. *Alder Flycatcher* (p. 209): song is *fee-bee-o*; short *kep* call; narrower, white eye ring is often inconspicuous; browner overall; smaller head relative to its body. *Willow Flycatcher* (p. 210): song is an explosive *fitz-be-yew*; emphatic *wit* call; browner overall; smaller head; very faint eye ring. *Least Flycatcher* (p. 211): song is a clear *che-bek*; thin *pit* call; prominent, white eye ring; rounded head; shorter wings. *Yellow-bellied Flycatcher* (p. 207): song is a liquid *chelek*; calls include a chipper *pe-wheep*, *preee*, *pur-wee* or *killik*; yellow wash from the throat to the belly.
Best Sites: Point Pelee NP; Wheatley PP; Rondeau PP; Port Bruce PP; Sudden Tract; Beverly Swamp; Wilson Tract.

ALDER FLYCATCHER

Empidonax alnorum

The Alder Flycatcher is often indistinguishable from other empidonax flycatchers until it opens its small, bicoloured beak: with a hearty *fee-bee-o*, its identity is revealed. Once this aggressive bird has been spotted, its feisty behaviour can often be observed without distraction as it drives away rivals and pursues flying insects.

• This nondescript bird is well named, because it is often found in alder and willow shrubs—a fact that can help in its identification. In southern Ontario, the Alder Flycatcher frequently competes against the Willow Flycatcher for control over dense riparian alder and willow thickets.

• Voice recognition is very important to many birds, and Alder Flycatchers instinctively know the simple phrase of their species (many birds have to learn their songs and calls). Even if a young Alder is isolated from the sounds of other Alder Flycatchers, it can produce a perfectly acceptable rendition when it matures.

• The Willow Flycatcher is a close relative of the Alder, and these two species were formerly grouped together as a single species known as the Traill's Flycatcher.

ID: olive brown upperparts; 2 dull white to buff wing bars; faint whitish eye ring; dark upper mandible; orange lower mandible; longish tail; white throat; pale olive breast; pale yellowish belly.

Size: *L* 14–15 cm.

Status: fairly common to common migrant and breeder from May to September.

Habitat: alder or willow thickets bordering lakes, streams or muskeg.

Nesting: in a fork in a dense bush or shrub, usually less than 1 m above the ground; small cup nest is loosely woven with grass and other plant materials; female incubates 3 or 4 white eggs, with dark spots concentrated around the larger end, for 12–14 days; both adults feed the young.

Feeding: flycatches from a perch for beetles, bees, wasps and other flying insects; also eats berries and occasionally seeds.

Voice: snappy *fee-bee-o*; call is a *wheep* or *peep*.

Similar Species: *Eastern Wood-Pewee* (p. 206): lacks the eye ring and the conspicuous wing bars. *Willow Flycatcher* (p. 210): different song; mostly found in drier areas south of Ottawa. *Least Flycatcher* (p. 211): bolder white eye ring; greener upperparts; pale grey and white underparts; different song and habitat. *Acadian Flycatcher* (p. 208) and *Yellow-bellied Flycatcher* (p. 207): yellowish eye rings; greener upperparts; yellower underparts; different songs and habitat.

Best Sites: almost any stream, lake or other wetland shoreline with dense willow or alder thickets.

WILLOW FLYCATCHER

Empidonax traillii

When warm spring winds flood southern Ontario with migrant songbirds, the characteristic *fitz-bew* call of the Willow Flycatcher occasionally rises above the sounds of the crowd. Upon arriving in a suitable shrubby area with thick willows and tangled dogwood, male flycatchers swing energetically on advantageous perches to battle vocally over preferred territory. Once the boundaries are drawn and the business of nesting begins, Willow Flycatchers become shy, inconspicuous birds that opt to remain out of sight. Only when an avian intruder violates an established boundary does the resident Willow Flycatcher aggressively reveal itself. After the raising of the young and a period of fattening-up in late summer and early fall, Willow Flycatchers begin their journey to Central and South America. • Thomas Stewart Traill was an Englishman who helped John James Audubon find a British publisher for his book *Ornithological Biography*.

ID: olive brown upperparts; 2 whitish wing bars; no eye ring; white throat; yellowish belly; pale olive breast.

Size: *L* 14–15 cm.

Status: uncommon to locally common migrant and breeder from May to September.

Habitat: shrubby areas on abandoned farmlands and in riparian corridors.

Nesting: in a fork or on a branch of a dense shrub, usually 1–2 m above the ground; female builds an open cup nest with grass, bark strips and plant fibres and lines it with down; female incubates 3 or 4 whitish to pale buff eggs, with brown spots concentrated toward the larger end, for 12–15 days.

Feeding: flycatches insects; also gleans insects from vegetation, usually while hovering.

Voice: *Male:* quick, sneezy *fitz-bew* that drops off at the end; up to 30 times a minute; call is a quick *whit*.

Similar Species: *Eastern Wood-Pewee* (p. 206): lacks the eye ring and the conspicuous wing bars. *Alder Flycatcher* (p. 209): different song; usually found in wetter areas. *Least Flycatcher* (p. 211): bolder white eye ring; greener upperparts; pale grey and white underparts; different song and habitat. *Acadian Flycatcher* (p. 208) and *Yellow-bellied Flycatcher* (p. 207): yellowish eye rings; greener upperparts; yellower underparts; different songs and habitat.

Best Sites: Ojibway Prairie; Point Pelee NP; Rondeau PP; Kettle Point; Long Point PP; Sudden Tract; Lynde Shores Conservation Area; Presqu'ile PP.

LEAST FLYCATCHER

Empidonax minimus

This bird might not look like a bully, but the Least Flycatcher is one of the boldest and most pugnacious songbirds of Ontario's deciduous woodlands. During the nesting season, it is noisy and conspicuous, forcefully repeating its simple, two-part call throughout much of the day. Intense song battles normally eliminate the need for physical aggression, but feather-flying fights are occasionally required to settle disputes over turf and courtship privileges. • Even though it is not as colourful and attractive as other Ontario birds, the Least Flycatcher is the most common and widespread empidonax flycatcher in Ontario, and you should have no problem meeting one in most parts of the province. • These birds often fall victim to nest parasitism by the Brown-headed Cowbird, whose hatched young often smother the much smaller Least Flycatcher nestlings.

ID: olive brown upperparts; 2 white wing bars; bold, white eye ring; fairly long, narrow tail; largely dark bill has a yellow-orange lower base; white throat; grey breast; grey-white to yellowish belly and undertail coverts.
Size: *L* 12–14 cm.
Status: common migrant and breeder from May to September.
Habitat: open deciduous or mixed woodlands; forest openings and edges; often in second-growth woodlands and occasionally near human habitation.
Nesting: in a crotch or fork of a small tree or shrub, often against the trunk; female builds a small cup nest with plant fibres and bark and lines it with fine grass, plant down and feathers; female incubates 4 creamy white eggs for 13–15 days; both adults feed the young.

Feeding: flycatches insects and gleans trees and shrubs for insects while hovering; may also eat some fruit and seeds.
Voice: constantly repeated, dry *che-bec che-bec*.
Similar Species: *Eastern Wood-Pewee* (p. 206): lacks the eye ring and the conspicuous wing bars. *Alder Flycatcher* (p. 209): faint eye ring; different song; usually found in wetter areas. *Willow Flycatcher* (p. 210): lacks the eye ring; greener upperparts; yellower underparts; different song. *Acadian Flycatcher* (p. 208) and *Yellow-bellied Flycatcher* (p. 207): yellowish eye rings; greener upperparts; yellower underparts; different songs. *Ruby-crowned Kinglet* (p. 248): broken eye ring; much daintier bill; shorter tail.
Best Sites: almost any open deciduous or mixed woodland.

211

EASTERN PHOEBE

Sayornis phoebe

Whether you're poking around your summer cottage, a campground picnic shelter or your backyard shed, there is a very good chance you will stumble upon an Eastern Phoebe family and its marvellous mud nest. The Eastern Phoebe's nest building and territorial defence is normally well underway by the time most other songbirds arrive in Ontario in mid-May. Once limited to nesting on natural cliffs and fallen riparian trees, this adaptive flycatcher has gradually found success in nesting on buildings and bridges. Too often, people unnecessarily destroy the phoebe's mud nests, but some folks have caught on to the benefits of having phoebe tenants, because these birds can be effective at controlling pesky insects. • Some other birds pump their tails while perched, but few Ontario species can match the zest and frequency of the Eastern Phoebe's tail pumping.

breeding

ID: grey-brown upperparts; white underparts with a grey wash on the breast and sides; belly may be washed with yellow in fall; no eye ring; no obvious wing bars; all-black bill; dark legs; frequently pumps its tail.
Size: *L* 17–18 cm.
Status: common migrant and breeder from April to October; a few may arrive as early as March; some may remain into December.
Habitat: open deciduous woodlands and forest edges and clearings; usually near water.
Nesting: under the ledge of a building, picnic shelter, culvert, bridge, cliff or well; cup-shaped mud nest is lined with moss, grass, fur and feathers; female incubates 4 or 5 white eggs, often with a few reddish-brown spots, for

about 16 days; both adults feed the young.
Feeding: flycatches flying beetles, flies, wasps, grasshoppers, mayflies and other insects; occasionally plucks aquatic invertebrates and small fish from the water's surface.
Voice: hearty, snappy *fee-bee*, delivered frequently; call is a sharp *chip*.
Similar Species: *Eastern Wood-Pewee* (p. 206): smaller; pale wing bars; bicoloured bill; does not pump its tail. *Olive-sided Flycatcher* (p. 205): dark 'vest'; white fluffy patches bordering the rump. *Empidonax flycatchers* (pp. 207–11): most have an eye ring and conspicuous wing bars. *Eastern Kingbird* (p. 215): white-tipped tail; black upperparts.
Best Sites: barns, sheds, bridges and other buildings throughout Ontario.

GREAT CRESTED FLYCATCHER

Myiarchus crinitus

The Great Crested Flycatcher's nesting habits are unusual for a flycatcher. It is a cavity nester, and it will occasionally use a nest box intended for a bluebird. In various parts of its range, the Great Crested Flycatcher has been known to have unusual tastes in decor: once in a while, it decorates the entrance of its nest with a shed snakeskin. The purpose of this uncommon, but noteworthy practice is not fully understood. In some instances, this versatile bird has even been known to substitute translucent plastic wrap for genuine reptilian skin. • In Ontario, songbirds such as the Great Crested Flycatcher are often thought of as Canadian birds that fly south for the winter. In reality, this flycatcher, and many other migrants, are subtropical or tropical birds of Central and South America that visit our country only briefly to raise their young before returning home.

ID: bright yellow belly and undertail coverts; grey throat and upper breast; reddish-brown tail; peaked 'crested' head; dark olive brown upperparts; heavy black bill.
Size: *L* 20–23 cm.
Status: common migrant and summer breeder from early May to mid-September; a few may arrive as early as late April, and some may remain into early November.
Habitat: deciduous and mixed woodlands and forests, usually near openings or edges.
Nesting: in a tree cavity, nest box or other artificial cavity, often lined with grass, bark strips and feathers; may hang a shed snakeskin or plastic wrap from the entrance hole; female incubates 5 creamy white to pale buff

eggs, marked with lavender, olive and brown, for 13–15 days.
Feeding: often in the upper branches of deciduous trees, where it flycatches for flying insects; may also glean caterpillars and occasionally fruit.
Voice: loud, whistled *wheep!* and a rolling *prrrrreet!*
Similar Species: *Yellow-bellied Flycatcher* (p. 207): much smaller; yellow throat; lacks the reddish-brown tail and large, all-black bill.
Western Kingbird (p. 214): all-grey head, neck and breast; lacks the head crest; darker tail with white outer margins.
Best Sites: almost any deciduous or mixed woodland edge or opening throughout southern Ontario.

213

WESTERN KINGBIRD

Tyrannus verticalis

More typical of the Canadian Prairies, the Western Kingbird is primarily a rare visitor to Ontario. Only a handful of Western Kingbirds is reported here each year, most often in August and September in popular birding areas, such as Point Pelee National Park and Long Point Provincial Park in southern Ontario. • Western Kingbirds are commonly seen surveying for prey from fenceposts, power lines or utility poles. Once a kingbird spots an insect, it might chase it for up to 15 m before a capture is made. • Once you have witnessed the kingbird's brave attacks against much larger birds, such as crows and hawks, it is easy to understand why this brawler was awarded the name 'kingbird.' • Its scientific name *verticalis* refers to the bird's hidden, red crown patch, which is flared during courtship displays and while in combat with rivals. This red patch, however, is not a good identification mark because it is rarely seen outside the breeding season. • The tumbling, aerial courtship display of the Western Kingbird is a good sign that this bird might be breeding. Twisting and turning all the way, the male rises about 20 m into the sky, stalls, and then tumbles, flips and twists as he plummets back to earth.

ID: grey head and breast; yellow belly and undertail coverts; black tail; white edge to the outer tail feathers; white chin; black bill; ashy grey upperparts; faint, dark grey mask; thin, orange-red crown (rarely seen).
Size: *L* 20–23 cm.
Status: rare vagrant in May, June, August and September; occasional breeder from mid-May to mid-September.
Habitat: open scrubland areas with scattered patches of brush or hedgerows; along the edges of open fields.
Nesting: in a deciduous tree near the trunk; bulky cup nest of grass, weeds and twigs is lined with fur, plant down and feathers; female incubates 3–5 whitish, heavily blotched eggs for 18–19 days.
Feeding: flycatches aerial insects, including bees, wasps, butterflies, moths, grasshoppers and flies; occasionally eats berries.
Voice: chatty, twittering *whit-ker-whit*; also a short *kit* or extended *kit-kit-keetle-dot*.
Similar Species: *Eastern Kingbird* (p. 215): black upperparts; white underparts; white-tipped tail. *Great Crested Flycatcher* (p. 213): slightly crested head; brownish upperparts; reddish-brown tail; yellowish wing bars; lacks the white edges to the outer tail feathers.
Best Sites: Point Pelee NP; Long Point PP; Rainy River area.

EASTERN KINGBIRD

Tyrannus tyrannus

When you think of a tyrant animal, images of a large carnivorous dinosaur are much more likely to come to mind than a little bird. True as that might be, no one familiar with the pugnacity of the Eastern Kingbird is likely to refute its scientific name, *Tyrannus tyrannus*. This kingbird is a brawler, and it will fearlessly attack crows, hawks and even humans that pass through its territory. Intruders are often vigorously pursued, pecked and plucked for some distance until the kingbird is satisfied that there is no further threat. In contrast, its butterfly-like courtship flight, which is characterized by short, quivering wingbeats, reveals the gentler side of this bird. • Kingbirds are common and widespread in Ontario, so during a drive in the country it is likely you will spot one sitting on a fenceline or utility wire along a roadside. • Eastern Kingbirds rarely walk or hop on the ground; they prefer to fly, even for very short distances.

ID: dark grey to black upperparts; white underparts; white-tipped tail; black bill; small head crest; thin orange-red crown (rarely seen); no eye ring; black legs.
Size: *L* 22 cm.
Status: common to very common migrant and breeder from May to early September; some might arrive as early as April, possibly remaining until mid-October.
Habitat: rural fields with scattered trees or hedgerows, clearings in fragmented forests, open roadsides, burned areas and near human settlements.
Nesting: on a horizontal tree or shrub limb; also on a standing stump or an upturned tree root; pair builds a cup nest of weeds, twigs and grass and lines it with root fibres, fine grass and fur;

female incubates 3 or 4 darkly blotched, white to pinkish-white eggs for 14–18 days.
Feeding: flycatches aerial insects; infrequently eats berries.
Voice: call is a quick, loud, chattering *kit-kit-kitter-kitter*; also a buzzy *dzee-dzee-dzee*.
Similar Species: *Tree Swallow* (p. 231): iridescent dark blue back; lacks the white-tipped tail; more streamlined body; smaller bill. *Olive-sided Flycatcher* (p. 205): lacks the white-tipped tail and the all-white underparts; 2 white tufts bordering the rump. *Eastern Wood-Pewee* (p. 206): smaller; lacks the white-tipped tail and the all-white underparts; bicoloured bill.
Best Sites: almost any open rural area in the southern two-thirds of the province.

LOGGERHEAD SHRIKE

Lanius ludovicianus

A shrike resembles a Northern Mockingbird in body shape and colour, but the Loggerhead's method of hunting is very different. This predatory songbird has highly acute vision, and it often perches atop shrubs and small trees to scan for small prey. Popular food items, caught in fast, direct flights or swooping dives, include large insects, voles, mice, shrews, lizards and the odd frog or small snake. • Like most songbirds, Loggerhead Shrikes sing to establish their territories and attract mates. Additionally, males display their competence at hunting by impaling prey on thorns and barbed wire. This behaviour might also serve as a means of storing excess food items during times of plenty. In spring, you can often see a variety of skewered critters baking in the sun—reminiscent of the way some people used to display the carcasses of hawks, foxes and coyotes on farm fences. • Loggerhead Shrike populations are declining in Ontario and many other parts of its North American range, earning this bird endangered species status. One of the reasons for the decline is believed to be habitat destruction, but many people think that automobiles are another major cause of Loggerhead mortality. On their wintering grounds in the southern U.S., shrikes like to fly low across roads to prey on insects that are attracted to the warm pavement.

ID: black tail and wings; grey crown and back; white underparts; black mask extends above the hooked bill onto the forehead. *In flight:* white wing patches; white-edged tail. *Juvenile:* brownish-grey, barred upperparts.
Size: *L* 23 cm.
Status: rare migrant and breeder from March to September; a few may arrive as early as mid-February, and some may remain until late December; considered endangered in Ontario.
Habitat: grazed pastures and marginal and abandoned farmlands with scattered hawthorn shrubs, fenceposts, barbed wire and nearby wetlands.
Nesting: low in the crotch of a shrub or small tree; thorny hawthorn shrubs are often preferred; bulky cup nest of twigs and grass is lined with animal hair, feathers, plant down and rootlets; female incubates 5 or 6 pale buff to greyish-white eggs, with dark spots concentrated at the larger end, for 15–17 days.
Feeding: mostly large insects; swoops down on prey from a perch or attacks in pursuit; eats small birds, rodents and shrews; also eats carrion, small snakes and amphibians.
Voice: *Male:* high-pitched, hiccuppy *bird-ee bird-ee* during summer; infrequently a harsh *shack-shack* year-round.
Similar Species: *Northern Shrike* (p. 217): winter visitor from the north; adult is larger; fine barring on the sides and breast; black mask does not extend above the hooked bill; immature has unbarred, light brown upperparts and strongly, but finely barred underparts. *Northern Mockingbird* (p. 259): slim bill; no mask; slimmer overall.
Best Sites: Grey County farmlands; Carden Plain; marginal farmlands south of Ottawa and north of Kingston areas.

NORTHERN SHRIKE

Lanius excubitor

Each fall, Northern Shrikes retreat from their taiga breeding grounds to replace southbound Loggerhead Shrikes in southern parts of our province. Like many of our raptors, Northern Shrikes appear in southern Ontario each winter in unpredictable and highly variable numbers. During their winter visits, they are typically seen perched like hawks on exposed treetops, from which they survey open and semi-open hunting grounds. Winter feeding stations also tempt many a shrike to test its hunting skills. • The Northern Shrike looks a little like a grey robin with the bill of a small hawk, and it specializes in catching and killing small birds and rodents. When this bird strikes a large target, it relies on its sharp, hooked beak to dispatch its quarry, although it may use its feet to help. • The Northern Shrike's habit of impaling its kills on thorns and barbs has earned it the names 'butcher bird' and 'nine-killer.' *Lanius* is Latin for 'butcher,' and *excubitor* is Latin for 'watchman' or 'sentinel'—'watchful butcher' is an appropriate description of the Northern Shrike's foraging behaviour.

ID: black tail and wings; pale grey upperparts; finely barred, light underparts; black mask does not extend above the hooked bill. *In flight:* white wing patches; white-edged tail. *Immature:* faint mask; light brown upperparts; brown barring on the underparts.
Size: *L* 25 cm.
Status: rare breeder from April to October; uncommon and erratic migrant and visitor from October to April.
Habitat: *Breeding:* sparse coniferous woodlands and muskeg near treeline. *Winter* and *In migration:* open country, including fields, shrubby areas, forest clearings and roadsides.
Nesting: on the taiga; in spruce, willows or shrubs; loose, bulky nest of sticks, bark and moss is lined with feathers and animal hair; female incubates 4–7 darkly spotted, greenish-white to pale grey eggs for 15–17 days.

Feeding: swoops down on prey from a perch or chases prey through the air; regularly eats small birds, shrews, rodents and large insects; may also take snakes and frogs; prey may be impaled on a thorn or barb for later consumption.
Voice: usually silent; infrequently gives a long grating laugh: *raa-raa-raa-raa. Male:* high-pitched, hiccuppy *hee-toodle-toodle-toodle* during summer.
Similar Species: *Loggerhead Shrike* (p. 216): breeds in southern Ontario; generally absent in winter; adult's mask extends above the bill onto the forehead; adult lacks the barring on the underparts; juvenile has barred underparts, crown and back. *Northern Mockingbird* (p. 259): slim bill; no mask; slimmer overall; paler wings and tail.
Best Sites: Amherst Island; Tommy Thompson Park; Moosonee.

WHITE-EYED VIREO
Vireo griseus

Proclaiming its spring arrival, the White-eyed Vireo sings *chick-ticha-wheeyou, chick-ticha-wheeyou-chick* among vibrant early spring blossoms of red-osier dogwood and spicebush in Ontario's Carolinian forest. Like most members of the vireo clan, the White-eyed Vireo can be a challenge to spot as it sneaks through dense tangles of branches and foliage in search of insects. If you are lucky enough to find a White-eyed Vireo in its favourite shrubby habitat, however, you should have no trouble getting a close look at it. Pishing or squeaking may enhance your chances of a quick view, but this often guarantees you will get an angry scolding from this energetic sprite. • Even more secretive than the bird itself is the location of its precious nest. Intricately woven with grass, twigs, bark, lichens, moss, plant down, leaves and the fibrous paper from a wasp nest, the vireo nest is hung between the forking branches of a tree or shrub. • The White-eyed Vireo is a relatively new addition to Ontario's avifauna—its first confirmed breeding record was reported here in 1971.

ID: yellow 'spectacles'; olive grey upperparts; white underparts with yellow sides and flanks; 2 whitish wing bars; dark wings and tail; pale eyes.

Size: *L* 13 cm.

Status: rare migrant and breeder from April to October; a few may remain as late as December.

Habitat: dense shrubby undergrowth and thickets in open, swampy deciduous woodlands, overgrown fields, young second-growth woodlands, woodland clearings and along woodlot edges.

Nesting: in a deciduous shrub or small tree; cup nest hangs from a horizontal fork;

pair incubates 4 lightly speckled, white eggs for 13–15 days; both adults feed the young.

Feeding: gleans insects from branches and foliage during very active foraging; often hovers while gleaning.

Voice: loud, snappy, 3–9-note song, usually beginning and ending with 'chick': *chick-ticha-wheeyou, chick-ticha-wheeyou-chick*!

Similar Species: *Pine Warbler* (p. 280) and *Yellow-throated Vireo* (p. 219): both have a yellow throat. *Blue-headed Vireo* (p. 220): white 'spectacles'; dark eyes; yellow highlights in the wings and tail.

Best Sites: Point Pelee NP; Rondeau PP; Long Point PP.

YELLOW-THROATED VIREO

Vireo flavifrons

The Yellow-throated Vireo is usually found in mature deciduous woodlands with little or no understorey, and it takes a particular liking to tall oaks and maples. Like its treetop neighbour the Cerulean Warbler, the Yellow-throated Vireo forages high above the forest floor, making it a difficult bird to observe. • Unmated males sing tirelessly as they search for nest sites, which usually includes placing a few pieces of nest material in several locations. When a female appears, the male dazzles her with his displays and leads her on a tour of potential nesting sites within his large territory. If a bond is established, they will mate and build an intricately woven, hanging nest in the forking branches of a deciduous tree. The male is a devoted helper, assisting the female in the building of the nest and the incubating and rearing of the young.

ID: bright yellow 'spectacles,' chin, throat and breast; olive upperparts, except for the grey rump and the dark wings and tail; 2 white wing bars; white belly and undertail coverts.
Size: *L* 14 cm.
Status: rare to uncommon migrant from May to mid-June and from September to mid-October (a few may remain until early November); rare breeder from May to September.
Habitat: mature deciduous woodlands with minimal understorey.
Nesting: pair builds a hanging cup nest in the fork of a horizontal, deciduous tree branch; pair incubates 4 creamy white to pinkish eggs, with dark spots toward the larger end, for 14–15 days; each parent takes on guardianship of half the fledged young.
Feeding: eats mostly insects, but will also feed on seasonally available berries; forages by inspecting branches and foliage in the upper canopy.
Voice: song is a slowly repeated series of hoarse phrases with long pauses in between: *ahweeo, eeoway, away*; calls include a throaty, quickened *heh heh heh*.
Similar Species: *Pine Warbler* (p. 280): olive yellow rump; thinner bill; faint, darkish streaking along the sides; yellow belly; faint 'spectacles.' *White-eyed Vireo* (p. 218): white chin and throat; greyer head and back; white eyes. *Blue-headed Vireo* (p. 220): white 'spectacles' and throat; yellow highlights in the wings and tail.
Best Sites: Point Pelee NP; Rondeau PP; Long Point PP; Dickson Wilderness Area; Sudden Tract; Beverly Swamp; Halton Regional Forest; Wye Marsh Wildlife Centre; Petroglyphs PP; Frontenac PP.

BLUE-HEADED VIREO

Vireo solitarius

From the canopies of Ontario's shady woodlands, the purposeful, liquid notes of the Blue-headed Vireo penetrate the dense foliage. The distinctive 'spectacles' that frame this bird's eyes provide a good fieldmark, and they are among the boldest of eye rings belonging to our songbirds. • During courtship, male Blue-headed Vireos fluff out their yellowish flanks and bob ceremoniously to their prospective mates. Once mating is complete and the eggs are in the nest, the parents become extremely quiet. If you are lucky, you may be able to approach close enough to have a look at the eggs. Once the young hatch, however, Blue-headed parents will readily scold an intruder long before its approach. Even so, Brown-headed Cowbirds manage to find temporarily vacated vireo nests in which to lay their eggs. As human development continues to fragment forests in Ontario, cowbirds might pose an increasing threat to their Blue-headed hosts. Blue-headed Vireos once occupied all of southern Ontario, but the loss of forests to agriculture has driven them northward. • Until recently, the Blue-headed, Cassin's and Plumbeous vireos were lumped together as one species, the Solitary Vireo.

ID: white 'spectacles'; 2 white wing bars; blue-grey head; olive green upperparts; white underparts; yellow sides and flanks; dark wings and tail have yellow highlights; stout bill; dark legs.

Size: *L* 13–15 cm.

Status: fairly common migrant in May and from early September to mid-October (a few may remain into late November); uncommon to common breeder from May to September.

Habitat: primarily remote mixed coniferous-deciduous forests; also pure coniferous forests and pine plantations.

Nesting: in a horizontal fork in a coniferous tree, low tree or tall shrub; hanging, basket-like cup nest is made of grass, roots, plant down, spider silk and cocoons; pair incubates 3–5 whitish eggs, lightly spotted with black and brown, for 12–14 days.

Feeding: gleans branches for insects; frequently hovers to pluck insects from vegetation.

Voice: *Male:* slow, purposeful, slurred, robin-like notes with moderate pauses in between: *chu-wee, taweeto, toowip, cheerio, teeyay; churr* call.

Similar Species: *White-eyed Vireo* (p. 218): yellow 'spectacles'; light-coloured eyes. *Yellow-throated Vireo* (p. 219): yellow 'spectacles' and throat.

Best Sites: Bon Echo PP; Algonquin PP; Lake Superior PP; Obatanga PP; Thunder Bay area; Quetico PP; Hwy 11 from Cobalt to Longlac.

220

WARBLING VIREO
Vireo gilvus

The charming Warbling Vireo is a common summer resident of the sparsely wooded parts of southern Ontario. Beginning in early May, its wondrous voice fills local parks and backyards—because this vireo often settles close to urban areas, its bubbly, warbling songs should be familiar to many southern residents. • Lacking any splashy field marks, it is only when this vireo moves from one leaf-hidden stage to another that it is readily observed. Searching treetops for this generally inconspicuous vireo may literally be 'a pain in the neck,' but the satisfaction of visually confirming its identity is exceptionally rewarding. • The hanging nests of vireos are usually much harder to find than the birds themselves. In winter, however, nests are revealed as they swing precariously from bare deciduous branches. • During their brief stay in Ontario, Warbling Vireos prefer old maples and poplars as foraging and nesting sites.

breeding

ID: partial dark eye line bordering the white eyebrow; no wing bars; olive grey upperparts; greenish flanks; white to pale grey underparts; grey crown.
Size: *L* 13–14 cm.
Status: uncommon migrant from May to late June (a few may arrive in late April); common breeder; uncommon migrant in early September (a few may remain as late as mid-November).
Habitat: open deciduous woodlands, and parks and gardens with deciduous trees.
Nesting: in a horizontal fork in a deciduous tree or shrub; hanging, basket-like cup nest is made of grass, roots, plant down, spider silk and a few feathers; pair incubates

4 darkly specked, white eggs for 12–14 days.
Feeding: gleans foliage for insects; occasionally hovers to glean insects from vegetation.
Voice: *Male:* long, musical warble of slurred whistles.
Similar Species: *Philadelphia Vireo* (p. 222): yellow breast, sides and flanks; full, dark eye line bordering the white eyebrow. *Red-eyed Vireo* (p. 223): black eye line extends to the bill; blue-grey crown; red eyes. *Tennessee Warbler* (p. 267): blue-grey cap and nape; olive green back; slimmer bill. *Orange-crowned Warbler* (p. 268): yellow overall; slimmer bill.
Best Sites: riparian woods, open woodland edges and well-wooded parks throughout southern Ontario, mainly south of the Canadian Shield.

221

PHILADELPHIA VIREO

Vireo philadelphicus

While many similar-looking birds sound quite different, the Philadelphia Vireo and Red-eyed Vireo are two species that sound very similar but are easy to tell apart once you locate them in your binoculars. Most forest songbirds are initially identified by voice, however, so the Philadelphia Vireo is often overlooked because its song is almost identical to the more abundant Red-eyed Vireo. • The Philadelphia Vireo nests in areas of Ontario's Canadian Shield that are dominated by mixed boreal forest, where it fills a niche left unoccupied by the strictly deciduous-dwelling Warbling Vireo of southern Ontario. • Like most other vireos, Phillies are difficult to observe; they usually perch and sing near the tops of tall, leafy trees. • This bird bears the name of the city in which the first scientific specimen was collected. Philadelphia was the centre of America's budding scientific community in the early 1800s, and much of the study of birds and other natural sciences originated in Pennsylvania.

breeding

ID: grey cap; full, dark eye line, bordered by a bold, white eyebrow; dark olive green upperparts; pale yellow breast, sides and flanks; white belly (underparts may be completely yellow in fall); robust bill; pale eyes.

Size: *L* 12–13 cm.

Status: uncommon migrant in mid- to late May and from late August to September; may arrive as early as late April and remain into early November); uncommon breeder from May to September.

Habitat: woodlands with aspen and alder.

Nesting: high up in a deciduous tree or low in a shrub; basket-like cup nest hangs from a horizontal fork; nest is made of grass, roots, plant down and spider silk; pair incubates 4 white eggs, with dark spots on the larger end, for about 14 days.

Feeding: gleans vegetation for insects; frequently hovers to glean food from foliage.

Voice: *Male:* like that of the Red-eyed Vireo, but it is usually slower, slightly higher pitched and not as variable: *Look-up way-up tree-top see-me.*

Similar Species: *Red-eyed Vireo* (p. 223): black-bordered, blue-grey cap; lacks the yellow breast; red eyes; song is very similar. *Warbling Vireo* (p. 221): partial, dark eye line (mostly behind the eye); lacks the yellow breast. *Tennessee Warbler* (p. 267): blue-grey cap and nape; olive green back; slimmer bill; lacks the yellow breast.

Best Sites: Algonquin PP; Killarney PP; Halfway Lake PP; Sault Ste. Marie area; Lake Superior PP; Pukaskwa NP; Sleeping Giant PP; Moosonee area.

RED-EYED VIREO

Vireo olivaceus

The Red-eyed Vireo is the undisputed champion of vocal endurance in Ontario. In spring and early summer, males sing continuously through the day until long after most songbirds have curtailed their courtship melodies, usually five or six hours after sunrise. One particularly vigorous Red-eyed Vireo male holds the record for most songs delivered in a single day: approximately 21,000! • Red-eyed Vireos adopt a particular stance when they hop up and along branches. They tend to be more hunched over than other songbirds, and they hop with their bodies diagonal to their direction of travel. • Red eyes are very uncharacteristic among songbirds and tend to be more prevalent in non-passerines, such as accipiters, grebes and some herons. There is no firm agreement about the reason for this vireo's eye colour. • This is the most common and widespread vireo in Ontario, and its adaptive nature has enabled it to become part of many Ontario communities. • Red-eyed Vireos sound a lot like American Robins, and beginning birders are often delighted to discover these nifty birds hiding behind a 'familiar' song right in front of their eyes.

breeding

ID: dark eye line; white eyebrow; black-bordered, blue-grey crown; olive green upperparts; olive cheek; white to pale grey underparts; may have a yellow wash on the sides, flanks and undertail coverts, especially in fall; no wing bars; red eyes (seen only at close range).
Size: *L* 15 cm.
Status: very common migrant and breeder from early May to early October; a few may arrive in early April, and some may remain until mid-November.
Habitat: deciduous woodlands with a shrubby understorey.
Nesting: in a horizontal fork in a deciduous tree or shrub; hanging, basket-like cup nest is made of grass, roots, spider silk and cocoons; female incubates 4 white eggs, with dark spots around the

larger end, for 11–14 days.
Feeding: gleans foliage for insects, especially caterpillars; often hovers; also eats berries.
Voice: call is a short, scolding *neeah. Male:* song is a continuous and variable, robin-like run of quick, short phrases, with distinct pauses in between: *Look-up, way-up, tree-top, see-me, here-I-am.*
Similar Species: *Philadelphia Vireo* (p. 222): yellow breast; lacks the black border to the blue-grey cap; song is very similar (slightly higher pitched). *Warbling Vireo* (p. 221): dusky eye line does not extend to the bill; lacks the black border to the grey cap. *Tennessee Warbler* (p. 267): blue-grey cap and nape; olive green back; slimmer bill.
Best Sites: any deciduous woodland or tree grove throughout most of the province.

GRAY JAY

Perisoreus canadensis

Few other Ontario birds rival the mischievous Gray Jay for curiosity and boldness. Attracted by any foreign sound or potential feeding opportunity, small family groups glide gently and unexpectedly out of spruce, pine and fir stands. Campgrounds and picnic areas in Ontario's northern shield country are the easiest places to find these mooching marauders. • Gray Jays lay their eggs and begin incubation as early as late February. Their nests are well insulated to conserve heat, and getting an early start on nesting means that young jays will learn how to forage efficiently and store food before the next cold season approaches. • In preparation for tough times, especially the winter months, Gray Jays often store food. Their specialized salivary glands coat the food with a sticky mucous helping to preserve it. • This common bird has some interesting alternate names: 'Whiskey Jack' is derived from the Algonquin name for this bird, *wiskedjack*; others affectionately call this bird 'Camp Robber.'

ID: fluffy, pale grey plumage; fairly long tail; white forehead, cheek, throat and undertail coverts; dark grey nape and upperparts; light grey breast and belly; dark bill. *Immature:* dark sooty grey overall; pale bill with a dark tip.
Size: *L* 28–33 cm.
Status: common year-round resident.
Habitat: dense and open coniferous and mixed forests, bogs and fens, picnic sites and campgrounds.
Nesting: on a branch in a conifer tree; bulky, well-insulated nest is made of plant fibres, roots, moss, twigs, feathers and fur; female incubates 3 or 4 pale grey to greenish eggs, marked with brown, greenish or reddish dots, for 17–22 days.

Feeding: searches the ground and vegetation for insects, fruit, seeds, fungi, bird eggs and nestlings, carrion and berries; stores food items at scattered cache sites.
Voice: complex vocal repertoire includes a soft, whistled *quee-oo*, a chuckled *cla-cla-cla* and a *churr*; also imitates other birds.
Similar Species: *Northern Shrike* (p. 217) and *Loggerhead Shrike* (p. 216): black mask; black and white wings and tail; hooked bill. *Northern Mockingbird* (p. 259): darker wings and tail; white patch in the wings; white outer tail feathers; longer, slimmer bill.
Best Sites: Petroglyphs PP; Algonquin PP; Grundy Lake PP; Halfway Lake PP; Lake Superior PP; Pukaskwa PP; Sleeping Giant PP; Quetico PP; Hwy 11.

BLUE JAY

Cyanocitta cristata

The large trees and bushy ornamental shrubs of Ontario's suburban neighbourhoods and rural communities are particularly appealing to the remarkable Blue Jay. This adaptable bird is common wherever plants bear fruit and backyard feeding stations are maintained with a generous supply of sunflower seeds and peanuts. • The Blue Jay is one of Ontario's most recognizable birds. With its raucous *jay-jay-jay* wake-up calls and beautiful, conspicuous plumage, this major league mascot is almost impossible to miss. • The Blue Jay embodies all the admirable traits and aggressive qualities of the corvid family, which includes the magpie, crow and raven. Beautiful, resourceful and vocally diverse, the Blue Jay can at times prove to be one of the most annoying and impish birds around. Fortunately, its intriguing character and enchanting boldness outweigh its occasional, briefly nerve-fraying behaviour. • Whether on its own or gathered in a mob, the Blue Jay will rarely hesitate to drive away smaller birds, squirrels or even cats when threatened. It seems there is no predator, not even the Great Horned Owl, that is too formidable for this bird to cajole or harass.

ID: blue crest; black 'necklace'; blue upperparts; white underparts; white bar and flecking on the wings; dark bars and white corners on the blue tail; black bill.
Size: *L* 28–31 cm.
Status: common to abundant migrant and breeder from March to November; uncommon to fairly common visitor from November to March.
Habitat: mixed deciduous forests, agricultural areas, scrubby fields and townsites.
Nesting: in the crotch of a tree or tall shrub; pair builds a bulky stick nest and incubates 4 or 5 greenish, buff or pale blue eggs, spotted with grey and brown, for 16–18 days.
Feeding: forages on the ground and among vegetation for nuts, berries, eggs, nestlings and birdseed; also eats insects and carrion.
Voice: noisy, screaming *jay-jay-jay*; nasal *queedle queedle queedle-queedle* sounds a little like a muted trumpet; often imitates various sounds.
Similar Species: none.
Best Sites: cities and towns, especially where there are birdfeeders.

BLACK-BILLED MAGPIE
Pica pica

This impressive bird has recently established a foothold in Ontario, settling in the agricultural fields and aspen groves of Rainy River Country. Many westerners are jaded by the omnipresence of magpies, but an Ontarian seeing this bird for the first time will be captivated by its beauty and approachability. • The Black-billed Magpie is one of the most exceptional architects among our birds. The elaborate domed nest that it builds is usually located in a tree or cluster of dense shrubs with access to open territory. Constructed of sticks and held together with mud, the domed compartment conceals and protects the eggs and young from harsh weather and most predators. The nests are so well built that they may remain abandoned in a tree for years before they are reused, often by non-builders, such as Great Horned Owls. • The magpie's noisy penchant for mobbing roosting owls often leads observers to entertaining views of both the magpies and their annoyed target.

ID: long, black tail; black head, breast and back; rounded, black and white wings; black undertail coverts; black bill; white belly; greenish gloss on the wings and tail.
Size: *L* 46–56 cm.
Status: very rare and extremely local year-round resident; infrequent fall and winter wanderer.
Habitat: groves of aspen, willow or alder among open farmlands.
Nesting: in a tree or tall shrub; domed stick and twig nest has an interior cup of mud lined with grass, weeds and hair; female incubates 5–8 greenish-grey eggs, heavily spotted with brown, for 16–24 days.
Feeding: forages on the ground for insects, carrion, human food waste, nuts, seeds and berries; may pick insects and ticks off livestock and deer; may eat some eggs and nestlings.
Voice: loud, nasal, frequently repeated *yeck-yeck-yeck*; also many other vocalizations.
Similar Species: none.
Best Sites: farmlands in the Rainy River area.

AMERICAN CROW

Corvus brachyrhynchos

American Crows are wary and intelligent birds that have flourished in spite of considerable human efforts, over many generations, to reduce their numbers. Crows are ecological generalists, and much of their strength lies in their ability to adapt to a variety of habitats. • Crows are common throughout much of the province in summer, but few remain in their breeding territory year-round. In fall, most group together in flocks numbering in the hundreds or thousands. These thrilling aggregations, known as 'murders,' migrate southward to the extreme southern parts of Ontario or into the United States for winter. In Essex County, up to 90,000 crows may roost together on any given winter night. During occasionally mild winters, some crows do not migrate and instead join gulls and ravens at landfill sites. The lengthening days of late winter entice them to disperse and migrate northward to breed. • *Corvus brachyrhynchos*, despite sounding cumbersome, is Latin for 'raven with the small nose.'

ID: all-black body; square-shaped tail; black bill and legs; slim, sleek head and throat.
Size: *L* 43–53 cm; *W* 94 cm.
Status: common to abundant migrant and breeder from February to early November; common to locally abundant visitor from November to February.
Habitat: urban areas, agricultural fields and other open areas with scattered woodlands; also among clearings, marshes, lakes and rivers in dense forested areas.
Nesting: in a conifer or deciduous tree or on a utility pole; large stick and branch nest is lined with fur

and soft plant materials; female incubates 4–6 brown- and grey-blotched, grey-green to blue-green eggs, for about 18 days.
Feeding: very opportunistic; feeds on carrion, small vertebrates, other birds' eggs and nestlings, berries, seeds, invertebrates and human food waste.
Voice: distinctive, far-carrying, repetitive *caw-caw-caw*.
Similar Species: *Common Raven* (p. 228): larger; wedge-shaped tail; shaggy throat; heavier bill.
Best Sites: cities and towns; agricultural areas and forest clearings.

227

COMMON RAVEN

Corvus corax

Whether stealing food from a flock of gulls, harassing a soaring hawk in mid-air, dining from a roadside carcass or confidently strutting among campers at a park, the Raven is worthy of its reputation as a bold and clever bird. Glorified in native cultures across the Northern Hemisphere, the Common Raven does not act by instinct alone. Through its complex vocalizations and occasional playful bouts of sliding down a snowbank, this raucous bird exhibits behaviours many people once thought of as exclusively human. • Breeding ravens maintain loyal, lifelong pair bonds, enduring everything from food scarcity and harsh weather to the raising of young. • Few birds occupy as large a natural range as the Common Raven. Distributed throughout the Northern Hemisphere, it is found along coastlines, in deserts, on mountain tops and even on the arctic tundra. Ravens once inhabited every corner of Ontario, but poisoning, trapping and shooting campaigns led to great declines in their population.

ID: all-black plumage; heavy, black bill; wedge-shaped tail; shaggy throat; rounded wings.
Size: *L* 61 cm; *W* 1.3 m.
Status: uncommon to common year-round resident.
Habitat: coniferous and mixed forests and woodlands, townsites, campgrounds and landfills; arctic tundra.
Nesting: on steep cliffs, ledges, bluffs, tall coniferous trees and utility poles; large stick and branch nest is lined with fur and soft plant materials; female incubates 4–6 brown or olive-blotched greenish eggs for 18–21 days.

Feeding: very opportunistic; feeds on carrion, small vertebrates, other birds' eggs and nestlings, berries, invertebrates and human food waste; some forage along roadways.
Voice: deep, guttural, far-carrying, repetitive *craww-craww* or *quork quork*; also many other vocalizations.
Similar Species: *American Crow* (p. 227): smaller; square-shaped tail; slim throat; slimmer bill; call is a higher-pitched *caw-caw-caw*.
Best Sites: any forest, woodland, townsite or landfill on the Canadian Shield.

HORNED LARK

Eremophila alpestris

The tinkling sounds of Horned Larks flying over Ontario pastures and fields are a sure sign that another spring season has arrived. Horned Larks are among the earliest arrivals in our province, settling on the fields long before the snows are gone. Flying and gliding in circles, displaying males issue their sweet chimes in flight before plummeting to the ground in dramatic, high-speed dives. • Horned Larks are commonly found along the shoulders of gravel roads, where they search for seeds. They are easy to see, but often tough to identify, because they fly off into the adjacent fields at the approach of any vehicle. • In Ontario, these open-country inhabitants are most common during spring and fall migration and in early winter as they congregate in flocks on farm fields, beaches and airfields, often in the company of Snow Buntings and Lapland Longspurs. • Despite this bird's widespread choice of habitat, its scientific name, which means 'lark of the mountains,' refers only to its alpine haunts.

ID: *Male:* small black 'horns' (often not raised); black line running under the eye from the bill to the cheek; light yellow to white face; dull brown upperparts; black breast band; dark tail with white outer tail feathers; light throat. *Female:* somewhat less distinctively patterned; duller plumage overall.

Size: *L* 18 cm.

Status: common migrant and breeder from February to November; rare to locally common visitor from November to February.

Habitat: *Breeding:* open areas, including pastures, croplands, sparsely vegetated fields, weedy meadows, airfields and alpine tundra. *Winter* and *In migration:* croplands, fields, roadside ditches and fields.

Nesting: on the ground; in a shallow scrape lined with grass,

plant fibres and roots; female chooses the nest site and incubates 3 or 4 pale grey to greenish-white eggs, blotched and spotted with brown, for 10–12 days.

Feeding: gleans the ground for seeds; feeds its young insects during the breeding season.

Voice: call is a tinkling *tsee-titi* or *zoot*; flight song is a long series of tinkling, twittered whistles.

Similar Species: *Sparrows* (pp. 303–20), *Longspurs* (pp. 322–23) and *Pipits* (p. 262): all lack the distinctive facial pattern, the 'horns' and the solid black breast band.

Best Sites: fields and pastures throughout southern Ontario south of the Canadian Shield; Polar Bear PP; Point Pelee NP; Lake St. Clair area; Sarnia airport; Tommy Thompson Park; Presqu'ile PP.

229

PURPLE MARTIN

Progne subis

Purple Martins once nested in natural tree hollows and in cliff crevices, but with today's modern accommodations, namely martin 'apartment' complexes, these birds have all but abandoned the natural nest sites. To be successful in attracting these large swallows to your backyard, martin condos should be placed high on a pole in a large, open area, preferably near water. The complexes must be designed with perfectly sized cavity openings and they must be cleaned out each winter. Unfortunately, there is always the chance that aggressive House Sparrows and European Starlings will lay claim to the luxurious digs and will chase away any Purple Martins that dare to move in. If all goes well, however, each spring will bring the return of a Purple Martin colony to your martin complex. The result will be an endlessly entertaining summer spectacle as the martin adults spiral around the house in pursuit of flying insects, and the young perch clumsily at the opening of their apartment cavity.

• The scientific name *Progne* refers to the Pandion's daughter Procne, who, according to Greek mythology, was transformed into a swallow.

♂

♀

ID: dark blue, glossy body; slightly forked tail; pointed wings; small bill. *Male:* dark underparts. *Female:* sooty grey underparts.
Size: *L* 18–20 cm.
Status: locally common migrant and breeder from April to September; a few may arrive as early as late March and some may remain until late October.
Habitat: semi-open areas, often near water.
Nesting: communal; usually in a human-made, apartment-style birdhouse; rarely in tree cavities or in cliff crevices; nest materials include feathers, grass, mud and vegetation; female incubates 4 or 5 white eggs for 15–18 days.
Feeding: mostly while in flight; usually eats flies, ants, bugs,

dragonflies and mosquitoes; may also walk on the ground, taking insects and rarely berries.
Voice: rich, fluty, robin-like *pew-pew*, often heard in flight.
Similar Species: *European Starling* (p. 261): longer bill (yellow in summer); lacks the forked tail. *Barn Swallow* (p. 235): deeply forked tail; buff-orange to reddish-brown throat; whitish to cinnamon underparts. *Tree Swallow* (p. 231): white underparts.
Best Sites: martin houses in urban, rural and cottage country backyards, usually near water; Point Pelee NP; Long Point PP; Niagara Peninsula; Trent Canal; Prince Edward County; Ottawa area; Rainy River area.

TREE SWALLOW

Tachycineta bicolor

Tree Swallows, our most common summer swallows, are often seen perched beside their fencepost nest boxes. When conditions are favourable, these busy birds are known to return to their young 10 to 20 times an hour, which provides observers with plenty of opportunity to watch and photograph the birds in action. • Tree Swallows prefer to nest in natural tree hollows or woodpecker cavities in standing dead trees, but where cavities are scarce, nest boxes are used as temporary sites. Increasingly, landowners, park managers and forestry companies are realizing the value of dead trees as homes for wildlife and are choosing to leave them standing. • Unlike other North American swallows, female Tree Swallows do not acquire their full adult plumage until their second or third year. • In the bright spring sunshine, the iridescent back of the Tree Swallow appears dark blue; prior to fall migration, it appears green. • The scientific name *bicolor* is Latin for 'two colours,' in reference to the contrast between the bird's dark upperparts and light underparts.

ID: iridescent dark blue or green head and upperparts; white underparts; no white on the cheek; dark rump; small bill; long, pointed wings; shallowly forked tail. *Female:* slightly duller. *Immature:* brown above; white below.
Size: *L* 14 cm.
Status: common migrant and breeder from April to mid-October; a few may arrive as early as late February; some may remain into late December.
Habitat: open areas, such as beaver ponds, marshes, lakeshores, field fencelines, townsites and open woodlands.
Nesting: in a tree cavity or nest box lined with weeds, grass and feathers; female incubates 4–6 eggs for up to 19 days.

Feeding: catches flies, midges, mosquitos, beetles and ants on the wing; also takes stoneflies, mayflies and caddisflies over water; may eat some berries and seeds.
Voice: alarm call is a metallic, buzzy *klweet*. *Male:* song is a liquid, chattering twitter.
Similar Species: *Purple Martin* (p. 230): female has sooty grey underparts; male is dark blue overall. *Eastern Kingbird* (p. 215): larger; white-tipped tail; longer bill; dark grey to blackish upperparts. *Bank Swallow* (p. 233) and *Northern Rough-winged Swallow* (p. 232): brown upperparts. *Barn Swallow* (p. 235): buff-orange to reddish-brown throat; deeply forked tail.
Best Sites marshes, beaver ponds and lakeshores throughout Ontario, especially those with nest boxes.

231

NORTHERN ROUGH-WINGED SWALLOW
Stelgidopteryx serripennis

The inconspicuous Northern Rough-winged Swallow typically nests in sandy banks along rivers and streams, enjoying its own private piece of waterfront. This swallow is usually seen in single pairs, but it doesn't mind joining a crowd, often gulping down insects in the company of other swallow species. Once in a while, a pair may nest among a large colony of Bank Swallows. In the wheeling flocks of feeding birds, the Rough-wings are often completely overlooked among their similar-looking cousins. • Unlike other Ontario swallows, male Northern Rough-wings have curved barbs along the outer edge of their primary wing feathers. The purpose of this saw-toothed edge remains a mystery. The ornithologist who initially named this bird must have been very impressed with its wings: *Stelgidopteryx* (scraper wing) and *serripennis* (saw feather) refer to this unusual characteristic.

ID: brown upperparts; light brownish-grey underparts; small bill; dark cheek; dark rump. *In flight:* long, pointed wings; notched tail.
Size: L 14 cm.
Status: rare to common migrant and breeder from April to September, some remain until early January; a few may arrive as early as mid-March.
Habitat: open and semi-open areas, including fields and open woodlands, usually near water.
Nesting: occasionally in small colonies; at the end of a burrow lined with leaves and dry grass; sometimes reuses kingfisher burrows, rodent burrows and other land crevices; female mostly

incubates 4–8 white eggs for 12–16 days.
Feeding: catches flying insects on the wing; sometimes eats insects from the ground; drinks on the wing.
Voice: generally quiet; occasionally a quick, short, squeaky *brrrtt*.
Similar Species: *Bank Swallow* (p. 233): dark breast band. *Tree Swallow* (p. 231): dark, iridescent bluish to greenish upperparts; clean white underparts. *Cliff Swallow* (p. 234): brown and blue upperparts; buff forehead and rump patch.
Best Sites: Rondeau PP; Long Point PP; The Pinery PP; Tobermory; Lynde Shores Conservation Area; Trent Canal; Presqu'ile PP; Rideau Canal.

BANK SWALLOW

Riparia riparia

A colony of Bank Swallows can be a constant flurry of activity as eager parents pop in and out of their earthen burrows with mouthfuls of insects for their insatiable young. Not surprisingly, all the activity tends to attract attention, but few predators are able to catch these swift and agile birds. • Bank Swallows usually excavate their own nest burrows, first using their small bills and later digging with their feet. Most nestlings are safe from predators within their nest chamber, which is typically 60 to 90 cm in length. • In medieval Europe, it was believed that swallows spent winter in the mud at the bottom of swamps, since they were not seen during that season. In those days, it was beyond imagination that these birds might fly south for the winter. • *Riparia* is from the Latin for 'riverbank,' which is a common nesting site for this bird. If you approach a colony by canoe, the birds will usually burst from their burrows in the hundreds and circle nervously until the river carries you away.

ID: brown upperparts; light underparts; brown breast band; long, pointed wings; shallowly forked tail; white throat; dark cheek; small legs.

Size: *L* 13 cm.

Status: common migrant and breeder from May to early September; a few may arrive as early as mid-March; some may remain as late as mid-November; migrants are often very locally abundant in mid-May and early August.

Habitat: steep banks, lakeshore bluffs and open areas, such as gravel pits.

Nesting: colonial; pair excavates or reuses a long burrow in a steep earthen bank; end of the burrow is lined with grass, rootlets, weeds, straw and feathers; pair incubates 4 or 5 white eggs for 14–16 days.

Feeding: catches flying insects; drinks on the wing.

Voice: twittering chatter: *speed-zeet speed-zeet*.

Similar Species: *Northern Rough-winged Swallow* (p. 232): lacks the dark breast band. *Tree Swallow* (p. 231): lacks the dark breast band; dark iridescent bluish to greenish upperparts. *Cliff Swallow* (p. 234): lacks the dark breast band; brown and blue upperparts; buff forehead and rump.

Best Sites: shorelines of Lake Erie, Lake Ontario, Lake Huron and the Detroit, St. Lawrence and Ottawa rivers.

CLIFF SWALLOW

Petrochelidon pyrrhonota

If the Cliff Swallow were to be renamed in the 20th century, it would probably be called the 'Bridge Swallow,' because so many river bridges in eastern North America seem to have a colony living under them. Clouds of Cliff Swallows will often swirl up along either side of the roadway, dazzling passers-by with their acrobatics and impressive numbers. If you stop to inspect the underside of a bridge, you might see hundreds of gourd-shaped mud nests stuck to the pillars and structural beams. During years of high run-off and prolonged rains, floods can wipe out entire colonies of nesting Cliff Swallows.
• Master mud masons, Cliff Swallows roll mud into balls with their bills and press the pellets together to form their characteristic nests within several days. Brooding parents peer out of the circular neck of the nest, with their gleaming eyes watching the world go by.
• Cliff Swallows are brood parasites— females often lay one or more eggs in the temporarily vacant nests of neighbouring Cliff Swallows. Upon returning to a parasitized nest, adults accept the foreign eggs and raise them as though they were their own.

ID: orangy rump; buff forehead; blue-grey head and wings; rusty cheek, nape and throat; buff breast; white belly; spotted undertail coverts; nearly square tail.
Size: *L* 14 cm.
Status: uncommon to very locally common migrant and breeder from May to mid-September; a few may arrive as early as mid-March; some may remain until late October.
Habitat: steep banks, cliffs, bridges and buildings near watercourses; forages over water, fields and marshes.
Nesting: colonial; under bridges and on cliffs and buildings; pair builds a gourd-shaped mud nest with a small opening near the bottom; pair incubates 4 or 5 brown-spotted, white to pinkish eggs for 14–16 days.
Feeding: catches flying insects on the wing; occasionally eats berries; drinks on the wing.
Voice: twittering chatter: *churrr-churrr*; also an alarm call: *nyew*.
Similar Species: *Barn Swallow* (p. 235): deeply forked tail; dark rump; usually has rust-coloured underparts and forehead. *Other swallows:* lack the buff forehead and rump patch.
Best Sites: bridges and buildings in open country near water; colonies are often abandoned after a few years.

BARN SWALLOW

Hirundo rustica

Although Barn Swallows do not occur in mass colonies, they are very familiar to most Ontarians because they usually build their nests on human structures. Barn Swallows once nested on cliffs, but their cup-shaped mud nests are now found in barns and boathouses, under bridges or in any other structure that provides shelter from predators and inclement weather. Unfortunately, not everyone appreciates nesting Barn Swallows. The young can be very messy, and the nests are often scraped off buildings just as the nesting season has begun. However, these graceful birds are natural pest controllers, and their close association with urban areas and tolerance for human activity affords us the wondrous opportunity to observe and study the normally secretive reproductive cycle of birds. • 'Swallow tail' is a term used to describe something that is deeply forked. In Ontario, the Barn Swallow is the only swallow that displays this feature. • *Hirundo* is Latin for 'swallow,' while *rustica* refers to this bird's preference for rural habitats.

ID: long, deeply forked tail; rust-coloured throat and forehead; blue-black upperparts; rust- to buff-coloured underparts; long, pointed wings.
Size: *L* 18 cm.
Status: common to abundant migrant and breeder from April to September; a few arrive as early as late March; some remain until January.
Habitat: in open rural and urban areas where bridges, culverts and buildings are found near rivers, lakes, marshes or ponds.
Nesting: singly or in small, loose colonies; on a vertical or horizontal building structure under a suitable overhang, on a bridge or in a culvert;

half or full cup nest is made of mud and grass or straw; pair incubates 4–7 white eggs, spotted with brown, for 13–17 days.
Feeding: catches flying insects on the wing.
Voice: continuous twittering chatter: *zip-zip-zip*; also *kvick-kvick*.
Similar Species: *Cliff Swallow* (p. 234): squared tail; buff rump and forehead; light-coloured underparts. *Purple Martin* (p. 230): shallowly forked tail; male is completely blue-black; female has sooty gray underparts. *Tree Swallow* (p. 231): lean white underparts; notched tail.
Best Sites: almost any building near water that is not frequently disturbed.

BLACK-CAPPED CHICKADEE

Poecile atricapillus

Flocks of curious Black-capped Chickadees can be seen year-round throughout Ontario as they flit from tree to tree, scouring branches and shrivelled leaves for insects. • Throughout the winter months, Black-capped Chickadees often join the company of kinglets, nuthatches, creepers, small woodpeckers and sometimes Boreal Chickadees in what appears to be a celebration of life in the forest. At this time of year, 'Black-caps' are common visitors to well-stocked feeders, and they are occasionally enticed to land on an outstretched hand offering a sunflower seed. In fall, adult Black-caps and their fledged young are often joined by vireos and warblers. • When foraging, Black-capped Chickadees swing upside-down on tree branches, snatching up insects and berries. • Most songbirds, including Black-capped Chickadees, have both songs and calls. The chickadee's *swee-tee* song is heard primarily during spring courtship, and its *chick-a-dee-dee-dee* call keeps flocks together and maintains contact between flock members. • The scientific name *atricapillus* is Latin for 'black crown.'

ID: black cap and bib; white cheek; grey back and wings; white underparts; light buff sides and flanks; dark legs; conspicuous white edgings on the wing feathers.
Size: *L* 13–15 cm.
Status: common year-round resident.
Habitat: deciduous and mixed forests and woodlands, riparian woodlands, wooded urban parks and backyards with birdfeeders.
Nesting: excavates a cavity in a soft, rotting stump or tree; cavity is lined with fur, feathers, moss, grass and cocoons; female incubates 6–8 white eggs, with fine reddish-brown dots, for 12–13 days.
Feeding: gleans vegetation, branches and the ground for small insects and spiders; visits backyard feeders; also eats conifer seeds and invertebrate eggs.
Voice: call is a chipper, whistled *chick-a-dee-dee-dee*; song is a slow, whistled *swee-tee* or *fee-bee*.
Similar Species: *Boreal Chickadee* (p. 237): grey-brown cap, sides and flanks. *Blackpoll Warbler* (p. 284): breeding male has 2 white wing bars, dark streaking on the white underparts, orangish legs and a longer, paler bill. *Carolina Chickadee:* exceptionally rare vagrant in Ontario; higher-pitched call; lacks the white edgings on the wing feathers; neater edge to the black bib.
Best Sites: at birdfeeders in wooded backyards; almost any woodlot or riparian woodland.

BOREAL CHICKADEE

Poecile hudsonicus

Birders generally love chickadees, and the Boreal Chickadee is especially sought-out as the northern representative of this endearing clan. • As its name suggests, the Boreal Chickadee resides primarily in Ontario's expansive boreal forest. Unlike the more common and familiar Black-capped Chickadee, the Boreal prefers the seclusion of coniferous forests, and it tends to be softer-spoken. During the nesting season, Boreal Chickadees are so quiet that you would never know they were there at all. • Chickadees burn so much energy that they must replenish their stores daily to survive the winter—they have insufficient fat reserves to survive a prolonged stretch of cold weather. Chickadees store food for winter in holes and bark crevices. • During cold nights, a chickadee enters a state of torpor, in which the bird's metabolism slows so that it uses less energy. • The scientific name *hudsonicus* refers to the northern (Hudsonian) region of Canada.

ID: grey-brown cap, back, sides and flanks; black bib; whitish to light grey breast and belly; whitish cheek patch; grey wings and tail.
Size: *L* 13–14 cm.
Status: uncommon to locally common year-round resident; some may move south of their breeding range for winter.
Habitat: spruce, fir and pine forests; sometimes in mixed coniferous forests with a small deciduous component.
Nesting: excavates a cavity in soft, rotting wood or uses a natural cavity or abandoned woodpecker nest in a conifer tree; female lines the nest with fur,

feathers, moss and grass; female incubates 5–8 white eggs, with fine, reddish-brown dots, for 11–16 days.
Feeding: gleans vegetation, branches and infrequently the ground for small tree-infesting insects (including their pupae and eggs) and spiders; also eats conifer seeds.
Voice: soft, nasal, wheezy *scick-a day day day.*
Similar Species: *Black-capped Chickadee* (p. 236): black cap; buffy flanks; more greyish than brownish overall.
Best Sites: Algonquin PP; Halfway Lake PP; Lake Superior PP; Pukaskwa NP; Sleeping Giant PP; Quetico PP; Fushimi Lake PP; forests bordering Hwy 11.

TUFTED TITMOUSE

Parus bicolor

This bird's entertaining feeding antics and rare status in Ontario keep curious observers occupied at birdfeeders. Grasping an acorn or sunflower seed with its tiny feet, the dexterous Tufted Titmouse strikes its dainty bill repeatedly against the hard outer coating, exposing the inner core. • A breeding pair of Tufted Titmice will maintain their bond throughout the year, even when joining small, multi-species flocks for the cold winter months. The titmouse family bond is so strong that the young from one breeding season will often stay with their parents long enough to help them with nesting and feeding duties the following year. In late winter, mating pairs break from their flocks to search for nesting cavities and soft lining material. If you are fortunate enough to have titmice living in your area, you might be able to attract one by setting out the hair you have accumulated in your hairbrush. There is a good chance that these curious birds will gladly incorporate your offering into the construction of their nest, allowing you the pleasure of knowing you are helping to keep titmice eggs and young as snug as can be.

ID: grey crest and upperparts; black forehead; white underparts and buffy flanks.
Size: *L* 15–17 cm.
Status: rare and very local year-round resident.
Habitat: deciduous woodlands, groves and suburban parks with large mature trees.
Nesting: in a natural cavity or woodpecker cavity lined with soft vegetation and animal hair; female may be fed by the male from courtship to time of hatching; female incubates 5 or 6 finely dotted, white eggs for 12–14 days; both adults and occasionally a 'helper' raise the young.
Feeding: insects, supplemented with seeds, nuts and fruits; will eat seeds and suet from feeders; forages on the ground and in trees, often hanging upside-down like a chickadee.
Voice: noisy, scolding calls, like those of chickadees; song is a whistled *peter peter* or *peter peter peter*.
Similar Species: none.
Best Sites: Rondeau PP; Niagara Peninsula shorelines; Niagara-on-the-Lake.

RED-BREASTED NUTHATCH

Sitta canadensis

The Red-breasted Nuthatch looks a lot like a red rocket as it streaks toward a neighbourhood birdfeeder from the cover of a coniferous tree. The nuthatch ejects empty shells left behind by sloppy finches and then selects its own meal before jetting off, never lingering longer than it takes to pick up a seed. • Red-breasted Nuthatches frequently join in on bird waves—groups of warblers, chickadees, kinglets, titmice and small woodpeckers often forage together through woodlands in winter or during migration. Nuthatches stand out from the other song-birds because of their unusual body form and habit of moving headfirst down tree-trunks. Their loud, nasal *yank-yank-yank* calls, which are frequently heard in spring, are also distinctive. • This bird smears the entrance of its nesting cavity with sap from pine or spruce trees. This sticky door-mat might inhibit ants and other animals from entering the nest chamber. Invertebrates can be the most serious threat to nesting success, because they can transmit fungal infections or parasitize nestlings. • The sci-entific name *canadensis* means 'of Canada.' (According to the rules of taxonomy, species named after places usually have scientific names that end with *-ensis*; species named after men end with *-i*; and species named after women end with *-ae*.)

ID: rusty underparts; grey-blue upperparts; white eyebrow; black eye line; black cap; straight bill; short tail; white cheek. *Male:* deeper rust on the breast; black crown. *Female:* light red wash on the breast; dark grey crown.
Size: *L* 11 cm.
Status: rare to fairly common year-round resident; some may be sedentary residents while others are in-province transients or short-distance migrants.
Habitat: *Breeding:* spruce-fir and pine forests; pine plantations. *Winter* and *In migration:* mixed woodlands, especially those near birdfeeders.
Nesting: excavates a cavity or uses an abandoned woodpecker nest; usually smears the entrance with sap; nest is made of bark shreds, grass and fur; female incubates 5 or 6 white eggs, spotted with reddish-brown, for about 12 days.
Feeding: forages down trees while probing under loose bark for larval and adult invertebrates; eats pine and spruce seeds during winter; often frequents feeders.
Voice: slow, continually repeated, nasal *yank-yank-yank* or *rah-rah-rah-rah*; also a short *tsip*.
Similar Species: *White-breasted Nuthatch* (p. 240): larger; lacks the black eye line and the red underparts.
Best Sites: backyard feeders; almost anywhere coniferous trees are found.

239

WHITE-BREASTED NUTHATCH

Sitta carolinensis

To a novice birdwatcher, seeing a White-breasted Nuthatch call repeatedly while clinging to the underside of a branch is an odd sight. To the nuthatch, however, this gravity-defying act is completely natural. Moving headfirst down a tree-trunk, the White-breasted Nuthatch forages for invertebrates while pausing to survey its surroundings and occasionally issuing a noisy call. • Unlike woodpeckers and creepers, nuthatches do not use their tails to brace themselves against tree-trunks— nuthatches grasp the tree through foot power alone. • Although White-breasted Nuthatches are regular visitors to most backyard feeders, they never stick around longer than to grab a seed and dash. Only an offering of suet can persuade this tiny bird to remain in a single spot for any length of time. • The scientific name *carolinensis* means 'of Carolina'—the first White-breasted Nuthatch specimen was collected in the Carolina mountains of the eastern U.S.

ID: white underparts; white face; grey-blue back; rusty undertail coverts; short tail; straight bill; short legs. *Male:* black cap. *Female:* dark grey cap.

Size: *L* 15 cm.

Status: fairly common year-round resident.

Habitat: mixed forests, woodlots and backyards.

Nesting: in a natural cavity or an abandoned woodpecker nest in a large deciduous tree; lines the cavity with bark, grass, fur and feathers; female incubates 5–8 white eggs, spotted with reddish brown, for 12–14 days.

Feeding: forages down trees headfirst in search of larval and adult invertebrates; also eats many nuts and seeds; regularly visits feeders.

Voice: song is a frequently repeated *werwerwerwerwer;* calls include *ha-ha-ha ha-ha-ha, ank ank* and *ip.*

Similar Species: *Red-breasted Nuthatch* (p. 239): black eye line; rusty underparts. *Black-capped Chickadee* (p. 236): black bib.

Best Sites: backyard feeders; almost any mixed woodland.

BROWN CREEPER

Certhia americana

Brown Creepers are never easy to find. Embracing old-growth forests during much of the year, they often go unnoticed until a flake of bark suddenly takes the shape of a bird. If a creeper is frightened, it will freeze and flatten against a tree-trunk, becoming even tougher to see. • Intent on feeding, the Brown Creeper spirals up tree-trunks, searching for hidden invertebrates. When it reaches the upper branches, the creeper floats down to the base of a neighbouring tree to begin another foraging ascent. Its long, stiff tail feathers prop it up against vertical tree-trunks as it hitches its way skyward. • Like the call of the Golden-crowned Kinglet, the thin whistle of the Brown Creeper is so high-pitched that birders often fail to hear it. To further the confusion, the creeper's song often takes on the boisterous warbling quality of a wood warbler song. • There are many species of creepers in Europe and Asia, but the Brown Creeper is the only one found in North America.

ID: brown back is heavily streaked with buffy white; white eyebrow; white underparts; downcurved bill; long, pointed tail feathers; rusty rump.

Size: *L* 13 cm.

Status: common migrant from early April to early May and from late September to late November; rare visitor from November to April; uncommon breeder.

Habitat: mature deciduous, coniferous and mixed forests and woodlands, especially in wet areas with large, dead trees; also found near bogs.

Nesting: under loose bark; nest of grass and conifer needles is woven together with spider silk; female incubates 5 or 6 whitish eggs, with reddish-brown dots, for 14–17 days.

Feeding: hops up tree-trunks and large limbs, probing loose bark for adult and larval invertebrates.

Voice: song is a faint, high-pitched *trees-trees-trees see the trees*; call is a high *tseee*.

Similar Species: *Nuthatches* (pp. 239–40): grey-blue back; straight or slightly up-turned bill. *Woodpeckers* (pp. 196–204): all lack the brown back streaking; straight bills.

Best Sites: Rondeau PP; The Pinery PP; Halton Regional Forest; Charleston Lake PP; Bon Echo PP; Algonquin PP; Pukaskwa PP.

CAROLINA WREN

Thryothorus ludovicianus

The energetic and cheerful Carolina Wren is a treasured year-round resident in southern Ontario. This bird performs lively 'duets' at any time of day and in any season. The duet often begins with the female's introductory chatter and is followed by innumerable ringing variations of *tea-kettle tea-kettle tea-kettle tea* from her mate. • These persistent birds continue to push the limits of their range northward in Ontario. In years of mild winter weather, colonies of Carolina Wrens become fairly large and stable, but a winter of frigid temperatures and ice-rain can completely decimate Ontario's otherwise healthy Carolina Wren population. Fortunately, such disasters represent only a minor, temporary loss of these stubborn, pioneering feathered delights from our province. • On occasion, a pair of Carolina Wrens will nest in the brushy thickets of an overgrown backyard or in an obscure nook or crevice in a house or barn. Carolina Wrens might even raise two broods in a single season.

ID: long, prominent, white eyebrow; rusty brown upperparts; rich buff-coloured underparts; white throat; slightly downcurved bill.
Size: *L* 14 cm.
Status: rare to locally uncommon year-round resident; may exhibit dramatic declines in years of severe winter weather.
Habitat: dense forest undergrowth, especially shrubby tangles and thickets.
Nesting: in a nest box or natural cavity; both adults fill the cavity with twigs and vegetation and line it with fine materials; nest cup may be domed and may include a snakeskin; female incubates 4 or 5 brown-blotched, white eggs for 12–16 days; both adults feed the young.
Feeding: usually forages in pairs on the ground and among vegetation;

eats mostly insects and other invertebrates; also takes berries, fruits and seeds; will visit bird feeders for peanuts and suet.
Voice: loud, repetitious *tea-kettle tea-kettle tea-kettle* may be heard at any time of day or year; female often chatters while the male sings.
Similar Species: *House Wren* (p. 243) and *Winter Wren* (p. 244): lack the prominent white eyebrow. *Marsh Wren* (p. 246): black, triangular back patch is streaked with white; prefers marshes. *Sedge Wren* (p. 245): dark crown and back are streaked with white; pale, indistinct eyebrow.
Best Sites: Point Pelee NP; Rondeau PP; Lake Erie shoreline between Long Beach and Historic Fort Erie; Niagara-on-the-Lake.

HOUSE WREN

Troglodytes aedon

The House Wren's bubbly song and energetic demeanour make it a welcome addition to any Ontario neighbourhood. A small cavity in a standing dead tree or a custom-made nest box is usually all it takes to attract this joyful bird to most backyards. Sometimes even an empty flowerpot or vacant drainpipe is deemed a suitable nest site, provided there is a local abundance of insect prey. Occasionally, you may find that your heartfelt nest site offering is packed full of twigs and left abandoned without any nesting birds in sight. Wrens often build numerous nests, which later serve as decoys or dummy nests for their would be ene-mies. In such a case, your only course of action should be to clean out the cavity and hope that another pair of wrens will find your real estate more appeal-ing. • In Greek mythology, Zeus transformed Aedon, the queen of Thebes, into a nightingale. The wonderfully warbled call of the House Wren is some-what similar to a nightingale's.

ID: brown upperparts with fine, dark barring on the upper wings and lower back; faint, pale eyebrow and eye ring; short, 'cocked up' tail is finely barred with black; whitish throat; whitish to buff underparts; faintly barred flanks.
Size: *L* 12 cm.
Status: common migrant and breeder from April to October; a few may arrive as early as late March; a few may be present in winter.
Habitat: thickets and shrubby openings in or at the edge of deciduous or mixed woodlands; often in shrubs and thickets near buildings.
Nesting: in a natural cavity or abandoned woodpecker nest; also in nest boxes or other artificial cavities; nest of sticks and grass is lined with feathers, fur and other soft materials; female probably incubates the 6–8 white eggs, with heavy, reddish-brown dotting, for 12–15 days.
Feeding: gleans the ground and vegetation for insects, especially beetles, caterpillars, grasshoppers and spiders.
Voice: smooth, running, bubbly warble: *tsi-tsi-tsi-tsi oodle-oodle-oodle-oodle* (lasting about 2–3 seconds).
Similar Species: *Winter Wren* (p. 244): smaller; darker overall; much shorter, stubby tail; prominent, dark barring on the flanks. *Sedge Wren* (p. 245): faint white streaking on the dark crown and back.
Best Sites: almost any thick rural hedgerow, shrubby fenceline, riparian thicket or tangle, shrubby abandoned field or woodland edge in southern Ontario.

WINTER WREN

Troglodytes troglodytes

Winter Wrens boldly announce their claim to patches of moist coniferous woodland, where they often make their homes in the green moss and gnarled upturned roots of decomposing tree-trunks. • The song of the Winter Wren is distinguished by its melodious, bubbly tone and extended duration. Few other singers in Ontario can sustain their song for up to 10 music-packed seconds. When they're not singing or nesting, Winter Wrens skulk through the forest understorey, quietly probing myriad nooks and crannies for invertebrates. • While the female raises the young, the male wren brings food to the nest and defends the territory through song. At night, the male sleeps away from his family in an unfinished nest. • Most of our Winter Wrens migrate south for winter, but some individuals brave the colder months in southwestern Ontario. • *Troglodytes* is Greek for 'creeping in holes' or 'cave dweller.' • The Winter Wren also breeds across Europe and Asia, where it is a common garden bird often called the Jenny Wren.

ID: very short, stubby, 'cocked up' tail; fine, pale buff eyebrow; dark brown upperparts; lighter brown underparts; prominent, dark barring on the flanks.
Size: *L* 10 cm.
Status: common migrant and breeder from April to mid-November; rare visitor from November to March.
Habitat: moist boreal forest, spruce bogs, cedar swamps and mixed forests dominated by mature pine and hemlock; often near water.
Nesting: in an abandoned woodpecker cavity, in a natural hole, under bark or upturned tree roots; bulky nest is made of twigs, moss, grass and fur; male frequently builds up to 4 'dummy' nests prior to egg-laying; female incubates 5–7 white eggs, with reddish-brown dots toward the

larger end, for 14–16 days.
Feeding: forages on the ground and on trees for beetles, wood borers and other invertebrates.
Voice: *Male:* song is a warbled, tinkling series of quick trills and twitters, often more than 8 seconds long; call is a sharp *chip-chip*.
Similar Species: *House Wren* (p. 243): tail is longer than the leg; less conspicuous barring on the flanks; lighter coloured overall. *Carolina Wren* (p. 242): long, bold, white eyebrow; much larger; long tail. *Marsh Wren* (p. 246): white streaking on the black back; bold, white eyebrow. *Sedge Wren* (p. 245): white streaking on the black back; longer tail; lighter-coloured underparts.
Best Sites: Rondeau PP; Roseville Swamp; Schaefer's Woods; Algonquin PP; Halfway Lake PP; Lake Superior PP; Sleeping Giant PP.

SEDGE WREN

Cistothorus platensis

Like most wrens, the Sedge Wren is secretive and difficult to observe. It is the least familiar of all Ontario wrens, because it keeps itself well concealed in dense stands of sedges and tall, wet grass. More often than not, birders must end a day of bird-watching with only an aural recognition of the Sedge Wren, rather than a visual record. • Sedge Wrens are feverish nest builders, and construction begins immediately after they settle on a nesting territory. Each energetic male might build several incomplete nests throughout his territory before the females arrive. The decoys or 'dummy' nests are not wasted: they often serve as dormitories for later in the season. • The scientific name *platensis* refers to the Rio de la Plata in Argentina, where another isolated population of this wren is found.

ID: short, narrow tail (often cocked up); faint, pale eyebrow; dark crown and back are faintly streaked with white; barring on the wing coverts; buff-orange sides, flanks and undertail coverts on otherwise whitish underparts.

Size: *L* 10–11 cm.

Status: rare from late April to mid-October; a few may remain into November.

Habitat: wet sedge meadows, wet grassy fields, marshes, bogs and beaver ponds; often in abandoned wet fields with low, shrubby willows and alders.

Nesting: usually less than 1 m from the ground; well-built globe nest with a side entrance is woven from sedges and grasses; female incubates 4–8 unmarked, white eggs for about 14 days.

Feeding: forages low in dense vegetation, where it picks and probes for adult and larval insects and spiders; occasionally catches flying insects.

Voice: a few short staccato notes followed by a rattling trill: *chap-chap-chap-chap, chap, churr-r-r-r-r-r.*

Similar Species: *Marsh Wren* (p. 246): broad, conspicuous white eyebrow; prominent white streaking on the black back; unstreaked crown; prefers cattail marshes. *Winter Wren* (p. 244): darker overall; shorter, stubby tail; unstreaked crown. *House Wren* (p. 243): unstreaked, dark brown crown and back.

Best Sites: Long Point PP; Luther Marsh; Spry Lake; Puslinch Wetland; Richmond Fen; Wye Marsh Wildlife Centre; Mission Island Marsh.

? **?**

MARSH WREN

Cistothorus palustris

Fueled by newly emerged aquatic insects, the Marsh Wren zips about in short bursts through tall stands of cattails and bulrushes. This expert hunter catches flying insects with lightning-speed, but don't expect to see this bird in action—the Marsh Wren is a reclusive bird that prefers to remain hidden deep within its dense marshland habitat. A patient observer might be rewarded with a brief glimpse of a Marsh Wren, but it is more likely that this bird's distinctive, old-fashioned sewing machine-like song will inform you of its presence. • Marsh Wrens occasionally destroy the nests and eggs of other Marsh Wrens and other marsh-nesting songbirds such as the Red-winged Blackbird. The Red-winged Blackbird, however, is prevented from doing the same, because the wren's globe nest keeps the wren eggs well hidden, and several 'dummy' nests helps to divert the bird from the real nest. • The scientific name *palustris* is Latin for 'marsh.' • Until recently this bird was known as the Long-billed Marsh Wren.

ID: white chin and belly; white to light brown upperparts; black triangle on the upper back is streaked with white; bold white eyebrow; unstreaked brown crown; long, thin, downcurved bill.

Size: *L* 13 cm.

Status: uncommon to locally common migrant and breeder from late April to October; a few may arrive as early as mid-March; some may remain into late November.

Habitat: large cattail and bulrush marshes interspersed with open water; occasionally in tall grass-sedge marshes.

Nesting: in marshes among cattails or tall emergent vegetation; globe-like nest is woven with cattails, bulrushes, weeds and grass and lined with cattail down; female incubates 4–6 white to pale brown eggs, heavily dotted with dark brown, for 12–16 days.

Feeding: gleans vegetation and flycatches for adult aquatic invertebrates, especially dragonflies and damselflies.

Voice: *Male:* rapid, rattled warble sounding like an old sewing machine; call is a harsh *chek*.

Similar Species: *Sedge Wren* (p. 245): smaller; streaked crown. *House Wren* (p. 243): faint eyebrow; lacks the white streaking on the black back. *Carolina Wren* (p. 242): larger; lacks the white streaking on the black back; buff underparts.

Best Sites: St. Clair NWA; Point Pelee NP; Rondeau PP; Long Point PP; Luther Marsh; Lynde Shores Conservation Area; Lake Scugog; Presqu'ile PP; Big Island Marsh.

GOLDEN-CROWNED KINGLET

Regulus satrapa

Golden-crowned Kinglets are seen in spring and fall in most parts of the province. As they engage in refueling exercises, they use tree branches as swings and trapezes, flashing their regal crowns and constantly flicking their tiny wings. During summer, these dainty forest sprites are often too busy to make an appearance for admiring observers. Not much larger than hummingbirds, Golden-crowned Kinglets can be difficult to spot as they flit and hover among coniferous treetops. In winter, Golden-crowned Kinglets are commonly seen and heard among multi-species flocks that often include Black-capped Chickadees, Boreal Chickadees, Red-breasted Nuthatches and Brown Creepers. These small flocks move through Ontario's forests, decorating tall spruces, pines, firs and naked deciduous hardwoods like Christmas ornaments. • This kinglet's extremely high-pitched call is very faint and is often lost in the slightest woodland breeze.

ID: olive back; darker wings and tail; light underparts; dark cheek; 2 white wing bars; black eye line; white eyebrow; black border to the crown. *Male:* reddish-orange crown. *Female:* yellow crown.

Size: *L* 10 cm.

Status: common to abundant migrant from mid-March to early May and from September to mid-November; common breeder from April to September; uncommon winter resident.

Habitat: *Breeding:* mixed and pure, mature coniferous forests, especially those dominated by spruce; also uses some conifer plantations. *Winter* and *In migration:* coniferous, deciduous and mixed forests and woodlands.

Nesting: usually in a spruce or conifer; hanging nest is made of moss, lichens, twigs and leaves; female incubates 8 or 9 whitish to pale buff eggs, spotted with grey and brown, for 14–15 days.

Feeding: gleans and hovers for insects, berries and occasionally sap among the forest canopy.

Voice: song is a faint, high-pitched, accelerating *tsee-tsee-tsee-tsee, why do you shilly-shally?*; call is a very high-pitched *tsee tsee tsee.*

Similar Species: *Ruby-crowned Kinglet* (p. 248): bold, broken, white eye ring; lacks the black border to the crown. *Chickadees* (pp. 236–37): lack the bright, colourful crown.

Best Sites: Bon Echo PP; Algonquin PP; Killarney PP; Halfway Lake PP; Wakami Lake PP; Lake Superior PP; Point Pelee NP; Long Point PP; Presqu'ile PP.

RUBY-CROWNED KINGLET

Regulus calendula

The loud, rolling song of the Ruby-crowned Kinglet is a familiar tune that echoes through Ontario's boreal forest in May and June. At that time of year, the forest emerges from its long winter sleep, and the sound of cold wind blowing through conifer boughs is replaced by the joyful sound of singing birds. • The male kinglet erects his brilliant red crown and sings to impress prospective mates during courtship. Throughout most of the year, however, his crown remains hidden among dull feathers on the bird's head and is impossible to see even through binoculars. • While in migration, Ruby-crowned Kinglets are regularly seen flitting about treetops, intermingling with a colourful assortment of warblers and vireos. This bird might be mistaken for an empidonax flycatcher, but the kinglet's frequent hovering techniques and energetic wing-flicking behaviour sets it apart from look-alikes.

ID: bold, broken eye ring; 2 bold, white wing bars; olive green upperparts; dark wings and tail; whitish to yellowish underparts; short tail; flicks its wings. *Male:* small, red crown (usually hidden). *Female:* lacks the red crown.
Size: *L* 10 cm.
Status: common to abundant migrant from mid-April to late May and from September to late October; uncommon to very common breeder from April to September; rare winter visitor.
Habitat: mixed woodlands and pure coniferous forests, especially those dominated by spruce; often found around forest openings and edges.
Nesting: usually in a spruce or conifer; female builds a hanging nest of moss, lichens, twigs and leaves and lines it with feathers, fur and plant down; female

incubates 7 or 8 brown-spotted, whitish to pale buff eggs for 13–14 days.
Feeding: gleans and hovers for insects and spiders; will also eat seeds and berries.
Voice: *Male:* song is an accelerating and rising *tea-tea-tea-tew-tew-tew look-at-Me, look-at-Me, look-at-Me.*
Similar Species: *Golden-crowned Kinglet* (p. 247): dark cheek; black border to the crown; male has an orange crown bordered by yellow; female has a yellow crown. *Orange-crowned Warbler* (p. 268): no eye ring or wing bars. *Empidonax flycatchers* (pp. 207–11): complete eye ring or no eye ring at all; larger bill; longer tail; lack the red crown.
Best Sites: Algonquin PP; Grundy Lake PP; Halfway Lake PP; Wakami Lake PP; Pukaskwa NP; Sleeping Giant PP; Fushimi Lake PP; Point Pelee NP; Long Point PP; Presqu'ile PP.

BLUE-GRAY GNATCATCHER

Polioptila caerulea

The Blue-gray Gnatcatcher is constantly on the move. This fidgety woodland inhabitant cocks its tail like a wren and issues a quiet, banjo-like twang as it flits intensely from shrub to shrub, gleaning insects from branches and leaves. • Gnatcatcher pairs remain close once a bond is established, and both parents share in the responsibility of nest-building, incubation and raising of the young. After hatching, young gnatcatchers remain grounded in the nest for about 16 days, leaving them vulnerable to attack from predators. As soon as they are ready to fly, young gnatcatchers leave the nest for the cover of dense shrubby tangles along woodland edges. Like most songbirds, Blue-gray Gnatcatchers mature quickly. They will fly as far as South America within months of hatching, and they are able to breed in their second summer. • Although this bird undoubtedly eats gnats, those particular insects only represent a small part of the bird's insectivorous diet. • Over the years, the Blue-gray Gnatcatcher has been slowly increasing in number and expanding its range in Ontario.

breeding

ID: blue-grey upperparts; long tail; white eye ring; pale gray underparts; no wing bars; black uppertail with white outer tail feathers. *Breeding male:* darker upperparts; black border on the side of the forecrown.
Size: *L* 11 cm.
Status: rare to uncommon migrant and breeder from mid-April to early November; a few may remain into December.
Habitat: deciduous woodlands along streams, ponds, lakes and swamps; also in orchards, shrubby tangles along woodland edges and oak savannas.
Nesting: on a limb or in a crotch of a deciduous tree; lichen-covered cup nest is made of plant fibres and grass and is bound with spider silk; pair incubates 3 or 4 bluish-white eggs, with reddish-brown dots, for 11–15 days.
Feeding: gleans vegetation and flycatches for insects, spiders and other invertebrates.
Voice: *Male:* song is a faint, airy *puree;* call is a banjo-like, high-pitched twang: *chee.*
Similar Species: *Kinglets* (pp. 247–48): olive green overall; short tail; wing bars.
Best Sites: Point Pelee NP; Rondeau PP; Long Point PP; The Pinery PP; Halton Regional Forest; Lynde Shores Conservation Area; Presqu'ile PP; Prince Edward Point NWA.

EASTERN BLUEBIRD

Sialia sialis

Perhaps no other bird is as cherished and admired in southern Ontario's country-sides as the lovely Eastern Bluebird. Dressed with the colours of the cool sky on its back and the warm setting sun on its breast, the male Eastern Bluebird looks like a piece of pure sky come to life. • When House Sparrows and European Starlings were introduced to North America, Eastern Bluebirds were forced to compete with them for nesting sites, and their numbers began to decline. The development of 'bluebird trails' has allowed bluebird populations to gradually recover throughout their range. Nest boxes are mounted on fenceposts along highways and rural roads, providing bluebirds with convenient nesting places. Bluebird boxes are easy to make, and Ontario's long winters provide excellent opportunities for school groups, natural history clubs and birders to build bluebird houses. If proper directions are not followed, however, the houses intended for bluebirds will be used to propagate a new generation of bluebird competitors.

♂

ID: chestnut red chin, throat, breast and sides; white belly and undertail coverts; dark bill and legs. *Male:* deep blue upperparts. *Female:* thin white eye ring; grey-brown head and back tinged with blue; blue wings and tail; paler chestnut on the underparts.
Size: *L* 18 cm.
Status: uncommon migrant and breeder from March to October; rare winter visitor.
Habitat: cropland fencelines, meadows, fallow and abandoned fields, pastures, forest clearings and edges, golf courses, large lawns and cemeteries.

Nesting: in an abandoned woodpecker cavity, natural cavity or nest box; mostly the female incubates 4 or 5 pale blue eggs for 13–16 days.
Feeding: swoops from a perch and pursues flying insects; also forages on the ground for invertebrates.
Voice: song is a rich, warbling *turr, turr-lee, turr-lee;* call is a chittering *pew.*
Similar Species: *Mountain Bluebird* (p. 360): lacks the red underparts; exceptionally rare in Ontario.
Best Sites: Rondeau PP; Long Point PP; Bruce Peninsula; Carden Plain; Foley Mountain Conservation Area; Manitoulin Island; Rainy River area.

VEERY

Catharus fuscescens

Navigating its way across the forest floor, the Veery travels in short, springy hops, flipping leaves and scattering leaf litter in search of worms and grubs. Spending most of its time in the thick undergrowth of the forest floor, the Veery is always tuned to the sounds of wiggling prey or approaching danger. This shy, camouflaged bird is the most terrestrial of the North American thrushes, and it is often difficult to find. Listen for the Veery in spring and early summer when its fluty, cascading song is easily detected. • When startled by an intruder, the Veery either flushes or faces the threat, exposing its faintly streaked buffy breast in the hope of concealment. • The name 'Veery' is an onomatopoeic version of this bird's airy song. The species name *fuscescens* is from the Latin word for 'dusky,' in reference to the bird's colour. • These birds migrate to South America each winter, so there's a very good chance that the Veery pairs nesting in your local ravine might soon be travelling to the rainforests of the Amazon!

ID: reddish-brown or tawny upperparts; very thin, greyish eye ring; faintly streaked, buff throat and upper breast; light underparts; grey flanks and face patch.
Size: *L* 16–19 cm.
Status: fairly common to common migrant and breeder from May to September; a few may arrive as early as late April; some may remain into November.
Habitat: cool, moist deciduous and mixed forests and woodlands with a dense understorey of shrubs and ferns; often in disturbed woodlands.
Nesting: on the ground or in a shrub; female builds a bulky nest of leaves, weeds, bark strips and rootlets; female incubates 3 or 4 pale greenish-blue eggs for 10–15 days.

Feeding: gleans the ground and lower vegetation for invertebrates and berries.
Voice: *Male:* song is a fluty, descending *da-vee-ur, vee-ur, vee-ur, veer, veer, veer;* call is a high, whistled *feeyou.*
Similar Species: *Swainson's Thrush* (p. 253): bold eye ring; olive brown upperparts; darker spotting on the throat and upper breast. *Hermit Thrush* (p. 254): reddish rump and tail; brownish back; bold eye ring; buff-brown flanks; large, dark spots on the throat and breast. *Gray-cheeked Thrush* (p. 252) and *Bicknell's Thrush:* grey-brown upperparts; dark breast spots; brownish-grey flanks.
Best Sites: Rondeau PP; Presqu'ile PP; Bon Echo PP; Algonquin PP; Killarney PP; Halfway Lake PP; Whitefish Island; Sleeping Giant PP.

GRAY-CHEEKED THRUSH

Catharus minimus

Few Ontarians have ever heard of the Gray-cheeked Thrush, but keen birders find this inconspicuous bird a source of great interest. This champion migrant of thrushes winters as far south as Peru and regularly summers in the Arctic, farther north than any other North American thrush. Each spring and fall the Gray-cheeked Thrush migrates through Ontario to the Hudson Bay Lowland, where it nests among willows and stunted black spruce. The inaccessibility of this muskeg region has prevented most birders and ornithologists from documenting more than a few nesting records for this elusive bird. • The Gray-cheeked Thrush travels primarily at night, so it is most often seen or heard rustling through shrub-covered leaf litter on early mornings. Gray-cheeked Thrushes will settle in almost any habitat while migrating, but they do not stay for long, rarely uttering more than a simple warning note during their brief refueling stops.

ID: grey-brown upperparts; grey face; inconspicuous eye ring may not be visible; heavily spotted breast; light underparts; brownish-grey flanks.

Size: *L* 18–20 cm.

Status: rare to uncommon migrant from late April to early June and from late August to late October; rare breeder from May to August.

Habitat: *Breeding:* dwarf black spruce near treeline and on coastal islands; muskeg and coniferous forest. *In migration:* variety of forested areas, parks and backyards.

Nesting: in a tree or willow, quite low to the ground; nest is woven from twigs, moss, grass, weeds, bark strips and rootlets; female incubates 4 pale blue eggs, with pale brown spots, for 12–14 days.

Feeding: hops along the ground, picking up insects and other invertebrates; might also feed on berries during migration.

Voice: typically thrush-like in tone, ending with a clear, descending whistle: *wee-a wee-o, wee-a, titi wheeee;* call is a downslurred *wee-o.*

Similar Species: *Bicknell's Thrush:* different song; base of the lower mandible is noticeably yellow. *Swainson's Thrush* (p. 253): prominent eye ring; buff cheek and upper breast. *Hermit Thrush* (p. 254): reddish tail; olive brown upperparts; lacks the grey cheek. *Veery* (p. 251): reddish-brown upperparts; very light breast streaking.

Best Sites: Point Pelee NP; Long Point PP; Presqu'ile PP; Sleeping Giant PP.

SWAINSON'S THRUSH

Catharus ustulatus

The upward spiral of the Swainson's Thrush's lifts the soul of each listener with every rising note. This thrush is an integral part of the morning chorus, and its inspiring song is also heard at dusk—the Swainson's Thrush is routinely the last of the forest songsters to be silenced by nightfall. • On its breeding grounds, the Swainson's Thrush is most often seen perched high in a treetop cast in silhouette against the colourful sky. In migration, this bird skulks low on the ground under shrubs and tangles, occasionally finding itself in backyards and neighbourhood parks. Most thrushes feed on the ground, but the Swainson's Thrush is also adept at gleaning food from the airy heights of trees, sometimes briefly hover-gleaning like a warbler or vireo. A wary bird, it does not allow for many viewing opportunities, and it often gives a sharp warning call at some distance. • William Swainson was an English zoologist and illustrator. His name also graces the Swainson's Hawk.

ID: grey-brown upperparts; noticeable buff eye ring; buff wash on the cheek and upper breast; spots arranged in streaks on the throat and breast; white belly and undertail coverts; brownish-grey flanks.
Size: *L* 18 cm.
Status: very common migrant from late April to early June and from mid-August to late October; common breeder from May to September; a few may remain until December.
Habitat: edges and openings of coniferous and mixed boreal forests to treeline; prefers moist areas with spruce and fir.
Nesting: usually in a shrub or small tree; small cup nest is made of grass, moss, leaves, roots and lichens and is lined with fur and soft fibres; female incubates 3 or 4 pale blue eggs, with brown spots toward the larger end, for 12–14 days.

Feeding: gleans vegetation and forages on the ground for invertebrates; also eats berries.
Voice: song is a slow, rolling, rising spiral: *Oh, Aurelia will-ya, will-ya will-yeee*; call is a sharp *wick*.
Similar Species: *Gray-cheeked Thrush* (p. 252) and *Bicknell's Thrush*: grey cheek; less or no buff wash on the breast; lack the conspicuous eye ring. *Hermit Thrush* (p. 254): reddish tail and rump; greyish-brown upperparts; darker breast spotting on a whiter breast. *Veery* (p. 251): lacks the bold eye ring; upperparts are more reddish; faint breast streaking.
Best Sites: Bruce Peninsula NP; Algonquin PP; Killarney PP; Halfway Lake PP; Wakami Lake PP; Lake Superior PP; Pukaskwa NP; Sleeping Giant PP; Quetico PP; Fushimi Lake PP.

HERMIT THRUSH

Catharus guttatus

If the beauty of forest birds was gauged by sound rather than appearance, there is no doubt that the Hermit Thrush would be deemed one of the most beautiful birds in Ontario. Its song is a familiar theme in many forests, and it is as much a part of the forest ecosystem as the trees and wildflowers. • The Hermit Thrush is a ground nester and its cryptic cup nest is usually nestled in a natural hollow between raised mossy hummocks under the low branches of a spruce or fir. It may seem unfair that the female must incubate the eggs on her own while the male defends the territory, but less activity around the nest is probably of benefit to the vulnerable eggs. • The scientific name *guttatus* is Latin for 'spotted' or 'speckled,' in reference to this bird's breast.

ID: reddish-brown tail and rump; greyish-brown upperparts; black-spotted throat and breast; light underparts; grey flanks; thin, whitish eye ring.

Size: *L* 18 cm.

Status: very common migrant from April to mid-May and from mid-September through October; common breeder from May to September; a few may remain through winter.

Habitat: deciduous, mixed or coniferous woodlands; wet coniferous bogs bordered by trees.

Nesting: usually on the ground; occasionally in a small tree or shrub; female builds a bulky cup nest of grass, twigs, moss, ferns and bark strips; female incubates 4 pale blue to greenish-blue eggs, sometimes showing dark flecks, for 11–13 days.

Feeding: forages on the ground and gleans vegetation for insects and other invertebrates; also eats berries.

Voice: song is a series of beautiful flute-like notes, both rising and falling in pitch; calls include a faint *chuck* and a fluty *treee*.

Similar Species: *Swainson's Thrush* (p. 253): buff cheek and wash on the breast; greyish-brown back and tail. *Veery* (p. 251): lightly streaked upper breast; all reddish-brown upperparts and tail. *Gray-cheeked Thrush* (p. 252) and *Bicknell's Thrush:* grey cheek; lack the conspicuous eye ring; Bicknell's may have a chestnut tail. *Fox Sparrow* (p. 314): stockier build; conical bill; brown breast spots.

Best Sites: Bon Echo PP; Algonquin PP; Grundy Lake PP; Killarney PP; Halfway Lake PP; Lake Superior PP; Pukaskwa NP; Sleeping Giant PP; Marten River PP.

WOOD THRUSH

Hylocichla mustelina

The loud, warbled notes of the Wood Thrush once resounded through southern Ontario forests, but forest fragmentation and urban sprawl have eliminated much of this bird's nesting habitat. Broken forests and diminutive woodlots have allowed for the invasion of common, open-area predators and parasites, such as raccoons, skunks, crows, jays and cowbirds, which traditionally had little access to nests that were insulated deep within vast stands of hardwood forest. Many tracts of forest that have been urbanized or developed for agriculture now host families of American Robins rather than the once-prominent Wood Thrush. • Henry David Thoreau, naturalist and author, considered the Wood Thrush's song to be the most beautiful of avian sounds.

ID: plump body; large, black spots on the white breast, sides and flanks; bold white eye ring; rusty head and back; brown wings, rump and tail.

Size: *L* 20 cm.

Status: uncommon to fairly common migrant and breeder from mid-April to early November; a few may remain into December.

Habitat: moist, mature and preferably undisturbed deciduous woodlands and mixed forests.

Nesting: low in a fork of a deciduous tree; female builds a bulky cup nest of grass, twigs, moss, weeds, bark strips and mud; nest is lined with softer materials; female incubates 3 or 4 pale greenish-blue eggs for 13–14 days.

Feeding: forages on the ground and gleans vegetation for insects and other invertebrates; also eats berries.

Voice: *Male:* 3–5-note bell-like phrases, with each note at a different pitch and followed by a trill: *Will you live with me? Way up high in a tree, I'll come right down and…seeee!;* calls include a *pit pit* and *bweebeebeep.*

Similar Species: *Other thrushes:* smaller spots on the underparts; most have a coloured wash on the sides and flanks; all lack the bold white eye ring and the rusty cap and back.

Best Sites: Rondeau PP; Halton Hills Regional Forest; Rouge River PP; Frontenac PP; Awenda PP; Algonquin PP; Hiawatha Highlands Conservation Area.

AMERICAN ROBIN

Turdus migratorius

American Robins are widespread and abundant in many of Ontario's natural habitats, but they are familiar to most of us because they commonly inhabit residential lawns, gardens and parks. These birds are widely recognized as harbingers of spring, and when March rolls around Ontarians look forward to their arrival in our province. Robins regularly overwinter in southern parts of our province, but sightings are not common because the birds tend to remain hidden. • Hunting robins may appear to be listening for prey, but they are actually looking for movements in the soil—they tilt their heads because their eyes are placed on the sides of their head. • Robins are occasionally seen hunting with a bill stuffed full of earthworms and grubs—a sign that hungry young robins are somewhere close at hand. Young robins are easily distinguished from their parents by their dishevelled appearance and heavily spotted underparts. • The American Robin was named by English colonists after the robin of their native land. Both birds look and behave similarly, even though they are only distantly related.

ID: grey-brown back; dark head; white throat streaked with black; white undertail coverts; incomplete, white eye ring; yellow, black-tipped bill. *Male:* deep brick red breast; black head. *Female:* dark grey head; light red-orange breast. *Juvenile:* heavily spotted breast.
Size: *L* 25 cm.
Status: abundant migrant and breeder from late March to early November; rare to uncommon resident from November to March.
Habitat: residential lawns and gardens, pastures, urban parks, broken forests, bogs and river shorelines.
Nesting: in a coniferous or deciduous tree or shrub; sturdy cup nest is built of

grass, moss and loose bark and cemented with mud; female incubates 4 light blue eggs for 11–16 days; may raise up to 3 broods each year in some areas.
Feeding: forages on the ground and among vegetation for larval and adult insects, earthworms, other invertebrates and berries.
Voice: song is an evenly spaced warble: *cheerily cheer-up cheerio;* call is a rapid *tut-tut-tut.*
Similar Species: *Varied Thrush* (p. 257): black breast band; 2 orange wing bars.
Best Sites: almost any suburban lawn or garden.

VARIED THRUSH

Ixoreus naevius

Varied Thrushes are rare in Ontario, so if you find one don't be surprised if fellow birders question your identification skills. Varied Thrushes are typically western birds, but invariably a few wander off course each fall and make their way into our province. Each year there are about 10 sightings reported in Ontario, usually at backyard feeders where dense coniferous trees provide shelter for this wayward wanderer. Berries, fruits, seeds, nuts, acorns and suet are some of the offerings that might encourage a lengthy visit from a Varied Thrush—provided Blue Jays and other backyard regulars don't dominate the wealth of goodies.

ID: dark upperparts; orange eyebrow; orange throat and belly; 2 orange wing bars. *Male:* black breast band; black-blue upperparts. *Female:* brown upperparts; faint breast band.
Size: *L* 24 cm.
Status: rare visitor from October to April.
Habitat: areas with dense coniferous cover near an active feeding station.
Nesting: does not nest in Ontario.
Feeding: forages on the ground and among vegetation for insects, seeds and berries; takes a variety of foods, especially suet at feeders.
Voice: rarely vocal in Ontario; male's song is a series of single notes (actually subtle trills) delivered at different pitches, with a lengthy pause between each note; call is a quiet *tuck.*
Similar Species: *American Robin* (p. 256): lacks the black breast band and the orange eyebrow, throat and wing bars.
Best Sites: potentially any birdfeeder with nearby dense coniferous cover.

VAGRANT

GRAY CATBIRD

Dumetella carolinensis

Gray Catbirds are most common in summer, when nesting pairs build their loose cup nest deep within impenetrable tangles of shrubs, brambles and thorny thickets. Gray Catbirds vigorously defend their nesting territories, and their defence tactics are so effective that the nesting success of neighbouring warblers and sparrows may increase as a result of the catbird's constant vigilance. • Female catbirds are very loyal to their nests, so they are less susceptible to parasitism by cowbirds. Even if a cowbird sneaks past the watchful female to deposit an egg in the nest, the foreign egg is often recognized and ejected. • True to its name, the Gray Catbird's call sounds much like the scratchy mewing of a house cat. Its characteristic call and boisterous, hectic, mimicked phrases are often the only evidence of this bird's presence. • In warmer parts of the province, Gray Catbirds may successfully raise two broods in a single nesting season, keeping the parents busy from May to early September.

ID: dark grey overall; black cap; long tail may be dark grey to black; chestnut undertail coverts; black eyes, bill and legs.
Size: *L* 22–23 cm.
Status: uncommon to common migrant and breeder from mid-May to October; a few may be present in winter.
Habitat: dense thickets, brambles, shrubby or brushy areas and hedgerows, often near water.
Nesting: in a dense shrub or thicket; bulky cup nest is loosely built with twigs, leaves and grass and is lined with fine material; female incubates 4 greenish-blue eggs for 12–15 days.
Feeding: forages on the ground and in vegetation for ants, beetles, grasshoppers, caterpillars, moths and spiders; also eats berries and visits feeders.
Voice: calls include a cat-like *meoow* and a harsh *check-check*; song is a variety of warbles, squeaks and mimicked phrases repeated only once and often interspersed with a *mew* call.
Similar Species: *Gray Jay* (p. 224), *Northern Mockingbird* (p. 259) and *Townsend's Solitaire* (p. 359): lack the black cap and the chestnut undertail coverts. *Brown Thrasher* (p. 260): rusty brown upperparts; streaked underparts; wings bars; repeats each song phrase twice.
Best Sites: deciduous thickets especially near water; Point Pelee NP; Rondeau PP; Long Point PP; Luther Marsh; Lynde Shores Conservation Area; Presqu'ile PP; Charleston Lake PP; Bon Echo PP.

NORTHERN MOCKINGBIRD

Mimus polyglottos

Mockingbirds are slowly establishing themselves as year-round residents in southern Ontario parks and gardens. In winter, they rely heavily on wild and ornamental fruits, especially the bounty of nutritious rose hips. Generous offerings of suet, raisins and fruit can go a long way toward luring mockingbirds and other birds into your yard. • The Northern Mockingbird thrills people with its incomparable vocal repertoire and its springtime courtship dances. Northern Mockingbirds have been known to sing more than 400 different song types, and they can imitate other birds, barking dogs and even musical instruments. They imitate sounds so closely that a computerized auditory analysis is often unable to detect differences between the original source and the mockingbird. • In their energetic courtship dance the male and female square off in what appears to be a swordless fencing duel. • The scientific name *polyglottos* is Greek for 'many tongues.'

ID: grey upperparts; dark wings; 2 thin, white wing bars; long, dark tail with white outer tail feathers; light grey underparts. *In flight:* large white patch at the base of the black primaries. *Juvenile:* paler overall; spotted breast.

Size: *L* 25 cm.

Status: rare to locally uncommon breeder (very rare isolated pairs in the north to Moosonee); a few are found year-round.

Habitat: hedges, suburban gardens and orchard margins with an abundance of available fruit; hedgerows of *multiflora* roses are especially important in winter.

Nesting: often in a small shrub or small tree; cup nest is built with twigs, grass, fur and leaves; female incubates 3 or 4 brown-blotched,

bluish-grey to greenish eggs for 12–13 days.

Feeding: gleans vegetation and forages on the ground for beetles, ants, wasps and grasshoppers; also eats berries and wild fruit; visits feeders for suet and raisins.

Voice: song is a medley of mimicked phrases, with the phrases often repeated 3 times or more; calls include a harsh *chair* and *chewk*.

Similar Species: *Northern Shrike* (p. 217) and *Loggerhead Shrike* (p. 216): thicker, hooked bill; black mask; juveniles are stockier and less vocal. *Townsend's Solitaire* (p. 359): prominent eye ring; peach rather than white in the wings. *Gray Catbird* (p. 258): grey overall; black cap; chestnut undertail covers; lacks the white outer tail feathers.

Best Sites: orchards and gardens in the Niagara area; Prince Edward Point; Kingston area; Ottawa area.

BROWN THRASHER

Toxostoma rufum

Amid the various chirps and warbles rising from woodland and lakefront edges in spring and early summer, the song of the male Brown Thrasher stands alone—its lengthy, complex chorus of twice-repeated phrases is unique. This thrasher has the most extensive vocal repertoire of any North American bird, and it is estimated that it is capable of up to 3000 distinctive combinations of various phrases. • Despite its size, the Brown Thrasher goes unnoticed in its shrubby domain. A typical sighting of this thrasher consists of nothing more than a flash of rufous as it zips from one tangle to another. • Because it nests on or close to the ground, its unguarded eggs and nestlings are particularly vulnerable to predation by snakes, weasels, skunks and other animals. Brown Thrashers are aggressive, vigilant nest-defenders, however, and desperate pairs have been known to attack nest robbers to the point of drawing blood. • Unlike other notable singers, such as the Northern Mockingbird and the similarly shaped, shrub-dwelling Gray Catbird, the Brown Thrasher lives well away from urban areas.

ID: reddish-brown upperparts; light-coloured underparts with heavy, brown spotting and streaking; long, downcurved bill; orange-yellow eyes; long, rufous tail; 2 white wing bars.

Size: *L* 29 cm.

Status: fairly common to common migrant and breeder from late April to October; a few may be present in winter.

Habitat: dense shrubs and thickets, overgrown pastures (especially those with hawthorns), woodland edges and brushy areas, rarely close to human habitation.

Nesting: usually in a low shrub; often on the ground; cup nest made of grass, twigs and leaves is lined with fine vegetation; pair incubates 4 reddish-brown dotted, bluish-white to pale blue eggs for 11–14 days.

Feeding: gleans the ground and vegetation for larval and adult invertebrates; occasionally tosses leaves aside; also eats seeds and berries.

Voice: sings a large variety of phrases, with each phrase usually repeated twice: *dig-it dig-it, hoe-it hoe-it, pull-it-up, pull-it-up*; calls include a loud crackling note, a harsh *shuck*, a soft *churr* or a whistled, 3-note *pit-cher-ee.*

Similar Species: *Hermit Thrush* (p. 254): shorter tail; grey-brown back and crown; dark brown eyes; much shorter bill; lacks the wing bars.

Best Sites: any brushy protected area or abandoned farmland throughout southern Ontario.

EUROPEAN STARLING

Sturnus vulgaris

The European Starling was brought to North America in 1890 and 1891, when about 60 of the birds were released into New York's Central Park as part of the local Shakespeare's society's plan to introduce all the birds mentioned in their favourite author's writings. The starling established itself in the New York landscape, and then spread quickly across the continent, often at the expense of many native, cavity nesting-birds, such as the Tree Swallow, Eastern Bluebird and Red-headed Woodpecker. Despite many concerted efforts to control or even eradicate this species, the European Starling will no doubt continue to assert its claim in the New World. • Courting starlings are infamous for their ability to reproduce the sounds of other birds, such as Killdeers, Red-tailed Hawks and Soras.

breeding

ID: short, squared tail; dark eyes. *Breeding:* blackish, iridescent plumage; yellow bill. *Fall adult:* blackish wings; feather tips are heavily spotted with white and buff. *Juvenile:* grey-brown plumage; brown bill. *In flight:* pointed, triangular wings.
Size: *L* 22 cm.
Status: abundant year-round resident, migrant, summer breeder and winter visitor.
Habitat: agricultural areas, townsites, woodland and forest edges, landfills and roadsides.
Nesting: in an abandoned wood-pecker cavity, natural cavity, nest box or other artificial cavity; nest is made of grass, twigs and straw; mostly female incubates 4–6 bluish to greenish-white eggs for 12–14 days.

Feeding: very diverse diet includes many invertebrates, berries, seeds and garbage; forages mostly on the ground.
Voice: variety of whistles, squeaks and gurgles; imitates other birds throughout the year.
Similar Species: *Rusty Blackbird* (p. 335): longer tail; black bill; lacks the spotting; yellow eyes; rusty tinge on the upperparts in fall. *Brewer's Blackbird* (p. 336): longer tail; black bill; lacks the spotting; male has yellow eyes; female is brown overall. *Brown-headed Cowbird* (p. 338): lacks the spotting; adult male has a longer tail, a shorter, dark bill and a brown head; juvenile has streaked underparts, a stout bill and a longer tail.
Best Sites: almost every city, town and agricultural area.

AMERICAN PIPIT

Anthus rubescens

Each fall, agricultural fields and open shorelines serve as refueling stations for large concentrations of migratory American Pipits. Flocks of pipits may go unnoticed to untrained eyes, because their dull brown and buff plumage blends into the landscape. To keen observers, however, their plain attire, white outer tail feathers and continuous habit of wagging their tails makes them readily identifiable. • Like the Sprague's Pipit of the Canadian Prairies, the American Pipit performs marvellous courtship flights. Although adults may already be paired upon arriving on their nesting grounds—a strategy that is thought to save valuable nesting time—the conspicuous courtship display helps each pair establish and defend the boundaries of their exclusive nesting territory. American Pipits nest in the remote, treeless tundra of the Hudson Bay coast, so few Ontarians will have a chance to view this bird on its breeding grounds. • This bird was formerly known as the Water Pipit (*Anthus spinoletta*).

breeding

ID: faintly streaked, grey-brown upperparts; lightly streaked 'necklace' on the upper breast; streaked sides and flanks; dark legs; dark tail with white outer tail feathers; buff-coloured underparts; slim bill and body.
Size: *L* 15–18 cm.
Status: rare migrant from April to early June; common migrant from September to early November; fairly common breeder from May to August; a few may remain into December.
Habitat: *Breeding:* coastal tundra. *In migration:* agricultural fields, pastures and shores of wetlands, lakes and rivers.
Nesting: in a shallow depression; small cup nest is made of coarse grass and sedges and is sometimes lined with fur; frequently has an overhanging canopy; female incubates 4–6 whitish to pale buff eggs, spotted with grey and brown, for 13–15 days.
Feeding: gleans the ground and vegetation for terrestrial and freshwater invertebrates and seeds.
Voice: familiar flight call is *pip-it pip-it*. *Male:* harsh, sharp *tsip-tsip* or *chiwee*.
Similar Species: *Horned Lark* (p. 229): black 'horns'; facial markings. *Sprague's Pipit:* lighter back with strong streaking; paler buff breast.
Best Sites: Polar Bear PP; Sarnia airport; Point Pelee NP; Long Point PP; Tommy Thompson Park; Presqu'ile PP.

BOHEMIAN WAXWING

Bombycilla garrulus

Descending upon mountain ash and other ornamental plantings, great flocks of Bohemian Waxwings thrill us with their unpredictable appearances. The faint, quavering whistles of these birds attract the ears of attentive naturalists who take pleasure in watching the birds gorge themselves in berry-filled trees. In most years, however, Bohemians are only seen in small groups, usually intermingled with over-wintering flocks of similar-looking Cedar Waxwings (the Bohemians' chestnut undertail coverts readily distinguish them from their cedar counterparts). • In late spring and early summer, waxwings retreat northward to remote and largely inaccessible areas of the Hudson Bay Lowland. • Waxwings get their name from the colourful spots on their secondary feathers. These 'waxy' spots are actually colourful enlargements of the feather shafts, whose pigments are derived from the birds' berry-filled diet.

ID: grey and cinnamon crest; black mask and throat; soft brownish-grey body; yellow terminal tail band; chestnut undertail coverts; small white, red and yellow markings on the wings. *Juvenile:* brown-grey upperparts; streaked underparts; light throat; no mask; white wing patches.
Size: *L* 20 cm.
Status: rare breeder from May to September; irregularly rare to fairly common visitor from mid-September to mid-May.
Habitat: *Breeding:* open coniferous forests, muskeg and birch groves, frequently near water. *Winter:* natural and residential areas with wild berries and fruit.

Nesting: in a conifer; cup nest of twigs, grass, moss and lichens is sometimes lined with fur; female incubates 4–6 pale bluish-grey eggs, heavily spotted with black, for 12–16 days.
Feeding: gleans vegetation for insects and wild fruit or catches flying insects on the wing; depends on berries and fruit in winter.
Voice: faint, high-pitched, quavering whistle.
Similar Species: *Cedar Waxwing* (p. 264): smaller; browner overall; slight yellow wash on the belly; white undertail coverts; lacks the yellow in the wings.
Best Sites: residential areas; Claremont Conservation Area; Ottawa Arboretum; Parry Sound's Belvedere Hill; Thunder Bay's Marina Park.

CEDAR WAXWING

Bombycilla cedrorum

Waxwings have a remarkable ability to digest a wide variety of berries, some of which are inedible or even poisonous to humans. Flocks of handsome Cedar Waxwings gorge on berries during late summer and fall. If a bird's crop is full, it will continue to pluck fruit and pass it along down the line like a bucket brigade, until it is gulped down by a still-hungry bird. If the fruits have fermented, the waxwings will show definite signs of tipsiness—they might fly erratically or flop around on the ground. Native berry-producing trees and shrubs planted in your backyard can attract Cedar Waxwings, often encouraging them to nest in your area. • Unlike Bohemian Waxwings, which nest in remote northern areas of our province, Cedar Waxwings are familiar summer residents. They are late nesters, ensuring that the berry crops will be ripe when nestlings are ready to be fed.• Practised observers learn to recognize this bird by its high-pitched, trilling calls.

ID: cinnamon crest; brown upperparts; black mask; yellow wash on the belly; grey rump; yellow terminal tail band; white undertail coverts; small red 'drops' on the wings. *Juvenile:* no mask; streaked underparts; grey-brown body.
Size: *L* 18 cm.
Status: very common migrant and breeder from May to October; uncommon visitor from November through April.
Habitat: wooded residential parks and gardens, overgrown fields, forest edges, and second-growth, riparian and open woodlands.
Nesting: in a tree or shrub; cup nest made of twigs, grass, moss and lichens is often lined with fine grass; female incubates 3–5 pale grey to bluish-grey eggs, with fine dark spotting, for 12–16 days.
Feeding: catches flying insects on the wing or gleans vegetation; also eats large amounts of berries and wild fruit, especially over fall and winter.
Voice: faint, high-pitched, trilled whistle: *tseee-tseee-tseee.*
Similar Species: *Bohemian Waxwing* (p. 263): larger; chestnut undertail coverts; small white, red and yellow markings on the wings; juvenile has chestnut undertail coverts and white wing patches.
Best Sites: almost any open wooded area.

BLUE-WINGED WARBLER

Vermivora pinus

During the mid-1800s, the Blue-winged Warbler began expanding its range eastward and northward from its home in the central midwestern U.S., finding new breeding territories among the overgrown fields and pastures of abandoned human settlements. Eventually, it came into contact with the Golden-winged Warbler, a bird with completely different looks but practically identical habitat requirements and breeding biology. Where both species share the same habitat, a distinctive, fertile hybrid, known as the Brewster's Warbler, may be produced. This hybrid tends to be more greyish overall, like the Golden-winged Warbler, but it retails its thin, black eye line and the touch of yellow on the breast from its Blue-winged parent. In rare cases when two of these hybrids are able to reproduce successfully, a second-generation hybrid, known as the Lawrence's Warbler, is produced. It is more yellowish overall, like the Blue-winged Warbler, but it has the black mask, chin and throat of the Golden-winged Warbler.

breeding

ID: bright yellow head and underparts, except for the white to yellowish undertail coverts; olive yellow upperparts; bluish-grey wings and tail; black eye line; thin, dark bill; 2 white wing bars; bold white tail spots on the underside of the tail.
Size: *L* 12 cm.
Status: rare and local migrant and breeder from May to September.
Habitat: second-growth woodlands, willow swamps, shrubby, overgrown fields, pastures, woodland edges and woodland openings.
Nesting: on or near the ground, concealed by vegetation; narrow, inverted, cone-shaped nest is made of grass, leaves and bark strips and is lined with soft materials; female incubates 5 white eggs, with fine brown spots toward the larger end, for about 11 days.
Feeding: gleans insects and spiders from the lower branches of trees and shrubs.
Voice: buzzy 2-note song: *beee-bzzz*.
Similar Species: *Prothonotary Warbler* (p. 288): lacks the black eye line and the white wing bars. *Pine Warbler* (p. 280): darker; white belly; faint streaking on the sides and breast. *Yellow Warbler* (p. 271): yellow wings; lacks the black eye line. *Prairie Warbler* (p. 281): black streaking on the sides and flanks; darker wings.
Best Sites: Rondeau PP; Halton Regional Forest; Westport area.

GOLDEN-WINGED WARBLER

Vermivora chrysoptera

Unlike people, who are unable to build fences around their property, male Golden-winged Warblers use song to defend their nesting territories. If song fails to repel rival males, then body language and aggression calls warn intruders to stay away. When a male's claim is seriously challenged, a warning call, a raised crown and a spread tail may be employed. The last resort is to physically remove the competitor in a high-speed chase or a winged duel. • The Golden-winged Warbler often swings upside down from branches like a chickadee, gleaning spiders and caterpillars from the undersides of leaves. Its buzzy tune closely resembles that of the Blue-winged Warbler, a closely related bird with which it often interbreeds.

breeding

ID: yellow forecrown and wing patch; dark chin, throat and mask over eye bordered by white; bluish-grey upperparts and flanks; white undersides; white tail spots on the underside of the tail. *Female and Immature:* duller overall, with a grey throat and mask.
Size: *L* 12 cm.
Status: rare migrant and breeder from May to early October.
Habitat: moist shrubby fields, woodland edges and early-succession forest clearings.
Nesting: on the ground; concealed by vegetation; open cup nest of grass, leaves and grapevine bark is lined with softer materials; female incubates 5 pinkish to pale cream eggs, marked with brown

and lilac, for about 11 days.
Feeding: gleans insects and spiders from tree and shrub canopies.
Voice: buzzy song begins with a higher note: *zee-bz-bz-bz*; call is a sweet *chip*.
Similar Species: *Yellow-rumped Warbler* (p. 276): white throat; dark breast patches; yellow sides. *Yellow-throated Warbler* (p. 279): lacks the yellow crown; 2 white wing bars; yellow throat. *Black-throated Green Warbler* (p. 277): lacks the dark mask; 2 white wing bars; black streaking on the sides. *Brewster's Warbler* and *Lawrence's Warbler* (hybrids): see Blue-winged Warbler (p. 265).
Best Sites: Halton Regional Forest; Greenock Swamp; Carden Plain.

TENNESSEE WARBLER

Vermivora peregrina

Tennessee Warblers lack the bold, bright features found in other warblers. Even so, they are difficult birds to miss because they have a loud, familiar song, and they are relatively common in our province. • Migrating Tennessee Warblers often sing their tunes and forage for insects high in the forest canopy. However, inclement weather and the need for food after a long flight often force these birds to lower levels in the forest. • Females build their nests on the ground and they usually remain close to the forest floor when feeding. • Spruce budworm outbreaks are welcomed by Tennessee Warblers, which thrive on these insects. During times of plenty, these birds may produce more than seven young in a single brood. • Alexander Wilson discovered this bird along the Cumberland River in Tennessee and he named it after that state. It is only a migrant in Tennessee, however, and it breeds almost exclusively in Canada. • Tennessee Warblers are easily confused with Warbling Vireos and Philadelphia Vireos.

breeding

ID: *Breeding male:* blue-grey cap; olive green back, wings and tail edgings; white eyebrow; black eye line; clean white underparts; thin bill. *Breeding female:* yellow wash on the breast and eyebrow; olive grey cap. *Non-breeding:* olive yellow upperparts; yellow eyebrow; yellow underparts except for white undertail coverts; male may have a white belly.
Size: *L* 12 cm.
Status: common to abundant migrant in September and from early May to July; uncommon to common breeder from May to September.
Habitat: *Breeding:* coniferous or mixed mature forests and occasionally spruce bogs. *In migration:* any woodland or tall shrubby area.
Nesting: on the ground or on a raised hummock; female builds a small cup nest of grass, moss and roots and lines it with fur; female incubates 5 or 6 white eggs, marked with brown or purple, for 11–12 days.
Feeding: gleans foliage and buds for small insects, caterpillars and other invertebrates; also eats berries; occasionally visits suet feeders.
Voice: male's song is an accelerating, loud, sharp *ticka-ticka-ticka swit-swit-swit-swit chew-chew-chew-chew-chew*; call is a sweet *chip*.
Similar Species: *Warbling Vireo* (p. 221): stouter overall; thicker bill; much less green on the upperparts. *Philadelphia Vireo* (p. 222): stouter overall; thicker bill; yellow breast and sides. *Orange-crowned Warbler* (p. 268): lacks the white eyebrow and the blue-grey head.
Best Sites: Mattawa River PP; Halfway Lake PP; Pukaskwa PP; Sleeping Giant PP, Missinaibi River PP; Woodland Caribou PP; Point Pelee NP; Rondeau PP.

ORANGE-CROWNED WARBLER

Vermivora celata

Don't be disappointed if you can't see the Orange-crowned Warbler's tell-tale orange crown, because its most distinguishing characteristic is its lack of field marks: wing bars, eye rings and colour patches are all conspicuously absent. • Whether in migration or on its breeding grounds, the Orange-crowned Warbler is generally rare to uncommon in Ontario. When encountered, it usually appears as a blurred olive yellow bundle flitting nervously among the leaves and branches of low shrubs. To make matters even worse, its drab appearance makes it frustratingly similar to females of other warbler species. • Wood-warblers are strictly confined to the New World. All 109 wood-warbler species (56 occurring north of Mexico) are thought to have originated in South America, which boasts the greatest diversity of wood-warblers. • *Vermivora* is Latin for 'worm eating'; *celata* is derived from the Latin word for 'hidden,' a reference to this bird's inconspicuous crown.

ID: olive yellow to olive grey body; faintly streaked underparts; bright yellow undertail coverts; thin, faint, dark eye line; bright yellow eyebrow and broken eye ring; thin bill; faint orange crown patch (rarely seen).
Size: *L* 13 cm.
Status: rare migrant in mid-May; rare to uncommon migrant from late August to early November; uncommon breeder from May to September.
Habitat: *Breeding:* mixed forests with an understorey of maple, willow, alder and hazelnut. *In migration:* any woodland or tall shrubby area.
Nesting: on the ground or in a small shrub; well-hidden, small cup nest is made of coarse grass, twigs, bark, moss and leaves and is lined with hair and fine grass; female incubates 4 or 5 creamy white eggs, with reddish-brown speckles, for 11–14 days.
Feeding: gleans foliage for invertebrates, berries, nectar and sap; often hover-gleans.
Voice: *Male:* faint trill that breaks downward halfway through.
Similar Species: *Tennessee Warbler* (p. 267): blue-grey head; dark eye line; bold white eyebrow; white underparts, including the undertail coverts. *Ruby-crowned Kinglet* (p. 248): broken, white eye ring; white wing bars. *Wilson's Warbler* (p. 298): complete, bright yellow eye ring; brighter yellow underparts; light-coloured legs; lacks the breast streaks. *Yellow Warbler* (p. 271): brighter head and underparts; reddish breast streaks (faint or absent on female). *Common Yellowthroat* (p. 296): female has a darker face and upperparts; lacks the breast streaks.
Best Sites: Moosonee area; Polar Bear PP; Point Pelee NP; Rondeau PP; Long Point PP; Presqu'ile PP; Sleeping Giant PP.

NASHVILLE WARBLER

Vermivora ruficapilla

N ashville Warblers have a most unusual distribution, with two widely separated summer populations: one eastern and the other western. These populations are believed to have been created thousands of years ago when a single core population was split apart during continental glaciation. • This warbler was first described near Nashville, Tennessee, but it does not breed in that state. This misnomer is not an isolated incident: the Tennessee, Cape May and Connecticut warblers all bear names that misrepresent their breeding distributions. • Nashville Warblers are common migrants and breeders in Ontario. They are best found in overgrown farmland and second-growth forest as they forage low in trees and thickets, often at the edge of a forest. • Nashville Warblers have benefited from the clearing of old-growth forests for timber and agriculture.

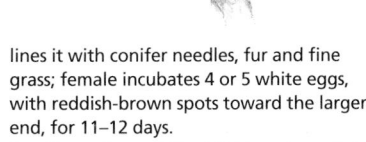

♂

ID: bold white eye ring; yellow-green upperparts; yellow underparts; white between the legs. *Male:* blue-grey head; may show a small, chestnut red crown. *Female* and *Immature:* duller overall; light eye ring; olive grey head; blue-grey nape.

Size: *L* 12 cm.

Status: very common migrant from late April to early June and from September to early October; common breeder from May to August; a few may arrive in early April; some may remain as late as January.

Habitat: second-growth mixed woodlands are preferred; also in wet coniferous forests, riparian woodlands, cedar-spruce swamps and moist, shrubby, abandoned fields.

Nesting: on the ground under a fern, sapling or shrubby cover; female builds a cup nest of grass, bark strips, ferns and moss and lines it with conifer needles, fur and fine grass; female incubates 4 or 5 white eggs, with reddish-brown spots toward the larger end, for 11–12 days.

Feeding: gleans foliage for insects, such as caterpillars, flies and aphids.

Voice: male's song begins with a thin, high-pitched *see-it see-it see-it see-it*, followed by a trilling *ti-ti-ti-ti-ti*; call is a metallic *chink*.

Similar Species: *Common Yellowthroat* (p. 296) and *Wilson's Warbler* (p. 298): females lack the greyish head and the bold white eye ring; all-yellow underparts. *Connecticut Warbler* (p. 294) and *Mourning Warbler* (p. 295): females have a greyish to brownish hood; yellow between the legs.

Best Sites: Halton Regional Forest; Bon Echo PP; Algonquin PP; Pukaskwa NP; woodlands bordering Hwy 11; Point Pelee NP; Rondeau PP; Long Point PP.

269

NORTHERN PARULA

Parula americana

Young Northern Parulas spend the first few weeks of their lives enclosed in a fragile, sock-like nest suspended from a tree branch. Once they have grown too large for the nest and their wing feathers are strong enough to allow for a short, awkward flight, the young leave their warm abode, dispersing themselves among the surrounding trees and shrubs. As warm summer nights slip away to be replaced by cooler fall temperatures, newly fledged Northern Parulas migrate to the warmer climes of Central America. • Northern Parulas are typically found in older forests where the lichens that they use during nesting have had a chance to mature. Males spend most of their time singing and foraging among the tops of tall coniferous spires, where they are often fearless and easily approached.

breeding

ID: blue-grey upperparts; olive patch on the back; 2 bold white wing bars; bold white eye ring broken by a black eye line; yellow chin, throat and breast; white belly and flanks. *Male:* 1 black and 1 orange breast band.
Size: *L* 11 cm.
Status: rare to very locally uncommon migrant and breeder from late April to mid-October; a few may remain into November.
Habitat: moist coniferous forests, humid riparian woodlands and swampy deciduous woodlands, especially where lichens hang from branches.
Nesting: usually in a conifer; small hanging nest is woven by the female into hanging strands of tree lichens; may add lichens to a dense cluster of conifer boughs; pair incubates 4 or 5 brown-marked,

whitish eggs for 12–14 days.
Feeding: forages for insects and other invertebrates by hovering, gleaning or hawking; feeds from the tips of branches and occasionally on the ground.
Voice: song is a rising, buzzy trill ending with an abrupt, lower *zip*.
Similar Species: *Cerulean Warbler* (p. 285): lacks the white eye ring; streaking on the breast and sides. *Blue-winged Warbler* (p. 265): yellow underparts. *Yellow-rumped Warbler* (p. 276): yellow rump and crown. *Yellow-throated Warbler* (p. 279) and *Kirtland's Warbler* (p. 360): heavy black streaking along the sides.
Best Sites: Black Creek PP; Algonquin PP; Wakami Lake PP; Lake Superior PP; Sleeping Giant PP.

270

YELLOW WARBLER

Dendroica petechia

Yellow Warblers usually arrive here in early May in search of caterpillars, aphids, beetles and other invertebrates. Flitting from branch to branch among open woodland edges and riparian shrubs, these inquisitive birds seem to be in perpetual motion. • Yellow Warblers are among the most frequent victims of cowbird parasitism. Unlike many birds, however, they can recognize the foreign eggs and many will either abandon their nests or build another nest overtop the old eggs. Some persistent Yellow Warblers build over and over, creating bizarre, high-rise, multi-layered nests. • During fall migration, silent, plain-looking Yellow Warblers and other similar-looking warblers can cause a great deal of confusion for birders who have been lulled into a false sense of familiarity with these birds.
• Yellow Warblers are often called 'wild canaries' because of their bright yellow plumage, but an observant eye and a discriminating ear will reveal the unique character of this bird.

breeding

ID: bright yellow body; black bill and eyes; bright yellow highlights in the dark yellow-olive tail and wings. *Breeding male:* red breast streaks. *Breeding female:* faint red breast streaks.

Size: *L* 13 cm.

Status: common migrant and breeder from May to August; a few may remain into November.

Habitat: moist, open woodlands with dense, low scrub, shrubby meadows, willow tangles and riparian woodlands, usually near water.

Nesting: in a fork in a deciduous tree or small shrub; female builds a compact cup nest of grass, weeds and shredded bark and lines it with plant down and fur; female incubates 4 or 5 speckled or spotted, greenish-white eggs for 11–12 days.

Feeding: gleans foliage and vegetation for invertebrates, especially caterpillars, inchworms, beetles, aphids and cankerworms; occasionally hover-gleans.

Voice: male's song is a fast, frequently repeated *sweet-sweet-sweet summer sweet.*

Similar Species: *Orange-crowned Warbler* (p. 268): lacks the reddish breast streaks; darker olive plumage overall. *American Goldfinch* (p. 349): black wings and tail; male often has a black forehead. *Wilson's Warbler* (p. 298): male has a black cap; female has a darker crown and upperparts; shorter, darker tail. *Common Yellowthroat* (p. 296): female lacks the yellow highlights in the wings; darker face and upperparts.

Best Sites: almost any moist, open woodland with dense deciduous shrubbery.

271

CHESTNUT-SIDED WARBLER

Dendroica pensylvanica

When colourful waves of warbler migrants flood across the Ontario landscape each May, the Chestnut-sided Warbler is consistently ranked among the most anticipated arrivals. Boldly patterned males flit about at eye level, often within arm's reach of dazzled onlookers. • Chestnut-sided Warblers tend to favour early-succession forests, which have become abundant in Ontario over the past century. Clear-cut logging and prescribed forest burns, while negatively affecting other species of warblers, have created suitable habitat for the Chestnut-sided Warbler in many parts of the province. A good indicator of the success of this species is that each spring and summer you can easily see more Chestnut-sided Warblers in a single day than John J. Audubon saw in his entire life—he saw only one! • When Carolus Linnaeus first described and named this species, he misspelled the name *pensylvanica*, meaning 'of Pennsylvania.' However, the rules of zoological nomenclature, based on the system of classification that Linnaeus established over 200 years ago, insist that such misspellings be perpetuated.

breeding

ID: *Breeding:* chestnut sides; white underparts; yellow cap; black legs; yellowish wing bars; black facial mask. *Breeding male:* bold colours. *Female:* washed-out colours; dark streaking on the yellow cap. *Fall adult:* yellow-green crown, nape and back; white eye ring; grey face and sides; white underparts. *Immature:* like the fall adult, but with brighter yellow wing bars.
Size: *L* 11–14 cm.
Status: common migrant in May and from mid-August to October; common breeder from May to August.
Habitat: shrubby, deciduous second-growth woodlands, abandoned fields and orchards; especially in areas that are regenerating after logging or fire.
Nesting: low in a shrub or sapling; small cup nest is made of bark strips, grass, roots and weed fibres and is lined with fine grasses, plant down and fur; female incubates 4 whitish eggs, with brown markings, for 11–12 days.
Feeding: gleans trees and shrubs at mid-level for insects.
Voice: loud, clear song: *so pleased, pleased, pleased to MEET-CHA!*; musical *chip* call.
Similar Species: *Bay-breasted Warbler* (p. 283): black face; dark chestnut hindcrown, upper breast and sides; buff belly and undertail coverts; white wing bars. *American Redstart* (p. 287): female has large yellow patches in the wings and tail; more greyish overall.
Best Sites: Halton Regional Forest; Algonquin PP; Chapleau Crown Game Reserve; Sleeping Giant PP; Point Pelee NP; Rondeau PP.

MAGNOLIA WARBLER

Dendroica magnolia

The Magnolia Warbler is widely regarded as one of the most beautiful wood-warblers. Like a customized Cadillac, the Magnolia comes fully loaded with all the fancy features—bold eyebrows, flashy wing bars and tail patches, an elegant 'necklace,' a bright yellow rump and breast and a dark mask. As if aware of its beauty, the Magnolia Warbler seems to flaunt its colours by 'posing' for birders. This beautiful warbler frequently forages along the lower branches of trees and among shrubs, allowing for reliable, close-up observations. • When spring cold fronts collide with flocks of migrant songbirds riding warm air across the Great Lakes, thousands of birds can be grounded. At such times, parks such as Point Pelee, Rondeau, Long Point and Sleeping Giant can be literally draped with Magnolias and other migrants. • Magnolia Warblers and many other songbirds migrate at night. Unfortunately, many birds are killed each year when they collide with buildings, radio towers and tall smokestacks.

breeding

ID: *Breeding male:* yellow underparts with bold black streaks; black mask; white eyebrow; blue-grey crown; dark upperparts; white wing bars often blend into a larger patch. *Female* and *Fall male:* duller overall; light facial mask; 2 distinct white wing bars; streaked, olive back. *In flight:* yellow rump; white tail patches.
Size: *L* 12–13 cm.
Status: very common migrant from mid- to late May and from mid-August to early October; very common breeder from May to August.
Habitat: open coniferous and mixed forests, mostly in natural openings and along edges, often near water; often prefers areas with short balsam fir and white spruce.
Nesting: on a horizontal limb in a conifer; loose cup nest made of grass, twigs and weeds is lined with rootlets; female incubates 4 white

eggs, marked with olive, brown, grey and lavender, for 11–13 days.
Feeding: gleans vegetation and buds; occasionally flycatches for beetles, flies, wasps, caterpillars and other insects; sometimes eats berries.
Voice: male's song is a quick, rising *pretty pretty lady* or *wheata wheata wheet-zu*; *clank* call.
Similar Species: *Yellow-rumped Warbler* (p. 276): white throat; yellow hindcrown patch; white belly. *Cape May Warbler* (p. 274): chestnut cheek patch on the yellow face; lacks the white tail patches. *Prairie Warbler* (p. 281): dusky jaw stripe; faint yellowish wing bars; immature lacks the white tail patches.
Best Sites: Petroglyphs PP; Algonquin PP; Sault Ste. Marie area; Pukaskwa NP; Sleeping Giant PP; woodlands bordering Hwy 11; Point Pelee NP; Rondeau PP.

CAPE MAY WARBLER

Dendroica tigrina

Observations of breeding Cape May Warblers in northern Ontario reveal that these birds are found only in forests that are at least 50 years of age. Older trees provide Cape Mays with secure nesting habitat and an abundance of canopy-dwelling insects. • Throughout most of its almost exclusively Canadian breeding range, this small bird seems to be a spruce budworm specialist—in years of budworm outbreaks, a Cape May can successfully fledge more young. The use of pesticides to control budworms and the harvesting of old-growth forests might adversely affect populations of this warbler. • The Cape May's tubular tongue is unique among wood-warblers. It uses its specialized tongue to feed on nectar and fruit juices while on its tropical wintering grounds. • This bird is named after Cape May County, New Jersey, where the first scientifically described specimen was collected.

breeding

Nesting: near the top of a spruce or fir, often near the trunk; cup nest is made of moss, weeds and grass and is lined with feathers and fur; female incubates 6 or 7 whitish eggs, with reddish-brown spots, for about 12 days.
Feeding: gleans treetop branches and foliage for spruce budworms, flies, beetles, moths, wasps and other insects; occasionally hover-gleans.

ID: dark streaking on the yellow underparts; yellow side collar; dark olive green upper-parts; yellow rump; clean white undertail coverts. *Breeding male:* chestnut cheek on the yellow face; dark crown; large, white wing patch. *Female:* paler overall; 2 faint, thin, white wing bars; greyish cheek and crown.
Size: *L* 12–14 cm.
Status: uncommon migrant through May and from mid-August to early October; irregular, locally rare to fairly common breeder from May to August; a few may remain into December.
Habitat: mature coniferous and mixed forests, especially in dense old-growth stands of white spruce and balsam fir.

Voice: very weak, high-pitched: *see see see see*; call is a very high-pitched *tsee.*
Similar Species: *Bay-breasted Warbler* (p. 283): male has a black face and chestnut throat, upper breast and sides; 2 white wing bars; unstreaked, buff underparts. *Black-throated Green Warbler* (p. 277): black throat and/or upper breast; white lower breast and belly; lacks the chestnut cheek; 2 white wing bars. *Magnolia Warbler* (p. 273): lacks the chestnut cheek patch and the yellow side collar; white tail patches; less streaking on the underparts.
Best Sites: Algonquin PP; Pukaskwa NP; Thunder Bay's Chippewa Park; Hwy 11 from Cochrane to Smooth Rock Falls; Point Pelee NP; Rondeau PP.

BLACK-THROATED BLUE WARBLER

Dendroica caerulescens

Dark and handsome, the male Black-throated Blue Warbler is a treasured sight to the eyes of any bird enthusiast or casual admirer. Females look nothing like their male counterparts, however, appearing more like a vireo or a plain-coloured Tennessee Warbler. • If you are fortunate enough to meet this bird during its migration or over the course of the nesting season, you will notice that it is more deliberate in its foraging behaviour than most other warblers. This warbler prefers to work methodically over a small area, snatching up insects among branches and foliage. • Black-throated Blue Warblers once nested among the deciduous forests of southern Ontario, beyond the limit of the Canadian Shield, but agriculture and urban development have forced them from many of these haunts.

breeding

ID: *Male:* black face, throat, upper breast and sides; dark blue upperparts; clean white underparts and wing patch. *Female:* olive brown upperparts; unmarked buff underparts; faint white eyebrow; small buff to whitish wing patch (may not be visible).
Size: *L* 13–14 cm.
Status: fairly common migrant and breeder from May to September; smaller numbers may remain into October and November.
Habitat: upland deciduous and mixed forests of the Canadian Shield with a dense understorey of deciduous saplings and shrubs; also in second-growth woodlands and brushy clearings.
Nesting: in the fork of a dense shrub or sapling, usually within 1 m of the ground; female builds an open cup nest of weeds, bark strips and spider webs and lines it with moss, hair and pine needles; female incubates 4 creamy white eggs, with

reddish-brown and grey blotches toward the larger end, for 12–13 days.
Feeding: thoroughly gleans the understorey for caterpillars, moths, spiders and other insects; occasionally eats berries and seeds; feeds less energetically than other wood-warblers.
Voice: song is a slow, wheezy *I am soo lay-zeee*, rising slowly throughout; call is a short *tip*.
Similar Species: male is distinctive. *Tennessee Warbler* (p. 267): lighter cheek; greener back; lacks the white wing patch. *Philadelphia Vireo* (p. 222): stouter bill; lighter cheek; more yellowy white below; lacks the white wing patch. *Cerulean Warbler* (p. 285): female has 2 white wing bars; broader, yellowish eyebrow.
Best Sites: Petroglyphs PP; Bon Echo PP; Algonquin PP; Killarney PP; Windy Lake PP; Lake Superior PP; Sleeping Giant PP; Rondeau PP.

275

YELLOW-RUMPED WARBLER

Dendroica coronata

The Yellow-rumped Warbler is the most abundant and widespread wood-warbler in North America, and Ontarians have a chance to meet one each spring from late April to late May. The best time to look is during the first few hours after dawn, when most Yellow-rumps are foraging among streamside and lakeshore trees. • Most of Ontario's Yellow-rumped Warblers nest on the Canadian Shield and the Hudson Bay Lowland, but some pairs raise their young among the fragmented woodlands of extreme southern Ontario. • Both races of the Yellow-rumped Warbler, which were once considered separate species, occur in Ontario: the 'Myrtle Warbler' has a white throat; the 'Audubon's Warbler,' has a yellow throat and is very rare in Ontario. • Adults are generally quiet when they have eggs or young to guard. If they are noisy and aggressive, it is a good sign that the young have left the nest. • The scientific name *coronata* is Latin for 'crowned,' referring to this bird's yellow crown.

♀

♂

'*Myrtle Warbler*'
breeding

ID: yellow crown, foreshoulder patches and rump; white underparts; dark cheek; faint white wing bars; thin eyebrow. *Male:* blue-grey upperparts with black streaking; black cheek, breast band and streaking along the sides and flanks. *Female:* grey-brown upperparts with dark streaking; dark streaking on the breast, sides and flanks.
Size: *L* 13–15 cm.
Status: common to abundant migrant from mid-April to late May and from mid-September to early November; common to very common breeder from May to September; a few may be present in winter.
Habitat: coniferous and mixed forests; rarely in pure deciduous woodlands.
Nesting: in a crotch or on a horizontal limb in a conifer; female builds a compact cup nest with grass, bark strips, moss, lichens and spider silk and lines it with feathers and fur; female incubates 4 or 5 brown- and grey-marked, creamy white eggs for about 12 days.

Feeding: hawks and hovers for beetles, flies, wasps, caterpillars, moths and other insects; gleans vegetation; sometimes eats berries.
Voice: male's song is a tinkling trill, often given in 2-note phrases that rise or fall at the end; there can be much variation between individuals; call is a sharp *chip* or *check*.
Similar Species: *Magnolia Warbler* (p. 273): yellow underparts; yellow throat; bold white eyebrow; lacks the yellow crown; white patches on the tail. *Chestnut-sided Warbler* (p. 272): chestnut sides on otherwise clean white underparts; lacks the yellow rump. *Cape May Warbler* (p. 274): heavily streaked, yellow throat, breast and sides; lacks the yellow crown. *Yellow-throated Warbler* (p. 279): lacks the yellow crown and rump; yellow throat; bold white eyebrow, ear patch and wing bars.
Best Sites: Bruce Peninsula woodlands; Bon Echo PP; Killarney PP; Wakami Lake PP; Sleeping Giant PP; forests bordering Hwy 11; Point Pelee NP; Long Point PP; Presqu'ile PP.

BLACK-THROATED GREEN WARBLER

Dendroica virens

Before the first warm rays of dawn brighten the spires of Ontario's forests, male Black-throated Green Warblers offer up their distinctive *See-See-See SUZY* tunes. Not only do males use song to defend their turf, they also seem to thrive on chasing each other from their territories. On occasion, they will even broaden the target of their aggression to include other songbirds. • When foraging in the forest canopy, male Black-throats are highly conspicuous as they dart from branch to branch, chipping noisily as they go. Females often prefer to feed at lower levels in the foliage of tall shrubs and sapling trees. • In other parts of its range in Canada, the Black-throated Green Warbler is a denizen of old-growth coniferous forests. In Ontario, it nests in a variety of forest types, including pure deciduous woodlands and conifer plantations.

breeding

♂

ID: yellow face; may show a faint dusky cheek or eye line; black upper breast band; streaking along the sides; olive crown, back and rump; dark wings and tail; 2 bold white wing bars; white lower breast, belly and undertail coverts. *Male:* black throat. *Female:* yellow throat; thinner wing bars.
Size: *L* 11–13 cm.
Status: very common migrant from late April to May and from late August to early October; common breeder from May to August; a few may remain into November.
Habitat: coniferous and mixed forests; also in some deciduous woodlands composed of beech, maple or birch; may inhabit cedar swamps, hemlock ravines and conifer plantations in extreme southern Ontario.
Nesting: in a crotch or on a horizontal limb, usually in a conifer; compact cup nest of grass, weeds, twigs, bark, lichens and

spider silk is lined with moss, fur, feathers and plant fibres; female incubates 4 or 5 creamy white to grey eggs, scrawled or spotted with reddish brown, for 12 days.
Feeding: gleans vegetation and buds for beetles, flies, wasps, caterpillars and other insects; sometimes takes berries; frequently hover-gleans.
Voice: fast *See-See-See SUZY!* or *zoo zee zoo zoo zee;* call is a *tick.*
Similar Species: *Blackburnian Warbler* (p. 278): female has yellowish underparts and an angular, dusky facial patch. *Cape May Warbler* (p. 274): heavily streaked, yellow throat, breast and sides. *Pine Warbler* (p. 280): lacks the black upper breast band; yellowish breast and upper belly.
Best Sites: Halton Regional Forest; Bruce Peninsula; Wakami Lake PP; Pukaskwa NP; Point Pelee NP; Rondeau PP; Long Point PP; Presqu'ile PP; Sleeping Giant PP.

277

BLACKBURNIAN WARBLER

Dendroica fusca

High among towering coniferous spires lives the colourful Blackburnian Warbler, ablaze in spring with a fiery orange throat. Blackburnians are widely regarded as one of the most beautiful warblers in Ontario. • Different species of wood-warblers are able to coexist through a partitioning of foraging 'niches' and feeding strategies. Through this intricate partitioning, competition for food sources is reduced and the exhaustion of particular resources is avoided. Some warblers inhabit high tree-tops, a few feed and nest along outer tree branches, some at high levels and some at lower levels, and others restrict themselves to inner branches and tree-trunks. Blackburnians have found their niche predominantly in the outermost branches of each tree. • This bird's name is thought to honour the Blackburne family of England. Ashton Blackburne probably collected the type specimen, and Anna Blackburne managed the museum in which it was housed. The scientific name *fusca* is Latin for 'dusky', an odd reference to the duller winter plumage of this bird.

breeding

ID: *Breeding male:* fiery, reddish-orange upper breast and throat; orange-yellow head with an angular black mask; 2 broad, black crown stripes; blackish upperparts; large, white wing patch; may show some white on the outer tail feathers; yellowish to whitish underparts; dark streaking on the sides and flanks. *Female:* brown version of the male; upper breast and throat are more yellowish than the male's.
Size: *L* 12–14 cm.
Status: fairly common migrant in May and from mid-August to mid-September; fairly common breeder from May to August; a few may remain into early November.
Habitat: mature coniferous and mixed forests.

Nesting: high in a mature conifer, often near a branch tip; cup nest of bark, twigs and plant fibres is lined with conifer needles, moss and fur; female incubates 3–5 white to greenish-white eggs, blotched with reddish brown toward larger end, for about 13 days.
Feeding: forages on the uppermost branches, gleaning budworms, flies, beetles and other invertebrates; occasionally hover-gleans.
Voice: soft, faint, high-pitched song: *ptoo-too-too-too tititi zeee* or *see-me see-me see-me see-me*; call is a short *tick*.
Similar Species: *Yellow-throated Warbler* (p. 279): blue-grey upperparts; white eyebrow, ear patch and eye crescent; lacks the orange throat. *Prairie Warbler* (p. 281): faint yellowish wingbars; black facial stripes do not form a solid angular patch.
Best Sites: Halton Regional Forest; Bruce Peninsula; Algonquin PP; Killarney PP; Wakami Lake PP; Lake Superior PP; Sleeping Giant PP; Point Pelee NP; Long Point PP; Presqu'ile PP.

YELLOW-THROATED WARBLER

Dendroica dominica

The striking Yellow-throated Warbler is a breeding bird in the southeastern U.S., but in some years a few overshoot their traditional range and migrate into southern Ontario, often with huge waves of Yellow-rumped Warblers. By far the most sightings in our province occur at Pelee Island and Point Pelee National Park, which could be the result of the unusually large number of birders that scour these places for rarities. Pelee contains some of the last remnants of Carolinian forest—a favoured habitat of the Yellow-throated Warbler that once carpeted much of southwestern Ontario. It's quite possible that global warming and efforts to encourage the regrowth of the Carolinian forest might result in a few pioneering Yellow-throat nesters in our province. • Fall and early winter can produce the odd wayward Yellow-throated Warbler, usually at a backyard feeder.

breeding

ID: yellow throat and upper breast; triangular black face mask; black forehead; bold white eyebrow and ear patch; white underparts, with black streaking on the sides; 2 white wing bars; bluish-grey upperparts.
Size: *L* 13–14 cm.
Status: very rare visitor from early April to late May and from early July to early January.
Habitat: primarily Carolinian forest; riparian woodlands, swamps and groves of oak or sycamore; seen at backyard feeders in winter.
Nesting: does not nest in Ontario.
Feeding: primarily insectivorous; gleans insects from tree-trunks and foliage by creeping along tree surfaces; often hawks insects out of the air; wintering birds may eat suet from feeders.

Voice: boisterous song a series of down-slurred whistles with a final rising note: *tee-ew tee-ew tee-ew tew-wee*; call is a loud *churp*.
Similar Species: *Magnolia Warbler* (p. 273): black 'necklace'; yellow breast, belly and rump; lacks the white ear patch. *Blackburnian Warbler* (p. 278): yellow-orange to orange-red throat, eyebrow, ear patch and crown stripe; often shows yellowish underparts; dark brown to blackish upperparts. *Yellow-throated Vireo* (p. 219): lacks the black and white in the face and the dark streaking on the sides. *Kentucky Warbler* (p. 293): unmarked, all-yellow underparts; lacks the white ear patch and the wing bars; yellow eyebrow.
Best Sites: Point Pelee NP; Rondeau PP; Long Point PP.

VAGRANT

279

PINE WARBLER

Dendroica pinus

This unassuming bird is perfectly named because it is bound to Ontario's majestic, sheltering pines. Although it is usually approachable, the Pine Warbler spends much of its time foraging near the top of tall, mature pine trees, so it is often difficult to observe. It behaves much like a Brown Creeper when it forages, deliberately probing the furrowed bark of tree-trunks in search of hidden insects. Occasionally, a Pine Warbler can be seen smeared in patches of sticky pine resin. • The Pine Warbler's modest appearance is very similar to a number of immature and fall-plumaged vireos and warblers, so birders are forced to obtain a good, long look before making a positive identification. This warbler is most often confused with the Bay-breasted or Blackpoll Warbler in drab fall plumage.

breeding

ID: olive green head and back; dark greyish wings and tail; whitish to dusky wing bars; yellow throat and breast; faded dark streaking or dusky wash on the sides of the breast; white undertail coverts and belly; faint line through the eye; faint yellow, broken eye ring; female is duller. *Immature:* duller; brownish olive head and back; pale yellow (male) to creamy-white (female) throat and breast; brown wash on the flanks. **Size:** *L* 13–14 cm.

Status: rare to locally uncommon migrant from April to early June; very locally rare to uncommon breeder from May to September; a few may remain into November.

Habitat: prefers open, mature pine woodlands and plantations for nesting; mixed and deciduous woodlands in migration.

Nesting: toward the end of a pine limb; female builds a deep, open cup nest of twigs, bark, weeds, grass, pine needles and spider webs and lines

it with feathers; pair incubates 3–5 whitish eggs, with brown specks toward the larger end, for about 10 days.

Feeding: eats mostly insects, berries and seeds; gleans from the ground or foliage by climbing around trees and shrubs; may hang upside-down on a branch tip like a chickadee or titmouse.

Voice: song is a short, musical trill; call note is a sweet *chip*.

Similar Species: *Prairie Warbler* (p. 281): distinctive, dark facial stripes; darker streaking on the sides; yellowish wing bars. *Kirtland's Warbler* (p. 360): darker streaking on the sides; broken, white eye ring; bluish-grey upperparts. *Bay-breasted Warbler* (p. 283) and *Blackpoll Warbler* (p. 284): immature and fall birds have dark streaking on the head and/or back; long, thin yellow eyebrow. *Yellow-throated Vireo* (p. 219): bright yellow 'spectacles'; gray rump; lacks the streaking on the sides.

Best Sites: The Pinery PP; St. Williams Forestry Station; Homer Watson Park, Mosport area; Bon Echo PP; Lake Superior PP; Point Pelee NP.

PRAIRIE WARBLER

Dendroica discolor

W oodland edges and open scrublands host the summer activities of the Prairie Warbler. This bird occupies early successional habitats or areas over the rocky Canadian Shield with such poor soil conditions that the vegetation remains short and scattered. A male Prairie Warbler may return each year to a favoured nesting site until the vegetation in that area grows too tall and dense. • Although Prairie Warblers are considered quite common in many parts of the eastern U.S., they are rare here, and estimates suggest there are fewer than 500 breeding pairs in the province. On their nesting grounds, song wars occasionally result in physical fights between competing males. When the dust and feathers clear, the victor resumes his slow, graceful, butterfly-like courtship flight.

♂

breeding

♀

ID: bright yellow face and underparts, except for the white undertail coverts; dark cheek stripe and eye line; black streaking on the sides; olive grey upperparts; inconspicuous chestnut streaks on the back; 2 faint yellowish wing bars; female and immature birds are duller.
Size: *L* 12–13 cm.
Status: rare migrant and breeder from May to September.
Habitat: dry, open scrubby sand dunes and rocky pine-oak-juniper scrublands; also found in woodland edges and young pine plantations with deciduous scrub.
Nesting: low in a tree; female builds an open cup nest of soft vegetation and lines it with with animal hair; female incubates 4 whitish eggs, with brown spots toward the larger end, for 11–14 days; both adults raise the young; small, loose nesting colonies may be formed.

Feeding: mainly insectivorous; will also eat berries and tree sap exposed by sapsuckers; caterpillars are a favoured item for nestlings; gleans, hover-gleans and occasionally hawks for prey.
Voice: buzzy song is an ascending series of *zee* notes; call is sweet *chip*.
Similar Species: *Pine Warbler* (p. 280): lacks distinctive, dark streaking in the face; lighter streaking on the sides; whitish wing bars. *Yellow-throated Warbler* (p. 279): white belly; bold white wing bars, eyebrow and ear patch. *Kirtland's Warbler* (p. 360): immature female has brownish upperparts and a pale white eye ring. *Bay-breasted Warbler* (p. 283) and *Blackpoll Warbler* (p. 284): immature and fall birds have white bellies and wing bars, and lighter upperparts with dark streaking.
Best Sites: The Pinery PP; Godfrey area; Mazinaw Lake; Severn Sound north to Parry Sound.

PALM WARBLER

Dendroica palmarum

Considering this bird's subtropical wintering range, it may make sense to call it the Palm Warbler, even though it doesn't forage in palm trees. Its summer range, however, lies almost exclusively in Canada. The Palm Warbler is just as comfortable here as it is in the subtropics, and it could just as easily been named the 'Bog Warbler' because of its preference for northern bogs of sphagnum moss and black spruce. • The Palm Warbler is easily recognized by its incessant tail-bobbing: its tail pumps whether the bird is hopping on the ground or perched momentarily on an elevated limb. In fall, when its distinctive chestnut crown has faded to olive brown, this habit becomes a prominent field mark.

breeding

ID: chestnut cap (may be inconspicuous in fall); yellow eyebrow; yellow throat and undertail coverts; yellow or white breast and belly; dark streaking on the breast and sides; olive brown upperparts; frequently bobs its tail; may show a dull yellowish rump.

Size: *L* 11–14 cm.

Status: fairly common migrant from late April to late May and from early September to late October; uncommon to locally abundant breeder from May to September; a few may show in winter.

Habitat: along the edges of mature bogs with scattered black spruce; less frequently in openings of spruce-tamarack forests with sphagnum moss and shrubs.

Nesting: on the ground or in a low shrub or stunted spruce; often on a sphagnum hummock concealed by grass; female builds a cup nest of grass, weeds and bark and lines it with feathers; 4 or 5 brown-marked, creamy white eggs are incubated for about 12 days.

Feeding: gleans the ground and vegetation for a wide variety of insects and berries while perched or hovering; occasionally hawks for insects; may take some seeds.

Voice: male's song is a weak, buzzy trill with a quick finish; call is a sharp *sup* or *check*.

Similar Species: *Yellow-rumped Warbler* (p.276): female has a bright yellow rump, crown patch and foreshoulder patch; white wing bars, throat and undertail coverts. *Prairie Warbler* (p. 281): dark jaw stripe; darker eye line; lacks the chestnut crown and the dark streaking on the breast. *Chipping Sparrow* (p. 305) and *American Tree Sparrow* (p. 304): stouter bodies; unstreaked, greyish underparts; lack the yellow plumage. *Pine Warbler* (p. 280): lacks the chestnut cap and the bold yellow eyebrow; faint whitish wing bars; white undertail coverts.

Best Sites: Hwy 11 from Iroquois Falls to Smooth Rock Falls; Point Pelee NP, Rondeau PP, Long Point PP, Presqu'ile PP; Sleeping Giant PP.

BAY-BREASTED WARBLER

Dendroica castanea

Deep within stands of old-growth spruce and fir is where you will have to search to find the handsome Bay-breasted Warbler. It typically forages midway up a tree, often on the inner branches, so it's often a difficult bird to spot. • Like all migratory birds, Bay-breasted Warblers face many dangers on their travels. Their annual trip north to the expansive spruce forests of Ontario, however, seems well worth it for the abundance of summer food that is found there. • Bay-breasted Warblers are invaluable when it comes to long-term suppression of spruce budworms. These birds typically move to where the larvae are most numerous, and it is estimated that in outbreak years, they can eat 13,000 budworms per hectare through the breeding season.

breeding

ID: *Breeding male:* black face and chin; chestnut crown, throat, sides and flanks; creamy yellow belly, undertail coverts and patch on the side of the neck; 2 white wing bars. *Breeding female:* paler, washed-out colours; dusky face; whitish to creamy underparts and neck patch; faint chestnut cap; rusty wash on the sides and flanks. *Fall adult:* yellow olive head and back; crown and back have dark streaking; whiter underparts. *Immature:* resembles the fall adult, but has less prominent streaking on the upperparts; lacks the chestnut sides and flanks.
Size: *L* 13–15 cm.
Status: fairly common to very common migrant from early May to early June and from mid-August to October; fairly common breeder from May to August; a few may remain into November.
Habitat: mature coniferous and mixed boreal forest; almost exclusively in stands of spruce and fir.
Nesting: usually on a horizontal conifer branch; open cup nest is built of grass, twigs, moss, roots and lichen and is lined with fine bark

strips and fur; female incubates 4 or 5 whitish eggs, with dark marks toward the larger end, for about 13 days.
Feeding: usually forages at the mid-level of trees; gleans vegetation and branches for caterpillars and adult invertebrates; eats spruce budworms when available.
Voice: song is an extremely high-pitched *seee-seese-seese-seee*; call is a high *see*.
Similar Species: *Cape May Warbler* (p. 274): chestnut cheek on the yellow face; dark streaking on mostly yellow underparts; lacks the reddish flanks and crown. *Chestnut-sided Warbler* (p. 272): yellow crown; white cheek and underparts; fall birds have a white eye ring, unmarked whitish face and underparts and lack the bold streaking on the yellow olive upperparts. *Blackpoll Warbler* (p. 284): fall and immature birds have dark streaking on the breast and sides and lack the chestnut on the sides and flanks; white undertail coverts.
Best Sites: Algonquin PP; Halfway Lake PP; Sleeping Giant PP; Point Pelee NP, Rondeau PP.

BLACKPOLL WARBLER

Dendroica striata

Only if you have skills in wilderness survival will you have the chance to observe the Blackpoll Warbler on its nesting turf—this bird summers in the remote, insect-swarmed muskeg of extreme northern Ontario. • The Blackpoll is the greatest warbler migrant: weighing less than a wet teabag, eastern migrants are known to fly south over the Atlantic, leaving land at Cape Cod and not resting until they reach the northern coast of Venezuela. In a single year, a Blackpoll Warbler may fly up to 24,000 km! This bird is truly an international resident, so conservation of its habitat requires the efforts of several nations. • Blackpoll Warblers in fall plumage are easily confused with Bay-breasted Warblers, which look very similar. Most Blackpolls, however, migrate later in fall than their Bay-breasted counterparts.

breeding

ID: 2 white wing bars; black streaking on the underparts; white undertail coverts. *Breeding male:* black cap and 'moustache' stripe; white cheek; black-streaked, olive grey upperparts; white underparts; orange legs. *Breeding female:* streaked, yellow olive head and back; white underparts; small, dark eyeline and pale eyebrow. *Fall adult:* olive yellow head, back, rump, breast and sides; yellow eyebrow; dark legs. *Immature:* paler streaking.

Size: *L* 13–14 cm.

Status: common migrant from late May to mid-June and from late August to early October; fairly common breeder from June to August; a few may remain into November.

Habitat: coniferous and mixed scrub, open coniferous growth on dry fens and bogs, the backsides of ridged riverbanks and sparsely vegetated beach ridges.

Nesting: concealed in a stunted spruce tree; nest is made of twigs, bark shreds, grass and lichens and is lined with feathers, fur and rootlets; female incubates 4 or 5 whitish eggs, spotted with lavender and brown, for about 12 days.

Feeding: gleans buds, leaves and branches for aphids, mosquitoes, beetles, wasps, caterpillars and many other insects; often flycatches for insects.

Voice: song is an extremely high-pitched, uniform trill: *tsit tsit tsit*; call is a loud *chip.*

Similar Species: *Black-and-white Warbler* (p. 286): dark legs; striped, black and white crown; male has a black chin, throat and cheek patch. *Black-capped Chickadee* (p. 236): lacks the wing bars and the black streaking on the underparts; black chin and throat. *Bay-breasted Warbler* (p. 283): fall adults and immatures lack the dark streaking on the underparts; chestnut sides and flanks; buff undertail coverts.

Best Sites: Winisk River PP; Severn River PP; Polar Bear PP; Point Pelee NP, Rondeau PP; Long Point PP, Presqu'ile PP; Sleeping Giant PP.

CERULEAN WARBLER

Dendroica cerulea

The Cerulean Warbler leads a mysterious life concealed in the heights of Ontario's deciduous forests. The handsome blue and white male is particularly difficult to observe as he blends into the sunny summer sky while foraging among treetop foliage. Often the only evidence of a meeting with this largely unobservable canopy dweller is the precious sound of the male's buzzy, trilling voice. • Only in the last few decades have ornithologists been able to document this bird's breeding behaviour—courtship, mating, nesting and the rearing of young all tend to take place high in the canopy, well out of sight of most observers. • The loss of Ontario's deciduous forests has caused a notable decline in the number of Cerulean Warblers in our province.

breeding

ID: white undertail coverts and wing bars. *Male:* blue upperparts; white throat and underparts; black 'necklace' and streaking on the sides. *Female:* blue-green crown, nape and back; dark eye line; yellow eyebrow, throat and breast; pale streaking on the sides. *Immature:* pale yellow underparts and eyebrow; yellowish to white wing bars; pale olive green upperparts.
Size: *L* 11–12 cm.
Status: rare and local to very locally uncommon migrant and breeder from late April to August; a few may remain into October.
Habitat: mature deciduous hardwood forests and extensive woodlands with a clear understorey; particularly drawn to riparian stands.
Nesting: high on the end of a deciduous branch; open cup nest is built with bark strips, weeds, grass, licken and spider silk and is lined with fur and moss; female incubates 3–5 brown-spotted, grey to creamy whitish eggs for about 12–13 days.
Feeding: insects are gleaned from upper-canopy foliage and branches; often hawks for insects.
Voice: song is a rapid, accelerating sequence of buzzy notes leading into a higher trilled note; call is a sharp *chip*.
Similar Species: *Black-throated Blue Warbler* (p. 275): male has a black face, chin and throat; female has a small white wing patch; lacks the wing bars. *Blackpoll Warbler* (p. 284) and *Bay-breasted Warbler* (p. 283): look like the female Cerulean, but have more yellow than green on the mantle. *Pine Warbler* (p. 280): browner; looks like the female Cerulean, but has more yellow on the mantle.
Best Sites: Rondeau PP; Sudden Tract; woodlands from Cambridge and Ancaster to Long Point PP; Halton Regional Forest; Point Pelee NP; Rondeau PP.

285

BLACK-AND-WHITE WARBLER

Mniotilta varia

In a general sense, this is a normal-looking warbler, but its foraging behaviour stands in sharp contrast to most of its kin. Rather than dancing or flitting quickly between twig perches, Black-and-white Warblers behave like creepers and nuthatches—a distantly related group of birds. Birders who have developed frayed nerves and tired eyes after watching flitty warblers will be refreshed by the sight of this bird as it methodically creeps up and down tree-trunks. • Novice birders can easily identify this unique, two-toned warbler, which retains its standard plumage throughout its stay in Ontario. Even a trip to its wintering grounds will reveal this warbler in the same outfit. A keen ear also helps to identify this forest-dweller: its gentle, oscillating song—like a wheel in need of greasing—is easily recognized and remembered.

breeding

ID: black and white, striped crown; dark upperparts with white streaking; 2 white wing bars; white underparts with black streaking on the sides, flanks and undertail coverts; black legs. *Breeding male:* black cheek and throat. *Breeding female:* grey cheek; white throat. *Immature female:* buffy sides and undertail coverts.
Size: *L* 11–14 cm.
Status: very common migrant from late April to May and from August to September; fairly common to very common breeder from May to August; a few may remain into November.
Habitat: deciduous or mixed forests, often near water; in cedar swamps, and alder and willow thickets bordering muskeg and beaver ponds.
Nesting: usually on the ground next to a tree, log or large rock; in a shallow scrape, often among a pile of dead leaves; female builds a cup nest with grass, leaves, bark strips, rootlets and pine needles and lines it with fur and fine grasses; female incubates 5 creamy white eggs, with brown flecks toward the larger end, for 10–12 days.
Feeding: gleans insect eggs, larval insects, beetles, spiders and other invertebrates while creeping along tree-trunks and branches.
Voice: series of high, thin, 2-syllable notes: *weetsee weetsee weetsee weetsee weetsee weetsee*; call is a sharp *pit* and a soft, high *seat*.
Similar Species: *Blackpoll Warbler* (p. 284): breeding male has a solid black cap and clean white undertail coverts.
Best Sites: Halton Regional Forest; Petroglyphs PP; Carillon PP; Grundy Lake PP; Killarney PP; Lake Superior PP; Pukaskwa NP; Point Pelee NP; Long Point PP; Sleeping Giant PP.

AMERICAN REDSTART

Setophaga ruticilla

American Redstarts are consistently listed as a favourite among birders. These supercharged birds flit from branch to branch in dizzying pursuit of prey. Even when perched, their tails sway rhythmically back and forth. Few birds can rival a mature male redstart for his contrasting black and orange plumage, his approachability and amusing behaviour. American Redstarts behave much the same way on their Central American wintering grounds, where they are locally known as *candelita* (little candle). • Although Redstarts are common in Ontario, their beautifully trilly songs are so variable that identifying one is a challenge to birders of all levels. • American Redstarts are typically found in small, rural woodlots and wooded parks in suburban residential areas, wherever there is a dense understorey of saplings.

ID: *Male:* black overall; red-orange fore-shoulder, wing and tail patches; white belly and undertail coverts. *Female:* olive brown upperparts; grey-green head; yellow foreshoulder, wing and tail patches; clean white underparts. *Immature male:* resembles a female, but has dark breast streaks.
Size: *L* 13 cm.
Status: common migrant and breeder from early May to early October; a few may remain into November.
Habitat: shrubby woodland edges, open and semi-open deciduous and mixed forests with a regenerating deciduous understorey of shrubs and saplings; often near water.

Nesting: in the fork of a shrub or sapling, usually 1–7 m above the ground; female builds an open cup nest with plant down, bark shreds, grass and rootlets and lines it with feathers; female incubates 4 brown-or grey-marked, whitish eggs for 11–12 days.
Feeding: actively gleans foliage and hawks for insects and spiders on leaves, buds and branches; often hover-gleans.
Voice: male's song is a highly variable series of *tseet* or *zee* notes, often given at different pitches; call is a sharp, sweet *chip*.
Similar Species: none.
Best Sites: almost any deciduous understorey or shrubby woodland edge, especially near water.

287

PROTHONOTARY WARBLER

Protonotaria citrea

The Prothonotary Warbler is unusual among the wood-warbler clan, because it nests in cavities. Standing dead trees and stumps riddled with natural cavities and woodpecker excavations provide perfect nesting habitat for this bird, especially if the site is near stagnant, swampy water. Much of its swampy habitat is inaccessible to birders, but if you are in the right place at the right time, you might be lucky enough to come across this bird as it forages for insects along a tree-trunk, decaying log or debris floating on the water's surface. • Suitable Prothonotary nesting sites are so rare in Ontario that a breeding pair will often return to the same nest cavity year after year. Males can be very aggressive in defending their territory, and they often resort to combative aerial chases when songs and warning displays fail to intimidate intruders. Unfortunately for neighbouring birds, this scorn is unprejudiced—other cavity-nesting birds, such as woodpeckers, wrens and bluebirds, are often victims of this fury.

breeding

ID: large, dark eyes and long bill are prominent on the unmarked, yellow head; yellow undersides, except for the white undertail coverts; olive green back; unmarked, bluish-grey wings and tail.
Size: *L* 14 cm.
Status: very rare migrant and rare, local breeder from May to early August; a few may remain into October.
Habitat: wooded deciduous swamps.
Nesting: cavities in standing dead trees, rotten stumps, birdhouses or abandoned woodpecker nests, from water level to 3 m above the ground; often returns to the same nest site; female chooses one of the male's moss-filled cavities, lines it with soft plant material and incubates 4–6 brown-spotted, creamy to pinkish eggs for 12–14 days.

Feeding: forages for a variety of insects and small mollusks; gleans from vegetation; may hop on floating debris or creep along tree-trunks.
Voice: male's song is a loud, ringing series of *sweet* or *zweet* notes issued on a single pitch; flight-song is *chewee chewee chee chee*; call is a brisk *tink*.
Similar Species: *Blue-winged Warbler* (p. 265): white wing bars; black eye line; yellowish-white undertail coverts. *Yellow Warbler* (p. 271): dark wings and tail with yellow highlights; yellow undertail coverts; male has reddish streaking in the breast. *Hooded Warbler* (p. 297): female has yellow undertail coverts and yellow-olive upperparts.
Best Sites: Point Pelee NP; Rondeau PP; Long Point PP.

WORM-EATING WARBLER

Helmintheros vermivorus

Worm-eating Warblers are rare in Ontario, and there are only about 30 confirmed sightings per year, most from Point Pelee National Park. Nearly all the sightings have been reported in May, but some birds inevitably surface throughout the summer and early fall. Most Worm-eating Warblers summer in the U.S., but they seem to have their eyes set on southern Ontario as the newest addition to their breeding range. To date, there is no evidence of breeding, but there is a good chance this bird may nest here in the future. • This bird spends much of its time foraging for small terrestrial insects and spiders among the dense undergrowth and leaf litter of deciduous forests. Although it inhabits the moist, leaf-covered ground where earthworms may be found, this bird rarely, if ever, includes earthworms in its diet.

ID: black and buff-orange striped head; brownish olive upperparts; rich buff-orange breast; whitish undertail coverts.
Size: *L* 13 cm.
Status: very rare visitor from mid-April to October.
Habitat: steep, deciduous woodland slopes, ravines and swampy woodlands with shrubby understorey cover.
Nesting: does not nest in Ontario.
Feeding: eats mostly small insects; forages on the ground and in trees and shrubs.

Voice: song is a faster, thinner version of the Chipping Sparrow's chipping trill; call is a buzzy *zeep-zeep.*
Similar Species: *Red-eyed Vireo* (p. 223): grey crown; white eyebrow; red eyes; yellow undertail coverts. *Louisiana Waterthrush* (p. 292) and *Northern Waterthrush* (p. 291): darker upperparts; bold white or yellowish eyebrow; dark streaking on the white breast; lack the striped head.
Best Sites: Point Pelee NP.

VAGRANT

OVENBIRD

Seiurus aurocapillus

The Ovenbird's loud and joyous ode to 'teachers' is a common sound that echoes through Ontario's deciduous and mixed forests in spring. Unfortunately, pinpointing the exact location of this resonating call is not always easy. An Ovenbird will rarely expose itself to the open forest, and it is most comfortable hidden in the tangles of low shrubs or among conifer branches. • The name 'Ovenbird' refers to this bird's unusual, oven-shaped ground nest. An incubating female nestled within her woven dome is usually confident enough in her nest that, unless closely approached, she will choose to sit tight rather than flee approaching danger. The nest is so well camouflaged that few human eyes ever find one, even though the nests are often located near hiking trails and bike paths.

ID: olive brown upperparts; white eye ring; heavy, dark streaking on the white breast, sides and flanks; rufous crown bordered by black; pink legs; white undertail coverts; no wing bars.

Size: *L* 15 cm.

Status: common migrant from May to early June and from early August to early October; common breeder from May to August; a few may remain as late as January.

Habitat: *Breeding:* undisturbed, mature forests with a closed canopy and very little understorey; often in ravines and riparian areas. *In migration:* dense riparian shrubbery and thickets and a variety of woodlands.

Nesting: on the ground; female builds an oven-shaped, domed nest of grass, weeds, bark, twigs and dead leaves and lines it with animal hair; female incubates 4 or 5 white eggs, with grey and brown spots, for 11–13 days.

Feeding: gleans the ground for worms, snails, insects and occasionally seeds.

Voice: loud, distinctive *tea-cher tea-cher Tea-CHER Tea-CHER*, increasing in speed and volume; night song is an elaborate series of bubbly, warbled notes, often ending in *teacher-teacher*; call is a brisk *chip, cheep* or *chock*.

Similar Species: *Northern Waterthrush* (p. 291) and *Louisiana Waterthrush* (p. 292): bold yellowish or white eyebrow; lack the rufous crown; darker upperparts. *Thrushes* (p. 251–57): all are larger and lack the rufous crown outlined in black.

Best Sites: almost any mature deciduous or mixed woodland with a closed canopy.

NORTHERN WATERTHRUSH

Seiurus noveboracensis

irders who are not satisfied by simply hearing a Northern Waterthrush in its nesting territory must literally get their feet wet if they want much hope of seeing one. This bird skulks along the shores of deciduous swamps or coniferous bogs, so fallen logs, shrubby tangles and soggy ground might discourage human visitors. Many birders, however, are quite content to look for this bird during relatively bug-free months in spring and fall, when migrating Northern Waterthrushes typically appear among drier, upland forests or along lofty park trails and boardwalks. Backyards featuring a small garden pond also attract migrating waterthrushes. • Its voice is loud and raucous for such a small bird, so it seems fitting that it was once known as the New York Warbler, a city well known for its decibels. The scientific name *noveboracensis* means 'of New York.'

ID: pale yellowish to buff eyebrow; pale yellowish to buff underparts with dark streaking; finely spotted throat; olive brown upperparts; pinkish legs; frequently bobs its tail.

Size: *L* 13–15 cm.

Status: common migrant from late April to May and from August to early October; common breeder from May to September; a few may remain as late as early January.

Habitat: wooded edges of swamps, lakes, beaver ponds, bogs and rivers; also in moist wooded ravines, and riparian thickets.

Nesting: on the ground, usually near water; female builds a cup nest of moss, leaves, bark, twigs and pine needles and lines it with moss, hair and rootlets; female incubates 4 or 5 whitish eggs,

spotted and blotched with brown and purple-grey, for 13 days.

Feeding: gleans foliage and the ground for invertebrates, frequently tossing aside ground litter with its bill; may also take aquatic invertebrates and small fish from shallow water.

Voice: song is a loud, 3-part *sweet sweet sweet, swee wee wee, chew chew chew chew*; call is a brisk *chip* or *chuck*.

Similar Species: *Louisiana Waterthrush* (p. 292): broader, white eyebrow; unspotted, white throat; orange-buff wash on the flanks. *Ovenbird* (p. 290): russet crown bordered by black stripes; white eye ring; lacks the pale eyebrow; unspotted throat.

Best Sites: Luther Marsh; Bon Echo PP; Carillon PP; Missinaibi River PP; Pukaskwa NP; Point Pelee NP; Sleeping Giant PP.

LOUISIANA WATERTHRUSH

Seiurus motacilla

In southern Ontario, the Louisiana Waterthrush is often seen sallying along the shorelines of babbling streams and gently swirling pools in search of its next meal. This bird inhabits swamps and sluggish streams throughout much of its North American range, but in Ontario, where its range overlaps with the Northern Waterthrush, it inhabits shorelines near fast-flowing water. • Louisiana Waterthrushes have never been recorded in great numbers in Ontario, partly because little suitable habitat remains for them. This bird's success depends on the stewardship of private landowners to protect its nesting habitat. Only a small percentage of Ontario's wild areas are officially protected by law in parks, conservation areas and ecological reserves. • Waterthrushes are easily identified by their habit of bobbing their head and moving their tail up and down as they walk.

ID: brownish upperparts; long bill; pink legs; white underparts with orange-buff wash on the flanks; long, dark streaks on the breast and sides; bicoloured, buffy and white eyebrow; clean white throat.

Size: *L* 15 cm.

Status: rare and local migrant and breeder from late March to September.

Habitat: moist, forested ravines, alongside fast-flowing streams; rarely along wooded swamps.

Nesting: concealed within a rocky hollow or within a tangle of tree roots; cup-shaped nest is made of leaves, bark, twigs and moss and is lined with animal hair, ferns and rootlets; female incubates 3–6 creamy white eggs, with purple-grey and brown spots, for about 14 days.

Feeding: terrestrial and aquatic insects and crustaceans are gleaned from rocks and debris near or in shallow water; dead leaves and other debris may be flipped and probed for food; occasionally catches flying insects over water.

Voice: song begins with 3–4 distinctive, shrill, slurred notes followed by a warbling twitter; call is a brisk *chick* or *chink*.

Similar Species: *Northern Waterthrush* (p. 291): yellowish to buff eyebrow narrows behind the eye; underparts are usually all yellowish or buff (occasionally all white); lacks the orange-buff flanks; finely spotted throat. *Ovenbird* (p. 290) and *Thrushes* (pp. 251–57): lack the broad, white eyebrow.

Best Sites: Sudden Tract; Halton Regional Forest; Helen Quilliam Otter Lake Sanctuary; Point Pelee NP; Rondeau PP; Long Point PP; High Park in Toronto.

KENTUCKY WARBLER

Oporornis formosus

Kentucky Warblers spend much of their time on the ground, overturning leaves and scurrying through dense thickets in search of insects. These birds are typically found in moist, deciduous woodlands of the eastern U.S., and each year a few make their way into Ontario. Most sightings are recorded in Point Pelee National Park during the last two weeks of May. • Although no nests have been confirmed, Kentucky Warblers are thought to be sporadic breeders in the deciduous woodland parks and wooded ravines of extreme southwestern Ontario. The lack of breeding evidence might be due to the fact that females are very shy and elusive, and during the breeding season they will often leave their nests before they are discovered. • Like waterthrushes and Ovenbirds, Kentucky Warblers have a habit of bobbing their tails up and down as they walk.

ID: bright yellow 'spectacles' and underparts; black crown, sideburns and half mask (duller on female); olive green upperparts.

Size: *L* 13 cm.

Status: very rare visitor from late April to July; exceptionally rare visitor from mid-August to late October.

Habitat: moist deciduous and mixed woodlands with dense shrubby cover and herbaceous plant growth, including wooded ravines, swamp edges and creek bottomlands.

Nesting: does not nest in Ontario.

Feeding: insects are gleaned while walking along the ground flipping over leaf litter or by snatching prey from the undersides of low foliage.

Voice: musical song is a series of 2-syllable notes: *chur-ree chur-ree* (similar to song of Carolina Wren); call is a sharp *chick*, *chuck* or *chip*.

Similar Species: *Canada Warbler* (p. 299): dark, streaky 'necklace'; bluish-grey upperparts. *Yellow-throated Warbler* (p. 279): bold white eyebrow, ear patch and wing bars; white belly and undertail coverts.

Best Sites: Point Pelee NP; Rondeau PP; Long Point area.

293

CONNECTICUT WARBLER

Oporornis agilis

Ontario's soggy, impenetrable sphagnum bogs and dry jack pine forests are favoured habitat for the mysterious and secretive Connecticut Warbler. Its elusive nature and primarily Canadian breeding distribution have made it one of the most sought after birds around. Ask Ontario birdwatchers about the Connecticut Warbler, and their responses will no doubt range from 'Never heard of it' to 'Good luck!' A trip to any of Ontario's northern bogs could reveal the boisterous songs of this ground-dwelling warbler, but pinpointing this bird's location may take patience and luck. • Difficulty in finding active Connecticut Warbler nests means that much of the bird's breeding biology remains unknown. • Like many other North American birds, the Connecticut Warbler was named for the place where it was first collected.

breeding

ID: bold white eye ring; yellow underparts; olive green upperparts; long undertail coverts make the tail look short; pink legs; longish bill. *Breeding male:* blue-grey hood. *Female and Immature:* grey-brown hood; light grey throat.

Size: *L* 13–15 cm.

Status: rare to uncommon and extremely elusive migrant and breeder from mid-May through September; a few may arrive as early as April.

Habitat: open pine forests and fairly open spruce bogs and tamarack fens with well-developed understorey growth.

Nesting: on the ground, on a hummock or in a low shrub; messy nest is made of leaves, weeds, grass, bark strips and moss; incubates 4 or 5 creamy white eggs, spotted with black, brown and/or lilac, for about 12 days.

Feeding: gleans caterpillars, beetles, spiders and other invertebrates from ground leaf litter; occasionally forages among low branches.

Voice: loud, clear, explosive *chipity-chipity-chipity chuck* or *per-chipity-chipity-chipity choo*; call is a brisk, metallic *cheep* or *peak*.

Similar Species: *Mourning Warbler* (p. 295): no eye ring or a thin, incomplete eye ring; shorter undertail coverts; male has a blackish breast patch; immature has a pale grey to yellow chin and throat. *Nashville Warbler* (p. 269): bright yellow throat; shorter, dark legs and bill.

Best Sites: Quetico PP; Lake of the Woods PP; Hwy 11 from Iroquois Falls to Smooth Rock Falls; Point Pelee NP; Sleeping Giant PP.

MOURNING WARBLER

Oporornis philadelphia

Although Mourning Warblers can be quite common in some locations, they are seen far less frequently than one might expect. These birds seldom leave the protection of their dense, shrubby, often impenetrable habitat, and they tend to sing only on their breeding territory. Riparian areas, regenerating cut-blocks and patches of forest that have been recently cleared by fire provide the low shrubs and sapling trees that this warbler relies on for nesting and foraging. Mourning Warblers are best seen during migration, when backyard shrubs and raspberry thickets may attract small, silent flocks. • This bird's dark hood reminded pioneering ornithologist Alexander Wilson of someone dressed in mourning. Some birders like to remember this bird's name by thinking that it is mourning the loss of its eye ring.

breeding

ID: yellow underparts; olive green upperparts; short tail; pinkish legs. *Breeding male:* usually no eye ring, but sometimes a broken eye ring; blue-grey hood; black upper breast patch. *Female:* grey hood; whitish chin and throat; may show a thin eye ring. *Immature:* grey-brown hood; pale grey to yellow chin and throat; thin, incomplete eye ring.
Size: L 13–14 cm.
Status: uncommon to common migrant from mid-May to early June and from late August to mid-September; uncommon to common breeder from May to August; a few may remain into October.
Habitat: dense and shrubby thickets, tangles and brambles, often in moist areas of forest clearings and along the edges of ponds, lakes and streams.
Nesting: on the ground, at the base of a shrub or plant tussock or in a small shrub; bulky nest is

made with leaves, weeds and grass and is lined with fur and fine grass; female incubates 3 or 4 brown spotted or blotched creamy white eggs for about 12 days.
Feeding: forages in dense low shrubs for caterpillars, beetles, spiders and other invertebrates.
Voice: husky, 2-part song is variable and lower at the end: *churry, churry, churry, churry, chorry, chorry*; call is a loud, low *check*.
Similar Species: *Connecticut Warbler* (p. 294): bold, complete eye ring; lacks the black breast patch; long undertail coverts make the tail look very short; immature has a light grey throat. *Nashville Warbler* (p. 269): bright yellow throat; dark legs.
Best Sites: Rondeau PP; Crane River Picnic Area; Halton Regional Forest; Halfway Lake PP; Lake Superior PP; Pukaskwa NP; Lake of the Woods PP.

COMMON YELLOWTHROAT

Geothlypis trichas

This energetic songster of Ontario's wetlands is a favourite among birders—its small size, bright plumage and spunky disposition quickly endear it to all who meet it. • Common Yellowthroats favour cattail marshes and wet, overgrown meadows, shunning the forest habitat preferred by most of their wood-warbler relatives. In May and June, male yellowthroats issue their distinctive *wichity-witchity-witchity* songs while perched atop tall cattails or shrubs. An extended look at a male in action will reveal the location of his favourite singing perches, which he visits in rotation. These strategic outposts mark the boundary of his territory, and they are fiercely guarded from the intrusions of other males. • Common Yellowthroat nests are commonly parasitized by Brown-headed Cowbirds.

ID: yellow throat, breast and undertail coverts; dingy white belly; olive green to olive brown upperparts; orangy legs. *Breeding male:* broad, black mask with a white upper border. *Female:* no mask; may show a faint white eye ring. *Immature:* duller overall.
Size: *L* 11–14 cm.
Status: very common migrant and breeder from May to September; a few may remain as late as January.
Habitat: cattail marshes, riparian willow and alder clumps, sedge wetlands, beaver ponds and wet overgrown meadows; sometimes on dry, abandoned fields.
Nesting: on or near the ground, often in a small shrub or among emergent aquatic vegetation;

female builds a bulky open cup nest of weeds, grass, sedges and other materials and lines it with hair and soft plant fibres; female incubates 3–5 brown- and black-spotted, creamy white eggs for 12 days.
Feeding: gleans vegetation and hovers for adult and larval insects, including dragonflies, spiders and beetles; occasionally eats seeds.
Voice: clear, oscillating *witchety witchety witchety-witch*; call is a sharp *tcheck* or *tchet*.
Similar Species: male's black mask is distinctive. *Kentucky Warbler* (p. 293): yellow 'spectacles'; all-yellow underparts; half mask. *Yellow Warbler* (p. 271): brighter yellow overall; yellow highlights in the wings; all-yellow underparts. *Wilson's Warbler* (p. 298): forehead, eyebrow and cheek are as bright as the all-yellow underparts; may show a dark cap. *Orange-crowned Warbler* (p. 268): dull yellow olive overall; faint breast streaks. *Nashville Warbler* (p. 269): bold, complete eye ring; blue-grey crown.
Best Sites: almost any cattail marsh throughout Ontario.

HOODED WARBLER

Wilsonia citrina

Hooded Warblers reach the northern limit of their range in southwestern Ontario, so they are rare in most parts of our province. Despite nesting low to the ground, they require extensive mature forests where fallen trees have opened gaps in the canopy, encouraging understorey growth. • Different species of wood-warblers can coexist in a limited environment because they partition their food supplies by foraging exclusively in certain areas. Hooded Warblers also partition among each other (intraspecies partitioning): males tend to forage in treetops, while the females forage near the ground. • Unlike their female counterparts, male Hooded Warblers may return to the same nesting territory year after year. Once the young have left the nest, each parent takes on guardianship of half the fledged young.

ID: bright yellow underparts; olive green upperparts; white undertail; pinkish legs. *Male:* black hood; bright yellow face. *Female:* yellow face and olive crown; may show faint traces of a black hood.
Size: *L* 14 cm.
Status: rare and local migrant and breeder from April to September; a few may remain into November.
Habitat: clearings with dense, low shrubs in mature, upland, deciduous and mixed forests; occasionally in moist ravines or mature white pine plantations with a dense understorey of deciduous shrubs.
Nesting: low in a deciduous shrub; mostly the female builds an open cup nest of fine grass, bark strips, dead leaves, animal hair,

spider webs and plant down; female incubates 4 creamy white eggs, with brown spots toward the larger end, for about 12 days.
Feeding: gleans insects and other forest invertebrates while hopping on the ground or from shrub branches; may scramble up tree-trunks or flycatch.
Voice: clear, whistling song is some variation of *whitta-witta-wit-tee-yo*; call note is a metallic *tink*, *chink* or *chip*.
Similar Species: *Wilson's Warbler* (p. 298), *Yellow Warbler* (p. 271) and *Common Yellowthroat* (p. 296): females lack the white undertail feathers. *Kentucky Warbler* (p. 293): yellow 'spectacles'; dark, triangular half mask.
Best Sites: Wardsville, Orwell and Long Point area woodlots; Point Pelee NP; Rondeau PP.

WILSON'S WARBLER

Wilsonia pusilla

You are almost sure to catch sight of the energetic Wilson's Warbler at any of Ontario's migration hotspots. This lively bird flickers quickly through tangles of leaves and trees, darting frequently into the air to catch flying insects. Birders often become exhausted while pursuing a Wilson's Warbler, but the bird itself never seems to tire during its lightning-fast performances. • This bird may make brief stop-overs in the shrubs of almost any backyard during spring or fall migration, but its nesting habitat is mostly restricted to northern parts of the province, where it settles near bogs and shrub-lined beaver ponds. • The Wilson's Warbler is richly deserving of its name. Named after Alexander Wilson, this species epitomizes the energetic devotion that that pioneering ornithologist exhibited in the study of North American birds.

ID: yellow underparts; yellow-green upper-parts; beady, black eyes; black bill; orange legs. *Male:* black cap. *Female:* cap is very faint or absent.

Size: *L* 11–13 cm.

Status: common migrant from early May to mid-June and from mid-August to late September; fairly common breeder from May to August; a few may remain into November.

Habitat: riparian woodlands, willow and alder thickets, bogs and wet, shrubby meadows.

Nesting: on the ground in moss or at the base of a shrub; female builds a nest of moss, grass and leaves and lines it with animal hair and fine grass; female incubates 4–6 brown-marked, creamy white eggs for 10–13 days.

Feeding: hovers, flycatches and gleans vegetation for insects.

Voice: song is a rapid chatter that drops in pitch at the end: *chi chi chi chi chet chet*; call is a flat, low *chet* or *chuck*.

Similar Species: male's black cap is distinctive. *Yellow Warbler* (p. 271): male has red breast streaks; brighter yellow upperparts. *Common Yellowthroat* (p. 296): female has a darker face. *Kentucky Warbler* (p. 293): yellow 'spectacles'; dark, angular half mask. *Orange-crowned Warbler* (p. 268): dull yellow olive overall; faint breast streaks. *Nashville Warbler* (p. 269): bold, complete eye ring; blue-grey crown.

Best Sites: Sudbury area; Hurkett Cove Conservation Area; Pukaskwa NP; Greenwater PP; Moosonee area; Point Pelee NP; Rondeau PP; Sleeping Giant PP.

CANADA WARBLER

Wilsonia canadensis

Male Canada Warblers, with their bold white eye rings, have a wide-eyed, alert appearance. They are fairly inquisitive birds, and they occasionally pop up from dense shrubs in response to passing hikers. • Canada Warblers live in open defiance of winter: they never stay in one place long enough to experience one! As the summer nesting season in Canada comes to a close, these warblers migrate to South America. • Although there are several wood-warblers that breed exclusively in Canada, the Canada Warbler isn't one of them. Most Canada Warblers nest in eastern Canada, but some can be found nesting in the U.S.

ID: yellow 'spectacles'; yellow underparts (except the white undertail coverts); blue-grey upperparts; pale legs. *Male:* streaky black 'necklace'; dark, angular half mask. *Female:* blue-green back; faint necklace.
Size: *L* 13–14 cm.
Status: fairly common to common migrant from early May to early June and from mid-August to late September; uncommon to fairly common breeder from May to August.
Habitat: wet, low-lying areas of mixed forests with a dense understorey, especially riparian willow-alder thickets; also cedar woodlands and swamps.
Nesting: on a mossy hummock or upturned root or stump; female builds a loose, bulky cup nest of leaves, grass, ferns, weeds and bark and lines it with animal hair and soft plant fibres; 4 brown-spotted,

creamy white eggs are incubated for about 10–14 days.
Feeding: gleans the ground and vegetation for beetles, flies, hairless caterpillars, mosquitoes and other insects; occasionally hovers.
Voice: song begins with one or more sharp *chip* note and continues with a rich, variable warble; call is a loud, quick *chick* or *chip*.
Similar Species: *Kentucky Warbler* (p. 293): lacks the black 'necklace'; yellow undertail coverts; greenish upperparts; half eye ring. *Northern Parula* (p. 270): white wing bars; broken, white eye ring; white belly. *Kirtland's Warbler* (p. 360): black streaking on the sides and flanks; broken, white eye ring; dark streaking on the back.
Best Sites: Rondeau PP; Halton Regional Forest; Lake Superior PP; Pukaskwa NP; Point Pelee NP; Long Point PP.

YELLOW-BREASTED CHAT

Icteria virens

At nearly 20 cm long, this unique bird is almost a warbler-and-a-half. It behaves like a typical wood-warbler, with a curiosity and flitting habits that seem misplaced in so large a bird. Its curious vocalizations and noisy thrashing behaviour, however, suggest a closer relationship to the mimic thrushes, such as the Gray Catbird and Northern Mockingbird. Chats typically thrash about in dense undergrowth, and they rarely hold back their strange vocalizations, often drawing attention to themselves. • Pelee Island, Point Pelee National Park and Rondeau Provincial Park are great places to meet this bird, especially during the last few weeks of May.

ID: white 'spectacles'; white jaw line; heavy, black bill; yellow breast; white undertail coverts; olive green upperparts; long tail; grey-black legs. *Male:* black lores. *Female:* grey lores.

Size: *L* 19 cm.

Status: rare to very locally uncommon migrant and breeder from May to September.

Habitat: riparian thickets, brambles and shrubby tangles.

Nesting: low in a shrub or deciduous sapling; well-concealed, bulky base of leaves and weeds holds an inner woven

cup nest made of vine bark; nest is lined with fine grass and plant fibres; female incubates 3 or 4 creamy white eggs, with brown spots toward the large end, for about 11 days.

Feeding: gleans insects from low vegetation; eats many berries in fall.

Voice: song is an assorted series of whistles, 'laughs,' squeaks, grunts, rattles and mews; calls include a *whoit*, *chack* and *kook*.

Similar Species: none.

Best Sites: Fish Point PP Reserve; Point Pelee NP; Rondeau PP; Walpole Island; Komoka Swamp; Prince Edward Point NWA.

SUMMER TANAGER

Piranga rubra

The northern limits of the Summer Tanager's breeding range lie south of our province, but each year small numbers make their way here, dazzling Ontario birders. Over 75 percent of all Summer Tanager sightings in Ontario have been recorded in the extreme southwestern corner of the province, but birders elsewhere in Ontario are occasionally blessed by a brief appearance—Summer Tanagers have been sighted as far north as Ottawa, Manitoulin Island and both Ouimet Canyon and Neys provincial parks. • It is possible that the Summer Tanager is an occasional breeder in Ontario, and some ornithologists think it is only a matter of time before some lucky birder stumbles across an active nest • Summer Tanagers thrive on a wide variety of insects, but they are best known for their courageous attacks on wasps. In the U.S., these birds snatch flying wasps from menacing swarms, and they are also known to raid wasp nests in search of larvae.

ID: *Male:* rose red overall; pale bill; immature male has patchy red and greenish plumage. *Female:* greyish- to greenish-yellow upperparts; dusky yellow underparts; may have an orange or reddish wash overall.
Size: *L* 18–19 cm.
Status: very rare visitor from late April to May and from September to late November; occasional visitor from June to August; may be an exceptionally rare, occasional breeder.
Habitat: pine woodlands, open mixed woodlands, especially those with oak or hickory, or riparian woodlands with cottonwoods.
Nesting: nesting in Ontario is not confirmed.
Feeding: eats mainly insects; also eats berries and small fruits; gleans insects from the tree canopy; may

hover-glean or hawk insects in mid-air; known to raid wasp nests.
Voice: song is a series of 3–5 sweet, clear whistled phrases, like a faster version of the American Robin's song; call is *pit* or *pit-a-tuck.*
Similar Species: *Scarlet Tanager* (p. 302): smaller bill; male has a black tail and black wings; female has darker wings, brighter underparts and uniformly olive upperparts. *Northern Cardinal* (p. 325): red bill; prominent head crest; male has a black mask and bib. *Western Tanager* (p. 360): wings bars. *Orchard Oriole* (p. 339) and *Baltimore Oriole* (p. 340): females have sharper bills and wing bars.
Best Sites: Pelee Island; Point Pelee NP; Rondeau PP; Long Point PP.

POSSIBLE BREEDER

301

SCARLET TANAGER

Piranga olivacea

Each spring, birders eagerly await the sweet, rough-edged song of the lovely Scarlet Tanager. The return of the brilliant red male is always a much-anticipated event in wooded ravines and at traditional migrant stop-over sites. • During the cold and rainy weather that often dampens spring migration, you may find yourself in the envious position of observing a Scarlet Tanager at eye level—the forest understorey often supports the foraging efforts of this bird during inclement weather. At other times, however, this bird can be surprisingly difficult to spot as it darts among forest canopies in pursuit of insect prey. • The Scarlet Tanager is the only member of the tanager clan that routinely nests in Ontario. In Central and South America there are over 200 tanager species representing every colour of the rainbow.

♂

breeding

ID: *Breeding male:* bright red overall; pure black wings and tail; pale bill. *Fall male:* patchy red and green-yellow plumage; black wings and tail. *Non-breeding male:* bright yellow underparts; olive upperparts; black wings and tail. *Female:* uniformly olive upperparts; yellow underparts; greyish-brown wings.
Size: *L* 16.5–19 cm.
Status: uncommon to fairly common migrant from early May to early June and from mid-August to September; fairly common breeder from May to August.
Habitat: fairly mature, upland deciduous and mixed forests.
Nesting: high in a tree branch (usually deciduous) well away from the trunk; female builds a flimsy, shallow cup nest of grass, weeds and twigs and lines it with rootlets and fine grass; female incubates 2–5 pale blue-green eggs, with reddish-brown to brown spots, for 12–14 days.

Feeding: gleans insects from the forest canopy; may hover-glean or hawk insects in mid-air; may forage at lower levels during cold weather; also takes some seasonally available berries.
Voice: song is a series of 4–5 sweet, clear, whistled phrase, like a blurred version of the American Robin's song; call is a *chip-burrr* or *chip-churrr*.
Similar Species: *Summer Tanager* (p. 301): larger bill; male has a red tail and red wings; female has paler wings and is duskier overall, often with an orange or reddish tinge. *Northern Cardinal* (p. 325): red bill, wings and tail; prominent head crest; male has a black mask and bib. *Western Tanager* (p. 360): wings bars. *Orchard Oriole* (p. 339) and *Baltimore Oriole* (p. 340): females have sharper bills and wing bars.
Best Sites: Rondeau PP; Halton Regional Forest; Frontenac PP; Algonquin PP; Killarney PP; Presqu'ile PP.

EASTERN TOWHEE

Pipilo erythrophthalmus

Eastern Towhees are often heard before they are seen. These noisy foragers rustle about in dense undergrowth, craftily scraping back layers of dry leaves to expose the seeds, berries or insects hidden beneath. • Although you wouldn't guess it, this colourful bird is a member of the American Sparrow family—a group that is usually drab in colour. • The Eastern Towhee and its western relative, the Spotted Towee, were once grouped together as a single species known as the Rufous-sided Towhee. • 'Squeaking' and 'pishing' are irresistible for towhees, who will quickly pop out from cover to investigate the curious noise. • The scientific name *Pipilo* is derived from the Latin *pipo*, meaning 'to chirp', or 'to peep'; *erythrophthalmus* is derived from Greek words that mean 'red eye.'

ID: rufous sides and flanks; white outer tail corners; white lower breast and belly; buff undertail coverts; red eyes; dark bill. *Male:* black hood and upperparts. *Female:* brown hood and upperparts.

Size: *L* 18–21 cm.

Status: uncommon migrant and breeder from late March to mid-November; a few may be present in winter.

Habitat: often along woodland edge and in shrubby, abandoned fields.

Nesting: on the ground or low in a dense shrub; female builds a camouflaged cup nest of twigs, bark strips, grass, weeds, rootlets and animal hair; mostly the female

incubates 3 or 4 creamy white to pale grey eggs, with brown spots toward the larger end, for 12 to 13 days.

Feeding: scratches at leaf litter for insects, seeds and berries; sometimes forages in low shrubs and saplings.

Voice: song is 2 high, whistled notes followed by a trill: *drink your teeeee;* call is a scratchy, slurred *cheweee!* or *chewink!*

Similar Species: *Dark-eyed Junco* (p. 321): much smaller; pale bill; black eyes; white outer tail feathers.

Best Sites: Ojibway Prairie; The Pinery PP; Rouge River PP; Lynde Shores Conservation Area; Charleston Lake PP; Bon Echo PP; Georgian Bay Islands NP.

AMERICAN TREE SPARROW

Spizella arborea

Most of us know these rufous-capped, spot-breasted sparrows as winter visitors to backyard feeders, but few of us realize that American Tree Sparrows also spend their summers here. They typically nest among patches of shrubs along the far northern coast and the subarctic treeline, so the best time to watch for them is in late March and April when they are in migration. As the small flocks migrate north, they offer bubbly, bright songs between bouts of foraging along the ground or in low, budding shrubs. • Although its name suggests a close relationship with trees or forests, it is actually a bird of treeless fields and semi-open, shrubby habitats. Perhaps a more appropriate name for this bird would be 'Subarctic Shrub Sparrow.'

ID: grey, unstreaked underparts; dark, central breast spot; pale rufous cap; rufous stripe behind the eye; grey face; mottled brown upperparts; notched tail; 2 white wing bars; dark legs; dark upper mandible; yellow lower mandible. *Non-breeding:* grey central crown stripe. *Juvenile:* streaky breast and head.

Size: *L* 15–16 cm.

Status: common migrant from mid-March to early May and from late October to late November; fairly common to common resident from November to April; fairly common to abundant breeder from May to October.

Habitat: *Breeding:* treeline and coastal shrubby areas of willow, alder and dwarf birch. *Winter* and *In migration:* brushy thickets, roadside shrubs, semi-open fields and agricultural croplands.

Nesting: usually on the ground, on a raised tussock or in a shrub; female builds an open cup nest of grass, moss, bark shreds and twigs and lines it with feathers and fine

grass; female incubates 4–6 pale greenish or bluish eggs, with brown spots toward the larger end, for 11–13 days.

Feeding: scratches exposed soil or snow for seeds in winter; eats mostly insects in summer; takes some berries and occasionally visits birdfeeders.

Voice: high, whistled *tseet-tseet* is followed by a short, sweet, musical series of slurred whistles; song may be given in late winter and during spring migration; call is a 3-note *tsee-dle-eat.*

Similar Species: *Chipping Sparrow* (p. 305): clear black eye line; white eyebrow; lacks the dark breast spot. *Swamp Sparrow* (p. 317): lacks the dark breast spot and the white wing bars; white throat. *Field Sparrow* (p. 307): white eye ring; orange-pink bill; lacks the dark breast spot.

Best Sites: almost any field or scrubby edge habitat throughout Ontario in winter; Polar Bear PP in summer.

CHIPPING SPARROW

Spizella passerina

The Chipping Sparrow and Dark-eyed Junco do not share the same tailor, but they must have attended the same voice lessons, because their songs are very similar. The rapid trill of the Chipping Sparrow is slightly faster, drier and less musical, and even experienced birders can have difficulty identifying this singer. • Chipping Sparrows commonly nest at eye level, so you can easily watch their breeding and nest-building rituals closeup. They are well known for their preference for conifers as a nesting site and hair as a lining material for the nest. By planting conifers in your backyard and offering samples of your pet's hair—or even your own—in backyard baskets in spring, you could attract nesting Chipping Sparrows to your area and contribute to their nesting success. • 'Chipping' refers to this bird's call; *passerina* is Latin for 'little sparrow.'

breeding

ID: *Breeding:* prominent rufous cap; white eyebrow; black eye line; light grey, unstreaked underparts; mottled brown upperparts; all-dark bill; 2 faint wing bars; pale legs. *Non-breeding:* paler crown with dark streaks; brown eyebrow and cheek; pale lower mandible. *Juvenile:* brown-grey overall with dark brown streaking; pale lower mandible.
Size: *L* 13–15 cm.
Status: uncommon to abundant migrant and breeder from early April to early November; a few may be present in winter.
Habitat: open conifers or mixed woodland edges; often in yards and gardens with tree and shrub borders.
Nesting: usually at mid-level in a coniferous tree; female builds a compact cup nest of woven grass and rootlets, which is often lined with hair; female incubates 4 pale blue eggs for 11–12 days.

Feeding: gleans seeds while hopping along the ground and on outer tree or shrub branches; prefers seeds from grass, dandelions and clovers; also eats adult and larval invertebrates; occasionally visits feeding stations.
Voice: rapid, dry trill of *chip* notes; call is a high-pitched *chip*.
Similar Species: *American Tree Sparrow* (p. 304): dark, central breast spot; lacks the bold white eyebrow; rufous stripe extends behind the eye. *Swamp Sparrow* (p. 317): lacks the white eyebrow, black eye line and white wing bars. *Field Sparrow* (p. 307): lacks the bold white eyebrow; rufous stripe extends behind the eye; white eye ring; grey throat; orange-pink bill.
Best Sites: almost any open woodland or open field bordered by trees and shrubs.

CLAY-COLORED SPARROW

Spizella pallida

For the most part, Clay-colored Sparrows go completely unnoticed, because their plumage, habit and voice all contribute to a cryptic lifestyle. Even when males are singing at the top of their 'air sacs,' they are usually mistaken for buzzing insects. Their tenuous numbers and widespread distribution in Ontario doesn't help either, but keen birders have little trouble finding these sparrows or recognizing them whenever they are present in suitable habitat. • Although subtle in plumage, the Clay-colored Sparrow still possesses an unassuming beauty. Birders looking closely at this sparrow to confirm its identity can easily appreciate its delicate shading, texture and form so often overlooked in birds with more colourful plumage. • These sparrows have adapted to a variety of habitats throughout Ontario. In the Kingston area, they are typically found in young red cedar stands; near Ottawa, they inhabit shrubby, open bogs and willow scrub habitat.

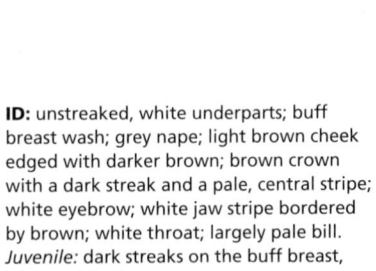

breeding

ID: unstreaked, white underparts; buff breast wash; grey nape; light brown cheek edged with darker brown; brown crown with a dark streak and a pale, central stripe; white eyebrow; white jaw stripe bordered by brown; white throat; largely pale bill. *Juvenile:* dark streaks on the buff breast, sides and flanks.
Size: *L* 13–14 cm.
Status: rare and local migrant and breeder from May to October.
Habitat: brushy open areas along forest and woodland edges; in forest openings, regenerating burn sites, abandoned fields and riparian thickets.
Nesting: in a grassy tuft or small shrub; female builds an open cup

nest of twigs, grass, weeds and rootlets and lines it with rootlets, fine grass and fur; mostly the female incubates 4 bluish-green eggs, speckled with brown, for 10–12 days.
Feeding: forages for seeds and insects on the ground and in low vegetation.
Voice: song is a series of 2–5 slow, low-pitched, insect-like buzzes; call is a soft *chip*.
Similar Species: *Chipping Sparrow* (p. 305): breeding adult has a prominent rufous cap, grey cheek and underparts, 2 faint white wing bars; all-dark bill; juvenile lacks the buff sides, flanks and grey nape.
Best Sites: Puslinch Wetland; Mosport to Myrtle Station; Macauley Mountain Conservation Area; Ottawa-area fields; Vermilion Bay to Red Lake; Rainy River area.

FIELD SPARROW

Spizella pusilla

This pink-billed sparrow is a denizen of overgrown fields, pastures and forest clearings. Deserted farmland may seem 'unproductive' to some people, but for Ontario's Field Sparrows it is heaven. For nesting purposes, the usual pastures they inhabit must be scattered with shrubs, herbaceous plants and plenty of tall grass. • Unlike most songbirds, a nestling Field Sparrow will apparently leave its nest prematurely if disturbed. • Over time the Field Sparrow has learned to recognize when its nest has been parasitized by the Brown-headed Cowbird. Because the unwelcome eggs are usually too large for this small sparrow to eject, the nest is simply abandoned. This sparrow may be so stubborn in refusing to raise young cowbirds that affected pairs may make numerous nesting attempts in a single season. • Some Field Sparrows remain in southern Ontario over winter, where they can be detected in small foraging groups or among larger flocks of American Tree Sparrows.

ID: orange-pink bill; grey face and throat; rusty crown with a grey central stripe; rusty streak behind the eye; white eye ring; 2 white wing bars; unstreaked grey underparts with buffy-red wash on the breast, sides and flanks; pinkish legs. *Immature:* duller version of the adult, with a streaked breast and faint buff-white wing bars.
Size: *L* 13–15 cm.
Status: uncommon to common migrant and breeder from April to October; rare to uncommon winter visitor from October to April; a few may be transient residents.
Habitat: abandoned or weedy and overgrown fields and pastures, woodland edges and clearings, extensive shrubby riparian areas and young conifer plantations.
Nesting: on or near the ground, often sheltered by a grass clump, shrub or sapling; female weaves

an open cup nest of grass and lines it with animal hair and soft plant material; female incubates 3–5 brown-spotted, whitish to pale bluish-white eggs for 10–12 days.
Feeding: forages on the ground; mostly insects taken in summer; mostly seeds taken in winter.
Voice: song is a series of clear whistles accelerating into a trill; call is a *chip* or *tsee*.
Similar Species: *American Tree Sparrow* (p. 304): dark central breast spot; lacks the white eye ring; dark upper mandible. *Swamp Sparrow* (p. 317): lacks the 2 white wing bars and the white eye ring; white throat; dark upper mandible. *Chipping Sparrow* (p. 305): all-dark bill; white eyebrow; black eye line; lacks the buffy-red wash on the underparts.
Best Sites: almost any overgrown or abandoned field or open area south of the Canadian Shield.

VESPER SPARROW

Pooecetes gramineus

For birders who live near Ontario's grassy fields and agricultural lands with multitudes of confusing little brown sparrows, the Vesper Sparrow offers a welcome relief—white outer tail feathers and a chestnut shoulder patch announce its identity while it's perched or in flight. The Vesper Sparrow is also known for its bold and easily distinguished song, which begins with two sets of unforgettable, double notes: *here-here! there-there!* • When the business of nesting begins, Vesper Sparrows scour the neighbourhood for a potential nesting site. More often than not, the nest ends up nestled in a grassy hollow at the base of a clump of weeds or small shrub. This setup provides camouflage, functions as a windbreak and acts as an umbrella to protect the young. • 'Vesper' is Latin for 'evening,' a time when this bird often sings; *Pooecetes* is Greek for 'grass dweller.'

ID: chestnut shoulder patch; white outer tail feathers; pale yellow lores; weak flank streaking; white eye ring; dark upper mandible; lighter lower mandible; light-coloured legs.
Size: *L* 15–17 cm.
Status: uncommon to fairly common migrant and breeder from April to November; a few may be present in winter.
Habitat: open fields bordered or interspersed with shrubs, semi-open shrublands and grasslands; also in agricultural areas, open, dry conifer plantations and scrubby gravel pits.
Nesting: in a scrape on the ground, often under a canopy of grass or at the base of a shrub; loosely woven, grass cup nest is lined with rootlets, fine grass and hair; mostly the female incubates 3–5 brown- and grey-blotched, whitish to greenish-white eggs for 11–13 days.
Feeding: walks and runs along the ground, picking up grasshoppers, beetles, cutworms, other invertebrates and seeds.
Voice: 4 characteristic, preliminary notes, with the second higher in pitch, followed by a bubbly trill: *here-here there-there, everybody-down-the-hill.*
Similar Species: *Other sparrows*: lack the white outer tail feathers and the chestnut shoulder patch. *Lark Sparrow* (p. 360): juvenile has streaking on the breast and lacks the chestnut shoulder patch. *American Pipit* (p. 262): thinner bill; greyer upperparts lack the brown streaking; lacks the chestnut shoulder patch. *Lapland Longspur* (p. 322): broad, pale eyebrow and reddish edgings to the wing feathers in non-breeding plumage; blackish or buff wash on the upper breast.
Best Sites: shrubby fields and fence-line margins in agricultural areas throughout southern Ontario; Ojibway Prairie; Long Point PP.

SAVANNAH SPARROW

Passerculus sandwichensis

The Savannah Sparrow is one of our province's most common open-country birds. At one time or another, most Ontarians have probably seen or heard one, although they may not have been aware of it—this bird's streaky, dull brown, buff and white plumage resembles so many of the other grassland sparrows that it is easily overlooked. • From early spring to early summer, males belt out their distinctive, buzzy tunes while perched atop a prominent shrub, tall weed or strategic fencepost. Later in summer and throughout early fall, they are most often seen darting across roads, highways and open fields in search of food. Like most sparrows, however, Savannahs generally stay out of sight. When danger appears, they take flight only as a last resort—they prefer to run swiftly and inconspicuously through the grass, like feathered voles. • The common and scientific names of this bird reflect its broad North American distribution: 'Savannah' refers to the city in Georgia; *sandwichensis* is derived from Sandwich Bay in the Aleutians off Alaska.

ID: finely streaked breast, sides and flanks; light-coloured, streaked underparts; mottled brown upperparts; yellow lores; light jaw line; light-coloured legs and bill; may show a dark breast spot.
Size: *L* 11–16 cm.
Status: common to abundant migrant and breeder from April to October; a few may be present in winter.
Habitat: agricultural fields (especially hay and alfalfa), moist sedge and grass meadows, pastures, beaches, bogs and fens.
Nesting: on the ground; in a shallow scrape well concealed by grass or a shrub; female builds an open cup nest that is woven and lined with grass; female incubates

3–6 whitish to greenish or pale tan eggs, marked with brown, for 10–13 days.
Feeding: walks or runs on the ground to glean insects and seeds; occasionally scratches.
Voice: song is a high-pitched, clear, buzzy *tea tea tea teeeeea today*; call is a high, thin *tsit*.
Similar Species: *Vesper Sparrow* (p. 308): white outer tail feathers; chestnut shoulder patches. *Lincoln's Sparrow* (p. 316): buff jaw line; buff wash across the breast; broad, grey eyebrow. *Grasshopper Sparrow* (p. 310): unstreaked breast. *Song Sparrow* (p. 315): lacks the yellow lores; triangular 'moustache' stripes; pale central crown stripe; rounded tail.
Best Sites: almost any open meadow or field throughout Ontario.

GRASSHOPPER SPARROW

Ammodramus savannarum

The Grasshopper Sparrow is named not for its diet but rather for its buzzy, insect-like song. During courtship flights, males chase females through the air, buzzing at a frequency that is usually inaudible to our ears. The males sing two completely different courtship songs: one ends in a short trill and the other is a prolonged series of high trills that change in pitch and speed. • The Grasshopper Sparrow is an open-country bird that prefers grassy expanses free of trees and shrubs. Wide, well-drained, grassy ditches in southern Ontario occasionally attract nesting Grasshopper Sparrows, so mowing or harvesting these grassy margins early in the nesting season may be detrimental to these birds. Convincing local landowners and the provincial government to delay cutting until mid-August or September would benefit the Grasshopper Sparrow. • *Ammodramus* is Greek for 'sand runner,' and *savannarum* is Latin for 'of the savanna.'

ID: unstreaked, white underparts with a buff wash on the breast, sides and flanks; flattened head profile; dark crown with a pale central stripe; buff cheek; mottled brown upperparts; beady, black eyes; sharp tail; pale legs; may show a small yellow patch on the edge of the forewing. *Immature:* less buff on the underparts; faint streaking across the breast.
Size: *L* 11–13 cm.
Status: elusive; rare to uncommon migrant and breeder from April to October.
Habitat: grasslands and grassy fields with little or no shrub or tree cover.
Nesting: in a shallow depression on the ground, usually concealed by grass; small cup nest is woven with grass and lined with rootlets, fine grass and hair; female incubates 4 or 5 creamy white eggs, spotted with grey and reddish brown, for 11–13 days.

Feeding: gleans insects and seeds from the ground and grass; eats many insects, including grasshoppers.
Voice: song is a high, faint, buzzy trill preceded by 1–3 high, thin, whistled notes: *tea-tea-tea zeeeeeeeeee.*
Similar Species: *Le Conte's Sparrow* (p. 312): buff- and black-striped head with a white central stripe on the crown; grey cheek; dark streaking on the sides and flanks. *Nelson's Sharp-tailed Sparrow* (p. 313): orange-buff face and breast; grey central crown stripe; grey cheek and shoulders. *Henslow's Sparrow* (p. 311): like the immature Grasshopper, but has darker breast streaking, rusty wings and small, dark ear and 'whisker' marks.
Best Sites: Puslinch Wetland; Durham County; Carden Plain; Prince Edward County; Wye Marsh Wildlife Centre; Point Pelee NP; Rondeau PP.

HENSLOW'S SPARROW

Ammodramus henslowii

It's difficult to predict when you'll see the next Henslow's Sparrow in Ontario—this bird makes irregular visits here, often appearing one year but not the next. Some males have been known to occupy a field for a few weeks before suddenly disappearing, probably owing to the lack of a potential mate. The Henslow's unpredictability has made it a difficult species to study, so there's much more to learn about its habitat requirements and the reasons for its recent, widespread decline. • Watch the male Henslow's Sparrow as he throws back his streaky, greenish head while hurling a distinctive song from atop a tall blade of grass. Without the male's lyrical advertisements, the Henslow's Sparrow would almost be impossible to observe—this bird spends most of its time foraging alone along the ground. When disturbed, it may fly a short distance before dropping into cover, but usually it prefers to run through dense, concealing vegetation. • Henslow's Sparrows are known for their unusual habit of singing at night.

ID: flattened head profile; olive green face, central crown stripe and nape; dark crown and whisker stripes; rusty tinge on the back, wings and tail; white underparts with dark streaking on the buff breast, sides and flanks; thick bill; deeply notched, sharp-edged tail. *Juvenile:* buff wash on most of the underparts; faint streaking only on the sides.
Size: *L* 12–13 cm.
Status: very rare migrant and possible breeder from April to October.
Habitat: large, fallow or wild grassy fields and meadows with a matted ground layer of dead vegetation and scattered shrub or herb perches; often in moist grassy areas.
Nesting: on the ground at the base of a grass clump or herbaceous plant; mostly the female builds an open cup nest of grass and weeds

and lines it with fine grass and hair; female incubates 3–5 whitish to pale greenish-white eggs, spotted with grey and reddish brown, for about 11 days.
Feeding: gleans insects and seeds from the ground.
Voice: weak, liquidly, cricket-like *tse-lick* song is distinctive, often given during periods of rain or at night.
Similar Species: *Other sparrows:* lack the greenish face, central crown strip and nape. *Grasshopper Sparrow* (p. 310): lacks the dark whisker stripe and the prominent streaking on the breast and sides. *Savannah Sparrow* (p. 309): lacks the buff breast. *Le Conte's Sparrow* (p. 312): buff- and black-striped head with a white central stripe; grey cheek.
Best Sites: Point Pelee NP; southern Prince Edward County.

LE CONTE'S SPARROW

Ammodramus leconteii

Le Conte's Sparrows are most common in the remote landscape of the Hudson Bay Lowland and northern subarctic coast, but they are occasionally found among damp, undisturbed meadows or at the edges of marshlands in southern Ontario. Le Conte's are secretive birds that are usually difficult to observe—even singing males typically choose low, concealing perches from which to offer their weak love ballads. Some skilled birders, however, may follow the buzzy tune to its source to catch a fleeting glimpse of the singer before he dives into tall vegetation and disappears from view. • Before it was converted to agricultural cropland, Holland Marsh in southern Ontario supported a small colony of Le Conte's Sparrows. • This bird's namesake, John Le Conte, is best remembered as one of the pre-eminent American entomologists of the 19th century, but he was interested in all areas of natural history.

ID: buff-orange face; grey cheek; black line behind the eye; light central crown stripe bordered by black stripes; buff-orange upper breast, sides and flanks; dark streaking on the sides and flanks; white throat, lower breast and belly; mottled brown-black upperparts; buff streaks on the back; pale legs. *Juvenile:* duller overall; more streaking on the breast.
Size: *L* 11–13 cm.
Status: very rare to rare migrant and breeder from late April to October.
Habitat: grassy meadows with dense vegetation, drier edges of wet sedge and grass meadows, willow and alder flats and forest openings.
Nesting: on or near the ground, concealed by tangled vegetation; open cup nest, woven with grass and rushes, is tied to standing plant stems and lined with fine grass and hair; female incubates 3–5 grey- and brown-spotted, greyish-white eggs for 12–13 days.
Feeding: gleans the ground and low vegetation for insects, spiders and seeds.
Voice: song is a weak, short, raspy, insect-like buzz: *t-t-t-zeeee zee* or *take-it ea-zeee*; alarm call is a high-pitched whistle.
Similar Species: *Nelson's Sharp-tailed Sparrow* (p. 313): grey central crown stripe and nape; white streaks on the dark back. *Grasshopper Sparrow* (p. 310): lacks the buff-orange face and the streaking on the underparts.
Best Sites: Luther Marsh area; Mission Island Marsh; Rainy River area; Moosonee area; Point Pelee NP; Sleeping Giant PP.

NELSON'S SHARP-TAILED SPARROW

Ammodramus nelsoni

Your timing will have to be perfect if you're hoping to see the Nelson's Sharp-tailed Sparrow as it migrates through our province. Among the marshlands of southern Ontario, a canoe or a floating blind may be essential in your quest to find this small sparrow as it rests among dense, concealing stands of cattails and bulrushes. • This sparrow's buzzy song is probably rarely heard in Ontario, because it breeds among the remote coastal sedge marshes of Hudson and James bays. In the Lake of the Woods corner of Ontario, a smaller, disjunct population of Nelson's Sharp-tailed Sparrows engages in a similar nesting ritual along the aspen-lined shores of lakes and wetlands. • Nelson's Sharp-tailed Sparrows have a very unusual breeding strategy among songbirds: the males rove around the marsh mating with all the available females, which are also promiscuous, and this sparrow does not establish pair bonds or territories. • Edward William Nelson was the chief of the U.S. Biological Survey and president of the American Ornithologists' Union. His greatest contribution was the creation of the Migratory Bird Treaty, which is still in effect today.

ID: buff-orange face, breast, sides and flanks; grey cheek, central crown stripe and nape; dark line behind the eye; light streaking on the sides and flanks; white stripes on a dark back; white to light buff throat; white belly.
Size: *L* 13–15 cm.
Status: rare migrant from late April through May and from late September to mid-November; uncommon to locally common breeder from June to September.
Habitat: *Breeding:* coastal sedge marshes; very local in wet meadows and along the edges of marshes and lakes. *In migration:* marshlands with tall emergent vegetation and shoreline vegetation.
Nesting: on the ground or low in upright grass or sedge stems; bulky cup nest is woven with dry grass and sedges and lined with fine grass; female incubates 3–5 pale blue-green to greenish-white eggs, heavily dotted with reddish brown, for 11–12 days.
Feeding: gleans ants, beetles, grasshoppers and other invertebrates from the ground and low vegetation; also eats seeds.
Voice: song is a short, raspy buzz: *ts tse-sheeeee*.
Similar Species: *Le Conte's Sparrow* (p. 312): lacks the grey nape and the white stripes on the dark back. *Grasshopper Sparrow* (p. 310): lacks the streaking on the underparts. *Savannah Sparrow* (p. 309): notched tail; heavily streaked underparts.
Best Sites: Lake of the Woods; Moosonee area; Dundas Marsh; Lynde Shores Conservation Area; Darlington PP; Presqu'ile PP.

FOX SPARROW

Passerella iliaca

Like the Eastern Towhee, the Fox Sparrow eagerly scratches out a living, using both feet to stir up leaves and scrape organic matter along the forest floor. This sparrow's preference for impenetrable, brushy habitat makes it a difficult species to observe, even though its noisy foraging habits often reveal its whereabouts. Its loud, whistled courtship songs are as easily recognized, and to the attentive listener they can often be as moving as a loon's wail or a wolf's howl. • Unlike other songbirds, which may filter through the province in a series of lingering waves, Fox Sparrows generally appear in southern Ontario for only a few short weeks before moving on to their nesting grounds in northern parts of the province. • The overall reddish-brown appearance of this bird inspired taxonomists to name it after the Red Fox.

ID: whitish underparts; heavy reddish-brown spotting and streaking often converges into a central breast spot; reddish-brown wings, rump and tail; grey crown; brown-streaked back; grey eyebrow and nape; stubby, conical bill; pale legs.

Size: *L* 17–19 cm.

Status: uncommon migrant from late March to late April and from early October to mid-November; uncommon to fairly common breeder from May to September; a few may be present in winter.

Habitat: *Breeding:* moist riparian thickets of willow and alder; also in dense vegetation in mixedwood forests. *In migration:* riparian thickets and brushy wood-land clearings, edges and parklands.

Nesting: on the ground or low in a shrub or sapling; often in sphagnum moss or Labrador tea; cup nest is woven with twigs, grass, moss and bark shreds and lined with fine grass and animal hair; female incubates 3 or 4 greenish-white to pale green eggs, heavily blotched with reddish brown, for about 12 days.

Feeding: scratches the ground to uncover seeds, berries and invertebrates; visits backyard feeding stations in migration and winter.

Voice: song is a variable, long series of melodic whistles: *All I have is what's here dear, won't you won't you take it?;* calls include *chip* and *click* notes.

Similar Species: *Song Sparrow* (p. 315): pale central crown stripe; dark 'moustache'; dark brownish rather than reddish streaking and upperparts. *Hermit Thrush* (p. 254): longer, thinner bill; light eye ring; dark breast spots; lacks the heavy streaking on the underparts; unstreaked, olive brown and reddish-brown upperparts.

Best Sites: Moosonee area; Severn River PP; Winisk River PP; Polar Bear PP; Point Pelee NP; Rondeau PP; Long Point PP; Presqu'ile PP; Sleeping Giant PP.

SONG SPARROW

Melospiza melodia

The Song Sparrow's heavily streaked, low-key plumage doesn't prepare you for its symphonic song. This well-named sparrow stands among the great Ontario songsters for the complexity, rhythm and emotion of its springtime rhapsodies. • Song Sparrows (and many other songbirds) learn to sing by eavesdropping on their fathers or on rival males. By the time a young male is a few months old, he will have formed the basis for his own courtship tune. • In recent decades, mild winters in the Toronto area and an abundance of backyard birdfeeders has enticed an increasing number of Song Sparrows to overwinter in our province. • Most songbirds are lucky if they are able to produce one brood per year; in some years, Song Sparrows in southwestern Ontario will successfully raise three broods. • The scientific name *melodia* means 'melody' in Greek.

ID: whitish underparts with heavy brown streaking that converges into a central breast spot; greyish face; dark line behind the eye; white jaw line is bordered by a dark whisker and 'moustache' stripes; dark crown, with a pale central stripe; mottled brown upperparts; rounded tail tip.

Size: *L* 14–18 cm.

Status: common to abundant migrant and breeder from mid-March through November; rare to uncommon visitor from November to March.

Habitat: shrubby areas, often near water, including willow shrublands, riparian thickets, forest openings and pastures.

Nesting: usually on the ground or low in a shrub or small tree; female builds an open cup nest of grass, weeds, leaves and bark shreds and lines it with rootlets, fine grass and hair; female incubates 3–5 greenish-white eggs, heavily spotted with reddish

brown, for 12–14 days; may raise 2 or 3 broods each summer.

Feeding: gleans the ground, shrubs and trees for cutworms, beetles, grasshoppers, ants, other invertebrates and seeds; also eats wild fruit and visits feeding stations.

Voice: 1–4 bright, distinctive introductory notes, such as *sweet, sweet, sweet*, followed by a buzzy *towee*, then a short, descending trill; calls include a short *tsip* and a nasal *tchep*.

Similar Species: *Fox Sparrow* (p. 314): heavier breast spotting and streaking; lacks the pale central crown stripe and dark 'moustache'; reddish rather than dark brownish streaking and upperparts. *Lincoln's Sparrow* (p. 316): lightly streaked breast with a buff wash; buff jaw line. *Savannah Sparrow* (p. 309): lightly streaked breast; yellow lores; lacks the greyish face and the dark triangular 'moustache'; notched tail.

Best Sites: almost any shrubby riparian area in Ontario.

LINCOLN'S SPARROW

Melospiza lincolnii

There is a certain beauty in the plumage of a Lincoln's Sparrow that is greater than the sum of its feathers. Sightings of this bird, linked with the sounds and smells of its natural habitat, can bring joy to the hearts of perceptive birdwatchers. • Most of our Lincoln's Sparrows build their nests in the cool, moist muskeg of northern Ontario, but a few regularly set up shop in more southerly locales, including Ottawa's Mer Bleue, Welland County's Wainfleet Bog and Luther Marsh. • Lincoln's Sparrows seem to be more timid than other Ontario sparrows. Males will sit openly on exposed perches and sing their bubbly, wren-like songs, but as soon as they're approached, they tend to slip under the cover of nearby shrubs. When they're not singing their courtship songs, Lincoln's Sparrows remain well hidden in tall grass and dense brushy growth. • This sparrow bears the name of Thomas Lincoln, a young companion to John J. Audubon on his voyage to Labrador.

ID: buff breast band, sides and flanks with fine dark breast streaking; buff jaw stripe; grey eyebrow, face and collar; dark line behind the eye; dark reddish cap, with a grey central stripe; white throat and belly; mottled grey-brown to reddish-brown upperparts; very faint, white eye ring.
Size: *L* 14 cm.
Status: uncommon to fairly common migrant from early May to early June and from early September to mid-October; fairly common to common breeder from late May to September; a few may be present in winter.
Habitat: shrubby edges of bogs, swamps, beaver ponds and meadows; also in the shrubby growth of recent forest burns or clearings.
Nesting: on the ground, often on soft moss or concealed beneath shrubs; female builds a well-hidden cup nest of grass and

sedges and lines it with fine grass and hair; female incubates 4 or 5 greenish-white to pale green eggs, heavily spotted with reddish brown, for 11–14 days.
Feeding: scratches at the ground, exposing invertebrates and seeds; occasionally visits feeding stations.
Voice: wren-like, musical mixture of buzzes, trills and warbled notes; calls include a buzzy *zeee* and *tsup*.
Similar Species: *Song Sparrow* (p. 315): heavier breast streaking; dark triangular 'moustache'; lacks the buff wash on the breast, sides and flanks. *Savannah Sparrow* (p. 309): yellow lores; white eyebrow and jaw line. *Swamp Sparrow* (p. 317): generally lacks the streaking on the breast; more contrast between the red and grey crown stripes.
Best Sites: Luther Marsh; Bon Echo PP; Mer Bleue; Algonquin PP; Lake Superior PP; Wakami Lake PP; Pukaskwa NP.

SWAMP SPARROW

Melospiza georgiana

S wamp Sparrows are well adapted to life near water. These wetland inhabitants skulk about the emergent vegetation of cattail marshes, foraging for a variety of invertebrates, including beetles, caterpillars, spiders, leafhoppers and flies. Like other sparrows, they are unable to swim, but many of their meals are snatched directly from the water's surface. • Swamp Sparrows must keep a lookout for daytime predators, such as Northern Harriers, Great Blue Herons and large snakes; at night, the key to survival is finding a secluded, concealing perch that will keep them safe from raccoons, skunks and weasels. • Swamp Sparrows are most easily seen in spring, when males sing their familiar trills from atop cattails or shoreline shrubs.

breeding

ID: grey face; reddish-brown wings; brownish upperparts; dark streaking on the back; dull grey breast; white throat and jaw line outlined by black stripes; dark line behind the eye. *Breeding:* rusty cap; streaked, buff sides and flanks. *Non-breeding:* streaked, brown cap with a grey central stripe; more brownish sides. *Immature:* buffy eyebrow and nape; faint streaking on the breast.
Size: *L* 13–14 cm.
Status: common migrant and breeder from late April to late October; rare to locally uncommon resident from November to April.
Habitat: cattail marshes, open wetlands, wet meadows and open, deciduous, riparian thickets.
Nesting: in emergent aquatic vegetation or shoreline bushes; cup nest, woven with coarse grass and marsh vegetation, is lined with fine grass; nest usually has a partial canopy and a side entrance;

female incubates 4 or 5 greenish-white to pale green eggs, heavily marked with reddish brown, for 12–15 days.
Feeding: gleans insects mainly from the ground, but also from vegetation and the water's surface; takes seeds in late summer and fall.
Voice: song is a sharp, metallic, slow trill: *Weet-Weet-Weet-Weet*; call is a harsh *chink*.
Similar Species: *Chipping Sparrow* (p. 305): clean white eyebrow; full black eye line; uniformly grey underparts; white wing bars. *American Tree Sparrow* (p. 304): central, dark breast spot; white wing bars; 2-toned bill. *Song Sparrow* (p. 315): heavily streaked underparts; lacks the grey collar. *Lincoln's Sparrow* (p. 316): fine breast streaking; less contrast between the brown and grey crown stripes.
Best Sites: almost any cattail marsh or open wetland throughout Ontario.

WHITE-THROATED SPARROW

Zonotrichia albicollis

This patriot of Canada's northern forests arrives each spring to sing its glorious, familiar tribute: *dear sweet Canada Canada Canada*. Cottagers and residents, from Cambridge north to the Hudson Bay coast, often find pleasure in the soothing sound of these few simple notes announcing the arrival of spring. • This handsome sparrow is easily identified by its bold white throat and striped crown. Two colour morphs are common throughout Ontario: one has black and white stripes on the head; the other has brown and tan stripes. • In spring and fall, White-throated Sparrows can appear anywhere in the province in great abundance. Urban backyards dressed with brushy fenceline tangles and a birdfeeder brimming with seeds can attract good numbers of these delightful sparrows. • Like many 'snowbirds,' most White-throated Sparrows move to warmer climates in fall and early winter. • *Zonotrichia* means 'hair-like,' a reference to the striped heads of birds in this genus; *albicollis* is Latin for 'white neck.'

ID: black and white (or brown and tan) striped head; white throat; grey cheek; yellow lores; black eye line; grey, unstreaked underparts; mottled, brown upperparts; greyish bill.
Size: *L* 17–18 cm.
Status: common to abundant migrant from mid-April to late May and from early September to mid-November; common breeder from May to September; rare to locally uncommon resident from November to April.
Habitat: *Breeding:* semi-open coniferous and mixed forests, especially in regenerating clearings and along shrubby forest edges. *In migration:* woodlots, wooded parks and riparian brush.
Nesting: on or near the ground, often concealed by low a shrub or

fallen log; female builds an open cup nest of grass, weeds, twigs and conifer needles and lines it with rootlets, fine grass and hair; female incubates 4–5 greenish-blue to pale blue eggs, marked with lavender and reddish brown, for 11–14 days.
Feeding: scratches the ground to expose invertebrates, seeds and berries; also gleans insects from vegetation and while in flight; eats seeds from birdfeeders in winter.
Voice: variable song is a clear and distinct whistled: *dear sweet Canada Canada Canada*; call is a sharp *chink*.
Similar Species: *White-crowned Sparrow* (p. 320): lacks the bold white throat and the yellow lores; pinkish bill; grey collar.
Best Sites: almost any semi-open coniferous or mixed forest or woodland.

HARRIS'S SPARROW

Zonotrichia querula

There are never uneventful days in the natural calendar of Ontario. During the spring and fall migrations, for example, there looms the possibility, however slim, of seeing a Harris's Sparrow. An unassuming migrant, the Harris's Sparrow passes through the province in small, isolated trickles, frequently mixing with flocks of White-throated and White-crowned sparrows. Occasionally, a few of these sparrows pick through the seed offerings at backyard feeders, creating a burst of excitement from lucky observers. • The Harris's Sparrow breeds exclusively along a range that extends from northern Manitoba to the northern border of the Northwest and Yukon territories. This region is where Canada's northern coniferous forest (taiga) fades into treeless tundra. Although similar habitat exists in the extreme northwestern corner of Ontario, breeding within the province was not confirmed until 1983.

breeding

ID: mottled brown and black upperparts; white underparts; pink-orange bill. *Breeding:* black crown, ear patch, throat and bib; grey face; black streaks on the sides and flanks; white wing bars. *Non-breeding:* brown face; brownish sides and flanks; white flecks on the black crown. *Immature:* white throat; mostly brownish crown with some black streaking.
Size: *L* 18–19 cm.
Status: rare to locally uncommon migrant from late March to late May and from mid-September to late November; very rare and local breeder from June to August; a few may be present in winter.
Habitat: *Breeding:* near treeline, where stunted spruce trees border tundra. *In migration:* brushy roadsides, shrubby vegetation, forest edges and riparian thickets.
Nesting: on or near the ground, usually under the cover of a low shrub or tree; open cup nest, made of twigs, lichen and moss, is lined with fine

grass and hair; female incubates 3–5 brown-marked, pale green eggs for 12–15 days.
Feeding: gleans the ground and vegetation for seeds, fresh buds, insects and berries; occasionally takes seeds from birdfeeders.
Voice: song is a series of 2–4 long quavering whistles; each series may be offered at the same or different pitch; call is a *jeenk* or *zheenk*; flocks in flight may give a rolling *chug-up chug-up.*
Similar Species: *White-throated Sparrow* (p. 318): greyish bill; yellow lores; black and white striped crown. *White-crowned Sparrow* (p. 320): black and white striped crown; grey collar; immature has a broad grey eyebrow bordered by a brown eye line and crown. *House Sparrow* (p. 351): male is brownish overall; grey crown; broad brown band behind the eye; broad whitish jaw band; dark bill.
Best Sites: check local bird hotlines for recent sightings; Sleeping Giant PP west to the Rainy River area.

WHITE-CROWNED SPARROW

Zonotrichia leucophrys

While most of Ontario's sparrows can quite honestly be classified as LBJs (little brown jobs), the White-Crowned Sparrow is smartly patterned. For a few short weeks in spring and fall, this large, bold sparrow brightens brushy expanses and suburban parks and gardens with its striped crown and cheeky song. Most Ontarians with well-stocked birdfeeders should be especially familiar with this bird—besides being conspicuous in appearance, White-throated Sparrows are tireless singers, even bursting into song in the light of the moon. • The White-crowned Sparrow is North America's most studied sparrow. Research on this bird has given science tremendous insight into bird physiology, homing behaviour and the geographic variability of song dialects.

ID: black and white striped head; black eye line; pink-orange bill; grey face; unstreaked, grey underparts; pale grey throat; mottled, grey-brown upperparts; 2 faint, white wing bars. *Immature:* broad, grey eyebrow bordered by a brown eye line and crown.
Size: *L* 14–18 cm.
Status: common migrant from late April to late May and from mid-September to mid-November; uncommon to common breeder from June to September; a few may be present in winter.
Habitat: *Breeding:* open shrubby meadows, bogs, forest edges, forest clearings riparian thickets and willow clumps on tundra. *In migration:* woodlots, brushy tangles and riparian thickets.
Nesting: on or near the ground, usually in a depression of moss and lichen sheltered by a shrub or small tree;

female builds an open cup nest of twigs, grass, leaves, weeds and bark shreds and lines it with feathers, hair and fine grass; female incubates 3–5 creamy-white to pale greenish eggs, heavily spotted with reddish brown, for 11–14 days.
Feeding: scratches the ground to expose insects and seeds; also eats berries, buds and moss caps; may take seeds from birdfeeders.
Voice: song is a frequently repeated variation of *I gotta go wee-wee now*; call is a high, thin *seet* or sharp *pink*.
Similar Species: *White-throated Sparrow* (p. 318): bold white throat; greyish bill; yellow lores; browner overall. *Golden-crowned Sparrow:* dark bill; golden-yellow crown, bordered by black.
Best Sites: almost any shrubby woodland edge throughout the province in migration; Point Pelee NP; Presqu'ile PP; Sleeping Giant PP; Polar Bear PP.

DARK-EYED JUNCO

Junco hyemalis

The Dark-eyed Junco passes through virtually any moderately sized woodlot in Ontario at some point in the year, and it is one of the most familiar birds in the province. • Juncos spend most of their time on the ground, and they are readily flushed from wooded trails and backyard feeders. Their distinctive, white outer tail feathers will flash in alarm as they rush for the cover of a nearby tree or shrub. • Juncos rarely perch at feeders, preferring to snatch up seeds that are knocked to the ground by other visitors, such as chickadees, sparrows, nuthatches and jays. • Most juncos migrate south for winter, but even during the coldest years in Ontario, you can manage to find a few here and there. • Western Canada boasts a great diversity of junco subspecies, some of which occasionally visit Ontario; our province is typically home to the subspecies known as the 'Slate-colored Junco.'

'Slate-colored Junco'

♂

ID: white outer tail feathers; pale bill. *Male:* dark slate grey overall, except for the white lower breast, belly and undertail coverts. *Female:* brown rather than grey. *Juvenile:* brown like the female, but streaked with darker brown.
Size: *L* 14–17 cm.
Status: common to very common migrant and visitor from September to May; common breeder from May to September.
Habitat: coniferous and mixed forests, especially in young jack pine stands, burned-over areas and shrubby regenerating clearings.
Nesting: on the ground, usually concealed by a shrub, tree, root, log or rock; female builds a cup nest of twigs, bark shreds, grass and moss and lines it with fine grass and hair; female incubates 3–5 whitish to bluish-white eggs, marked with grey and brown, for 12–13 days.
Feeding: scratches the ground for invertebrates; also eats berries and seeds.
Voice: song is a long, dry trill, very similar to the call of the Chipping Sparrow, but more musical; call is a smacking *chip* note, often given in series.
Similar Species: *Eastern Towhee* (p. 303): larger; female has rufous sides, red eyes and a greyish bill.
Best Sites: Petroglyphs PP; Killarney PP; Lake Superior PP; Pukaskwa NP; Quetico PP.

LAPLAND LONGSPUR

Calcarius lapponicus

Throughout much of the year, Lapland Longspurs wheel about in masses over the fields of southern Ontario. From day to day, their movements are largely unpredictable, but they typically appear wherever open fields offer an abundance of seeds or waste grain. Flocks of longspurs can be surprisingly inconspicuous until they are closely approached—anyone attempting a closer look at the flock will be awed by the sight of the birds suddenly erupting into the skies, flashing their white outer tail feathers. • In fall, these birds arrive from their breeding grounds looking like mottled, brownish sparrows, and they retain their drab plumage throughout the winter months. When the farmers work their fields in spring, Lapland Longspurs have already molted into their bold breeding plumage, which they will wear through summer. • The Lapland Longspur breeds in northern polar regions, including the area of northern Europe known as Lapland.

non-breeding

ID: white outer tail feathers; pale yellowish bill. *Non-breeding adult* and *Breeding female:* often has rufous in the wings; mottled brown and black upperparts; lightly streaked flanks; male has faint chestnut on the nape and a diffuse black breast; female has a narrow, lightly streaked buff breast band. *Breeding male:* black crown, face and bib; chestnut nape; broad, white stripe curving down to shoulder from the eye (may be tinged with buff behind the eye). *Immature:* greyish nape; broader buff-brown breast band.
Size: *L* 16 cm.
Status: rare to locally uncommon migrant and visitor from October to mid-May; locally common breeder from May to September.
Habitat: *Breeding:* coastal tundra. *Winter* and *In migration:* pastures, meadows and croplands.
Nesting: on dry tundra hummock,

preferably concealed by dwarf shrub cover; female builds an open cup nest of grass and sedges and lines it with fine grass and feathers; female incubates 4–6 greenish-white to greyish-green eggs, marked with brown and black, for about 12 days.
Feeding: *Winter:* gleans the ground and snow for seeds and waste grain. *Summer:* mainly eats insects and some seeds.
Voice: flight song is a rapid slurred warble; musical calls; flight calls include a rattled *tri-di-dit* and a descending *teew*.
Similar Species: *Snow Bunting* (p. 324): black and white wing pattern. *Smith's Longspur* (p. 323): completely buff to buff-orange underparts; male has a black and white face and a buff-orange nape.
Best Sites: Polar Bear PP; Sarnia airport; Wolfe Island; open fields throughout southern Ontario.

SMITH'S LONGSPUR

Calcarius pictus

Smith's Longspurs are among the least-known birds in Ontario, and few of us could ever say we've seen one. These uncommon and secretive birds may be seen briefly while they retreat south for winter, but you'll have to look closely through larger flocks of Lapland Longspurs to spot them. Their summers are spent far removed from most Ontarians on the narrow band of grass, sedges and dwarf shrubs along the Hudson Bay coast. Under the warm subarctic sun, herbaceous plants burst into colourful bloom and hordes of insects emerge from their dormant larval states. This burst of activity draws longspurs and other migrant birds to Ontario's north, where adult birds will nest and raise their young on the brief abundance of summer life. • This bird's winter range is limited to a few southcentral U.S. states. • John J. Audubon named this bird in honour of his friend and subscriber, Gideon Smith.

breeding

ID: white outer tail feathers; small white shoulder patch (often concealed); mottled brown and black upperparts. *Breeding male:* black crown; black and white face; buff-orange underparts and collar; faint streaking on the sides and flanks. *Non-breeding male, Female* and *Immature:* streaked crown and nape; buff underparts with faint streaking on the breast.
Size: *L* 15 cm.
Status: occasional migrant and visitor from late April to late May and from late September to early November; uncommon to locally common breeder from May to September.
Habitat: dry sedge tundra, usually close to raised sandy-gravel ridges with clumps of stunted spruce.
Nesting: on the ground on dry tundra hummock, often concealed by a low shrub; female builds an open cup nest of grass and sedges,

lined with feathers, hair and lichen; female incubates 4 pale green to tan eggs, marked with brown and lavender, for about 12 days.
Feeding: insects and seeds are gleaned from the ground and low vegetation.
Voice: song is a warbling *switoo-whidee-deedew, whee-tew*; alarm call is a slow *tick tick tick*, like a watch.
Similar Species: *Lapland Longspur* (p. 322): less white in the tail; whitish belly and undertail coverts; often shows black on the neck or breast; breeding male has a black throat and bib, and a chestnut nape. *Vesper Sparrow* (p. 308): chestnut shoulder patch; white underparts. *American Pipit* (p. 262): thinner bill; lacks white patch on the shoulder; streaking on the breast.
Best Sites: check local bird hotlines for recent sightings; Polar Bear PP; dredge dump area off Thunder Bay's Chippewa Park; fields in the Rainy River area.

SNOW BUNTING

Plectrophenax nivalis

In early winter, when flocks of Snow Buntings descend on rural Ontario fields, their startling black and white plumage flashes in contrast with the snow-covered backdrop. It may seem strange that Snow Buntings are whiter in summer than in winter, but the darker winter plumage may help these birds absorb heat on the coldest, clear winter days. • Snow Buntings venture farther north than any other songbird in the world. A single individual, likely misguided and lost, was recorded not far from the North Pole in May of 1987. Most of these birds breed north of Ontario's borders, but a single breeding record comes from Ontario's Hudson Bay coast near Manitoba. • In winter, Snow Buntings prefer expansive areas, including grain croplands, fields and pastures, where they scratch and peck at exposed seeds and grains. On occasion they will ingest small grains of sand or gravel from roadsides as a source of minerals and to help digestion.

non-breeding

ID: black and white wings and tail; white underparts. *Breeding male:* black back; all-white head and rump; black bill. *Breeding female:* streaky brown and whitish crown and back; dark bill. *Non-breeding:* yellowish bill; golden brown crown and rump; female has a blackish forecrown and a golden back with dark streaks.

Size: *L* 15–18 cm.

Status: uncommon to irregularly abundant migrant and visitor from October to early May; very rare breeder from May to September.

Habitat: *Breeding:* rough, rocky terrain or outcroppings on coastal tundra. *Non-breeding:* manured fields, feedlots, pastures, grassy meadows, lakeshores, roadsides and railways.

Nesting: on the ground in a protected cavity in rock or natural debris; female builds a bulky cup nest of grass and moss and lines it with feathers, hair, plant down, fine grass and rootlets; female incubates 4–7 whitish to pale blue-green eggs with dark markings, for about 12 days.

Feeding: gleans the ground and snow for seeds and waste grain; also takes insects when available, especially in summer.

Voice: spring song is a musical, high-pitched *chi-chi-churee*; call is a whistled *tew.*

Similar Species: *Lapland Longspur* (p. 322): overall brownish upperparts; lacks the black and white wing pattern.

Best Sites: fields, pastures and roadsides throughout southern Ontario; Sarnia airport; Tommy Thompson Park; Wolfe and Amherst islands.

NORTHERN CARDINAL
Cardinalis cardinalis

A bird as beautiful as the Northern Cardinal rarely fails to capture our attention and admiration. Without the help of a bird identification guide, most Ontarians can easily recognize this delightful year-round neighbour. Cardinals prefer the tangled shrubby edges of woodlands, but they are easily attracted to backyards with feeders and sheltering trees and shrubs. • Cardinals form one of the bird world's most faithful pair bonds. The male and female remain in close contact year-round, singing to one another through the seasons with soft, bubbly whistles. • Few Ontarians realize that the Northern Cardinal is a relative newcomer to Canada. This bird's range has expanded northward over the years into southern Ontario, probably because of the wealth of backyard birdfeeders here, the warm microclimate of our urban centres, and forest fragmentation, which has created ideal habitat for this bird. • The cardinal owes its name to the vivid red plumage of the male, which resembles the robes of Roman Catholic cardinals.

ID: *Male:* red overall; pointed crest; black mask and throat; red, conical bill. *Juvenile male:* like the female, but has a dark bill and crest. *Female:* shaped like the male; brown-buff to buff-olive overall; red bill, crest, wings and tail.
Size: *L* 19–23 cm.
Status: fairly common to very common year-round resident.
Habitat: brushy thickets and shrubby tangles along forest and woodland edges, in backyards and in suburban and urban parks.
Nesting: in dense shrubs, thickets, vine tangles or low in a coniferous tree; female builds an open cup nest of twigs, bark shreds, weeds, grass, leaves and rootlets and lines it with hair and fine grass; female

incubates 3 or 4 whitish to bluish- or greenish-white eggs, marked with grey, brown and purple, for 12–13 days.
Feeding: hops on the ground or in low shrubs, gleaning seeds, insects and berries.
Voice: song is a variable series of clear, bubbly whistled notes: *What cheer! What cheer! birdie-birdie-birdie What cheer;* call is a metallic *chip.*
Similar Species: *Summer Tanager* (p. 301) and *Scarlet Tanager* (p. 302): lack the head crest, black mask and throat and the red conical bill; Scarlet Tanager has black wings and tail.
Best Sites: almost any brushy tangle along a woodland edge in southern Ontario, from Windsor to Ottawa.

ROSE-BREASTED GROSBEAK

Pheucticus ludovicianus

It's difficult to miss the boisterous, whistled tune of the Rose-breasted Grosbeak. This bird's hurried, robin-like song is easily recognized, and it's one of the more common songs heard among Ontario's deciduous forests in spring and summer. Although the female lacks the magnificent colours of the male, she shares his talent for beautiful song. • Rose-breasted Grosbeaks usually build their nests low in a tree or tall shrub, but they typically forage high in the canopy, where they can be difficult to spot. Luckily for birdwatchers, the abundance of autumn berries often draws these birds to ground level. • Rose-breasted Grosbeaks migrate primarily at night, and their wandering habits often result in a few birds turning up unexpectedly in remote northern communities. • The species name *ludovicianus*, Latin for 'from Louisiana,' is misleading, because this bird is only a migrant through Louisiana and other southern U.S. states.

breeding

ID: pale, conical bill; dark wings with small white patches; dark tail. *Male:* black hood and back; red breast and inner underwings; white underparts and rump. *1st-spring male:* may show brown instead of black. *1st-fall male:* like the female, but has a streaked, orangy breast and sides. *Female:* bold whitish eyebrow; thin crown stripe; brown upperparts with dark brown streaking.
Size: *L* 18–21 cm.
Status: common migrant and breeder from May to September; a few may remain as late as December.
Habitat: deciduous and mixed forests.
Nesting: fairly low in a tree or tall shrub, often near water; mostly the female builds a flimsy cup nest of twigs, bark strips, weeds, grass and leaves and lines it with rootlets and hair; pair incubates 3–5 pale greenish-blue eggs, spotted with reddish-brown, for 13–14 days.
Feeding: gleans vegetation for insects, seeds, buds, berries and some fruit; occasionally hover-gleans or catches flying insects on the wing; may also visit feeding stations.
Voice: song is a long, melodious series of whistled notes, much like a fast version of a robin's song; call is a distinctive squeak.
Similar Species: male is distinctive. *Purple Finch* (p. 342): female is much smaller and has heavier streaking on the underparts. *Sparrows* (pp. 303–20): smaller; all lack the large conical bill.
Best Sites: almost any deciduous woodland in southern Ontario, including Thunder Bay to Lake of the Woods.

BLUE GROSBEAK

Guiraca caerulea

Male Blue Grosbeaks owe their spectacular spring plumage not to a fresh molt but, oddly enough, to feather wear. While Blue Grosbeaks are wintering in Mexico and Central America, their brown feather tips slowly wear away, leaving the crystal blue plumage that is seen as they arrive on their breeding grounds. • Blue Grosbeaks are very expressive during courtship. If you are lucky enough to spot one of these birds in spring, watch for the tail-spreading, tail-flicking and crown-raising behaviours that suggest the bird might be breeding—you could be witness to the first Blue Grosbeak nesting attempt in Ontario. • Most of the small numbers of Blue Grosbeaks that make appearances in Ontario can be found in May along the wooded sandspits and peninsulas that jut into Lake Erie. • Birders are advised to look carefully for the rusty wing bars that will distinguish this bird from the similar-looking, and much more common Indigo Bunting. • *Caerulea* is from the Latin for 'blue,' a description that just doesn't grasp this bird's true beauty.

ID: large, pale greyish, conical bill. *Male:* blue overall; 2 rusty wing bars; black around the base of the bill. *Female:* soft brown plumage overall; whitish throat; rusty wing bars; rump and shoulders are faintly washed with blue. *1st-spring male:* like the female, but has a blue head.
Size: *L* 15–19 cm.
Status: very rare visitor from late April to late July.
Habitat: thick brush, riparian thickets, shrubby areas and dense weedy fields near water.

Nesting: does not nest in Ontario.
Feeding: gleans insects from the ground while hopping; occasionally takes seeds; may visit feeding stations.
Voice: sweet, melodious, warbling song with phrases that rise and fall; call is a loud *chink*.
Similar Species: *Indigo Bunting* (p. 328): smaller body and bill; male lacks the wing bars; female has dark brown streaking on the breast.
Best Sites: Point Pelee NP; Rondeau PP; Long Point PP.

VAGRANT

INDIGO BUNTING

Passerina cyanea

In the shadow of a towering tree, a male Indigo Bunting can look almost black. If this happens during your first encounter with this bird, reposition yourself quickly so that the sun strikes and enlivens this bunting's incomparable indigo colour—the rich shade of blue is rivalled only by the sky. • Raspberry thickets are a favoured nesting location for many of Ontario's Indigo Buntings. The dense, thorny stems provide the nestlings with protection from many predators, and the berries are a convenient source of food. • The Indigo Bunting employs a clever and comical foraging strategy to reach the grass and weed seeds upon which it feeds: the bird lands midway on a stem and then shuffles slowly towards the seed head, which eventually bends under the bird's weight, giving the bunting easier access to the seeds.

ID: stout, grey conical bill; beady, black eyes; black legs; no wing bars. *Male:* blue overall; black lores; wings and tail may show some black. *1st-spring male:* mottled blue and brown overall. *Fall male:* like the female, but usually with some blue in the wings and tail. *Female:* soft brown overall; brown streaks on breast; whitish throat.
Size: *L* 14 cm.
Status: fairly common to common migrant and breeder from May to September.
Habitat: deciduous forest and woodland edges, regenerating forest clearings, shrubby fields, orchards, abandoned pastures and hedgerows; occasionally along mixed woodland edges.
Nesting: usually in an upright fork of a small tree or shrub or within a vine tangle; female builds a cup nest of grass, leaves and bark strips and lines it with rootlets, hair and feathers; female

incubates 3 or 4 white to bluish-white eggs, rarely spotted with brown or purple, for 12–13 days.
Feeding: gleans low vegetation and the ground for insects, especially grasshoppers, beetles, weevils, flies and larvae; also eats the seeds of thistles, dandelions, goldenrods and other native plants.
Voice: song consists of paired warbled whistles: *fire-fire, where-where, here-here, see-it see-it*; call is a quick *spit*.
Similar Species: *Blue Grosbeak* (p. 327): larger overall; larger, more robust bill; 2 rusty wing bars; male has a black around base of the bill; female lacks the streaking on the breast. *Mountain Bluebird* (p. 359): exceptionally rare in Ontario; larger; slimmer bill; male has pure blue wings and tail.
Best Sites: almost any shrubby deciduous woodland edge in southern Ontario, including Thunder Bay to Lake of the Woods.

DICKCISSEL
Spiza americana

Since the first Dickcissel sighting in Ontario in 1895, there have only been a handful of sporadic nesting records and largely unpredictable sightings. Its erratic and irregular behaviour both befuddles the motivation and ignites the imagination of would be observers. • Arriving in suitable nesting habitat before the smaller females, breeding males bravely announce their presence with stuttering, trilled renditions of their own name. Territorial males perch atop a tall blade of grass, fencepost or rock to scour their turf for signs of potential mates or unwelcome males. Dickcissels are polygynous, and males may mate with up to eight females in a single breeding season. This breeding strategy means that the male gives no assistance to the females in nesting or brooding. • Dickcissels are sometimes seen foraging in small flocks during migration, but they are most regularly seen among troupes of House Sparrows at backyard feeders over winter.

breeding

ID: yellow eyebrow; grey head, nape and sides of yellow breast; brown upperparts; pale greyish underparts; rufous shoulder patch; dark, conical bill. *Male:* white chin and black bib; duller colours in non-breeding plumage. *Female:* duller version of the male; white throat. *Immature:* dull like the female, but has a very faint eyebrow and dark streaking on the crown, breast, sides and flanks.
Size: *L* 15–18 cm.
Status: very rare, erratic and irregular visitor from April to May and from September to October; irregular breeder from May to September; extremely rare, but annual vagrant from November to April; most regular in the southwest.
Habitat: abandoned fields dominated by forbs, weedy meadows, croplands, grasslands and grassy roadsides.
Nesting: on or near the ground, concealed well among tall, dense

vegetation; female builds a bulky open cup nest of forbs, grass and leaves and lines it with rootlets, fine grass or hair; female incubates 4 pale blue eggs for 12–13 days.
Feeding: insects and seeds are gleaned from the ground and low vegetation; small flocks may visit birdfeeders, especially in winter.
Voice: song consists of 2–3 single notes followed by a trill, often paraphrased as *dick dick dick-cissel*; flight call is a buzzer-like *bzrrrrt*.
Similar Species: *Eastern Meadowlark* (p. 332): much larger; long, pointed bill; yellow chin and throat with a black necklace. *American Goldfinch* (p. 349): lacks the black bib; white or yellow-buff bars on the dark wings; may show a black forecrown.
Best Sites: Point Pelee NP; Pelee Island; Wiarton airport; Wawanosh Valley Conservation Area; Toronto area.

329

BOBOLINK

Dolichonyx oryzivorus

During the nesting season, male and female Bobolinks rarely interact with one another. For the most part, the males perform aerial displays and sing their bubbly, tinkling songs from exposed grassy perches while the females carry out the nesting duties. Once the young have hatched, the males become scarce, spending much of their time along the ground hunting for insects. • At first glimpse, a female Bobolink resembles a sparrow, but a male, with his dark belly and buff and black upperparts, is coloured like no other bird in Ontario. • Bobolinks once benefited from increased agriculture in Ontario, but modern practices, such as harvesting hay early in the season, continue to thwart the reproductive efforts of this bird. • The paraphrase of the Bobolink's song given below is from the poem 'Robert of Lincoln,' by William Cullen Bryant, an American poet. Some people think that the name of this bird is an abbreviation of 'Robert O. Lincoln,' but others think it is a reference to the bird's song.

ID: *Breeding male:* black bill, head, wings, tail and underparts; buff nape; white rump and wing patch. *Breeding female:* yellowish bill; brown-buff overall; streaked back, sides, flank and rump; pale eyebrow; dark eye line; light central crown stripe bordered by dark stripes; whitish throat. *Non-breeding male:* similar to a breeding female, but darker above and rich golden-buff below.
Size: *L* 15–20 cm.
Status: common migrant and breeder from late April to September.
Habitat: tall, grassy meadows and ditches, hayfields and some croplands.
Nesting: on the ground, usually in hayfields; well-concealed cup nest, made of grass and forb stems, is placed in a shallow depression and lined with fine grass; female incubates 5–6 greyish to light reddish-brown eggs, heavily blotched

with lavender and brown, for 11–13 days.
Feeding: gleans the ground and low vegetation for adult and larval invertebrates; also eats many seeds.
Voice: song is a series of banjo-like twangs: *bobolink bobolink spink spank spink*, often given in flight; also issues a *pink* call in flight.
Similar Species: *Lark Bunting* (p. 360): thicker conical bill; male lacks the yellow nape and white rump; females have a white wing patch. *Savannah Sparrow* (p. 309): dark breast streaking; yellow lores. *Vesper Sparrow* (p. 308): breast streaking; white outer tail feathers. *Grasshopper Sparrow* (p. 310): white belly; unstreaked sides and flanks.
Best Sites: almost any moist, grassy meadow or hayfield in southern Ontario; also in Thunder Bay, Lake of the Woods and Hwy 11 from North Bay to Cochrane.

RED-WINGED BLACKBIRD

Agelaius phoeniceus

A birder's winter blahs might be remedied by the sound of the season's first Red-winged Blackbird. The males get an early start on the season, arriving in Ontario's marshes and wetlands a week or so before the females, often in mid-March. In the females' absence, the males stake out territories through song and visual displays. A male's bright red shoulders and short, raspy song are his most important tools in the often intricate strategy he employs to defend his territory from rivals. A flashy and richly voiced male that has managed to establish a large and productive territory can attract several mates to his cattail kingdom. In field experiments, males whose red shoulders were painted black soon lost their territories to rivals they had previously defeated. • After a male has wooed the female, she starts the busy work of weaving a nest amidst the cattails. Cryptic colouration allows the female to sit inconspicuously upon her nest, blending perfectly with the surroundings. • *Agelaius* is a Greek word meaning 'flocking,' which is an accurate description of this bird's impressive winter behaviour. The species name *phoeniceus* is a reference to the colour red, which was introduced to the Greeks as a dye by the ancient Phoenicians.

ID: *Male:* all black, except for the large, red shoulder patch edged in yellow (occasionally concealed). *Female:* heavily streaked underparts; mottled brown upperparts; faint red shoulder patch; light eyebrow.
Size: *L* 18–24 cm.
Status: abundant migrant and breeder from mid-March to November; rare to locally fairly common visitor from November to March.
Habitat: cattail marshes, wet meadows and ditches, croplands and shoreline shrubs.
Nesting: colonial and polygynous; in cattails or shoreline bushes; female weaves an open cup nest of dried cattail leaves and grass and lines it with fine grass; female incubates 3 or 4 darkly marked,

pale blue-green eggs for 10–12 days.
Feeding: gleans the ground for seeds, waste grain and invertebrates; also gleans vegetation for seeds, insects and berries; occasionally catches insects in flight; may visit feeding stations.
Voice: song is a loud, raspy *konk-a-ree* or *ogle-reeeee*; calls include a harsh *check* and a high *tseert*; female may give a loud *che-che-che chee chee chee*.
Similar Species: male is distinctive (when the shoulder patch shows). *Brewer's Blackbird* (p. 336) and *Rusty Blackbird* (p. 335): females lack the streaked underparts. *Brown-headed Cowbird* (p. 338): juvenile is smaller and has a stubbier, conical bill.
Best Sites: any cattail marsh.

EASTERN MEADOWLARK

Sturnella magna

Eastern Meadowlarks seem genuinely proud to call Ontario home. Their trademark tune is the voice of rural Ontario, and it rings through spring from fenceposts and powerlines, wherever grassy meadows and pastures are found. Listen for the meadowlark as it belts out its boisterous *See-you at school-today* across the grassy landscape. • The male's bright yellow underparts, black V-shaped 'necklace,' and white outer tail feathers help attract mates. Females share these colourful attributes for a slightly different purpose: when a predator approaches too close to a nest, the incubating female explodes from the grass in a burst of flashing colour. Most predators cannot resist chasing the moving target, and once the female has led the predator away from the nest, she simply folds away her white tail flags, exposes her camouflaged back and disappears into the grass without a trace. • Because of their bright plumage, meadowlarks don't seem to fit in with the blackbird family. When they're seen in silhouette, however, the similarities become very apparent.

breeding

ID: yellow underparts; broad, black breast band; mottled brown upperparts; short, wide tail with white outer tail feathers; long, pinkish legs; yellow lores; long, sharp bill; blackish crown stripes and eye line border a pale eyebrow and median crown stripe; dark streaking on the white sides and flanks.
Size: *L* 23–24 cm.
Status: uncommon to common migrant and breeder from mid-March to mid-November; rare visitor from November to March.
Habitat: grassy meadows and pastures; also in some croplands, weedy fields, grassy roadsides and old orchards.
Nesting: in a depression or scrape on the ground, concealed by dense grass; domed grass nest, with a side entrance, is woven into the surrounding vegetation; female incubates 3–7 white eggs, heavily spotted with brown and purple, for about 13–15 days.

Feeding: walks or runs along the ground, gleaning grasshoppers, crickets, beetles and spiders from the ground and vegetation; extracts grubs and worms by probing its bill into the soil; also eats seeds.
Voice: song is a rich series of 2–8 melodic, clear, slurred whistles: *See-you at school-today* or *This is the Year*; gives a rattling flight call and a high, buzzy *dzeart*.
Similar Species: *Western Meadowlark* (p. 333): paler upperparts, especially the crown stripes and eye line; different song and call; yellow on the throat extends onto the lower cheek. *Dickcissel* (p. 329): much smaller; solid dark crown; white throat; lacks the brown streaking on the sides and flanks.
Best Sites: pastures and meadows throughout southern Ontario, mostly south of the Canadian Shield; Manitoulin Island; Sturgeon Falls to Sudbury; Sault Ste. Marie area.

332

WESTERN MEADOWLARK
Sturnella neglecta

Western Meadowlarks have probably inhabited the Lake of the Woods region in western Ontario since the early settlers cleared the forests for agriculture, but they have just recently colonized fields and pastures in southwest Ontario. Where their range overlaps with the Eastern Meadowlark, the birds may nest in the same pastures and occasionally interbreed. The two meadowlark species are very similar in appearance, so birders must listen for their songs to distinguish one from the other. • Birders are encouraged to exercise extreme caution when walking through meadowlark nesting habitat. Meadowlarks' grassy domed nests are extremely difficult to locate, and most are so well concealed that they are crushed before they are seen. • The Western Meadowlark was overlooked by the Lewis and Clark expedition, which mistakenly thought it was the same species as the Eastern Meadowlark. This oversight is represented in the scientific name *neglecta*.

breeding

ID: yellow underparts; broad, black breast band; mottled brown upperparts; short, wide tail with white outer tail feathers; long, pinkish legs; yellow lores; brown crown stripes and eye line bordered by a pale eyebrow and median crown stripe; dark streaking on the white sides and flanks; long, sharp bill; yellow on the throat extends onto the lower cheek.
Size: *L* 23–24 cm.
Status: rare migrant from late March to late May and from mid-October to late November; rare to very locally common breeder from May to September.
Habitat: grassy meadows and pastures; also in some croplands, weedy fields and grassy roadsides.
Nesting: in a depression or scrape on the ground, concealed by dense grass, forbs or rarely low shrubs; domed grass nest, with a side entrance, is woven into the surrounding vegetation; female

incubates 3–7 white eggs, heavily spotted with brown and purple, for about 13–15 days.
Feeding: walks or runs along the ground, gleaning grasshoppers, crickets, beetles, other insects and spiders from the ground and vegetation; extracts grubs and worms by probing its bill into the soil; also eats seeds.
Voice: song is a rich, melodic series of bubbly, flute-like notes; calls include a low, loud *chuck* or *chup*, a rattling flight call or a few clear whistled notes.
Similar Species: *Eastern Meadowlark* (p. 332): darker upperparts, especially the crown stripes and eye line; different song and call; yellow on the throat does not extend onto the lower cheek. *Dickcissel* (p. 329): much smaller; solid dark crown; white throat; lacks the brown streaking on the sides and flanks.
Best Sites: Sarnia airport; Chesley-area fields; fields west of Barrie; the Lake of the Woods–Rainy River area.

333

YELLOW-HEADED BLACKBIRD

Xanthocephalus xanthocephalus

Y ou might expect a bird as handsome as the Yellow-headed Blackbird to have a song to match its splendid gold and black plumage. Unfortunately, a trip to a favoured wetland will quickly reveal the shocking truth: when the male arches his golden head backward, he struggles to produce a painful, pathetic grinding noise. Although the song of the Yellow-headed Blackbird might be the worst in North America, its quality soon becomes an appreciated aspect of its marshy home—together with the smell of decomposing vegetation, the insects and the overall sogginess. • Yellow-headed Blackbirds are rare in Ontario, but you can watch for them at a few locales, including Lake of the Woods–Rainy River region and marshes in extreme southwestern Ontario. • Where Yellow-headed Blackbirds occur with Red-winged Blackbirds, the larger Yellow-heads dominate, commandeering the centre of the wetland and pushing the red-winged competitors to the periphery.

ID: *Male:* yellow head and breast; otherwise black body; white wing patches; black lores; long tail; black bill. *Female:* dusky brown overall; yellow breast, throat and eyebrow; hints of yellow in the face.
Size: *L* 20–28 cm.
Status: rare migrant and visitor from mid-August to early June; rare and very local breeder from May to September.
Habitat: deep, permanent marshes, sloughs, lakeshores and river impoundments where cattails dominate.
Nesting: loosely colonial; female builds a bulky, deep basket of emergent aquatic plants and lines it with dry grass and other vegetation; nest is woven into

emergent vegetation over water; female incubates 4 pale green to pale grey eggs, marked with grey or brown, for 11–13 days.
Feeding: gleans the ground for seeds, beetles, snails, waterbugs and dragonflies; also probes into cattail heads for larval invertebrates.
Voice: song is a strained, metallic grating note followed by a descending buzz; call is a deep *krrt* or *ktuk*; low quacks and liquidy clucks may be given during breeding season.
Similar Species: male is distinctive. *Rusty Blackbird* (p. 335) and *Brewer's Blackbird* (p. 336): females lack the yellow throat and face.
Best Sites: Tremblay Beach Conservation Area; St. Clair NWA; Rondeau PP; Lake of the Woods–Rainy River area.

RUSTY BLACKBIRD

Euphagus carolinus

The Rusty Blackbird owes its name to the colour of its rusty fall plumage, but its name could just as well reflect this bird's grating, squeaky song, which sounds very much like a rusty hinge. • During fall migration and over winter, Rusty Blackbirds often intermingle with flocks of other blackbirds, sometimes blackening the rural skies of southwestern Ontario. Their days are spent foraging along the wooded edges of fields and wetlands, and they will occasionally pick through the manure-laden ground of cattle feedlots. At day's end, foraging is curtailed, and most birds seek the shelter of trees and shrubs and the stalks of emergent marshland vegetation. • Unlike many blackbirds, the Rusty Blackbird nests in isolated pairs or very small, loose colonies. • Rusty Blackbirds are generally less abundant and less aggressive than their relatives, and they generally avoid human-altered environments.

breeding

ID: yellow eyes; dark legs; long, sharp bill. *Breeding:* dark plumage; male is darker and has a subtle green gloss on its body and a subtle bluish or greenish gloss on its head. *Non-breeding:* rusty wings, back and crown; male is darker; female has buffy underparts and a rusty cheek.
Size: *L* 23 cm.
Status: uncommon to common spring and fall migrant from early March to early May and from late September to early December; uncommon summer breeder from May to September; rare winter visitor.
Habitat: *Breeding:* bogs, fens, beaver ponds, wet meadows and the shrubby shorelines of lakes, rivers and swamps. *Non-breeding:* marshes, open fields, feedlots and woodland edges near water.
Nesting: low in a shrub or small conifer, often above or very near water; female builds a bulky nest of twigs, grass and lichens, with

an inner cup of mud and decaying vegetation, and lines it with fine grass; female incubates 4 or 5 pale blue-green eggs, spotted with grey and brown, for about 14 days.
Feeding: walks along shorelines, gleaning waterbugs, beetles, dragonflies, snails, grasshoppers and occasionally small fish; also eats waste grain and seeds.
Voice: song is a squeaky, creaking *kushleeeh ksh-lay*; call is a harsh *chack*.
Similar Species: *Brewer's Blackbird* (p. 336): male has glossier, iridescent plumage, showing more purple on the head and a greener body; female has dark eyes; fall birds lack the conspicuous rusty highlights. *Common Grackle* (p. 337): longer keeled tail; larger body and bill; more iridescent. *European Starling* (p. 261): bill is yellow in summer; speckled appearance; dark eyes.
Best Sites: Algonquin PP; Sault Ste. Marie area; Lake Superior PP; wetlands off Hwy 11; cattle feed lots and wetlands in southwestern Ontario.

BREWER'S BLACKBIRD

Euphagus cyanocephalus

This bird of the western plains is a relatively new addition to Ontario's avifauna. In recent years, the Brewer's Blackbird has made itself known here, showing up along some of Ontario's roadsides, where it searches for road-killed insects and squabbles with pigeons and starlings for scraps of food. • Unlike the more solitary Rusty Blackbird, the Brewer's almost always nests in colonies, which often include up to 14 pairs. As fall approaches, the colonies join with other family groups to form large, migrating flocks. • The Brewer's feathers show an iridescent quality as reflected rainbows of sunlight move along the feather shafts. As it walks, the Brewer's Blackbird jerks its head back and forth like a chicken, enhancing the glossy effect and distinguishing it from other blackbirds. • John J. Audubon named this bird after his friend and prominent oologist (student of eggs) Thomas Mayo Brewer.

ID: *Male:* iridescent green body and purplish head often look black; yellow eyes; some fall males may show some faint rusty feather edgings. *Female:* flat brown plumage; dark eyes.
Size: *L* 20–25 cm.
Status: rare migrant from April to May and from late September to late November; rare to uncommon breeder from May to September; a few may overwinter.
Habitat: moist, grassy meadows and roadsides with nearby wetlands and patches of trees and shrubs.
Nesting: in small colonies; on the ground or in a shrub or small tree; female builds a bulky, open cup nest of twigs, grass and forbs and lines it with rootlets, fine grass and hair; female incubates 4–6 brown-spotted, pale grey to greenish-grey eggs for 12–14 days.

Feeding: walks along shorelines and open areas, gleaning invertebrates and seeds.
Voice: song is a creaking, 2-noted *k-shee*; call is a metallic *chick* or *check*.
Similar Species: *Rusty Blackbird* (p. 335): longer, more slender bill; iridescent plumage has a subtler green gloss on the body and a subtle bluish or greenish gloss on the head; female has yellow eyes. *Common Grackle* (p. 337): much longer, keeled tail; larger body and bill. *Brown-headed Cowbird* (p. 338): shorter tail; stubbier, thicker bill; male has dark eyes and a brown head; female has paler streaked underparts and a very pale throat. *European Starling* (p. 261): bill is yellow in summer; speckled appearance; dark eyes.
Best Sites: Bruce Peninsula; Sturgeon Falls area; Sudbury area; Sault Ste. Marie area; Thunder Bay area; Lake of the Woods–Rainy River area.

COMMON GRACKLE

Quiscalus quiscula

The Common Grackle is a poor but spirited singer. Usually while perched in a shrub, a male grackle will slowly take a deep breath to inflate his breast, causing his feathers to spike outward; then he closes his eyes and gives out a loud, strained *tssh-schleek*. Despite his lack of musical talent, the male remains smug and proud, posing with his bill held high. • In fall and over winter, large flocks of Common Grackles gather in rural areas, where they forage for waste grain in open fields. Smaller bands occasionally venture into urban neighbourhoods, where they assert their dominance at backyard birdfeeders—even bullying Blue Jays yield feeding rights to these cocky and aggressive birds. • The grackle is easily distinguished from Rusty and Brewer's blackbirds by its long, heavy bill and its lengthy, wedge-shaped tail. In flight, the grackle's long tail trails behind it like a hatchet blade. • At night, grackles commonly roost with groups of European Starlings, Red-winged Blackbirds and even Brown-headed Cowbirds.

ID: iridescent plumage (purple-blue head and breast, bronze back and sides, and purple wings and tail) often looks blackish; long, keeled tail; yellow eyes; long, heavy bill; female is smaller, duller and browner than the male. *Juvenile:* dull brown overall; dark eyes.

Size: *L* 28–34 cm.

Status: abundant migrant and breeder from late March to October; rare to locally common visitor from October to March.

Habitat: wetlands, hedgerows, fields, wet meadows, riparian woodlands, along the edges of coniferous forests and woodlands, urban and suburban parks, and shrubby parks and gardens.

Nesting: singly or in small colonies; in dense tree or shrub branches or emergent vegetation, often near water; female builds a bulky open cup nest of twigs, grass, forbs and mud and lines it with fine grass or feathers; female incubates 4 or 5 brown-blotched, pale blue eggs for 12–14 days.

Feeding: slowly struts along the ground, gleaning, snatching and probing for insects, earthworms, seeds, waste grain and fruit; also catches insects in flight and eats small vertebrates; may take some bird eggs.

Voice: song is a series of harsh, strained notes ending with a metallic squeak: *tssh-schleek* or *gri-de-leeek*; call is a quick, loud *swaaaack* or *chaack*.

Similar Species: *Rusty Blackbird* (p. 335) and *Brewer's Blackbird* (p. 336): smaller overall; lack the heavy bill and the keeled tail. *Red-winged Blackbird* (p. 331): shorter tail; male has a red shoulder patch and dark eyes. *European Starling* (p. 261): very short tail; long, thin bill (yellow in summer); speckled appearance; dark eyes.

Best Sites: almost any field, wetland, park, woodland edge or hedgerow throughout Ontario.

BROWN-HEADED COWBIRD

Molothrus ater

The Brown-headed Cowbird's song, a bubbling, liquidy *glug-ahl-whee*, might translate to other birds as 'here-comes trouble!' Historically, Brown-headed Cowbirds followed bison herds across the plains and prairies west of Ontario–they now follow cattle—and their nomadic lifestyle made it impossible for them to construct and tend a nest. Instead, cowbirds engage in 'nest parasitism,' laying their eggs in the nests of other songbirds. Many of the parasitized songbirds do not recognize the cowbird eggs and incubate them and raise the cowbirds as their own. Cowbird chicks typically hatch first and develop much more quickly than their nestmates, which are pushed out of the nest or out-competed for food. • The expansion of ranching, the fragmentation of forests and the extensive network of transportation corridors through Ontario has significantly increased the cowbird's range, and it now parasitizes more than 140 bird species in North America, including species that probably had no contact with it prior to widespread human settlement.

ID: thick, conical bill; short, squared tail; dark eyes. *Male:* iridescent green-blue body plumage usually looks glossy black; dark brown head. *Female:* brown plumage overall; faint streaking on light brown underparts; pale throat.
Size: *L* 15–20 cm.
Status: very common migrant and breeder from late March to late October; rare to locally common visitor from November to March.
Habitat: open agricultural and residential areas, including fields, woodland edges, utility cutlines, roadsides, fencelines, landfills, campgrounds, picnic areas and areas near cattle.
Nesting: does not build a nest; each female may lay up to 40 eggs a year in the nests of other birds, usually laying 1 egg per nest, but sometimes up to 8 (probably from several different cowbirds); whitish eggs, marked with grey and brown, hatch after 10–13 days.
Feeding: gleans the ground for seeds, waste grain and invertebrates, especially grasshoppers, beetles and true bugs.
Voice: song is a high, liquidy gurgle *glug-ahl-whee* or *bubbloozeee*; call is a squeaky, high-pitched *seep, psee* or *wee-tse-tse*, often given in flight; also a fast, chipping *ch-ch-ch-ch-ch-ch*.
Similar Species: *Rusty Blackbird* (p. 335) and *Brewer's Blackbird* (p. 336): lack the contrasting brown head and darker body; slimmer, longer bills; longer tails; all have yellow eyes except for the female Brewer's Blackbird. *Common Grackle* (p. 337): much larger overall; longer, heavier bill; longer keeled tail.
Best Sites: cattle pastures, stockyards, feedlots, fencelines and roadsides throughout southern Ontario, including Cochrane to Lake of the Woods.

ORCHARD ORIOLE

Icterus spurius

Unlike the starling, the Orchard Oriole doesn't seem to be interested in sampling ripening fruit. Orchards may once have been a favoured haunt of this oriole, but because orchards are now heavily sprayed and manicured, it is unlikely that you will ever see this bird in such a locale. • These smart-looking birds are best seen in spring, when eager males hop from branch to branch singing their courtship songs. The wooded edges of Lake Erie and the Golden Horseshoe are by far the most productive areas to find oriole males engaged in their romantic serenades.

ID: *Male:* black hood and tail; chestnut underparts, shoulder and rump; dark wings with a white wing bar and feather edgings. *1st-spring male:* like an adult female with a blackish bib. *Female* and *Immature:* olive upperparts; yellow to olive-yellow underparts; faint white wing bars on dusky grey wings.
Size: *L* 15–18 cm.
Status: rare to locally uncommon migrant and breeder from mid-April to September.
Habitat: open woodlands, suburban parklands, forest edges, hedgerows and groves of shade trees.
Nesting: in the fork of a deciduous tree or shrub; female builds a hanging pouch nest woven from grass and other fine plant fibres; female incubates 4 or 5 pale bluish-white eggs,

blotched with grey, brown and purple, for about 12–15 days.
Feeding: finds insects and berries while inspecting trees and shrubs; probes flowers for nectar.
Voice: song is a loud, rapid, varied series of whistled notes; call is a quick *chuck*.
Similar Species: *Baltimore Oriole* (p. 340): male has brighter orange plumage with orange in the tail; female has orange overtones. *Summer Tanager* (p. 301) and *Scarlet Tanager* (p. 302): females have thicker, pale bills and lack the wing bars.
Best Sites: Point Pelee NP; Lake Erie shoreline from Long Point PP to Port Colborne; Walpole Island; Toronto's Grenadier Pond; Prince Edward Point NWA.

BALTIMORE ORIOLE

Icterus galbula

The male Baltimore Oriole has a striking, Halloween-style, black and orange plumage that flickers like smoldering embers amidst our neighbourhood treetops. As if its brilliant plumage wasn't enough to secure our admiration, its rich courtship whistles drip to the ground like manna from the heavens. • Baltimore Orioles are fairly common in Ontario, but they are often difficult to find because they inhabit the forest heights. Developing an ear for their whistled *peter peter peter here peter* tune and more frequent gazing up into your neighbourhood's deciduous trees will no doubt produce many enchanting views of this beloved oriole. • Like many of the songbirds that nest in Ontario, the Baltimore Oriole is really only a visitor to our province; it spends at least half of each year in the tropics of Central and South America. • Irishman George Calvert, the Baron of Baltimore, established a colony in Maryland. Mark Catesby, one of America's first naturalists, chose this bird's name because the male's plumage mirrored the colours of the baron's coat of arms. 'Oriole' is derived from words meaning 'golden bird.'

ID: *Male:* black hood, back, wings and central tail feathers; bright orange underparts, shoulder, rump and outer tail feathers; white wing patch and feather edgings. *Female:* olive brown upperparts (darkest on the head); dull yellow-orange underparts and rump; white wing bar.

Size: *L* 18–20 cm.

Status: uncommon to common migrant and breeder from May to early October; a few may remain in winter.

Habitat: deciduous and mixed forests, particularly riparian woodlands, natural openings, shorelines, roadsides, orchards, gardens and parklands.

Nesting: high in a deciduous tree, suspended from a branch; female builds a hanging pouch nest of grass, bark shreds, rootlets, plant stems and grapevines and lines it with fine grass, rootlets and fur; occasionally adds string and fishing line; female incubates 4 or 5 pale grey to bluish-white eggs with dark markings, for 12–14 days.

Feeding: gleans canopy vegetation and shrubs for caterpillars, beetles, wasps and other invertebrates; also eats some fruit and nectar; may visit hummingbird feeders and feeding stations that offer orange halves.

Voice: song consists of slow, loud, clear whistles: *peter peter here here peter;* calls include a 2-note *tea-too* and a rapid chatter: *ch-ch-ch-ch-ch.*

Similar Species: *Orchard Oriole* (p. 339): male has darker chestnut plumage; female is olive yellow and lacks the orange overtones. *Summer Tanager* (p. 301) and *Scarlet Tanager* (p. 302): females have thicker, pale bills and lack the wing bars.

Best Sites: almost any deciduous or mixed woodland in southern Ontario, including Thunder Bay to Lake of the Woods.

PINE GROSBEAK

Pinicola enucleator

Pine Grosbeaks are colourful nomads of the Boreal Forest where spruce, pine and fir carpet the landscape of muskeg and Canadian Shield rock. Much of their survival depends on the availability of conifer seeds, so Pine Grosbeaks are always in search of a good crop. • It is a great moment in a typical Ontario winter when the Pine Grosbeaks emerge from the wilds to settle on your backyard feeder. Every so often, Pine Grosbeaks flock to southern woodlands in winter, occasionally bringing birds as far south as Toronto, Hamilton and Windsor. These erratic winter invasions thrill southern Ontario naturalists—the birds' bright colours and exciting flock behaviour are certainly a welcome sight. These invasions are not completely understood, but it is thought that cone crop failures or changes to forest ecology caused by logging, forest fires or climatic factors may force these hungry 'finches' southward in search of food. • *Pinicola* is Latin for 'pine dweller,' and *enucleator* is Latin for 'one who takes off shells.'

ID: stout, dark, conical bill; 2 white wing bars; black wings and tail. *Male:* rosy red head, upperparts and breast; grey sides, flanks, belly and undertail coverts. *Female and Immature:* grey overall; yellow or russet wash on the head and rump.

Size: *L* 20–25 cm.

Status: rare to very uncommon, transient year-round resident; irregularly rare to very uncommon visitor outside of breeding range, usually from October to March.

Habitat: *Breeding:* spruce-fir coniferous forests. *Winter:* conifer plantations, deciduous woodlands with fruiting mountain ash, crabapple and woody nightshade and backyard feeding stations.

Nesting: in a conifer or tall shrub; bulky cup nest, loosely made of twigs, grass, forbs and rootlets, is lined with lichens, rootlets and moss;

female incubates 4 bluish-green eggs, spotted with black, brown and purple, for 13–15 days.

Feeding: gleans buds, berries and seeds from trees; also forages on the ground; visits feeding stations in winter.

Voice: song is a short, sweet, musical warble; call is a 3-note whistle with a higher middle note; short, muffled trill is often given in flight; chatters when feeding in flocks.

Similar Species: *White-winged Crossbill* (p. 345): much smaller; lacks the stubby bill and the prominent grey colouration. *Red Crossbill* (p. 344): lacks the stubby bill and the white wing bars. *Evening Grosbeak* (p. 350): female has a light-coloured bill, a dark whisker stripe, tan underparts and broad, white wing patches.

Best Sites: Sault Ste. Marie area; Chapleau Crown Game Reserve; Moosonee area; backyard feeders in varying numbers.

341

PURPLE FINCH

Carpodacus purpureus

The courtship of Purple Finches is a gentle and appealing ritual. The liquid warbling song of the male bubbles through conifer boughs announcing his presence to potential mates. Upon the arrival of an interested female, the colourful male dances lightly around her, beating his wings until he softly lifts into the air. • The Purple Finch prefers the cool northern coniferous and mixed forests of Ontario's Canadian Shield and Hudson Bay Lowland, although small numbers routinely nest among southern conifer plantations and open deciduous woodlands. • The Purple Finch's gentle nature and simple but stunning plumage endears it to many birdwatchers. Fortunately, most bird admirers in Ontario have ample opportunity to meet this charming finch. • Flat, raised table-style feeding stations with nearby tree cover are sure to attract Purple Finches, and erecting one may keep a small flock in your area over winter. • Purple (*purpureus*) is simply a false description of this bird's reddish coloration. Roger Tory Peterson said it best when he described the Purple Finch as 'a sparrow dipped in raspberry juice.'

ID: *Male:* light bill; raspberry red head, throat, breast and nape; brown- and red-streaked back and flanks; reddish-brown cheek; red rump; notched tail; light, unstreaked belly and undertail coverts. *Female:* dark brown cheek and jaw line; white eyebrow and lower cheek stripe; heavily streaked underparts; unstreaked undertail coverts.
Size: *L* 13–15 cm.
Status: fairly common migrant and breeder from March to October; rare to locally uncommon visitor from October to March.
Habitat: *Breeding:* coniferous and mixed forests. *Winter* and *In migration:* coniferous, mixed and deciduous forests, shrubby open areas and feeding stations with nearby tree cover.
Nesting: on a conifer branch, far from the trunk; cup nest, woven

with twigs, grass and rootlets, is lined with moss and hair; female incubates 4 or 5 pale greenish-blue eggs, marked with black and brown, for about 13 days.
Feeding: gleans the ground and vegetation for seeds, buds, berries and insects; readily visits table-style feeding stations.
Voice: song is a bubbly, continuous warble; call is a single metallic *cheep* or *weet*.
Similar Species: *House Finch* (p. 343): squared tail; male lacks the reddish cap; female lacks the distinct cheek patch. *Red Crossbill* (p. 344): larger bill with crossed mandibles; male has more red overall and dark Vs on the whitish undertail coverts.
Best Sites: Presqu'ile PP; Bon Echo PP; Algonquin PP; Lake Superior PP; Sleeping Giant PP; backyard feeders throughout southern Ontario.

HOUSE FINCH

Carpodacus mexicanus

Since its first appearance here in the early 1970s, the House Finch has established itself in communities from Windsor to Ottawa, mainly along the north shores of Lake Erie and Lake Ontario. A native to western North America, the House Finch was brought to eastern parts of the continent as an illegally captured cage bird known as the 'Hollywood Finch.' In the early 1940s, New York pet shop owners released their birds to avoid prosecution and fines, and it is the descendants of those birds that are now colonizing Ontario. • Only the resourceful House Finch has been aggressive and stubborn enough to successfully outcompete the House Sparrow. Like the House Sparrow, this finch has prospered in urban environments. Both birds often build their messy nests among eaves, rafters, chimneys and other human-fashioned habitats and both thrive on seeds.

ID: streaked undertail coverts; brown-streaked back; square tail. *Male:* brown cap; bright red eyebrow, forecrown, throat and breast; heavily streaked flanks. *Female:* indistinct facial patterning; heavily streaked underparts.
Size: *L* 13–15 cm.
Status: uncommon to locally common migrant; locally uncommon winter resident; uncommon to locally abundant summer resident.
Habitat: cities, towns and agricultural areas.
Nesting: in a cavity, building, dense foliage or abandoned bird nest; especially in evergreens and ornamental shrubs near buildings; mostly the female builds an open cup nest of grass, twigs, forbs, leaves, hair and feathers, often adding string and other debris; female incubates 4 or 5 pale blue

eggs, dotted with lavender and black, for 12–14 days.
Feeding: gleans vegetation and the ground for seeds; also takes berries, buds and some flower parts; often visits feeding stations.
Voice: song is a bright, disjointed warble lasting about 3 seconds, often ending with a harsh *jeeer* or *wheer*; flight call is a sweet *cheer*, given singly or in series.
Similar Species: *Purple Finch* (p. 342): notched tail; male has a more burgundy red cap, upper back and flanks; female has a distinct cheek patch. *Red Crossbill* (p. 344): bill has crossed mandibles; male has more red overall and darker wings.
Best Sites: birdfeeders in Windsor, Niagara Falls, Hamilton, Toronto, Kingston and Ottawa; Rondeau PP; Presqu'ile PP.

RED CROSSBILL

Loxia curvirostra

Red Crossbills are the great gypsies of Ontario's bird community, wandering through the province's forests in search of pine cones. They might breed at any time of the year if they discover a bumper crop—it's not unusual to hear them singing and see them nest-building in mid-winter. Their nomadic ways make them difficult birds to find, and even during years of plenty there is no guarantee these birds will surface in our province. Winter is typically the time to see crossbills, and in some years, large flocks suddenly appear in southern parts of the province. • The oddly shaped bill of crossbills are an adaptation for prying open conifer cones. Once a cone is cracked, a crossbill uses its nimble tongue to extract the soft, energy-rich seeds hidden within. • The scientific name *curvirostra* is Latin for 'curve billed.'

ID: bill has crossed tips. *Male:* dull orange-red to brick red plumage; dark wings and tail; always has colour on the throat. *Female:* olive grey to dusky yellow plumage; plain, dark wings. *Juvenile:* streaky brown overall.

Size: *L* 13–16 cm.

Status: rare, erratic and irruptive, transient year-round resident; particularly irruptive in winter.

Habitat: coniferous forests and plantations, favouring red and white pine, but also other pine and spruce-fir forests.

Nesting: high on the outer branch of a conifer; female builds an open cup nest of twigs, grass, bark shreds and rootlets and lines it with moss, lichens, rootlets, feathers and hair; female incubates 3 or 4 pale bluish-white to greenish-white eggs, dotted with black and purple, for 12–18 days.

Feeding: primarily conifer seeds (especially pine); also eats buds, deciduous tree seeds and occasionally insects; often licks road salt or minerals in soil and along roadsides; rarely visits feeders.

Voice: distinctive *jip-jip* call note, often given in flight; song is a varied series of warbles, trills and chips (similar to other finches).

Similar Species: *White-winged Crossbill* (p. 345): 2 broad, white wing bars. *Pine Siskin* (p. 348): similar to juvenile Red Crossbill, but is smaller, lacks the crossed bill and has yellow highlights in the wing. *Pine Grosbeak* (p. 341): stubby, conical bill; white wing bars. *House Finch* (p. 343) and *Purple Finch* (p. 342): conical bills; less red overall; lacks the red on the lower belly; lighter brownish wings.

Best Sites: highly variable from year to year; St. Williams Forestry Station; Petroglyphs PP; Bon Echo PP; Algonquin PP.

WHITE-WINGED CROSSBILL

Loxia leucoptera

People are often amazed by the colourful and bizarre shapes of bird bills. Although this bird's bill lacks the colourful flair of the tropical toucan's and the massive proportions of the hornbill's, its cross-mandible design is shared by only two bird species in North America. White-winged Crossbills primarily eat spruce and tamarack seeds, and their bills are adapted to pry open cones. • Crossbills overwinter in flocks. The presence of a foraging group high in a spruce tree creates an unforgettable shower of conifer cones and crackling chatter. Like many finches, White-winged Crossbills can be abundant one year and nearly absent the next. • When not foraging in spruce spires, White-winged Crossbills often drop to ground level, where they drink water from shallow forest pools or lick salt from winter roads. Unfortunately, their habit of licking salt from roadsides often results in crossbill fatalities.

ID: bill has crossed tips; 2 bold white wing bars. *Male:* pinkish red overall; black wings and tail. *Female:* streaked brown upperparts; dusky yellow underparts slightly streaked with brown; dark wings and tail. *Juvenile:* streaky brown overall (with white wing bars). **Size:** *L* 15–17 cm.

Status: uncommon, transient year-round resident; uncommon to locally abundant, erratic, irruptive visitor from October to March.

Habitat: coniferous forests, primarily spruce, fir, tamarack and eastern hemlock; occasionally townsites and deciduous forests.

Nesting: on an outer branch in a conifer; female builds an open cup nest of twigs, grass, bark shreds and forbs and lines it with moss, lichens, rootlets, hair and soft plant down; female incubates 2–4 whitish to pale blue-green eggs, spotted with brown and lavender, for 12–14 days.

Feeding: prefers conifer seeds (mostly spruce and tamarack); also eats deciduous tree seeds and occasionally insects; often licks salt and minerals from roads when available.

Voice: song is a high-pitched series of warbles, trills and chips; call is a series of harsh, questioning *cheat* notes, often given in flight.

Similar Species: *Red Crossbill* (p. 344): lacks the white wing bars; male is deeper red (less pinkish). *Pine Siskin* (p. 348): similar to the juvenile White-winged Crossbill, but is smaller, has yellow highlights in the wing and lacks the crossed bill. *Pine Grosbeak* (p. 341): stubby, conical bill; thinner wing bars; female is very grey; male has grey sides. *House Finch* (p. 343) and *Purple Finch* (p. 342): conical bills; less red overall; lighter brownish wings.

Best Sites: erratic and irruptive, especially in winter; Algonquin PP; Lake Superior PP; Hwy 11 from Iroquois Falls to Cochrane.

345

COMMON REDPOLL

Carduelis flammea

A predictably unpredictable winter visitor, the Common Redpoll is seen in Ontario in varying numbers. It might appear in flocks of hundreds or in groups of a dozen or less, depending on the year. Redpolls are renowned for their effective winter adaptations, but they have a very small surface area relative to their internal volume, so they are in constant danger of running out of fuel and dying from hypothermia. This limitation means that they must eat almost constantly—redpolls are continually gleaning waste grain from bare fields or stocking up on seed at winter feeders. Because of their focus on food, wintering redpolls are remarkably fearless of humans. • Redpolls can endure colder temperatures than any other songbird. Their highly insulative feathers enable them to withstand bitter cold, especially when the feathers are fluffed out, which traps layers of warm, insulating air.

non-breeding

ID: red forecrown; black chin; yellowish bill; streaked upperparts and rump; lightly streaked sides, flanks and undertail coverts; notched tail. *Male:* pinkish-red breast is brightest in breeding plumage. *Female:* whitish to pale grey breast.

Size: *L* 13 cm.

Status: fairly common, transient year-round resident and breeder; uncommon to locally abundant, erratic, irruptive migrant and visitor from October to early April.

Habitat: *Breeding:* coastal tundra with low shrubs and patches of dwarf spruce, willow and alder. *Winter:* open fields, meadows, roadsides, utility cutlines, railways, forest edges and backyards with feeders.

Nesting: low in a shrub or dwarf spruce; occasionally in grass clumps; open cup nest, made of fine twigs, grass, plant stems, lichens and moss, is lined with feathers, hair or plant down;

female incubates 4 or 5 pale blue eggs with fine dark speckles, for about 12 days.

Feeding: gleans the ground, snow and vegetation in large flocks for seeds in winter; often visits feeding stations; some insects are taken in summer.

Voice: song is a twittering series of trills; calls are a soft *chit-chit-chit-chit* and a faint *swe-eet*; indistinguishable from the Hoary Redpoll.

Similar Species: *Hoary Redpoll* (p. 347): unstreaked or partly streaked rump; usually has faint or no streaking on the sides and flanks; generally paler and more plump overall; bill may look stubbier; lacks the streaking on the undertail coverts. *Pine Siskin* (p. 348): heavily streaked overall; yellow highlights in the wings and tail.

Best Sites: Moosonee area; Polar Bear PP; irruptive in winter; fields and backyard feeders throughout Ontario.

HOARY REDPOLL

Carduelis hornemanni

Mixed in with the abundant Common Redpolls, you will often see a more lightly coloured bird with noticeably less streaking. The 'Great Redpoll Debate' predictably ensues as you and your birder friends compare notes on the ambiguous field marks of these two species. Things were much simpler when the two redpolls were considered a single species. • Hoary Redpolls are well adapted to life in the cold. They have a high level of food intake, in part because of a special storage pouch in the esophagus (the esophageal diverticulum), which allows them to carry large quantities of energy-rich seeds. When seed crops fail or icy winds become intolerable, however, Hoary Redpolls do not hesitate to move south, where numbers occasionally 'irrupt' every few years. • Jens Wilken Hornemann was one of Denmark's leading botanists, and he helped organize an expedition to Greenland, where the first scientific specimen of this bird was taken.

non-breeding

ID: red forecrown; black chin; yellowish bill; frosty white plumage overall; lightly streaked upperparts, except for the unstreaked rump; unstreaked underparts (flanks may have faint streaking); notched tail. *Male:* pinkish-tinged breast. *Female:* white to light grey breast.
Size: *L* 13–14 cm.
Status: very rare to uncommon, erratic, irruptive migrant and visitor from November to March; may be a very rare breeder.
Habitat: *Breeding:* coastal tundra. *Winter:* open fields, meadows, roadsides, utility cutlines, railways, forest edges and backyards with feeders.
Nesting: on or near the ground; female builds an open cup nest of grass and lines it with plant down, feathers and hair; female

incubates 4 or 5 pale blue eggs with fine dark speckles, for about 14 days.
Feeding: gleans the ground, snow and vegetation for seeds and buds; occasionally visits feeding stations in winter; also takes some insects in summer.
Voice: song is a twittering series of trills; calls are a soft *chit-chit-chit-chit* and a faint *swe-eet*; indistinguishable from the Common Redpoll.
Similar Species: *Common Redpoll* (p. 346): streaked rump, sides, flanks and undertail coverts; generally darker and slimmer overall. *Pine Siskin* (p. 348): heavily streaked overall; yellow highlights in the wings and tail.
Best Sites: erratic and irruptive in winter; fields and backyard feeders, especially in northern Ontario.

PINE SISKIN
Carduelis pinus

Y ou can spend days, weeks and even months in pursuit of Pine Siskins and you may only be met with frustration, aching feet and a sore, kinked neck. The smartest way to meet these birds is to set up a finch feeder filled with black niger seed in your backyard and wait for them to appear. If the feeder is in the right location, you can expect your backyard to be visited by Pine Siskins at just about any time of year, but particularly in winter. • Tight flocks of these gregarious birds are frequently heard before they're seen. Once you recognize their characteristic, rising *zzzreeeee* calls and boisterous chatter, you can confirm the presence of these finches by simply listening. • Aside from the Pine Siskin's occasional flashes of yellow, its wardrobe is drab and sparrow-like. But for those who get to know it, the bird's behaviour reveals a gentle nature that radiates the playfulness and enthusiasm of a goldfinch.

ID: heavily streaked underparts; yellow highlights at the base of the tail feathers and in the wings (easily seen in flight); dull wing bars; darker, heavily streaked upperparts; slightly forked tail; indistinct facial pattern. *Immature:* similar to the adult, but the overall yellow tint fades through summer.
Size: *L* 11–13 cm.
Status: uncommon to common, irruptive and erratic year-round resident; uncommon to common migrant and visitor from October to May.
Habitat: *Breeding:* coniferous and mixed forests and urban and rural ornamental and shade trees. *Winter:* coniferous and mixed forests, forest edges, meadows, roadsides, agricultural fields and backyards with feeders.
Nesting: usually loosely colonial; typically at mid-height on an outer branch of a conifer; female builds a loose cup of twigs, grass and rootlets and lines it with feathers,

hair, rootlets and fine plant fibres; female incubates 3–5 pale blue eggs, with dark dots, for about 13 days.
Feeding: gleans the ground and vegetation for seeds (especially thistle seeds), buds and some insects; attracted to road salts, mineral licks and ashes; regularly visits feeding stations.
Voice: song is a variable, bubbly mix of squeaky, metallic raspy notes, sometimes resembling a jerky laugh; call is a buzzy, rising *zzzreeeee.*
Similar Species: *Common Redpoll* (p. 346) and *Hoary Redpoll* (p. 347): red forecrown; lack the yellow in the wings and tail. *Purple Finch* (p. 342) and *House Finch* (p. 343): females have a thicker bill and no yellow in the wings or tail. *Sparrows* (pp. 303–20): all lack the yellow in the wings and tail.
Best Sites: parks and coniferous forests and woodlands throughout the Canadian Shield; fields and backyard feeders.

AMERICAN GOLDFINCH

Carduelis tristis

The American Goldfinch is a bright, cheery songbird that is commonly seen in weedy fields, along roadsides and among backyard shrubs throughout summer and fall. Goldfinches seem to delight in perching upon late-summer thistle heads as they search for seeds, and it's hard to miss the familiar, jubilant *po-ta-to-chip* they issue as they flutter over parks and gardens in a distinctive undulating flight style. • Goldfinches nest late in the summer to ensure there is a dependable source of thistles and dandelion seeds to feed their young. • It is enjoyable to observe a flock of goldfinches raining down to ground level to poke and prod the heads of dandelions. These birds do their best to play up the comedy as they attempt to step down on the flower stems to reach the crowning seeds. A dandelion-filled lawn always seems a lot less weedy with a flock of glowing goldfinches hopping through the yard.

breeding

ID: *Breeding male:* black cap (extends onto the forehead); black wings and tail; bright yellow body; white wing bars, undertail coverts and tail base; orange bill and legs. *Non-breeding male:* olive brown back; yellow-tinged head; grey underparts. *Female:* yellow-green upperparts and belly; yellow throat and breast.
Size: *L* 11–14 cm.
Status: common migrant and breeder from April to December; uncommon to fairly common visitor from November to April.
Habitat: weedy fields, woodland edges, meadows, riparian areas and parks and gardens.
Nesting: in late summer and fall; in the fork of a deciduous shrub or tree, often in hawthorn, serviceberry or sapling maple; female builds a compact cup nest of plant fibres, grass and spider silk and lines it with plant down

and hair; female incubates 4–6 pale bluish-white eggs, occasionally spotted with light brown, for about 12–14 days.
Feeding: gleans vegetation for seeds, primarily thistle, birch and alder, as well as for insects and berries; commonly visits feeding stations.
Voice: song is a long and varied series of trills, twitters, warbles and sibilant notes; calls include *po-ta-to-chip* or *per-chic-or-ee* (often delivered in flight) and a whistled *dear-me, see-me.*
Similar Species: *Evening Grosbeak* (p. 350): much larger; massive bill; lacks the black forehead. *Wilson's Warbler* (p. 298): olive upperparts; olive wings without wing bars; thin, dark bill; black cap does not extend onto the forehead.
Best Sites: almost any weedy field, shrubby riparian area and forest edge with road access in Ontario.

349

EVENING GROSBEAK

Coccothraustes vespertinus

Unannounced, a flock of Evening Grosbeaks descends one chilly winter day upon your backyard birdfeeder filled with sunflower seeds. You watch the stunning gold and black grosbeaks with delight, but you soon come to realize that these birds are both an aesthetic blessing and a financial curse. The birds will eat great quantities of expensive birdseed and then suddenly disappear in late winter, in an expression of their wild and independent spirit. Evening Grosbeaks are transient residents in Ontario, and they are generally encountered every two to three years in large wintering flocks • It's hard not to notice the massive bill of this seed eater. As any seasoned bird-bander will tell you, the Evening Grosbeak's bill can exert an incredible force per unit area—it may be the most powerful of any North American bird. • It was once thought that the Evening Grosbeak sang only in the evening, a fact that is reflected in both its common and scientific names (*vespertinus* is Latin for 'of the evening').

ID: massive, light-coloured, conical bill; black wings and tail; broad, white wing patches. *Male:* black crown; bright yellow eyebrow and forehead band; dark brown head gradually fades into the golden yellow belly and lower back. *Female:* grey head and upper back; yellow-tinged underparts; white undertail coverts.

Size: *L* 18–22 cm.

Status: irregularly rare to locally fairly common migrant and visitor from October to mid-May; fairly common breeder from April to early October.

Habitat: *Breeding:* coniferous and mixed forests and woodlands; occasionally in deciduous woodlands, suburban parks and orchards. *Winter:* coniferous, mixed and deciduous forests and woodlands, parks and gardens with feeders.

Nesting: on an outer limb in a conifer; female builds a flimsy cup nest of twigs and lines it with rootlets, fine grass, plant fibres, moss and pine needles; female incubates 3 or 4 pale blue to blue-green eggs, blotched with purple, grey and brown, for 11–14 days.

Feeding: gleans the ground and vegetation for seeds, buds and berries; also eats insects and licks mineral-rich soil; often visits feeding stations for sunflower seeds.

Voice: song is a wandering, halting warble; call is a loud, sharp *clee-ip* or a ringing *peeer*.

Similar Species: *American Goldfinch* (p. 349): much smaller; small bill; smaller wing bars; male has a black cap. *Pine Grosbeak* (p. 341): female has a black bill and smaller wing bars; grey overall.

Best Sites: erratic and irruptive; potentially any woodland or backyard feeder in southern Ontario; Bon Echo PP; Halfway Lake PP.

HOUSE SPARROW

Passer domesticus

For most of us, the House Sparrow is the first bird we meet and recognize in our youth. Although it is one of our most abundant and conspicuous birds, many generations of House Sparrows may live out their lives within our backyards with few of us every knowing much about this omnipresent neighbour. • House Sparrows were introduced to North America in the 1850s around Brooklyn, New York, as part of a plan to control the numbers of insects that were damaging grain and cereal crops. Contrary to popular opinion at the time, this sparrow's diet is largely vegetarian, so its impact on crop pests proved to be minimal. Since then, this Eurasian sparrow has managed to colonize most human-altered environments on the continent, and it has benefited greatly from a close association with humans. Unfortunately, its aggressive behaviour has helped it to usurp territory from many native bird species, especially in rural habitats. • House Sparrows are not closely related to the other North American sparrows; they belong to the family of Old World Sparrows or 'Weaver Finches.'

ID: *Breeding male:* grey crown; black bib and bill; chestnut nape; light grey cheek; white wing bar; dark, mottled upperparts; grey underparts. *Non-breeding male:* smaller black bib; light-coloured bill. *Female:* plain grey-brown overall; buffy eyebrow; streaked upperparts; indistinct facial patterns; greyish, unstreaked underparts.
Size: *L* 14–17 cm.
Status: abundant year-round resident.
Habitat: townsites, urban and suburban areas, farmyards and agricultural areas, railyards and other developed areas (absent from undeveloped areas).

Nesting: often communal; in human-made structures, ornamental shrubs or natural cavities; pair builds a large, dome-shaped nest of grass, twigs, plant fibres and litter and often lines it with feathers; pair incubates 4–6 whitish to greenish-white eggs, dotted with grey and brown, for 10–13 days.
Feeding: gleans the ground and vegetation for seeds, insects and fruit; frequently visits feeding stations for seeds.
Voice: song is a familiar, plain *cheep-cheep-cheep-cheep*; call is a short *chill-up*.
Similar Species: female is distinctively drab. *Harris's Sparrow* (p. 319): grey face, black cap and pink-orange bill.
Best Site: your backyard.

351

OCCASIONAL BIRD SPECIES

WESTERN GREBE
Aechmophorus occidentalis

This large grebe, a vagrant from the western plains and prairies, is very rarely seen along Lake Ontario shores in spring and fall. Lake of the Woods has supported a non-breeding pair each summer since 1989.

ID: long, slender neck; black upperparts from the base of the bill to the tail; white underparts from the chin through the belly; long, thin, yellow bill; white cheek; black on the face extends down to surround the red eyes.
Size: *L* 51–61 cm.

NORTHERN FULMAR
Fulmarus glacialis

This bird of the high seas is very rarely sighted in Ontario, but it may occur regularly off the Hudson Bay coast in fall. Most sightings occur from late October to January.

ID: prominent forehead; yellow bill with a prominent nostril tube; stocky body; short, thick neck; yellow feet. *Light morph:* white head and underparts; bluish-gray upperparts. *Dark morph:* dark gray overall; pale flight feathers. *In flight:* quick wingbeats followed by stiff-winged glides.
Size: *L* 43–51 cm; *W* 1.1 m.

light morph

NORTHERN GANNET
Morus bassanus

This occasional to rare visitor from the Atlantic coast has been reported here in most years since 1983. It has been seen along Ontario's north coast and the Ottawa River, but most reports are from Lake Ontario in late fall.

ID: thick, tapered bill; long, narrow wings; pointed tail. *Adult:* mostly white; black wing tips and feet; buffy wash on the nape. *Immature:* various stages of mottled gray, black and white. *In flight:* pointed at all ends; black wing tips.
Size: *L* 89–97 cm; *W* 1.8 m.

LITTLE BLUE HERON
Egretta caerulea

breeding

This rare spring and fall vagrant is an annual visitor to wetlands in southern Ontario. Point Pelee, Rondeau and Long Point provincial parks are good locations to look for post-breeding wanderers of this species.

ID: greyish-blue overall; black-tipped, grey bill; yellow eyes; grey lores. *Non-breeding:* dark purplish head and neck. *Breeding:* pinkish-purple head and neck; black feet and legs. *Immature:* all-white plumage; dark-tipped primaries; yellowish feet and legs.
Size: *L* 61 cm; *W* 1 m.

TRICOLORED HERON
Egretta tricolor

Tricolored Herons are rare but regular visitors to our province each spring, and sightings are recorded every few years in fall. Lake Erie and Toronto-area marshes have produced the most sightings of these birds.

breeding

ID: *Breeding:* long, slender bill, neck and legs; purplish- to greyish-blue plumage; white underparts and foreneck; pale rump; long plumes on the head and back. *Immature:* chestnut hindneck and wing coverts.
Size: *L* 66 cm; *W* 91 cm.

YELLOW-CROWNED NIGHT-HERON
Nyctanassa violacea

Only a couple of these night-herons are seen each year in Ontario, usually from mid-April to early June in Point Pelee, Rondeau and Long Point parks. Occasionally, individual birds are discovered farther north.

breeding

ID: black head; white cheeks and crown; yellowish forehead; stout, black bill; pale area at the base of the lower mandible; slate grey neck and body; yellow legs. *Breeding:* long, white head plumes extend down the back of the neck. *Immature:* brown plumage with white spotting; green legs. *In flight:* legs extend well behind the tail.
Size: *L* 61 cm; *W* 1.1 m.

GLOSSY IBIS
Plegadis falcinellus

This vagrant is most often seen in spring or fall, with records from the Pelee area to Ottawa and the Bruce Peninsula. The Glossy Ibis looks like a cross between a heron and a curlew.

breeding

ID: long, downcurved bill; long legs; brown eyes; dark skin in front of the eye is bordered by 2 pale stripes. *Breeding:* chestnut head, neck and sides; green and purple sheen on the wings, tail, crown and face. *Winter:* dark greyish-brown head and neck are streaked with white. *In flight:* neck is fully extended; legs trail behind the tail; hunchbacked appearance; flocks fly in lines or V formations.
Size: *L* 56–64 cm; *W* 91–94 cm.

BLACK VULTURE
Coragyps atratus

This vulture of the southern U.S. was once considered an exceptionally rare vagrant in Ontario, but it is now sighted almost every year in southern parts of our province. Look for the light wing tips to distinguish it from the more common Turkey Vulture.

ID: all-black plumage; greyish head, legs and feet; base of the primaries are light grey and contrast noticeably against the otherwise dark underparts.
Size: *L* 64 cm; *W* 1.5 m.

CINNAMON TEAL
Anas cyanoptera

The breeding male Cinnamon Teal is unmistakeable, but the female looks a lot like a female Blue-winged Teal. A couple of breeding records have been reported in Ontario, mostly from sewage lagoons in the southwest. This teal is now sighted every couple of years on average, mostly in southwestern Ontario or west of Thunder Bay.

ID: longish, broad bill; blue forewing patch; green speculum. *Male:* rich cinnamon red head, neck and underparts; red eyes. *Female:* dark eyes; mottled brown overall.
Size: L 38–43 cm.

TUFTED DUCK
Aythya fuligula

This Old World relative of the Ring-necked Duck has a distinct crest on the back of its head. It is an occasional winter visitor to the lower Great Lakes, with one or two sightings recorded each year in our province.

ID: *Male:* rounded, purplish-blackish head with an obvious crest on the hindcrown; pale eyes; black body except for the white sides; dark-tipped, blue-grey bill. *Female:* brown overall; less obvious head crest; may show white around the base of the bill.
Size: L 43 cm.

SWALLOW-TAILED KITE
Elanoides forficatus

This hawk-like bird is a distinctive visitor from the southeastern U.S. Most sightings have been recorded west of Long Point Provincial Park in May, late August and early September.

ID: white head, underparts and underwing linings; black upperparts; dark eyes; long, deeply forked tail. *Immature:* similar to an adult, but with white-tipped primary feathers and a shorter tail. *In flight:* never hovers.
Size: L 58 cm; W 1.2 m.

MISSISSIPPI KITE
Ictinia mississippiensis

Point Pelee National Park seems to be the best place to see this distant wanderer from the southern U.S. Keep a close eye out in May, and you may be one of the lucky few to witness a Mississippi Kite catching flying insects in daring acrobatic flights.

ID: long, pointed, swept-back wings; upperside of the secondaries are pale grey; dark grey upperparts; dark tail; pale grey head and underparts. *Immature:* dark brownish upperparts; streaky brown underparts; pale translucent bands on a dark tail. *In flight:* never hovers; first primary is shorter than the rest.
Size: L 37 cm; W 89 cm.

SWAINSON'S HAWK
Buteo swainsoni

Every year at least one or two of these western wanderers are detected in Ontario, usually at Holiday Beach, Hawk Cliff or Beamer Point Conservation Area between early September and mid-November.

light morph

ID: long, narrow wings; fan-shaped tail. *Light morph:* dark bib; white wing linings contrast with dark flight feathers; white belly; finely barred tail. *Dark morph:* dark wing linings blend with brown flight feathers; brown overall. *In flight:* wings are held in a shallow V.
Size: *Male: L* 48–51 cm; *W* 1.3 m (female is slightly larger).

ROCK PTARMIGAN
Lagopus mutus

This ptarmigan is an extremely rare, irruptive visitor to Ontario's north. It usually moves into the province over winter, at which time the female lacks the red eye comb. In winter, the male Rock Ptarmigan can be distinguished from a Willow Ptarmigan by its black eye line.

winter

ID: black outer tail feathers; black bill and eyes.
Summer: small, red eye comb; mottled buff, brown and black overall; white wings and legs. *Winter:* all white overall; male has a prominent black eye line and a bright red eye comb; female lacks the eye line and eye comb.
Size: *L* 36 cm.

GREATER PRAIRIE-CHICKEN
Tympanuchus cupido

Greater Prairie-Chickens are thought to have been past inhabitants of the grasslands of southwestern Ontario. The last Greater Prairie-Chicken sighting in Ontario was in April 1959, in Sanford Township, Kenora District.

ID: dark brown, black and cinnamon-buff mottled upperparts; brown and white barred underparts; whitish, feathered legs; rounded tail. *Male:* yellow-orange eye comb; blackish tail; inflated yellow-orange neck sacs and erect, long, blackish neck feathers during its courtship dance. *Female:* shorter, browner neck feathers; barred tail.
Size: *L* 43 cm.

WHOOPING CRANE
Grus americana

Whooping Cranes were extirpated from Ontario decades ago, and it is unlikely that they will be seen in Ontario in the near future. However, anything is possible, and wanderers could appear during migration. Observers should take care not to confuse this bird with the relatively common Sandhill Crane.

ID: very tall; mostly white; black primary feathers; bare red skin on the forehead and chin; long, pointed bill; black legs. *Immature:* orange-red head and neck. *In flight:* neck and legs are extended.
Size: *L* 1.3–1.5 m; *W* 2–2.3 m.

BLACK-NECKED STILT
Himantopus mexicanus

About every other year, at least one of these elegant shorebirds wanders north into Ontario to the delight of vigilant birdwatchers. Extremely long, red legs and a black and white body easily identify this marshland wader.

ID: very long, pink to red legs; dark upperparts; clean white underparts; long, thin, straight bill; small white eyebrow; male is blacker than the female.
Size: *L* 36–38 cm.

AMERICAN AVOCET
Recurvirostra americana

Only a few of these shapely shorebirds make appearances along Ontario's shorelines and marshy mudflats each year. The Rainy River–Lake of the Woods area and southwestern Ontario produce the most sightings during spring and fall migration.

ID: long, upturned, black bill; long, pale blue legs; black wings with wide, white patches; white underparts. *Breeding:* peachy red head, neck and breast. *Non-breeding:* grey head, neck and breast. *In flight:* long, skinny legs and neck; black and white wings.
Size: *L* 43–46 cm.

non-breeding

ESKIMO CURLEW
Numenius borealis

Eskimo Curlews are believed to be extinct, because there were only a handful of possible sightings in North America in the latter half of the 20th century. All suspected sightings of this bird should be reported and documented with a photograph, if possible. The Eskimo Curlew may be easily confused with the larger Whimbrel.

ID: small curlew; shortish, slender, downcurved bill; lacks a well-defined central crown stripe; dark eye line; darkish, mottled brown upperparts; lighter brown to buff underparts with arrow-shaped markings on the breast. *In flight:* pale cinnamon underwing linings; all-dark primaries lack the light barring.
Size: *L* 36 cm.

CURLEW SANDPIPER
Calidris ferruginea

fall moult

The annual report of one or two Curlew Sandpipers is promising for Ontario birders hoping to get a glimpse of this vagrant from Eurasia. The shores of Lake Erie and western Lake Ontario in fall are the best locations to see the Curlew Sandpiper.

ID: long, black, downcurved bill; black legs; clean white undertail coverts; white rump; bold, white upperwing stripe. *Breeding:* rich chestnut overall; dark mottling on the crown and back; female is paler. *Non-breeding:* pale grey upperparts; darker grey wings; whitish underparts; white eyebrow; brownish wash on the head.
Size: *L* 22 cm.

MEW GULL
Larus canus

This small gull of the Pacific coast and northwestern parts of the continent is now recorded almost annually in Ontario. The lower Great Lakes waterways from Sarnia to the Cornwall Dam have supported the most sightings.

breeding

ID: dark eyes; dove-like profile. *Breeding:* white head and underparts; grey upperparts; all-yellow bill; yellow legs. *Non-breeding:* head and nape are washed with brown. *Immature:* black-tipped bill; black tail band; head and underparts are smudged with varying amounts of brown.
Size: *L* 40–45 cm; *W* 90–105 cm.

CALIFORNIA GULL
Larus californicus

The Niagara River area is one of the more reliable places to see this vagrant from the West. Late fall and early winter are the best times to search for this bird among the lower Great Lakes.

breeding

ID: yellow bill; red and black spot on the lower mandible; yellow-green legs; dark eyes; grey back; black wing tips. *Breeding:* white head; white underparts. *Non-breeding:* dark, spotty wash on the head and nape. *Immature:* mottled brown overall; pinkish legs; black-tipped, pale bill.
Size: *L* 50–58 cm; *W* 1.2–1.4 m.

IVORY GULL
Pagophila eburnea

Most sightings of this occasional vagrant have been recorded from late November to late February, with the majority of appearances in December from northern Ontario. Ivory Gulls winter on the Arctic and North Atlantic oceans. The nearest breeding colony is on Baffin Island.

ID: all-white plumage; black legs and eyes; yellow-tipped, dark grey bill. *1st winter:* patchy, dark speckling on the face and body; dark tail band; dark spots on the primary feather tips.
Size: *L* 43 cm; *W* 94 cm.

BLACK GUILLEMOT
Cepphus grylle

Only a single guillemot nesting record exists for Ontario: hatched guillemot eggshells were discovered among the rocks of Manchuinagush Island, west of Cape Henrietta Maria, in 1957. Black Guillemots are rare winter visitors to Ontario's far north.

ID: black bill; orange-red feet; upperwings are black, each showing a large white wing patch; underwings are white with dark tips and trailing edges. *Breeding:* black overall, except for the white wing patch. *Non-Breeding:* white overall, except for the mainly black wing and tail; dark mottling on the crown, back and rump. *Immature:* like the non-breeding adult, but with dark mottling on the face, neck, sides and flanks.
Size: *L* 30–36 cm; *W* 58 cm.

BARN OWL
Tyto alba

It appears that urbanization and intensive farming practices in rural communities have caused the virtual extirpation of the Barn Owl from Ontario. The records committee has not received a report of this white-faced, dark-eyed, nocturnal hunter since 1990.

ID: white, heart-shaped face; dark eyes; no ear tufts; unstreaked, whitish underparts; rusty back; long legs.
Size: *L* 17–24 cm; *W* 43–60 cm.

RUFOUS HUMMINGBIRD
Selasphorus rufus

Backyard sugarwater feeders maintained for Ruby-throated Hummingbirds may attract Rufous strays that have wandered east of their Rocky Mountain homes. Fall is the best time to meet these colourful, dainty sprites.

ID: long, thin, black bill; mostly rufous tail. *Male:* rufous back, tail and flanks; scaled, scarlet throat; green crown; white breast and belly. *Female:* green back; red-spotted throat; rufous flanks; light underparts.
Size: *L* 9 cm.

SCISSOR-TAILED FLYCATCHER
Tyrannus forficatus

This tropical-looking flycatcher nests only as far north as Nebraska, but almost every spring or fall a stray bird visits Ontario. Many seem to skirt Lake Huron and Lake Superior, often appearing on the Bruce Peninsula and in the Thunder Bay area.

ID: dark wings; extremely long outer tail feathers give a forked appearance in flight; whitish to greyish head, back and breast; salmon pink underwing linings, flanks and lower underparts; bright pinkish-red wing pits. *Immature:* duller, shorter-tailed version of the adult, with a brownish back.
Size: *L* 33 cm; male's tail is up to 23 cm long.

BEWICK'S WREN
Thryomanes bewickii

Spring is by far the best time to see the Bewick's Wren. Most of these occasional visitors are seen at Point Pelee and Rondeau provincial parks, where open woodlands, shrubby fencelines and dense thickets are their favoured habitat. Five Bewicks nests were found at Point Pelee in the 1950s, but no nesting attempts have been documented since then.

ID: brown upperparts; white underparts; long, bold white eyebrow; dark, barred tail has white corners.
Size: *L* 13 cm.

NORTHERN WHEATEAR
Oenanthe oenanthe

Northern Wheatears are occasional visitors to southern parts of the province, and they may be regular visitors to our northern coast. Most sightings occur in fall along the Ottawa River, but look for these birds anywhere in the province.

ID: white undertail coverts, rump and upper tail; lower tail forms a black, inverted T; white forehead and eyebrow. *Breeding male:* blue-grey upperparts; black wings and triangular ear patch; cinnamon-buff to whitish underparts. *Female* and *Fall male:* brown upperparts; buffier underparts.
Size: *L* 15 cm.

breeding

MOUNTAIN BLUEBIRD
Sialia currucoides

Although Mountain Bluebirds have been seen in our province in spring, the best time to see these western delights is probably fall and early winter. The only Ontario nesting records are of a male Mountain Bluebird mated with a female Eastern Bluebird near Port Stanley in 1985 and 1986. Future nest records are most likely to come from the Rainy River area.

ID: black eyes, bill and legs. *Male:* sky blue body; upperparts are darker than the underparts. *Female:* sky blue wings, tail and rump; blue-grey back and head; brown-grey underparts.
Size: *L* 18 cm.

TOWNSEND'S SOLITAIRE
Myadestes townsendi

Every winter, a small number of Townsend's Solitaires abandon the Rocky Mountains of the West and make appearances here in Ontario. Birders in Toronto and Hamilton record most of the province's sightings, usually between late September and early May. Overwintering vagrants appear to prefer eating buckthorn (*Rhamnus* sp.) nutlets, which are poisonous to humans.

ID: grey body; darker wings and tail; peach-coloured wing patches (very evident in flight); white eye ring; white outer tail feathers; long tail. *Immature:* brown body is heavily spotted with buff; pale eye ring.
Size: *L* 22 cm.

BLACK-THROATED GRAY WARBLER
Dendroica nigrescens

The Black-throated Gray Warbler is another vagrant from western North America. It is an occasional visitor to Ontario, with many records originating from the Toronto area from early May to mid-June and from early August to early January.

ID: *Breeding male:* black and white head; grey back streaked with black; white underparts; sides streaked with black; small yellow spot between the eye and bill; white eyebrow and 'moustache.' *Female:* lighter overall.
Size: *L* 13 cm.

breeding

KIRTLAND'S WARBLER
Dendroica kirtlandii

breeding

The Kirtland's Warbler was once thought to breed commonly at Petawawa, but it is now a rare visitor to the province and one of the most endangered of all North American birds. Kirtland's Warblers are sighted mainly in spring and fall, with the odd record of summer territoriality.

ID: *Male:* blue-grey upperparts; yellow underparts; black streaks on the back, sides and flanks; whitish undertail coverts; bold, broken white eye ring; black patch in front of the eyes. *Female:* duller grey overall; lacks the black face markings.
Size: *L* 15 cm.

WESTERN TANAGER
Piranga ludoviciana

breeding

There have been many reports of this bird in Ontario, but only a few confirmed sightings. Western Tanagers are occasional visitors to our province from late April to late May and from early August to late November.

ID: *Breeding male:* yellow underparts and rump; black back, wings and tail; yellow and white wing bars; variably reddish head; light-coloured bill. *Breeding female:* olive green overall; faint wing bars.
Size: *L* 18 cm.

SPOTTED TOWHEE
Pipilo maculatus

Until recently, this bird and the Eastern Towee were grouped together as the Rufous-sided Towhee. This western sparrow is distinguished from the Eastern Towhee by the white spots on its back and its slightly different call. It is an occasional visitor throughout Ontario.

ID: *Male:* black hood, back, wings and tail; rufous flanks; white spotting on the wings and back; white tips to the outer tail feathers; white belly. *Female:* somewhat paler overall.
Size: *L* 18–22 cm.

LARK SPARROW
Chondestes grammacus

Lark Sparrows nest sporadically in scattered locations throughout southern Ontario. On average, fewer than three birds are reported in our province each year.

ID: distinctive 'helmet' of broad, white stripes, thin, black stripes and chestnut red patches; unstreaked, pale greyish-white underparts; dark central breast spot; black tail with white outer feathers; mottled black and brown upperparts.
Size: *L* 15–17 cm.

LARK BUNTING
Calamospiza melanocorys

breeding

Lucky observers might see a Lark Bunting at any time of year. However, this bird is best seen in the Rainy River area and the grasslands of southwestern Ontario in spring and fall.

ID: dark, conical bill; large, white wing patch. *Breeding male:* all-black plumage; white patch at the tip of the tail. *Female, Immature* and *Non-breeding male:* mottled brown upperparts; brown streaked underparts; pale eyebrow; partial whitish wing patches.
Size: *L* 18 cm.

SELECT REFERENCES

American Ornithologists' Union. 1998. *Check-list of North American Birds.* 7th ed. American Ornithologists' Union, Washington, D.C.

Cadman, M.D., P.F.J. Eagles and F.M. Helleiner. 1987. *Atlas of the Breeding Birds of Ontario.* University of Waterloo Press, Waterloo.

Choate, E.A. 1985. *The Dictionary of American Bird Names.* Rev. ed. Harvard Common Press, Cambridge, Mass.

Dunn, J., and K. Garrett. 1997. *A Field Guide to Warblers of North America.* Houghton Mifflin Co., Boston.

Ehrlich, P.R., D.S. Dobkin and D. Wheye. 1988. *The Birder's Handbook.* Fireside, New York.

Farrand, J., ed. 1983. *The Audubon Society Master Guide to Birding.* Vols. 1–3. Alfred A. Knopf, New York.

Fisher, C. 1996. *Ontario Birds.* Lone Pine Publishing, Edmonton.

Godfrey, W.E. 1986. *The Birds of Canada.* Rev. ed. National Museum of Natural Sciences, Ottawa.

Goodwin, C.E. 1995. A *Bird-Finding Guide to Ontario.* Rev. ed. University of Toronto Press, Toronto.

Graham, J.R. 1997. *Seasonal Status of Birds: Point Pelee National Park and Vicinity.* Friends of Point Pelee, Leamington, Ont.

James, R.D. 1991. *Annotated Checklist of the Birds on Ontario.* 2nd ed. Royal Ontario Museum, Toronto.

Kaufman, K. 1996. *Lives of North American Birds.* Houghton Mifflin Co., Boston.

McNicholl, M.K., and J.L. Cranmer-Byng, ed. 1994. *Ornithology in Ontario.* Ontario Field Ornithologists, Toronto.

National Geographic Society. 1999. *Field guide to the birds of North America.* 3rd ed. National Geographic Society, Washington, D.C.

Peck, G.K., and R.D. James. 1983. *Breeding Birds of Ontario: Nidiology and Distribution* (*Vol. 1: Nonpasserines*). Royal Ontario Museum, Toronto.

Peck, G.K., and R.D. James. 1987. *Breeding Birds of Ontario: Nidiology and Distribution* (*Vol. 2: Passerines*). Royal Ontario Museum, Toronto.

Peterson, R.T. 1980. *A Field Guide to the Birds of Eastern and Central North America.* Houghton Mifflin Co., Boston.

Sauer, J.R., J.E. Hines, I. Thomas, J. Fallon and G. Gough. 1999. *The North American Breeding Bird Survey, Results and Analysis 1966–1998.* Version 98.1. USGS Patuxent Wildlife Research Center, Laurel, Md. <http://www.mbr-pwrc.usgs.gov/bbs/bbs.html>

Sauer, J.R., S. Schwartz and B. Hoover. 1996. *The Christmas Bird Count Home Page.* Version 95.1. USGS Patuxent Wildlife Research Center, Laurel, Md. <http://www.mbr-pwrc.usgs.gov/bbs/cbc.html>

Spiers, J.M. 1985. *Birds of Ontario* (Vols. 1 & 2). Natural Heritage/Natural History, Toronto.

Stokes, D., and L. Stokes. 1996. *Stokes Field Guide to Birds: Eastern Region.* Little, Brown and Co., Toronto.

Terres, J.K. 1995. *The Audubon Society Encyclopedia of North American Birds.* Wings Books, New York.

GLOSSARY

accipiter: a forest hawk (genus *Accipiter*); characterized by a long tail and short, rounded wings; feeds mostly on birds.

axillars: the feathers of the inner underwing, of the 'wingpit.'

brood: *n.* a family of young from one hatching; *v.* sit on eggs so as to hatch them.

conifer: a cone-producing tree, usually a softwood evergreen (e.g., spruce, pine, fir).

corvid: a member of the crow family (Corvidae); includes crows, jays, magpies and ravens.

coverts: usually refers to the upper secondary coverts, which are the short feathers covering the base of the secondaries.

covey: a brood or flock of partridges, quails or grouse.

creche: a 'daycare' for the young of colonially nesting birds.

crepuscular: active chiefly during the twilight before dawn and after dusk.

crop: an enlargement of the esophagus; serves as a storage structure and (in pigeons) has glands that produce secretions.

dabbling: a foraging technique used by ducks, where the head and neck are submerged but the body and tail remain on the water's surface.

deciduous tree: a tree that loses its leaves annually (e.g., oak, maple, aspen, birch).

dimorphism: the existence of two distinct forms of a species, such as between the sexes.

diurnal: active chiefly during daylight.

eclipse: the dull, female-like plumage that male ducks briefly acquire after molting from their breeding plumage.

fledgling: a young bird that has left the nest but is dependent upon its parents.

flushing: a behaviour where frightened birds explode into flight in response to a disturbance.

flycatching: a feeding behaviour where the bird leaves a perch, snatches an insect in mid-air and returns to the same perch; also known as 'hawking' or 'sallying.'

hawking: a feeding behaviour where a bird attempts to capture insects through aerial pursuit.

irruption: a sporadic mass migration of birds into a non-breeding area.

kleptoparasitism: a parasitic behaviour characterized by the theft of food items produced by another.

leading edge: the front edge of the wing as viewed from below.

litter: fallen plant material, such as twigs, leaves and needles, that forms a distinct layer above the soil, especially in forests.

lore: the small patch between the eye and the bill.

molting: the periodic replacement of worn out feathers (often twice a year).

morphology: the science of form and shape.

nape: the back of the neck.

niche: an ecological role filled by a species.

parasitism: a relationship between two species where one benefits at the expense of the other.

pishing: a repeated sibilant sound made expressly to attract birds.

plucking post: a perch habitually used by raptors to remove feathers or fur from prey.

polyandrous: having a mating strategy where one female breeds with several males.

polygynous: having a mating strategy where one male breeds with several females.

precocial: young birds generally capable of adult behaviours, and so able to promptly abandon the site of hatching and move about with adults.

primaries: the outermost flight feathers.

raptor: a carnivorous (meat-eating) bird; includes eagles, hawks, falcons and owls.

riparia: riverine forests, thickets and other stands of woody wetland vegetation; the term is ordinarily used to describe taller streamside cover, such as willows, cottonwoods, etc.

rufous: rusty red in color.

sallying: repeated aerial pursuit of insects performed by flying from a perch.

scapulars: feathers of the shoulder, seeming to join the wing and back.

speculum: the patterned or colourful secondaries of ducks.

squeaking: making a sound to attract birds by loudly kissing the back of the hand, or by using a specially designed squeaky bird call.

talons: the claws of birds of prey.

torpor: a state of lowered metabolism enabling a creature to endure conditions during which it cannot find sufficient food to sustain normal activity.

understorey: the shrub or thicket layer beneath a canopy of trees.

crown

eyebrow/ supercilium

eye line

lore

wing bars

chin

greater coverts

throat

rump

breast

tips of primary feathers

flank

tail feathers

belly

undertail coverts

secondary feathers

CHECKLIST

The following checklist contains 472 species of birds that have been officially recorded in Ontario. Species are grouped by family and listed in taxonomic order in accordance with the A.O.U. *Check-list of North American Birds* (7th ed.).

Species with fewer than 10 confirmed records in the province are listed in italics. An asterisk (*) identifies species that once occurred regularly in the province, but are now unlikely to be seen. A plus (+) identifies species that have appeared in abundance (more than 10 confirmed records) on isolated occasions. An (e) identifies species that are extinct.

Loons (Gaviidae)
- ❏ Red-throated Loon
- ❏ Pacific Loon
- ❏ Common Loon
- ❏ *Yellow-billed Loon*

Grebes (Podicipedidae)
- ❏ Pied-billed Grebe
- ❏ Horned Grebe
- ❏ Red-necked Grebe
- ❏ Eared Grebe
- ❏ Western Grebe

Shearwaters & Petrels (Procellariidae)
- ❏ Northern Fulmar
- ❏ Black-capped Petrel+
- ❏ *Greater Shearwater*
- ❏ *Audubon's Shearwater*

Storm-Petrels (Hydrobatidae)
- ❏ *Wilson's Storm-Petrel*
- ❏ *Leach's Storm-Petrel*
- ❏ *Band-rumped Storm-Petrel*

Gannets (Sulidae)
- ❏ Northern Gannet

Pelicans (Pelecanidae)
- ❏ American White Pelican
- ❏ *Brown Pelican*

Cormorants (Phalacrocoracidae)
- ❏ Double-crested Cormorant
- ❏ *Great Cormorant*

Darters (Anhingidae)
- ❏ *Anhinga*

Frigatebirds (Fregatidae)
- ❏ *Magnificent Frigatebird*

Herons (Ardeidae)
- ❏ American Bittern
- ❏ Least Bittern
- ❏ Great Blue Heron
- ❏ Great Egret
- ❏ Snowy Egret
- ❏ Little Blue Heron
- ❏ Tricolored Heron
- ❏ Cattle Egret
- ❏ Green Heron
- ❏ Black-crowned Night Heron
- ❏ Yellow-crowned Night-Heron

Ibises & Spoonbills (Threskiornithidae)
- ❏ *White Ibis*
- ❏ Glossy Ibis
- ❏ *White-faced Ibis*

Storks (Ciconiidae)
- ❏ *Wood Stork*

Vultures (Cathartidae)
- ❏ Black Vulture
- ❏ Turkey Vulture

Waterfowl (Anatidae)
- ❏ *Black-bellied Whistling-Duck*
- ❏ *Fulvous Whistling-Duck*
- ❏ Greater White-fronted Goose
- ❏ Snow Goose
- ❏ Ross's Goose
- ❏ Canada Goose
- ❏ Brant
- ❏ Mute Swan
- ❏ Trumpeter Swan
- ❏ Tundra Swan
- ❏ Wood Duck
- ❏ Gadwall
- ❏ Eurasian Wigeon
- ❏ American Wigeon

- ❏ American Black Duck
- ❏ Mallard
- ❏ Blue-winged Teal
- ❏ Cinnamon Teal
- ❏ Northern Shoveler
- ❏ Northern Pintail
- ❏ *Garganey*
- ❏ Green-winged Teal
- ❏ Canvasback
- ❏ Redhead
- ❏ Ring-necked Duck
- ❏ Tufted Duck
- ❏ Greater Scaup
- ❏ Lesser Scaup
- ❏ King Eider
- ❏ Common Eider
- ❏ Harlequin Duck
- ❏ Surf Scoter
- ❏ White-winged Scoter
- ❏ Black Scoter
- ❏ Oldsquaw
- ❏ Bufflehead
- ❏ Common Goldeneye
- ❏ Barrow's Goldeneye
- ❏ *Smew*
- ❏ Hooded Merganser
- ❏ Common Merganser
- ❏ Red-breasted Merganser
- ❏ Ruddy Duck

Kites, Hawks & Eagles (Accipitridae)
- ❏ Osprey
- ❏ Swallow-tailed Kite
- ❏ Mississippi Kite
- ❏ Bald Eagle
- ❏ Northern Harrier
- ❏ Sharp-shinned Hawk
- ❏ Cooper's Hawk
- ❏ Northern Goshawk
- ❏ Red-shouldered Hawk
- ❏ Broad-winged Hawk
- ❏ Swainson's Hawk
- ❏ Red-tailed Hawk

❏ *Ferruginous Hawk*
❏ Rough-legged Hawk
❏ Golden Eagle

Falcons & Caracaras (Falconidae)
❏ *Crested Caracara*
❏ American Kestrel
❏ Merlin
❏ Gyrfalcon
❏ Peregrine Falcon
❏ *Prairie Falcon*

Grouse & Allies (Phasianidae)
❏ Gray Partridge
❏ Ring-necked Pheasant
❏ Ruffed Grouse
❏ Spruce Grouse
❏ Willow Ptarmigan
❏ Rock Ptarmigan
❏ Sharp-tailed Grouse
❏ Greater Prairie-Chicken*
❏ Wild Turkey

New World Quails (Odontophoridae)
❏ Northern Bobwhite

Rails & Coots (Rallidae)
❏ Yellow Rail
❏ *Black Rail*
❏ King Rail
❏ Virginia Rail
❏ Sora
❏ *Purple Gallinule*
❏ Common Moorhen
❏ American Coot

Cranes (Gruidae)
❏ Sandhill Crane
❏ *Whooping Crane*

Plovers (Charadriidae)
❏ Black-bellied Plover
❏ American Golden-Plover
❏ *Mongolian Plover*
❏ *Snowy Plover*
❏ *Wilson's Plover*
❏ Semipalmated Plover
❏ Piping Plover
❏ Killdeer

Oystercatchers (Haematopodidae)
❏ *American Oystercatcher*

Stilts & Avocets (Recurvirostridae)
❏ Black-necked Stilt
❏ American Avocet

Sandpipers & Allies (Scolopacidae)
❏ Greater Yellowlegs
❏ Lesser Yellowlegs
❏ *Spotted Redshank*
❏ Solitary Sandpiper
❏ Willet
❏ *Wandering Tattler*
❏ Spotted Sandpiper
❏ Upland Sandpiper
❏ Eskimo Curlew*
❏ Whimbrel
❏ *Slender-billed Curlew*
❏ *Long-billed Curlew*
❏ *Black-tailed Godwit*
❏ Hudsonian Godwit
❏ Marbled Godwit
❏ Ruddy Turnstone
❏ Red Knot
❏ Sanderling
❏ Semipalmated Sandpiper
❏ Western Sandpiper
❏ *Little Stint*
❏ Least Sandpiper
❏ White-rumped Sandpiper
❏ Baird's Sandpiper
❏ Pectoral Sandpiper
❏ *Sharp-tailed Sandpiper*
❏ Purple Sandpiper
❏ Dunlin
❏ Curlew Sandpiper
❏ Stilt Sandpiper
❏ Buff-breasted Sandpiper
❏ Ruff/Reeve
❏ Short-billed Dowitcher
❏ Long-billed Dowitcher
❏ Common Snipe
❏ American Woodcock
❏ Wilson's Phalarope
❏ Red-necked Phalarope
❏ Red Phalarope

Gulls & Allies (Laridae)
❏ Pomarine Jaeger
❏ Parasitic Jaeger
❏ Long-tailed Jaeger
❏ Laughing Gull
❏ Franklin's Gull
❏ Little Gull
❏ Black-headed Gull
❏ Bonaparte's Gull

❏ Mew Gull
❏ Ring-billed Gull
❏ California Gull
❏ Herring Gull
❏ Thayer's Gull
❏ Iceland Gull
❏ Lesser Black-backed Gull
❏ *Slaty-backed Gull*
❏ Glaucous Gull
❏ Great Black-backed Gull
❏ Sabine's Gull
❏ Black-legged Kittiwake
❏ *Ross's Gull*
❏ Ivory Gull
❏ Caspian Tern
❏ *Royal Tern*
❏ *Sandwich Tern*
❏ Common Tern
❏ Arctic Tern
❏ Forster's Tern
❏ *Least Tern*
❏ *Sooty Tern*
❏ *White-winged Tern*
❏ Black Tern
❏ *Black Skimmer*

Alcids (Alcidae)
❏ *Dovekie*
❏ *Thick-billed Murre*
❏ *Razorbill*
❏ Black Guillemot
❏ *Long-billed Murrelet*
❏ Ancient Murrelet
❏ *Atlantic Puffin*

Pigeons & Doves (Columbidae)
❏ Rock Dove
❏ *Band-tailed Pigeon*
❏ *Eurasian Collared-Dove*
❏ *White-winged Dove*
❏ Mourning Dove
❏ Passenger Pigeon (e)
❏ *Inca Dove*
❏ *Common Ground-Dove*

Cuckoos (Cuculidae)
❏ Black-billed Cuckoo
❏ Yellow-billed Cuckoo
❏ *Groove-billed Ani*

Barn Owls (Tytonidae)
❏ Barn Owl*

Owls (Strigidae)
❏ Eastern Screech-Owl
❏ Great Horned Owl

❏ Snowy Owl
❏ Northern Hawk Owl
❏ *Burrowing Owl*
❏ Barred Owl
❏ Great Gray Owl
❏ Long-eared Owl
❏ Short-eared Owl
❏ Boreal Owl
❏ Northern Saw-whet Owl

Nightjars (Caprimulgidae)
❏ *Lesser Nighthawk*
❏ Common Nighthawk
❏ *Common Poorwill*
❏ Chuck-will's-widow
❏ Whip-poor-will

Swifts (Apodidae)
❏ Chimney Swift

Hummingbirds (Trochilidae)
❏ *Green Violet-ear*
❏ *Broad-billed Hummingbird*
❏ Ruby-throated Hummingbird
❏ *Black-chinned Hummingbird*
❏ Rufous Hummingbird

Kingfishers (Alcedinidae)
❏ Belted Kingfisher

Woodpeckers (Picidae)
❏ *Lewis's Woodpecker*
❏ Red-headed Woodpecker
❏ Red-bellied Woodpecker
❏ Yellow-bellied Sapsucker
❏ Downy Woodpecker
❏ Hairy Woodpecker
❏ Three-toed Woodpecker
❏ Black-backed Woodpecker
❏ Northern Flicker
❏ Pileated Woodpecker

Flycatchers (Tyrannidae)
❏ Olive-sided Flycatcher
❏ *Western Wood-Pewee*
❏ Eastern Wood-Pewee
❏ Yellow-bellied Flycatcher
❏ Acadian Flycatcher
❏ Alder Flycatcher
❏ Willow Flycatcher
❏ Least Flycatcher

❏ *Gray Flycatcher*
❏ *Dusky Flycatcher*
❏ Eastern Phoebe
❏ *Say's Phoebe*
❏ *Vermilion Flycatcher*
❏ *Ash-throated Flycatcher*
❏ Great Crested Flycatcher
❏ *Sulphur-bellied Flycatcher*
❏ *Variegated Flycatcher*
❏ *Couch's (Tropical) Kingbird*
❏ *Cassin's Kingbird*
❏ Western Kingbird
❏ Eastern Kingbird
❏ *Gray Kingbird*
❏ Scissor-tailed Flycatcher
❏ *Fork-tailed Flycatcher*

Shrikes (Laniidae)
❏ Loggerhead Shrike
❏ Northern Shrike

Vireos (Vireonidae)
❏ White-eyed Vireo
❏ *Bell's Vireo*
❏ Black-capped Vireo
❏ Yellow-throated Vireo
❏ *Plumbeous Vireo*
❏ Blue-headed Vireo
❏ Warbling Vireo
❏ Philadelphia Vireo
❏ Red-eyed Vireo

Crows, Jays & Magpies (Corvidae)
❏ Gray Jay
❏ Blue Jay
❏ *Clark's Nutcracker*
❏ Black-billed Magpie
❏ *Eurasian Jackdaw*
❏ American Crow
❏ *Fish Crow*
❏ Common Raven

Larks (Alaudidae)
❏ Horned Lark

Swallows (Hirundinidae)
❏ Purple Martin
❏ Tree Swallow
❏ *Violet-green Swallow*
❏ Northern Rough-winged Swallow
❏ Bank Swallow
❏ Cliff Swallow
❏ Cave Swallow+
❏ Barn Swallow

Chickadees & Titmice (Paridae)
❏ *Carolina Chickadee*
❏ Black-capped Chickadee
❏ Boreal Chickadee
❏ Tufted Titmouse

Nuthatches (Sittidae)
❏ Red-breasted Nuthatch
❏ White-breasted Nuthatch

Creepers (Certhiidae)
❏ Brown Creeper

Wrens (Troglodytidae)
❏ *Rock Wren*
❏ Carolina Wren
❏ Bewick's Wren
❏ House Wren
❏ Winter Wren
❏ Sedge Wren
❏ Marsh Wren

Kinglets (Regulidae)
❏ Golden-crowned Kinglet
❏ Ruby-crowned Kinglet

Gnatcatchers (Sylviidae)
❏ Blue-gray Gnatcatcher

Thrushes (Turdidae)
❏ *Siberian Rubythroat*
❏ Northern Wheatear
❏ Eastern Bluebird
❏ Mountain Bluebird
❏ Townsend's Solitaire
❏ Veery
❏ Gray-cheeked Thrush
❏ *Bicknell's Thrush*
❏ Swainson's Thrush
❏ Hermit Thrush
❏ Wood Thrush
❏ *Eurasian Blackbird*
❏ *Fieldfare*
❏ American Robin
❏ Varied Thrush

Mockingbirds & Thrashers (Mimidae)
❏ Gray Catbird
❏ Northern Mockingbird
❏ *Sage Thrasher*
❏ Brown Thrasher

Starlings (Sturnidae)
❏ European Starling

Pipits (Motacillidae)
❏ American Pipit
❏ *Sprague's Pipit*

Waxwings (Bombycillidae)
❏ Bohemian Waxwing
❏ Cedar Waxwing

Silky-flycatchers (Ptilogonatidae)
❏ *Phainopepla*

Wood-Warblers (Parulidae)
❏ Blue-winged Warbler
❏ Golden-winged Warbler
❏ Tennessee Warbler
❏ Orange-crowned Warbler
❏ Nashville Warbler
❏ *Virginia's Warbler*
❏ Northern Parula
❏ Yellow Warbler
❏ Chestnut-sided Warbler
❏ Magnolia Warbler
❏ Cape May Warbler
❏ Black-throated Blue Warbler
❏ Yellow-rumped Warbler
❏ Black-throated Gray Warbler
❏ Black-throated Green Warbler
❏ *Townsend's Warbler*
❏ *Hermit Warbler*
❏ Blackburnian Warbler
❏ Yellow-throated Warbler
❏ Pine Warbler
❏ Kirtland's Warbler
❏ Prairie Warbler
❏ Palm Warbler
❏ Bay-breasted Warbler
❏ Blackpoll Warbler
❏ Cerulean Warbler
❏ Black-and-white Warbler
❏ American Redstart
❏ Prothonotary Warbler
❏ Worm-eating Warbler
❏ *Swainson's Warbler*
❏ Ovenbird
❏ Northern Waterthrush
❏ Louisiana Waterthrush
❏ Kentucky Warbler
❏ Connecticut Warbler
❏ Mourning Warbler
❏ *MacGillivray's Warbler*
❏ Common Yellowthroat
❏ Hooded Warbler
❏ Wilson's Warbler
❏ Canada Warbler
❏ *Painted Redstart*
❏ Yellow-breasted Chat

Tanagers (Thraupidae)
❏ Summer Tanager
❏ Scarlet Tanager
❏ Western Tanager

Sparrows & Allies (Emberizidae)
❏ *Green-tailed Towhee*
❏ Spotted Towhee
❏ Eastern Towhee
❏ *Cassin's Sparrow*
❏ *Bachman's Sparrow*
❏ American Tree Sparrow
❏ Chipping Sparrow
❏ Clay-colored Sparrow
❏ Field Sparrow
❏ Vesper Sparrow
❏ Lark Sparrow
❏ *Black-throated Sparrow*
❏ Lark Bunting
❏ Savannah Sparrow
❏ Grasshopper Sparrow
❏ *Baird's Sparrow*
❏ Henslow's Sparrow
❏ Le Conte's Sparrow
❏ Nelson's Sharp-tailed Sparrow
❏ Fox Sparrow
❏ Song Sparrow
❏ Lincoln's Sparrow
❏ Swamp Sparrow
❏ White-throated Sparrow
❏ Harris's Sparrow
❏ White-crowned Sparrow
❏ *Golden-crowned Sparrow*
❏ Dark-eyed Junco
❏ Lapland Longspur
❏ Smith's Longspur
❏ *Chestnut-collared Longspur*
❏ Snow Bunting

Grosbeaks & Buntings (Cardinalidae)
❏ Northern Cardinal
❏ Rose-breasted Grosbeak
❏ *Black-headed Grosbeak*
❏ Blue Grosbeak
❏ *Lazuli Bunting*
❏ Indigo Bunting
❏ *Varied Bunting*
❏ *Painted Bunting*
❏ Dickcissel

Blackbirds & Allies (Icteridae)
❏ Bobolink
❏ Red-winged Blackbird
❏ Eastern Meadowlark
❏ Western Meadowlark
❏ Yellow-headed Blackbird
❏ Rusty Blackbird
❏ Brewer's Blackbird
❏ Common Grackle
❏ *Great-tailed Grackle*
❏ Brown-headed Cowbird
❏ Orchard Oriole
❏ *Hooded Oriole*
❏ Baltimore Oriole
❏ *Bullock's Oriole*
❏ *Scott's Oriole*

Finches (Fringillidae)
❏ *Brambling*
❏ *Gray-crowned Rosy-Finch*
❏ Pine Grosbeak
❏ Purple Finch
❏ *Cassin's Finch*
❏ House Finch
❏ Red Crossbill
❏ White-winged Crossbill
❏ Common Redpoll
❏ Hoary Redpoll
❏ Pine Siskin
❏ *Lesser Goldfinch*
❏ American Goldfinch
❏ Evening Grosbeak

Old World Sparrows (Passeridae)
❏ House Sparrow
❏ *Eurasian Tree Sparrow*

INDEX OF SCIENTIFIC NAMES

This index references only the primary species accounts.

INDEX OF COMMON NAMES

Page numbers in boldface type refer to the primary, illustrated species accounts.

ABOUT THE AUTHOR

Inspired at an early age during adventures to Cranberry Marsh, the Rouge River Valley and Algonquin Provincial Park, Andy Bezener has developed a keen interest in the study and conservation of nature. Fieldwork with the Canadian Wildlife Service and a degree in Conservation Biology, have given Andy joyful insight into the lives of many North American birds. His admiration and concern for wilderness and wildlife has led him across much of Ontario, North America and southern Africa. Andy is coauthor of Lone Pine's *Rocky Mountain Nature Guide, Birds of Northern California, Birds of Boston* and *Birds of New York City, Western Long Island and Northeastern New Jersey.*

ABOUT THE REVIEWER

Ross James is a Departmental Associate and former Curator of Ornithology at the Royal Ontario Museum in Toronto. He spent years studying the foraging behaviour of vireos in southern Ontario, and for his masters and doctoral research at the University of Toronto, he studied the ecological and behavioural relationships of Blue-headed and Yellow-throated vireos. He has spent time as a committee member and contributor to the *Atlas of Breeding Birds of Ontario,* and he is a coauthor of *Ontario Birds at Risk.* He has also authored an *Annotated Checklist of Ontario Birds,* two volumes of the *Breeding Birds of Ontario* and two accounts for the *Birds of North America.* Ross has published more than 80 papers on birds, and he has spent more than a decade as chairman and co-chairman of the Birds Subcommittee of The Committee on the Status of Endangered Wildlife in Canada (COSEWIC).